P9-AGU-885

Markets and Hierarchies:
Analysis and Antitrust Implications

Markets and Hierarchies: Analysis and Antitrust Implications

A Study in the Economics of Internal Organization

Oliver E. Williamson
University of Pennsylvania

THE FREE PRESS
A Division of Macmillan Publishing Co., Inc.
NEW YORK

Collier Macmillan Publishers
LONDON

To the Memory of My Mother and to
Dolores and the Children

Copyright © 1975 by The Free Press
                A Division of Macmillan Publishing Co., Inc.

All rights reserved. No part of this book may be reproduced or
transmitted in any form or by any means, electronic or mechanical,
including photocopying, recording, or by any information storage and
retrieval system, without permission in writing from the Publisher.

The Free Press
A Division of Macmillan Publishing Co., Inc.
866 Third Avenue, New York, N.Y. 10022

Collier Macmillan Canada, Inc.

First Free Press Paperback Edition 1983

Printed in the United States of America

printing number paperback
1 2 3 4 5 6 7 8 9 10

printing number hard cover
7 8 9 10

Library of Congress Cataloging in Publication Data

Williamson, Oliver E
   Markets and hierarchies, analysis and antitrust
implications.

   Bibliography: p.
   Includes index.
   1. Industrial organization. 2. Industrial
management. 3. Trusts, industrial. I. Title.
HD31.W5173   658.4′02   74-27597
ISBN 0-02-935360-2
ISBN 0-02-934780-7 (pbk.)

Contents

Preface to the College Edition

The study of economic organization commonly proceeds as though market and administrative modes of organization were disjunct. Market organization is the province of economists. Internal organization is the concern of organization theory specialists. And never the twain shall meet.

Markets and Hierarchies maintains that one can understand the powers and limits of market and internal modes of organization only by examining each in relation to the other. Rather than focusing on technology and production costs, attention is focused on transaction cost economizing. The book has a bearing on the theory of the firm, the study of labor organization, and the evolution of the modern corporation, including vertical integration and conglomerate aspects. The policy ramifications mainly affect antitrust situations. Such a book appears most naturally in an industrial organization sequence and has been used extensively in this connection.

I am gratified, however, that organization theorists have recognized that the book deals with a number of issues relevant to them. This is because *Markets and Hierarchies* makes contact with "human nature as we know it." In contrast with the standard apparatus of neoclassical economics, which is relatively unhelpful in attempting to assess hierarchical structures and internal control processes, the language of transaction cost economizing turns out to be a good deal more useful. Applications to other business areas have also been made—marketing, regulation, and business policy being among the more important. Thus, although the book examines vertical integration mainly in a manufacturing context, the decision of whether or not to integrate forward into distribution raises substantially identical transaction cost issues in marketing. More generally, the "fundamental transformation" of an *ex ante* large-numbers supply situation to an *ex post* condition of bilateral exchange, which transformation has transaction cost origins and appears recurrently throughout the book, has profound ramifications for the study of both regulation and strategic business behavior.

Indeed, any activity that can be described directly or indirectly as contractual is usefully investigated in transaction cost economizing terms. Some of the applications are obvious, but others are more subtle. (The study of marriage—both traditional and unconventional kinds—is an example of the latter.) The trick in every case is to understand what it is that is being contracted for, to identify the alternative governance structures within which the transaction under study might feasibly be organized, and to effect a discriminating match.

Students and teachers who find comparative institutional analysis congenial often discover applications that were not at all evident to me at the time that *Markets and Hierarchies* was written. This naturally makes for lively classroom discussion. The first two chapters are crucial. Thereafter the readings can be tailored to the needs of the class.

OLIVER E. WILLIAMSON
November 1982

Preface

This book is concerned with the organization of economic activity within and between markets and hierarchies. Whereas market transactions involve exchange between autonomous economic entities — the study of which exchanges is the familiar object of microeconomic analysis — hierarchical transactions are ones for which a single administrative entity spans both sides of the transaction, some form of subordination prevails, and, typically, consolidated ownership obtains.

Also, whereas received microtheory generally regards the organization of economic activity between firms and markets as a datum, the study of markets and hierarchies expressly attempts to assess the efficiency properties of alternative contracting modes. Correspondingly, while conventional analysis is largely preoccupied with the investigation of final product markets, the study of markets and hierarchies entails, additionally, an intensive examination of labor market, intermediate product market, and capital market related transactions.

I contend in this connection that the modeling apparatus of received microtheory is insufficiently microanalytic to deal with many of the transactional phenomena of interest. What is referred to as the "organizational failures framework" is proposed and repeatedly employed in an attempt to assess the efficacy of completing related sets of transactions across a market or within a firm.

Although I espouse a somewhat unconventional worldview, students and followers of John R. Commons will recognize that I subscribe to his dictum that the transaction is the ultimate unit of microeconomic analysis. This position has never enjoyed widespread acceptance, even during Commons's period of maximum influence — which has waned considerably. Whether I have made a more compelling case is uncertain. Nevertheless, it is of interest to observe that the analysis of transactions was regarded by Commons and other institutionalists as central to the study of economics.

My treatment differs from the institutionalists in at least three ways. First, I am able to draw on an extensive market failure literature that was unavailable forty years ago. This is a considerable advantage. Second, rather than regard the microanalytic study of markets and hierarchies as being in essential conflict with received microtheory, I am inclined to consider these as complements. The transactional approach is held to be useful to the extent that it produces fruitful insights and systematically organizes a diverse set of phenomena. The phenomena of interest, often, are ones on which conventional microtheory is silent. Accordingly, standard modes of economic analysis that deal with related issues at a higher level of aggregation need not be abandoned — although, to be sure, eclecticism results in occasional strain. Third, and connected, I draw on the rather unique intellectual atmosphere that prevailed at the "Carnegie School" during the early 1960's. This involved an interdisciplinary approach to the study of social science phenomena and a contagious, even exhilarating, research commitment to "reformulate old issues."

I was advised by a number of scholars to whom I distributed an earlier version of the manuscript that a distinctive worldview was being offered and that this ought to be emphasized. In the revision, I have attempted to heed this advice—partly by contrasting my interpretation of the economic phenomena in question with prior treatments. Aspects of the book may appear to be argumentative as a result, but are not by intent contentious. Those treatments with which I have taken exception have been selected not because they were straw men but because they were among the best prior statements available.

The transactional issues that I am concerned with in this book are complex and often elusive. Systematic treatment has been facilitated by devising a special vocabulary. This imposes a burden on the reader who, in order to follow the argument, must familiarize himself with the vocabulary and, more generally, learn to "think transactionally." That such an investment is not only necessary but at least sometimes pays off is suggested by the following passage in a letter from a colleague regarding the penultimate version:

> . . . complicated sentences that have references to bounded rationality, information impactedness, small-numbers bargaining problems, etc., can be mind-boggling to the uninitiated. I'm not sure what to suggest since it all seems very clear to me now, but I think that you should be aware that it is extremely toughgoing at first.

I am both aware and sympathetic. If I could have dealt successfully with the issues otherwise, I would have.

I have sought and received the advice of a large number of scholars, students and faculty alike, on the materials in this book. I am especially indebted to Richard Nelson and Paul Joskow for their penetrating criticism and strong encouragement. Other faculty who have read all or parts of the manuscript and to whom I am grateful for advice are Bruce Ackerman, Kenneth Arrow, Stanley Engerman, Ralph Ginsberg, Hywel Jones, Dennis Mueller, Almarin Phillips, Lee Preston, and Fred Weston.

I have discussed all the materials in the book with my students and have benefited greatly from these sessions. The oral and written suggestions of Jeffrey Harris, Larry Haverkamp, Harry Pinson, Marc Rubin, Sharon Sallow, David Teece, and Kenneth Vogel were especially helpful.

Several chapters were written with the assistance of coauthors. The collaboration of Jeffrey Harris and Michael Wachter (on Chapter 4), of Narottam Bhargava (on Chapter 8), and of Donald Turner (on Chapter 10) is gratefully acknowledged.

Research on this book was supported in part by a grant from the Brookings Institution, partly by the Fels Center of Government, and more recently, by a grant from the National Science Foundation. I appreciate the support of each. The Brookings support was associated with its program of Studies in the Regulation of Economic Activity, which was financed by the Ford Foundation. The views expressed herein do not necessarily represent those of the officers, trustees, or other staff members of the Brookings Institution or of the Ford Foundation.

Many of the chapters are derived from my previously published research. Much in Chapters 2, 3, 5, and 6 is based on material that appeared (in highly condensed form) in the *American Economic Review,* vol. 61, May 1971, and vol. 63, May 1973. Chapter 4 appeared in the *Bell Journal of Economics,* vol. 6, Spring 1975. Chapter 7 is based on a paper that appeared in *Industrial Management: East and West* (Aubrey Silberston and Francis Seton, eds., Praeger, 1972) while Chapter 8 is based on a paper that was published in *Market Structure and Corporate Behavior* (Keith Cowling, ed., Gray-Mills, 1972). Chapters 9 and 12 are derived from a paper in the *University of Pennsylvania Law Review,* vol. 122, June 1974. Chapter 10 is based on a paper that appeared in the *Proceedings of the International Conference on Monopolies, Mergers, and Restrictive Practices* (J. B. Heath, ed., HMSO, 1971) and Chapter 11 had its origins in a paper in the *Harvard Law Review,* vol. 86, June 1972. The several publishers have allowed me to elaborate and integrate these materials in this book, for which I express my appreciation.

I have benefited continuously from the affirmative research atmosphere that my wife Dolores and our children have helped to create and sustain. Their sympathy and support for my efforts have been extraordinary, and in some degree are hopefully reciprocated.

OLIVER E. WILLIAMSON

Introduction

A brief review of the antecedent literature on which I rely and a sketch of the "organizational failures framework" are set out in Chapter 1. The proposed approach to the study of transactions requires that much more attention be paid to microanalytic detail. The advantages of the proposed approach are illustrated by examining three familiar economic issues: price discrimination, insurance, and vertical integration. The transactional approach is shown to yield, in each case, richer or different implications than received microtheory.

The organizational failures framework is developed more extensively in Chapter 2. This material is somewhat tedious. Those who have interests in only one or a few of the topics treated in subsequent chapters can skip directly to them. Chapter 2 should be read carefully, however, by those who regard a systematic study of markets and hierarchies to be intrinsically interesting.

The organization of peer groups and the evolution of simple hierarchy are examined in Chapter 3. Whereas the peer group represents a shift from market to internal organization, a shift from peer group to simple hierarchy represents a reconstitution of internal organization from one structure to another — that is to say, an organization form change.

Hierarchy usually implies a superior-subordinate relationship. What is referred to as an "employment relation" is commonly associated with voluntary subordination. The reasons for and properties of the employment relation are examined in Chapter 4. Alternative labor-contracting modes are compared and collective organization is shown to have important efficiency attributes for tasks that involve the acquisition by the work force of idiosyncratic knowledge.

Once specialized productive units are organized into simple hierarchies and the appropriate employment relation is designated for each, the questions are when and how will such units be joined in a single firm rather than exchange between them being mediated by a market. This is the vertical integration issue. It is addressed in Chapter 5 in the context of the following question: What organizational relations have what efficiency consequences if a set of technologically separable but transactionally related simple hierarchies are engaged in recurring exchange of a small-numbers sort under uncertainty? The question is not merely whether internal organization can be substituted for the market with beneficial results, but what type of internal organization is to be employed. This second question poses organization form issues.

Whereas the discussion of vertical integration in Chapter 5 emphasizes the prospective gains from integration, the treatment in Chapter 6 qualifies the argument. Some of the ways in which markets deal with incomplete contracts are discussed; possible or purported antisocial consequences of vertical integration are also considered.

My analysis of vertical integration is completed in Chapter 7, in which some of the limitations to which internal organization is subject as the firm grows in size and complexity (organization form held constant) are examined. I argue in this connection that the organizational failures framework, as sketched in Chapter 1 and elaborated in Chapter 2, applies to the study of market failures and internal organizational failures alike.

Considering the importance that is attached to organization form, the extent to which internal organization experiences failure might be expected to vary with organization form. The ways by which some of the more serious limitations that beset the radial expansion of the functionally organized firm can be attenuated by adopting the multidivisional structure are developed in Chapter 8. The importance of internal controls to successful divisionalization is emphasized.

The argument is applied to the question of conglomerate organization in Chapter 9, and the discussion in earlier chapters is expanded to include failures in the capital market. Whereas simple hierarchy and vertical integration can be regarded as substitutions of internal organization for failures in the labor and intermediate product markets, respectively, conglomerate organization — of the appropriate multidivisional kind — constitutes the substitution of internal organization for failures in the capital market.

The literature on the relation between technological innovation and market structure is surveyed in Chapter 10. A systems approach to the innovation process is then proposed, the object of which is to permit the distinctive advantages of both small and large firms, which apply at different stages of the innovation process, to be realized. The relation of organizational innovation to technological innovation is also developed.

The origins and persistence of dominant firm industries are examined in Chapter 11. I argue that dominant firms arise less because of static scale economies, as is commonly argued, but because of default failures and stochastic market failures. A more assertive antitrust policy with respect to dominant firms is urged for circumstances — as in the case of default and chance event failures — in which markets fail to perform self-policing functions. Subject to "appropriate" qualifications, the dissolution of dominant firms is proposed.

A reconstituted dominant firm industry would, however, normally remain highly concentrated. Whether there are any benefits to be had from converting a monopoly into an oligopoly is sometimes doubted. I address this question in Chapter 12 by posing the oligopoly issue as a problem of contracting. I argue that the problems of tacit and explicit collusion are much more serious than are commonly thought, even if such agreements are lawful, *a fortiori* if collusion is held to be unlawful. The reasons for this are traced to the important differences between markets and hierarchies that are developed in earlier chapters.

The markets and hierarchies approach is briefly recapitulated in Chapter 13. Antitrust implications are summarized and some directions for future research are indicated.

1. Toward a New Institutional Economics

A broadly based interest among economists in what might be referred to as the "new institutional economics" has developed in recent years. Aspects of mainline microtheory, economic history, the economics of property rights, comparative systems, labor economics, and industrial organization[1] have each had a bearing on this renaissance. The common threads that tie these various studies together are: (1) an evolving consensus that received microtheory, as useful and powerful as it is for many purposes, operates at too high a level of abstraction to permit many important microeconomic phenomena to be addressed in an uncontrived way; and (2) a sense that the study of "transactions," which concerned the institutionalists in the profession some forty years ago, is really a core matter and deserves renewed attention. Unlike the earlier institutionalists, however, the current group is inclined to be eclectic. The new institutional economists both draw on microtheory and, for the most part, regard what they are doing as complementary to, rather than a substitute for, conventional analysis.

The spirit in which this present book is written very much follows the thinking of these new institutionalists. I hope, by exploring microeconomic issues of markets and hierarchies in greater detail than conventional analysis commonly employs, to achieve a better understanding of the origins and functions of various firm and market structures — stretching from elementary work groups to complex modern corporations. I focus on transactions and the costs that attend completing transactions by one institutional

1. Among the studies that deal, directly or indirectly, with the new institutional economics are Alchian and Demsetz (1972, 1973), Arrow (1969, 1974), Davis and North (1971), Doeringer and Piore (1971), Kornai (1971), Nelson and Winter (1973), and Ward (1971). Earlier efforts of my own to move in this direction are reported in Williamson (1971, 1973). For a recent symposium "On the Economics of Internal Organization," in which many of the market and hierarchy issues are raised, see the Spring and Fall 1975 issues of the *Bell Journal of Economics.*

1

mode rather than another. While the relation of technology to organization remains important, it is scarcely determinative. I argue in this connection that, but for a few conspicuous exceptions, neither the indivisibilities nor technological nonseparabilities on which received theory relies to explain nonmarket organization are sufficient to explain any but very simple types of hierarchy. Rather I contend that transactional considerations, not technology, are typically decisive in determining which mode of organization will obtain in what circumstances and why.

Central to the analysis is what I refer to as the "organizational failures framework." Its distinction is that it expressly acknowledges the importance played by *human* factors in attempting to grapple with problems of economic organization. Such considerations usually operate, if at all, only in a vague, background way. Indeed, they are altogether suppressed in many of the conventional models of economic man that populate intermediate theory textbooks. Although references to "human nature as we know it" (Knight, 1965, p. 270) occasionally appear, these rarely occupy an active role in the analysis. I submit, however, that more self-conscious attention to rudimentary human attributes is essential if we are to accurately characterize and more adequately understand many of the problems of markets and hierarchies.

The remainder of this chapter is an overview of the mode of analysis and types of problems that this book is concerned with. Some of the antecedents to the proposed approach are examined in Section 1. A preliminary statement of the basic framework is set out in Section 2. The framework is then applied to three specific examples in Section 3. These applications reveal that a sensitivity to transaction costs is often essential. They also show that the language of studying markets and hierarchies proposed herein often permits microeconomic phenomena of quite diverse kinds to be understood in different and in some respects deeper ways than conventional analysis would otherwise afford.

1.   Some Antecedents

The materials in this section are in no sense a survey. They merely indicate an early concern among some members of the profession of the types of institutional issues that I deal with in this treatise. With the exception of the market failure literature, which is examined briefly in Section 1.4, there is little reason to believe that there was a concerted effort among the successive authors whose work is cited to redefine economic problems in a complementary way. Each was, however, committed to the proposition that economics should expressly address and help assess the transactional properties of alternative modes of organization.

1.1 Commons on Institutional Economics

As Commons was aware, his treatment of institutional economics was a highly personal effort (1934, p. 1). He was exploring new issues and inventing a quasijudicial language as he proceeded. Inasmuch as the transaction was held to be the ultimate unit of economic investigation (1934, pp. 4, 5, 8), he made transfers of legal control and the efficacy of contracting the focus of his studies.

He considered scarcity to be ubiquitous and conflict of interest, natural (1934, p. 6). He saw the central contribution of institutional economics to the study of economics to be the introduction and explication of the importance of collective action. The requisite degree of cooperation for efficiency to be realized arose not from a presupposed harmony of interests but from the invention of institutions that produced order out of conflict, where order was defined as "working rules of collective action, a special case of which is 'due process of law'" (1934, p. 6). To the extent that collective action was successful in mitigating conflict, a greater total yield — hence, potentially, a more preferred result for all of the parties — was thereby made feasible.

His treatment of "futurity" is of special significance, where "The concept of futurity is that of expected events, but the principle of futurity is the similarity of repetition, with variability, of transactions and their valuations, performed in the moving Present with reference to future events" (1934, p. 738). The emphasis, as I interpret it, is on (1) recurrent contracting, conducted under conditions of (2) uncertainty, and for which (3) successive adaptations are needed to bring the parties into efficient adjustment. As will be apparent, each of these plays an important role in the discussion of transactions in the sections and chapters that follow.

1.2 Coase on the Nature of the Firm

Coase has characterized his 1937 treatment of the firm as "much cited and little used" (1972, p. 63). The reason why it is so widely cited, I submit, is that there is a general appreciation among economists that conventional treatments of firms and markets are not really derived from first principles but are instead arbitrarily imposed. Coase's article makes this fact clear, which qualifies it as a natural in any survey of price theory. But the article is also rather tautological (Alchian and Demsetz, 1972, p. 783), a characteristic that explains why it is not more widely used. Transaction costs are appropriately made the center piece of the analysis, but these are not operationalized in a fashion that permits one to assess the efficacy of completing transactions as between firms and markets in a systematic way.

The article is nevertheless an uncommonly insightful treatment of a fundamental problem at an early point in time and can scarcely be faulted because it did not go further. Of special importance for my purposes are its following attributes:

1. Transactions, and the costs associated therewith, not technology, are the central object of the analysis (1937, pp. 336, 338, 341, 350).
2. Uncertainty and, implicitly, bounded rationality are key features of the argument (1937, pp. 336-337).

Coase contends that the firm serves to economize on transaction costs in two respects. First, reliance on the price mechanism requires that the relevant prices be discovered (1937, p. 336). The firm becomes a sole source supplier to itself for those transactions that are shifted out of the market and into the firm; relevant prices are known or, in any event, bids are presumably solicited less frequently as a result. Second, the firm substitutes a single incomplete contract (an employment agreement) for many complete ones. Such incomplete contracts purportedly economize on the "cost of negotiating and concluding" separate contracts (1937, p. 336). They also facilitate adaptation to changing market circumstances, because the requisite services to be provided are described in the employment agreement in only general terms—the details are to be elaborated at a later date (1937, p. 337).

The underlying factors that explain how and why these economies are realized are not worked out, however, and Coase's discussion of why internal organization does not fully displace the market is even less complete. Though its discussion here would be premature, I submit that a more complete theory of firms and markets than Coase was able to forge in this seminal study awaits more self-conscious attention to the ramifications of the elementary attributes of human decision makers—of which opportunism is one, and bounded rationality is another.

1.3 Hayek on Information

Hayek's discussion of the rational economic order is of interest in several respects. For one thing, he was especially anxious to dispel the notion that central planning is a realistic alternative to competitive market systems (1945, p. 521). Although I shall not be concerned with this issue here, the transactional approach developed herein and the firm or market issues that I address in the chapters that follow have an obvious bearing on the plan or market controversies that have occupied the attention of the profession for many years. More germane to the purposes of this book, however, are Hayek's observations of the following general kind:

1. The problem of a rational economic order is trivial in the absence of bounded rationality limits on human decision makers. It is accordingly essential at the outset to appreciate that bounds on rationality do exist and must be expressly taken into account if organizational issues are to be addressed in operational terms (1945, pp. 519, 527).

2. Much of the knowledge required to make efficient economic decisions cannot be expressed as statistical aggregates but is highly idiosyncratic in nature: "practically every individual has some advantage over all others in that he possesses unique information of which beneficial use might be made, but of which use can be made only if the decisions depending on it are left to him or are made with his active cooperation. We need to remember . . . how valuable an asset in all walks of life is knowledge of people, of local conditions, and of special circumstances" (1945, pp. 521-522).

3. The economic problem is relatively uninteresting except where economic events are changing and sequential adaptations to changing market circumstances are called for (1945, pp. 523-524).

4. The "marvel" of the economic system is that prices serve as sufficient statistics, thereby economizing on bounded rationality (1945, pp. 525-528).

Although each of these observations is important to the argument of this book, I use them in a somewhat different way than does Hayek — mainly because I am interested in a more microeconomic level of detail than he. Given bounded rationality, uncertainty, and idiosyncratic knowledge, I argue that prices often do *not* qualify as sufficient statistics and that a substitution of internal organization (hierarchy) for market-mediated exchange often occurs on this account. Also, unlike Hayek, the alternative organizational modes examined here are strictly firm and market; central planning boards never expressly enter the picture.

1.4 Market Failure

The postwar market failure literature is also an important antecedent literature that poses many of the same types of issues that arise in the markets and hierarchies discussion. As will be apparent, the insurance problem, as described by Arrow (1971, pp. 134-43) and examined in Section 3.1, below, is really a paradigm for studying the employment relation, vertical integration, and competition in the capital market, all of which are developed in the chapters that follow. Similarly, public goods issues (Samuelson, 1954; Hurwicz, 1972), including option demand discussions (Weisbrod, 1964; Cicchetti and Freeman, 1971), are variants of the price discrimination problem (see section 3.2, below). The extensive literature on externalities has long been linked with the question of vertical integration (Davis and Whinston, 1962). Akerlof's (1970) and Arrow's (1969) treatments of the effects of information asymmetries on market exchange are intimately connected with what I refer to as the information impactedness problem.

I draw, directly and indirectly, on this literature throughout the book. At the same time I find it instructive to apply the microanalytic contracting approach herein proposed to reinterpret aspects of the market failure literature. Commonalities among types of failures that are not otherwise apparent are thereby disclosed.

1.5 A Summing Up

My debts to Commons are principally that he defined the economic problem in a spirit that is very much akin to my own. I do not borrow more in detail from what he did because his is a highly personalized analysis and there have been significant developments in the economics and organization theory literatures of the past forty years that are more apposite. Coase's remarkable article on the nature of the firm is instructive in that he both posed the firm and market issues in a direct way and identified transaction costs and contractual relations as the critical factors to be investigated. Hayek's examination of the rational economic order, though directed toward central planning rather than firm and market issues, is very much concerned with problems similar to those found in this book. An appreciation for bounded rationality and idiosyncratic knowledge is essential if the study of markets and hierarchies is to proceed in an operationally engaging way. Finally, the market failure literature raises many of the same types of issues that are of interest here. The context and details differ, but the underlying phenomena are very much the same.

1.6 Some Differences

Despite my considerable reliance on prior literature, this book differs from earlier treatments of markets and hierarchies in significant respects. Even more striking are the differences between my approach to industrial organization issues and the familiar structure-conduct-performance paradigm. Some of the main dissimilarities are indicated here.

1.6.1. DIFFERENCES FROM EARLIER FIRM AND MARKET LITERATURE

The markets and hierarchies approach is interdisciplinary in that it draws extensively on contributions from both economics and organization theory. In addition to the literature referred to above, the contingent claims contracting (Arrow, 1971, pp. 121-134; Meade, 1971, pp. 147-188) and recent organizational design (Hurwicz, 1972) literatures supply the requisite economic background. The administrative man (Simon, 1957) and strategic behavior (Goffman, 1969; Schelling, 1960) literatures are the main organization theory inputs.

The principal differences between the earlier literature and the approach taken here are that: (1) I am much more concerned than are prior treatments with tracing out the ramifications of bounded rationality; (2) I expressly introduce the notion of opportunism and am interested in the ways that opportunistic behavior is influenced by economic organization; and (3) I emphasize that it is not uncertainty or small numbers, individually or together, that occasion market failure but it is rather the *joining* of these factors with bounded rationality on the one hand and opportunism on the other that gives rise to exchange difficulties.

The human factors that are included in the framework nowhere appear, to my knowledge, as a *set* of key attributes in prior studies of economic organization. Not that discussions of bounded rationality and opportunism have never previously appeared. But these have never previously been identified as key attributes and no prior effort has been made to link each to uncertainty and small-numbers in the way that I do.

Furthermore, although opportunism is a variety of self-interest seeking assumption, and thus is akin to the prevailing behavioral assumption employed throughout microeconomics, the consequences of opportunism are incompletely developed in conventional economic models of firms and markets. As Diamond has noted, standard "economic models . . . [treat] individuals as playing a game with fixed rules which they obey. They do not buy more than they know they can pay for, they do not embezzle funds, they do not rob banks" (1971, p. 31). But, whereas behavior of these kinds is disallowed under conventional assumptions, opportunism, in a rich variety of forms, is made to play a central role in the analysis of markets and hierarchies herein.

1.6.2 DIFFERENCES WITH THE STRUCTURE-CONDUCT-PERFORMANCE PARADIGM

The structure-conduct-performance paradigm has characterized much of the industrial organization research during the past forty years [see Bain (1956, 1968) and Caves (1967)]. A goal of profit maximization is ordinarily imputed to the firm, internal organization is largely neglected, and the outer environment is described in terms of market structure measures such as concentration, barriers to entry, excess demand, and so forth. The distribution of transactions between firm and market is mainly taken as a datum.

The present approach differs from this in that the assignment of transactions to one mode or another is taken to be intrinsically interesting and, in a loose way at least, something to be "derived" — somewhat in the spirit of Coase's recent reflections on the state of industrial organization (1972, pp. 62-66). I furthermore regard organization form — by which I mean the hierarchical structure of the firm, the way in which internal economic activities are decomposed into operating parts subject to internal controls — to be distinctly interesting and warranting separate attention. Indeed, I anticipate that measures of internal organizational structure will eventually be joined with measures of market structure in attempting to explain conduct and performance in industrial markets and subdivisions thereof.

I furthermore conjecture that attention to internal organization will prove fruitful in attempting to study the conduct and performance of quasimarket and nonmarket organizations (nonprofits, such as hospitals, universities, foundations, and so forth; and government bureaus). It is generally agreed that the conventional paradigm has been of limited utility in attempting to assess organizations of these kinds. Internal organizational analysis promises to have greater application for the study of nonmarket institutions.

2. A Preliminary Statement of the Organizational Failures Framework

Although I shall defer a more complete statement of the organizational failures framework until Chapter 2 (indeed, some of the elements that appear in it are not even identified here), a sketch of the basic approach, set out early, will not only provide an overview of what will follow but also permit some immediate applications of the framework to be made.

The general approach to economic organization employed here can be summarized compactly as follows: (1) Markets and firms are alternative instruments for completing a related set of transactions; (2) whether a set of transactions ought to be executed across markets or within a firm depends on the relative efficiency of each mode; (3) the costs of writing and executing complex contracts across a market *vary with the characteristics of the human decision makers who are involved with the transaction on the one hand, and the objective properties of the market on the other*; and (4) although the human and environmental factors that impede exchanges between firms (across a market) manifest themselves somewhat differently within the firm, the same set of factors apply to both. A symmetrical analysis of trading thus requires that we acknowledge the transactional limits of internal organization as well as the sources of market failure. Basic to such a comparative analysis is the following proposition: Just as market structure matters in assessing the efficacy of trades in the marketplace, so likewise does internal structure matter in assessing internal organization.

The markets and hierarchies approach attempts to identify a set of *environmental factors* which together with a related set of *human factors* explain the circumstances under which complex contingent claims contracts will be costly to write, execute, and enforce. Faced with such difficulties, and considering the risks that simple (or incomplete) contingent claims contracts pose, the firm may decide to bypass the market and resort to hierarchical modes of organization. Transactions that might otherwise be handled in the market are thus performed internally, governed by administrative processes, instead.

The environmental factors that lead to prospective market failure are uncertainty and small-numbers exchange relations. *Unless joined, however, by a related set of human factors, such environmental conditions need not impede market exchange.* The pairing of uncertainty with *bounded rationality* and the joining of small numbers with what I shall refer to as *opportunism* are especially important.

Consider first the pairing of bounded rationality with uncertainty. The principle of bounded rationality has been defined by Herbert Simon as follows: "*The capacity of the human mind for formulating and solving complex problems is very small compared with the size of the problems whose solution is required for objectively rational behavior in the real world*" (1957, p. 198, emphasis in original). It refers to neurophysiological limits on the one hand and language limits on the other. If, in consideration of these limits, it is very costly or impossible to identify future contingencies and specify, *ex ante,* appropriate adaptations thereto, long-term contracts may be supplanted by internal organization. Recourse to the latter permits adaptations to uncertainty to be accomplished by administrative processes in a sequential fashion. Thus, rather than attempt to anticipate all possible contingencies from the outset, the future is permitted to unfold. Internal organization in this way economizes on the bounded rationality attributes of decision makers in circumstances in which prices are not "sufficient statistics" and uncertainty is substantial.

Explicating the relation between opportunism and a small numbers exchange condition is somewhat involved and is accordingly deferred to the examples in Section 3 and to Chapter 2. Suffice it to observe here that (1) opportunism refers to a lack of candor or honesty in transactions, to include self-interest seeking with guile; (2) opportunistic inclinations pose little risk as long as competitive (large-numbers) exchange relations obtain; (3) many transactions that at the outset involve a large number of qualified bidders are transformed in the process of contract execution, so that a small-numbers supply condition effectively obtains at the contract renewal interval; and (4) recurrent short-term contracting is costly and risky when opportunism and transactions of this latter kind are joined.

In consideration of the problems that both long- and short-term contracts are subject to — *by reason of bounded rationality and uncertainty in the first instance and the pairing of opportunism with small-numbers relations in the second*—internal organization may arise instead. Issues here are dealt with as they arise rather than in an exhaustive contingent-planning fashion from the outset. The resulting adaptive, sequential decision-making process is the internal organizational counterpart of short-term contracting and serves to economize on bounded rationality. Opportunism does not pose the same difficulties for such internal sequential supply relations that it does when negotiations take place across a market because (1) internal divisions do not have pre-emptive claims on profit streams (but more nearly joint profit maximize instead); and (2) the internal incentive and control machinery is much more extensive and refined than that which obtains in market exchanges. The firm is thereby better able to take the long view for investment purposes (and hence is more prepared to put specialized plant and equipment in place) while simultaneously adjusting to changing market circumstances in an adaptive, sequential manner.

But whichever way the assignment of transactions to firm or market is made initially, the choice ought not to be regarded as fixed. Both firms and markets change over time in ways that may render inappropriate an initial assignment of transactions to firm or market. The degree of uncertainty associated with the transactions in question may diminish; market growth may support large-numbers supply relations; and information disparities between the parties often shrink. Also, changes in information processing technology may occur which alter the degree to which bounded rationality limits apply, with the result that a different assignment of activities between markets and hierarchies than was selected initially becomes appropriate later. Thus, we ought periodically to reassess the efficacy of completing transactions by one mode rather than another.

3. Three Illustrations

Whether the proposed approach leads to a better understanding of or to implications different from those found in received microtheory can best be established by addressing it to particular economic phenomena. Three are examined here: price discrimination, the insurance problem, and Stigler's life cycle treatment of vertical integration. Although the first of these does not ordinarily entail market and hierarchy choices, price discrimination has the advantage of being familiar and does raise transaction cost issues. Except to the extent that self-insurance is a viable alternative, neither does the insurance problem expressly pose market and hierarchy issues. It is, however, a paradigmatic problem, the attributes of which will recur in a variety of contracting contexts in the chapters that follow. Stigler's treatment of vertical integration is directly concerned with market and hierarchy issues.

3.1 Price Discrimination

The differences between received microtheory and the transaction cost approach can be illustrated by examining the familiar problem of price discrimination. As will be evident, the transaction cost approach does not abandon but rather augments the received microtheory model.

Assume that the market in question is one for which economies of scale are large in relation to the size of the market, in which case the average cost curve falls over a considerable output range. Assume, in particular, that demand and cost conditions are as shown in Figure 1. The unregulated monopolist who both maximizes profits and sells his output at a single, uniform price to all customers will restrict output below the social optimum (shown by Q^* in Figure 1), at which marginal cost equals price.[2] Instead, the monopolist will restrict his output to Q_m, where marginal cost equals marginal revenue and an excess of price over marginal cost obtains.

It is sometimes argued, however, that price discrimination will correct the allocative efficiency distortion referred to. In particular, the monopolist who segregates his market in such a way that each customer is made to pay his full valuation (given by the demand curve) for each unit of output has the incentive to add successive units of output until the price paid for the last item sold just equals the marginal cost. The fully discriminating monopolist will thus be led to expand output from Q_m to Q^*.[3] Although income distribution will be affected in the process (in possibly objectionable ways), the output distortion noted earlier is removed and an allocative efficiency gain is realized.[4]

Evaluating this allocative efficiency claim gives us our first opportunity to contrast the conventional analysis of received microtheory with a transactions cost approach. Implicit in the above conventional microtheory argument is an assumption that the costs of both discovering true customer

---

2. So-called "second-best" issues are assumed away here and throughout this section.
3. So that a break-even problem will not be posed if output is set at Q^*, I assume that scale economies are exhausted before this output is reached.
4. If the output of the industry in question is used as an intermediate rather than strictly as a final product, factor distortions at other stages of production may be induced. For a discussion, see McKenzie (1951). For simplicity, let these types of issues be assumed away.

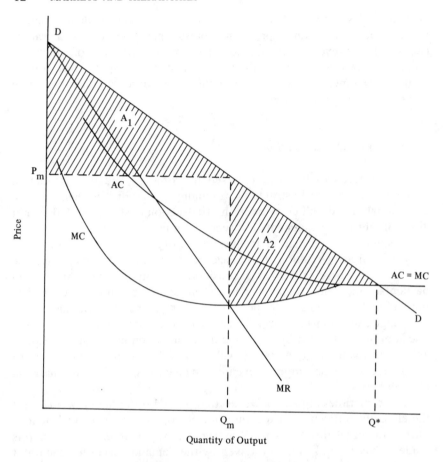

Figure 1.

valuations for the product and enforcing restrictions against resale (so that there can be no arbitrage) are negligible and can be disregarded. Such costs vanish, however, only if either (1) customers will honestly self-reveal preferences and self-enforce nonresale promises (no opportunism); or (2) the seller is omniscient, a possibility that requires unbounded rationality of an especially strong kind. Inasmuch as assumptions of both kinds are plainly unrealistic, the question naturally arises: Does an allocative efficiency gain obtain when nontrivial transaction costs must be incurred to discover true customer valuations and/or to police nonresale restrictions? Unfortunately for received microtheory, the outcome is uncertain if these transaction costs are introduced.

To see this, assume (for simplicity) that the transaction costs of accomplishing full price discrimination are independent of the level of output: The costs are either zero, in which event no effort to price discriminate is made, or T, in which case customer valuations become fully known and enforcement against cheating is complete[5] Price discrimination will of course be attractive to the monopolist if a net profit gain can be shown — a situation that will obtain if the additional revenues (which are given by the two shaded regions, A_1 and A_2, in Figure 1) exceed the costs of achieving discrimination, T. Interesting for social welfare evaluation purposes is the fact that an incremental gross welfare gain is realized only on output that exceeds Q_m. This gain is given by the lower triangle (A_2). Consequently, the net social welfare effects will be positive only if A_2 exceeds the transaction costs, T. An allocative efficiency loss, occasioned by high transaction costs, but a private monopoly gain, derived from price discrimination applied to *all* output, is therefore consistent with fully discriminatory pricing in circumstances where nontrivial transaction costs are incurred in reaching the discriminatory result. More precisely, if T is less than A_1 plus A_2 but more than A_2 alone, the monopolist will be prepared to incur the customer information and policing costs necessary to achieve the discriminatory outcome, because his profits will be augmented ($A_1 + A_2 > T$), but these same expenditures will give rise to a net social welfare loss ($A_2 < T$).[6]

Of course, in circumstances in which T is zero or negligible, this contradiction does not arise. Such may obtain if the product or service is costly to store (for example, electricity supply, telephone service), in which case arbitrage is made difficult and, whatever the opportunistic inclinations of buyers may be, promises not to resell become unimportant. The problem of discovering true valuations still remains, but this can often be approximated if customer classes can be segregated and low-cost metering devices are employed. I nevertheless emphasize that the conventional welfare gain associated with price discrimination rests crucially on the assumption that transaction costs of both valuation and policing kinds are negligible. If these cannot be so characterized, such transaction costs need expressly to be taken into account before a welfare assessment is ventured.

3.2 The Insurance Example

As indicated, the insurance example is interesting not merely for its own sake but also because the parameters of the insurance problem can

5. Generalizing the analysis by expressing the transaction costs of discerning true customer valuations and by policing resale restrictions as a continuous function of output is relatively easy but yields little that the simplified assumptions do not. (One difference is that the price discriminating output will be less than Q^*.) The analysis can likewise be generalized to make the degree of precision of price discrimination a decision variable.
6. The discussion in the text assumes, implicitly, that the uniform pricing monopolist can price at P_M without inducing entry. If, however, the entry forestalling price ($\overline{P}$) is less than P_M, the initial position to be evaluated is a larger output and lower price than that discussed above. For fixed T, the welfare gains of price discrimination are further reduced. (In all likelihood, an entry threat will reduce the private gains as well.)

be reinterpreted in such a way as to expose the problems that employment contracts, vertical integration, and competition in the capital market confront. It is also interesting because it poses what may be referred to as the "information impactedness" problem. (Information impactedness is a derivative condition in the organizational failures framework. It is mainly attributable to the pairing of uncertainty with opportunism. It exists in circumstances in which one of the parties to an exchange is much better informed than is the other regarding underlying conditions germane to the trade, and the second party cannot achieve information parity except at great cost—because he cannot rely on the first party to disclose the information in a fully candid manner.[7])

Risk aversion will be assumed and the question is whether a group of individuals who are exposed to independent risks will be able to pool these successfully with an insurer. Assume further that the members of the group are uniformly distributed over the risk interval p_1 to p_2, where $p_1 < p_2$, and p denotes the probability for a particular individual that the contingency to be insured will eventuate. (Because this probability will vary depending on the risk-mitigating actions taken by an individual, assume that p reflects efficient risk mitigation.) Whereas individuals will be assumed to know their risk characteristics exactly, the insurer is unable, at low cost, to distinguish one member of the group from another. Information impactedness thus obtains. Assume also that the highest premium that an individual of risk class p will pay is $(p + \epsilon)D$, where $\epsilon < (p_2 - p_1)/2$, and D is the (common) damage that will be incurred if the contingency obtains.

In the absence of other information, and assuming transactions costs to be negligible, insurers would break even if they could sell insurance to all members of this group at a premium of $[(p_1 + p_2)/2]D$, which is the mean loss. Such a premium will regarded as excessive, however, by those good-risk types for whom $p + \epsilon < (p_1 + p_2)/2$. Inasmuch as these preferred risks cannot easily establish that they are honestly entitled to a lower premium—because (opportunistic) poor-risk types can make the same representations and insurers are unable (except at great cost) to distinguish between them—they will withdraw. Breakeven then requires that remaining parties be charged a higher premium; the system will stabilize eventually at a premium of $(p_2 - \epsilon)D$. Information impactedness and opportunism thus result in what is commonly referred to as the "adverse selection" problem.

Moreover, the matter does not end here if the extent of the losses incurred is influenced by the degree to which insured parties take steps designed to mitigate losses. If promises were self-enforcing, insurers need merely extract a promise from insureds that, once insured, they will behave "re-

7. A more complete development of information impactedness, the forms that it can take, and the underlying reasons therefore will be deferred to Chapter 2. That the condition arises in the context of insurance transactions and poses severe problems should, however, be evident from what follows.

sponsibly." Alternatively, if it could easily be discerned *ex post* whether efficient contingency-mitigating practices had or had not been followed, insurers could supply insureds with appropriate incentives to behave responsibly by paying only those claims that fell within the terms of the agreement. If, however, such determinations can be made only at great cost and (some) insureds exploit *ex post* information differentials opportunistically, the problem referred to in the insurance literature as "moral hazard" (Arrow, 1971, pp. 142, 202, 243) obtains. Premiums will be increased on this account as well. Note also that responsible parties who would otherwise be prepared to self-enforce promises to take efficient loss-mitigating actions may find that such behavior is not competitively viable and will consequently be induced to imitate opportunistic types by underinvesting in loss mitigation.[8] A sort of Gresham's Law of Behavior obtains.

Revising the terms of a contract to reflect the additional information gleaned from experience may be referred to as experience rating. The prospect that this will be done serves to curb opportunism in contract execution. Inferior agents will nevertheless be able to exploit information impactedness, however, unless original terms are relatively severe (that is, no bargains are to be had on joining) or parties are unable easily to opt out when terms are adjusted adversely against them.

One way to accomplish the latter is that markets pool their experience so that opportunistic types cannot secure better terms by "quitting" and turning elsewhere. This pooling requires that a common language be devised for describing agent characteristics, which will be greatly facilitated if the behavior in question can be easily quantified. If, instead, the judgments to be made are highly subjective, the costs of communication needed to support a collective experience rating system are apt to be prohibitive in relation to the gains — if the organizational mode is held constant.[9]

Experience-rating is also of interest to superior risk/responsible types. Good risks and/or those who would be prepared to self-enforce promises to mitigate losses efficiently may be induced to join at a high premium by

8. It is furthermore relevant in this connection to distinguish between insurance claims attributable to excessive exposure to hazard, for failure to take appropriate protective actions, and the "overutilization" of insured services (for example, health care) because, given insurance, the effective price is less than the market price. Pauly contends that only the former and not the latter reflects moral hazard, and describes the price responsiveness as a result "not of moral perfidy, but of rational economic behavior" (1968, p. 535). Clearly however, behavior of both types could and would be eliminated if insurers could extract self-enforcing promises from insureds not to exploit *ex post* information impactedness opportunistically. Inasmuch as *ex post* behavior of both types is attributable to the impossibility of extracting such guarantees, it seems artificial that one type should be regarded as moral perfidy but not the other (cf., Arrow, 1971, pp. 220-221).
9. Recourse to internal organization may permit these costs of communication to be attenuated. For an interesting discussion of experience rating in markets, see Leff (1970). Some of the problems of markets in experience-rating respects are developed in Chapter 2.

the assurance that premiums will subsequently be made on a more discriminating basis as information accumulates. This offer will be especially attractive if, rather than merely revise a priori probabilities on the basis of claim experience, performance audits are also made — because, without a performance audit, the true explanation for outcomes that are jointly dependent on the state of nature that obtains and the behavior of the economic agent cannot be accurately established (Arrow, 1969, p. 55). Monitoring thus helps restore markets that are otherwise beset with opportunistic distortions to more efficient configurations — albeit that some degree of imperfection, in a net benefit sense, is irremediable (the costs of complete information parity are simply prohibitive).

3.3 Stigler on Vertical Integration

Stigler's explication, as it applies to vertical integration, of Adam Smith's theorem that "the division of labor is limited by the extent of the market" leads to his deduction of the following life cycle implications: Vertical integration will be extensive in firms in young industries; disintegration will be observed as an industry grows; and reintegration will occur as an industry passes into decline (1968, pp. 129-141). These life cycle effects are illustrated by reference to a multiprocess product, each of which processes involves a separable technology and hence has its own distinct cost function.[10] Some of the processes display individually falling cost curves, others rise continuously, and still others have U-shaped cost curves.

Stigler then inquires: Why does not the firm exploit the decreasing cost activities by expanding them to become a monopoly? He answers by observing that, at the outset, the decreasing cost functions may be "too small to support a specialized firm or firms" (1968, p. 133). But, unless the argument is meant to be restricted to global or local monopolies, for which there is no indication, resort to a specialized firm does not exhaust the possibilities. Assuming that there are at least several rival firms in the business, why does not one of these exploit the available economies, to the mutual benefit of all the parties, by producing the entire requirement for the group? The reasons, I submit, turn on transaction cost considerations.

If, for example, the exchange of specialized information between the parties is involved (Stigler specifically refers to "market information" as one of the decreasing cost possibilities), strategic misrepresentation issues are posed. The risk here is that the specialist firm will disclose information to its rivals in an incomplete and distorted manner. Because the party buying the information can establish its accuracy only at great cost, possibly only by collecting the original data itself, the exchange fails to go through. If,

---

10. Stigler employs the separability assumption for convenience; relaxing it complicates but does not alter the general argument.

however, rivals were not given to being opportunistic, the risk of strategic distortion would vanish and the (organizationally efficient) specialization of information could proceed.

The exchange of physical components that experience decreasing costs is likewise discouraged where both long-term and spot market contracts prospectively incur transactional difficulties. Long-term contracts are principally impeded by bounded rationality considerations: Given bounded rationality, the extent to which uncertain future events can be expressly taken into account — in the sense that appropriate adaptations thereto are costed out and contractually specified — is simply limited. Because, given opportunism, incomplete long-term contracts predictably pose interest conflicts between the parties, other arrangements are apt to be sought.

Spot market (short-term) contracting is an obvious alternative. Such contracts, however, are hazardous if a small-numbers supply relation obtains — a condition that, by assumption, holds for the circumstances described by Stigler. The buyer then incurs the risk that the purchased product or service will, at some time, be supplied under monopolistic terms. Industry growth, moreover, need not eliminate the tension of small-numbers bargaining if the item in question is one for which learning by doing is important and if the market for human capital is imperfect.[11] Delaying own-production until own-requirements are sufficient to exhaust scale economies would, considering the learning costs of undertaking own-production at this later time, incur substantial transition costs. It may, under these conditions, be more attractive from the outset for each firm to produce its own requirements — or, alternatively, for the affected firms to merge.[12] Without present or prospective transaction costs of the sorts described, however, specialization by one of the firms (that is, monopoly supply), to the mutual benefit of all, would presumably occur. Put differently, technology is no bar to contracting; it is transactional considerations that are decisive.

Aspects of the above argument can be illustrated with the help of Figure 2. The average costs of supplying the item in question by a specialized outside supplier at time 1 are shown by the curve AC_1^s. Firms that are already in the industry can supply the same item at the average costs shown by AC_1^x. The curve AC_1^s is everywhere above the curve AC_1^x because firms already in the industry avoid the setup costs that a specialized outside supplier would incur. Each of the firms in the industry generates requirements for the item at time 1 of Q_1^i. The total industry requirements at time 1 is Q_1^T.

11. The point is developed further in Chapter 4.
12. Mergers would permit the firms involved to realize economies of scale with respect to the decreasing cost activity in question. Such mergers might also, however, result in market power. That such mergers are attractive is clear in a private net benefit sense, but social net benefits need not obtain.

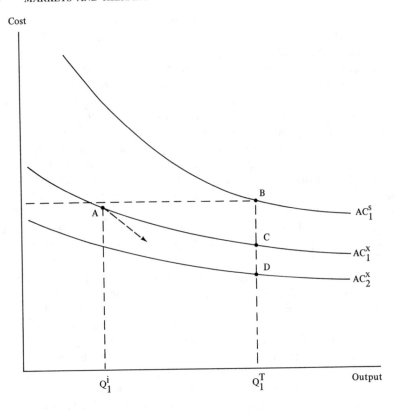

Figure 2.

The implicit comparison that Stigler makes in his explanation for
vertical integration is point *A* versus point *B*. Thus, although having a
specialized supplier service the whole industry (produce Q_1^T) would permit
economies of scale to be more fully exploited, the declining cost advantage
is more than offset by the setup costs — on which account the average costs
of the specialized supplier (at *B*) exceed the average costs that each individual firm would incur by supplying its own requirements (at *A*). My argument, however, is that point *A* should also be compared with point *C* —
where point *C* shows the average costs of supplying the requirements for
the entire industry by one of the firms that is *already in the industry*. Such
a firm does not incur those setup costs which disadvantage the outside
specialist supplier. Given the decreasing cost technology that Stigler
assumes, the average costs at *C* are necessarily less than those at *A*. Why
then not have one of the firms already in the industry supply both itself
and all others? The impediments, I submit, are the above described hazards
of interfirm contracting (of both long-term and spot market types), which

is to say, transaction cost considerations, not technology, explain the outcome.

The comparison, moreover, can be extended to include a consideration of the curve AC_2^x, which represents the average costs that will be incurred by an integrated firm at time 2 which has been supplying the product or service continuously during the interval from time 1 to time 2. The curve AC_2^x is everywhere lower than AC_1^x by reason of learning-by-doing advantages. To the extent that such learning advantages are firm-specific,[13] they will accrue only to firms that have undertaken own-production during the supply interval in question. Thus, if one of the firms in the industry becomes the monopoly supplier to all others at time 1 and if at time 2 the other firms become dissatisfied with the monopoly supplier's terms, these buying firms cannot undertake own-supply at a later date on cost parity terms—because they have not had the benefit of learning-by-doing.

Note finally the arrow that points away from point A toward point D. If the industry is expected to grow, which plainly is the case for the circumstances described by Stigler, and if each of the firms in the industry can be expected to grow with it, then each firm, if it supplies its own requirements (Q_1^i) at time 1 and incurs average costs of A, can, by reason of both growth and learning-by-doing, anticipate declining own-supply costs — perhaps to the extent that each substantially exhausts the economies of scale that are available. Because own-supply avoids the transactional hazards of small-numbers outside procurement, vertical integration of the decreasing cost technology items to which Stigler refers is thus all the more to be expected.

13. This condition assumes that the market for human capital is imperfect. Firm X cannot simply hire firm Y's experienced employees away without incurring very considerable transfer costs. Knowledge acquired through learning-by-doing is thus impacted in firm Y.

2. The Organizational Failures Framework

A more complete statement of the organizational failures framework is developed in this chapter. My purposes are to better define and give operational content to the transactional terminology introduced in Chapter 1; to show why it is always the joining of human with environmental factors, not either taken by itself, that poses transactional problems; and to introduce systems considerations by reference to "atmosphere." Each of the transactional relations of interest is first described in general terms and illustrated by example. The prospective advantages that internal organization affords with respect to the transactional condition in question are then indicated.

Although failures can be and often are assessed with respect to a frictionless ideal, my concern throughout the book is with comparative institutional choices. Only to the extent that frictions associated with one mode of organization are prospectively attenuated by shifting the transaction, or a related set of transactions, to an alternative mode can a failure be said to exist. Remediable frictions thus constitute the conditions of interest.

I assume, for expositional convenience, that "in the beginning there were markets." This choice of initial conditions results in what may appear to be a preoccupation with market failure. In fact, however, organizational failure is a symmetrical term meant to apply to market and nonmarket organizations alike. Thus, although a presumption of market failure[1] is warranted where it is observed that transactions are shifted out of a market and into a firm, a presumption of internal organizational failure is warranted for transactions that are unshifted (continue to be market-mediated). My

1. This is merely a presumption. Transactions are sometimes shifted out of the market into the firm because the firm thereby realizes a strategic advantage over actual and potential rivals and in relation to customers. Such monopoly incentives are examined in subsequent chapters. They by no means constitute the main reason for supplanting market mediated transactions.

choice of initial conditions tends to highlight transactions of the former kind, as compared with transactions that continue to be market-mediated; however, were the initial conditions to have been reversed, so that "in the beginning there was central planning," the analysis would appear instead to be preoccupied with internal organizational failures. In either case, the same organizational failures framework would be employed, the focus would remain the same (namely, the assignment of economic activity to firm and market in such a way as to economize on transaction costs),[2] and the same eventual configuration of transactions as between firm and market should be observed.[3]

The pairing of bounded rationality with uncertainty/complexity is examined in Section 1. The joining of opportunism with small numbers exchange conditions is treated in Section 2. The derivative relation, information impactedness, is then developed in Section 3. Atmosphere is treated briefly, and selectively, in Section 4. A schematic of the markets and hierarchies framework is then set out in Section 5.

1. Bounded Rationality and Uncertainty/Complexity

1.1 General

Bounded rationality refers to human behavior that is "*intendedly* rational, but only *limitedly* so" (Simon, 1961, p. xxiv). Although it is widely appreciated that human decision makers are not lightning calculators, and occasionally this fact is explictly taken into account in abstract models of market processes (Radner, 1968), the implications for economic organization have only been scratched.

Bounded rationality involves neurophysiological limits on the one hand and language limits on the other. The physical limits take the form of rate and storage limits on the powers of individuals to receive, store, retrieve, and process information without error. Simon observes in this connection that "it is only because individual human beings are limited in knowledge, foresight, skill, and time that organizations are useful instruments for the achievement of human purpose" (1957, p. 199). Inasmuch as the literature on contingent claim markets was at a very early stage of its development in 1957 and since Simon is inexplicit on what alternative modes were subject to displacement by "organizations" (markets, after all, are usefully regarded

---

2. This assumes that economies of scale are fully realized, at least to the extent that market demand permits.
3. The only difference would be that transactions for which neither firm nor market had an advantage would be assigned to the market under the first set of initial conditions and to the firm for the second.

as organizations also), it is not clear that Simon had the substitution of internal organization for imperfect contingent claims markets in mind. The reasons why the absence of unlimited computational capacity prevents comprehensive contracting of the sort required for the standard theorems on the existence and optimality of a competitive equilibrium to go through have, however, since been examined by Radner (1968).

Whereas the absence of a full set of contingent claims markets was of interest to Radner mainly because this permitted him to explain the existence of spot markets and demands for liquidity, which do not appear in the Arrow-Debreu version of the contingent claims model, it is of interest here because incomplete (or costly) contingent claims markets also occasion the development of internal organization. To the extent that internal organization serves to economize on scarce computational capacity, and does not experience offsetting disabilities, internal organization is presumably favored. This turns out to be especially significant in relation to adaptive, sequential decision-making.

Language limits refer to the inability of individuals to articulate their knowledge or feelings by the use of words, numbers, or graphics in ways which permit them to be understood by others. Despite their best efforts, parties may find that language fails them (possibly because they do not possess the requisite vocabulary or the necessary vocabulary has not been devised),[4] and they resort to other means of communication instead. Demonstrations, learning-by-doing, and the like may be the only means of achieving understanding when such language difficulties develop.

Bounds on rationality are interesting, of course, only to the extent that the limits of rationality are reached—which is to say, under conditions of uncertainty and/or complexity. In the absence of either of these conditions, the appropriate set of contingent actions can be fully specified at the outset.[5] Thus, it is bounded rationality in relation to the condition of the environment that occasions the economic problem. Given unbounded rationality, contingent claims contracting goes through, whatever the degree of complexity to be dealt with. Similarly, given a sufficiently simple environment, bounded rationality constraints are never reached and com-

4. Note that if language fails because receivers cannot comprehend complexity, then the problem is an information receiving and processing difficulty, not an inability to find suitable language to convey meaning. The capacity to comprehend complexity can, of course, be expanded by replacing low capacity by high capacity receivers. Given, however, that high capacity receivers are in short supply, these need to be allocated to alternative uses with care.

   For a more general discussion of bounded rationality, see March and Simon (1958, Chap. 6) and Simon (1972).

5. An example is the two-dimensional tic-tac-toe game. The problem of *ex ante* specification of contingent responses for all moves in this game is, in relation to the computational powers of most adults, relatively simple. The corresponding chess problem, by contrast, is impossibly complex; *ex ante* specification of the full decision tree is infeasible (see Section 1.2, below).

parative institutional choices between firm and market are not posed—not in any interesting way at least. When, however, transactions are conducted under conditions of uncertainty/complexity, in which event it is very costly, perhaps impossible, to describe the complete decision tree, the bounded rationality constraint is binding and an assessment of alternative organizational modes, in efficiency respects, becomes necessary. Feldman and Kanter's discussion of the decision process is particularly relevant (1965, p. 615):

> For even moderately complex problems . . . the entire decision tree cannot be generated. There are several reasons why this is so: one is the size of the tree. The number of alternative paths in complex decision problems is very large. . . . A second reason is that in most decision situations, unlike chess, neither the alternative paths nor a rule for generating them is available. . . . A third reason is the problem of estimating consequences. . . . For many problems, consequences of alternatives are difficult, if not impossible, to estimate. The comprehensive decision model is not feasible for most interesting decision problems.

As they point out, most decision problems, unlike board games such as chess, are not deterministic but involve decision-making under uncertainty. For these, the comprehensive decision tree is not apt even to be feasible. As Simon indicates, however, and as is maintained here, the distinction between deterministic complexity and uncertainty is inessential. What may be referred to as "uncertainty" in chess is "uncertainty introduced into a perfectly certain environment by inability—computational inability—to ascertain the structure of the environment. But the result of the uncertainty, whatever its source, is the same: approximation must replace exactness in reaching a decision" (Simon, 1972, p. 170). As long as either uncertainty or complexity is present in requisite degree, the bounded rationality problem arises and an interesting comparative institutional choice is often posed.[6]

1.2 Some Examples

1.2.1 COMPLEXITY

Chess, as von Neumann and Morgenstern have observed, is a trivial game: ". . . if the theory of Chess (i.e., the complete tree of possible games) were really fully known there would be nothing left to play" (1953, p. 125). As they subsequently point out, however, and as Simon elaborates, the complete decision tree is prohibitively complex to develop. Assuming, at any given stage in a game of chess, that there are about thirty legal moves, there will be, for a move and its replies, about 10^3 possibilities to consider.

6. I also point out in this connection that the distinction between risk and uncertainty is not one with which I will be concerned—if indeed it is a truly useful one to employ in any context whatsoever (see Hirschleifer, 1970, p. 215; also Green, 1971, p. 213).

If the average length of game is forty moves, 10^{120} possibilities must be considered (Simon, 1972, p. 166) — which is unimaginably vast.

1.2.2 UNCERTAINTY

Meade's discussion of the limitations of contingent claims contracting affords a striking example of bounded rationality. After first describing "a single gigantic once-for-all forward 'higgle-haggle' in which all contingent goods and services (i.e., all goods and services at each possible time-cum-environmental condition) are bought and sold once and for all now for money payments made now" (1971, p. 166),[7] he then goes on to concede (1971, p. 183):

> When environmental uncertainties are so numerous that they cannot all be considered . . . or, what comes perhaps to much the same thing, when any particular environmental risks are so hard to define and to distinguish from each other that it is impossible to base a firm betting or insurance contract upon the occurrence or non-occurrence of any one of them, then for this reason alone it is impossible to have a system of contingency or of conditional forward markets.

Although a full explanation for the impossibility conditions described by Meade also involves opportunism (see Section 2, below), a major contributing factor is the existence of bounded rationality. Environmental uncertainties, when these become so numerous that they cannot all be considered, presumably exceed the data processing capabilities of the parties. The complete decision tree simply cannot be generated — in which event "the bulk of meaningful future transactions cannot be carried out on any existing present market" (Arrow, 1969, p. 51).

1.2.3 LANGUAGE

A final example of bounded rationality is afforded by Commons in his description of the political leader as one who "can formulate in language what others feel but could not tell" (1934, p. 750). The bounds on rationality here take the form of language rather than computational limits and evidently vary among individuals. If the specialization of labor is feasible, those whose rationality limits are less severely constrained than others are natural candidates to assume technical, administrative, or political leadership positions — which is to say that a hierarchy can emerge on this account.[8]

----

7. If one takes the assumption of unbounded rationality to the limit, one might reasonably ask why the gigantic higgle-haggle? If everyone can be fully apprised of the resources and preferences of everyone else, the gigantic simultaneous equations system can be identically "solved" by everyone at the outset and the iterative procedures of the higgle-haggle bypassed. Most economists regard such computational capacities to be mind-boggling, hence their recourse to iterative processes by which contingent prices are generated. [See, however, Meade (1971, p. 148).]

8. For additional discussion of the way in which the differential distribution of talents gives rise to hierarchy, see Chapter 3, Section 3.

1.3 Internal Organization

As Hayek emphasized (see Chapter 1), the price system has advantages over central planning in circumstances where the relevant information is summarized by price signals. The price system relieves the need for parties who are remotely related to the underlying change in the data to be apprised of the details associated with changing market conditions. Demands on scarce rationality capabilities are correspondingly limited.

Where competitive supply conditions are not satisfied, reliance on summary statistics can be hazardous. For the reasons that will be developed in Section 2 and in the following chapters, internal organization often has attractive properties in that it permits the parties to deal with uncertainty/ complexity in an adaptive, sequential fashion without incurring the same types of opportunism hazards that market contracting would pose. Such *adaptive, sequential decision processes economize greatly on bounded rationality*. Rather than specifying the decision tree exhaustively in advance, and deriving the corresponding contingent prices, events are permitted to unfold and attention is restricted to only the actual rather than all possible outcomes.[9]

A further advantage of internal organization is that, as compared to recurrent market exchange, efficient codes are more apt to evolve and be employed with confidence by the parties. Such coding also economizes on bounded rationality. Complex events are summarized in an informal way by using what may be an idiosyncratic language.[10] Although, in principle, the parties to recurrent market contracts could devise the same language, thereby realizing the same economies, such exchanges are more subject to risks of opportunism—hence, are less apt to be developed as fully.

An additional advantage of internal organization is that it promotes convergent expectations, serving in this way to attenuate uncertainties that are generated when interdependent parties make independent decisions with respect to changing market circumstances (Malmgren, 1961). If each of the parties to a related set of transactions takes his own observations on how events are changing, infers probable consequences (including how other parties can be expected to adapt), and acts accordingly, there is a risk that the resulting set of decisions will be made in a jointly incompatible manner.

9. As Chernoff and Moses put it, in the context of deriving Bayes strategies, the sequential process of successively revising *a priori* probabilities on the basis of new observations "permits you to 'cross your bridge as you come to it' rather than phrase your detailed strategy in advance, thereby 'crossing all possible bridges you might conceivably come to'" (1959, p. 192).

10. As Guetzkow puts it: "Communication systems become effective when they employ languages which carry large amounts of meaning with relatively fewer symbols. Organizations find such things as blueprints, product number systems, and occupational jargons helpful in increasing the efficiency of their communications" (1965, p. 551).

It is not, however, that markets are perverse or inherently "predisposed" to go through an extended period of disequilibrium during which a common set of expectations among the parties gradually evolves. In principle, this adjustment process could be shortened by having one of the autonomous parties to the exchange temporarily serve as the decision maker for all: he would declare who is to adapt and how. The risk of giving such an assignment to an autonomous party is that he will refer to his private gains rather than to a collective calculus in making a recommendation. To the extent that internal organization mitigates such opportunistic behavior, without incurring offsetting costs, a shift from market to hierarchy will promote efficient adaptation.

2. Opportunism and Small Numbers

2.1 General

Opportunism extends the conventional assumption that economic agents are guided by considerations of self-interest to make allowance for *strategic* behavior. This involves self-interest seeking with guile and has profound implications for choosing between alternative contractual relationships. Such strategic interaction has been discussed in other contexts by other writers; Schelling's (1960) and Goffman's (1969) treatments are especially notable.

Opportunism is to be distinguished from both stewardship behavior and instrumental behavior. Whereas stewardship behavior involves a trust relation in which the word of a party can be taken as his bond, instrumental behavior is a more neutral mode in which there is no necessary self-awareness that the interests of a party can be furthered by stratagems of any sort (Goffman, 1969, p. 88). Opportunistic behavior differs from both because it involves making "false or empty, that is, self-disbelieved, threats and promises" in the expectation that individual advantage will thereby be realized (Goffman, 1969, p. 105).

Advantages that are due to (1) pre-existing and fully disclosed productive conditions (for example, a unique location or differential skill) that obtain at the outset should be distinguished from advantages which result from (2a) selective or distorted information disclosure or (2b) self-disbelieved promises regarding future conduct. Advantages of the first type do not involve opportunism. Rather, parties are simply realizing returns to which their pre-existing position entitles them; no special concern over the form which a contract takes develops on this account.

The strategic manipulation of information or misrepresentation of intentions, however, are to be regarded as opportunistic and do have comparative institutional significance for assigning transactions to one mode of organization instead of another. Opportunism of the (2b) kind is of special importance in this connection. Thus, if opportunism of the second kind were missing, then self-enforcing promises to the effect that "I solemnly pledge to execute this contract efficiently and to seek only fair returns at the contract renewal interval" could be extracted as a condition of being awarded the initial contract *and,* except as it affects the terms struck during the original negotiations, opportunism of the (2a) kind would vanish as well. Accordingly, the importance of assigning transactions to one mode of organization rather than another would be negligible.

By assumption, however, self-enforcing commitments of this kind cannot be secured. At least some of the agents who accede to such terms do it casually, in a self-disbelieved way. Since these types cannot be distinguished *ex ante* from sincere types (see the discussion of information impactedness below), relying on such promises exposes sales contracts to hazards during contract execution and at the contract renewal interval. Lest such contracts be inefficiently executed, an effort must be made to anticipate contingencies and spell out terms much more fully than would otherwise be necessary. Also, inasmuch as corners can be cut on even a detailed agreement in ways that are difficult to discern *ex post,* the agreement needs to be monitored. Internal organization may thus arise because it pemits economies to be realized in initial contracting and/or monitoring respects.

But merely to harbor opportunistic inclinations does not imply that markets are flawed on this account. It is furthermore necessary that a small-numbers condition prevail. Absent this, rivalry among large numbers of bidders will render opportunistic inclinations ineffectual. Parties who attempt to secure gains by strategic posturing will find, at the contract renewal interval, that such behavior is nonviable. Opposite parties will arrange alternative trades in which competitive terms are satisfied.

When, however, opportunism is joined with a small-numbers condition, the trading situation is greatly transformed. All of the types of difficulties associated with exchange between bilateral monopolists in stochastic market circumstances now appear. The transactional dilemma that is posed is this: it is in the interest of each party to seek terms most favorable to him, which encourages opportunistic representations and haggling. The interests of the *system,* by contrast, are promoted if the parties can be joined in such a way as to avoid both the bargaining costs and the indirect costs (mainly maladaptation costs) which are generated in the process.

What is of special interest to the analysis here is that while frequently a large-numbers condition will appear to obtain at the outset, this may be illusory or may not continue into contract renewal stages. The illusion is that implicit homogeneity assumptions may not be satisfied. Nonhomogeneity coupled with information impactedness conditions gives rise to serious transactional difficulties — as the discussion of the insurance problem in the preceding chapter indicates and as Akerlof's examination of the used car market reveals (1970, pp. 489-492).

Much more germane to my interests here, however, is that large-numbers homogeneity conditions which obtain at the outset *may no longer hold at the contract renewal interval.* If parity among suppliers is upset by first-mover advantages, so that winners of original bids subsequently enjoy nontrivial cost advantages over nonwinners, the sales relationship that eventually obtains is effectively of the small-numbers variety. The argument has relevance not only for examining when separable components will be made internally rather than purchased, but also when the work flow between successive individuals will be exchanged under an employment rather than a sales relationship.

2.2 An Example

2.2.1 *Ex Ante* SMALL NUMBERS

Arrow illustrates the problems of small-numbers exchange by reference to a lighthouse example (1969, p. 58). He abstracts from uncertainty by assuming that the lighthouse keeper knows exactly when each ship has need for his services. Furthermore, Arrow assumes that only one ship will be within range of the lighthouse at any one time, so that exclusion is possible by turning off the light to a nonpaying ship. An exchange problem nevertheless arises because there is only a single seller and a single buyer "and no competitive forces to drive the two into competitive equilibrium" (1969, p. 58).

This example is a version of the bilateral monopoly problem. As is well-known, the parties have an incentive to exchange the joint profit maximizing quantity, but they are also inclined to expend considerable resources bargaining over the price at which the exchange is to take place. Only, however, to the extent that the parties are joined in *recurrent* small-numbers bargaining under *changing* market circumstances is an interesting comparative institutional choice posed.

Absent recurrent bargaining, a merger agreement has nothing to commend it over a one-shot exchange agreement. Absent changing market circumstances, an exchange agreement, once reached, can be made to hold indefinitely. The advantage of internal organization when recurrent exchange and changing circumstances are joined is that a merger agreement both permits adaptation and forecloses future haggling. Recurrent spot contracting, by contrast, is impaired as each party seeks to adjust the terms to his advantage with each change in the data, and complex contingent claims contracts are apt to be infeasible.

2.2.2 *Ex Post* SMALL NUMBERS

A problem of recurring interest throughout the book is the following: Although a large-numbers exchange condition obtains at the outset, it is transformed during contract execution into a small-numbers exchange relation on account of (1) idiosyncratic experience associated with contract execution, and (2) failures in the human and nonhuman capital markets. The issues here are best addressed in the context of information impactedness in Section 3, below.

2.3 *Internal Organization*

Internal organization enjoys advantages of three kinds over market modes of contracting in circumstances where opportunism and small-numbers conditions are joined. First, in relation to autonomous contractors, the parties to an internal exchange are less able to appropriate subgroup gains, at the expense of the overall organization (system), as a result of opportunistic representations. The incentives to behave opportunistically are accordingly attenuated. Second, and related, internal organization can be more effectively audited. Finally, when differences do arise, internal organization realizes an advantage over market mediated exchange in dispute settling respects. Consider these *seriatim*.

Unlike autonomous contractors, internal divisions that trade with one another in a vertical integration relationship do not ordinarily have pre-emptive claims on their respective profit streams. Even though the divisions in question may have profit center standing, this is apt to be exercised in a restrained way. For one thing, the terms under which internal trading occurs are likely to be circumscribed. Cost-plus pricing rules, and variants thereof, preclude supplier divisions from seeking the monopolistic prices which their sole source supply position might otherwise entitle them. In addition, the managements of the trading divisions are more susceptible to appeals for cooperation. Since the aggressive pursuit of individual interests redounds to the disadvantage of the system, and as present and prospective compensation (including promotions) can be easily varied by the general office to reflect noncooperation, simple requests to adopt a cooperative mode are apt to be heeded. Altogether, a more nearly joint profit maximizing attitude and result is to be expected.

The auditing advantage of internal organization in relation to interfirm organization is attributable to constitutional and incentive differences which operate in favor of the internal mode. An external auditor is typically constrained to review written records and documents and in other respects restrict the scope of his investigation to clearly pertinent matters. An internal auditor, by contrast, has greater freedom of action, both to include less formal evidence and to explore the byways into which his investigation leads. The difference in scope is partly explained by the fact that the internal auditor can be presumed to act in the interests of the firm — which leads into an examination of incentive differences.

Whereas an internal auditor is not a partisan but regards himself, and is regarded by others, in mainly instrumental terms, the external auditor is associated with the "other side" and his motives are regarded suspiciously. The degree of cooperation received by the auditor from the audited party varies accordingly. The external auditor can expect to receive only perfunctory cooperation. Potential "informants," who as insiders know which conditions are amiss and why, are unlikely to volunteer information — since, internally, it is apt to be regarded as an act of disloyalty and, externally, is an unlikely route to reward.[11] Where, however, audits of operating divisions are made by the general office, the same stigma is not attached to such disclosure.[12] Information impactedness conditions are thus much more easily overcome in internal than in interfirm trades.

Finally, internal organization is not beset with the same kinds of difficulties that autonomous contracting experiences when disputes arise between the parties. Although interfirm disputes are often settled out of court in an informal fashion (Macaulay, 1963; Leff, 1970), this resolution is sometimes difficult and interfirm relations are often strained. Costly litigation is sometimes unavoidable. Internal organization, by contrast, is less given to such disputes (since the parties are more inclined to adapt cooperatively) and is able to settle many such disputes by appeal to fiat — an enormously efficient way to settle instrumental differences. In circumstances, however, where interfirm profitability differences are involved (as they are when the transaction takes place between autonomous parties), fiat is apt to be an inadmissible conflict resolution device. (Who is to be the arbiter? Is he adequately informed? What are his biases? Can he be bribed?) More generally, internal organization supplants markets (in labor, intermediate product, and capital market respects) partly because it assumes and effectively discharges certain *quasijudicial functions.*

The upshot is that internal organization is less vulnerable to the hazards of opportunism when — either from the outset or, as is more commonly the case, as a result of idiosyncratic experience during contract execution — a small-numbers exchange condition obtains.

---

11. The informant is unlikely to be able to strike an enforceable bargain with the external auditor that he regards as satisfactory — partly on account of the difficult problems that trading in information is peculiarly subject to (see Arrow, 1971, pp. 150-53). Unable to appropriate the gains from squealing, he is unwilling to jeopardize his employment.

12. Not only is such reporting not regarded as a subversive act, but it may be affirmatively represented as a duty to disclose observed subgoal pursuit that has potentially pernicious systems consequences. Prospective internal rewards are associated with auditing assistance which, in this context, is regarded as an act of cooperation.

3. Information Impactedness

Information impactedness is a derivative condition that arises mainly because of uncertainty and opportunism, though bounded rationality is involved as well. It exists when true underlying circumstances relevant to the transaction, or related set of transactions, are known to one or more parties but cannot be costlessly discerned by or displayed for others.

It will be useful, for the purposes of understanding the information impactedness condition, to distinguish between buyer, seller, and arbiter to the transaction. Also, *ex ante* information impactedness, which exists at the time of the original negotiations, should be distinguished from *ex post* information impactedness, which develops during the course of contract execution. The occasion to engage an arbiter appears only in conjunction with the *ex post* information impactedness condition.

The relation of information impactedness to first-mover conditions ought also to be emphasized. The reason why outsiders are not on a parity with insiders is usually because outsiders lack firm-specific, task-specific, or transaction-specific experience. Such experience is a valuable resource and can be used in strategic ways by those who, by being awarded initial contracts, have acquired it.

3.1 General

It is generally conceded that if information is asymmetrically distributed between the parties to an exchange, then the exchange is subject to hazards. As Arrow explains it: ". . . the critical impact of information on the optimal allocation of risk bearing is not merely its presence or absence but its inequality among economic agents" (1969, p. 55). I submit, however, that: (1) it is not merely asymmetry alone but asymmetry coupled with (a) the high costs of achieving information parity and (b) the proclivity of parties to behave opportunistically that poses the problem; (2) information problems can develop even when parties have identical information and, *a fortiori,* if information differences exist; and (3) the distribution of information between the parties is of special concern in small-numbers bargaining contexts.

The last proposition is reasonably obvious.[13] Consider therefore a small-numbers exchange relation in the context of (2) above, where both

---

13. One of the remarkable attributes of large-numbers competition is that it serves to safeguard buyers against opportunistic representations of suppliers who enjoy an information advantage. Thus, even though suppliers may be much more fully apprised of certain

buyer and seller have identical information, and assume, furthermore, that this information is entirely sufficient for the transaction to be completed. Such exchanges might nevertheless experience difficulty if, despite identical information, one agent makes representations that the true state of the world is different than both parties know it to be and if, in addition, it is costly for an outside arbiter to determine what the true state of the world is. The problem develops here because human agents are given to making opportunistic representations if the arbiter can discern which party is lying, and to what degree, only by incurring the expense associated with making independent observations.[14] Consequently, only when buyer, seller, and arbiter all have identical information regarding the state of the world, and this information is adequate, can one say with confidence that the transaction will go through without difficulty.

Next, consider a variant of this situation where all parties, including the arbiter, have identical information, but the information is incomplete, and the parties have failed to fully specify, *ex ante,* both the rules for inferring, on the basis of incomplete information, what state of the world obtains and the rules by which additional observations are to be taken. Contractual ambiguities can plainly develop since parties can make *ex post* representations in favor of mappings which favor their interests.[15] Costly haggling then results.

Suppose, instead, that the parties have different information but that, were the information possessed by both parties to be candidly revealed, the resulting information pool would be sufficient for the exchange to be completed. Suppose, furthermore, that neither party has an information "advantage" at the outset. Nevertheless, problems can develop which even an agreed upon mapping fails to rectify. Opportunism here takes the form of selective disclosure or distortion of the data to which each party uniquely has access — which, provided again that it is costly for an arbiter to be independently apprised as to what true conditions exist, is to be anticipated.

The problems are compounded if an information asymmetry condition exists. One of the agents to the contract has deeper knowledge than does the other, and it is costly for the party with less information to achieve

---

attributes of the transaction, this is of little consequence if buyers can continuously elicit competitive bids in the marketplace. The competitive process in these circumstances makes it unprofitable for any party to engage in strategic behavior (Hurwicz, 1972, p. 324).

14. Occasionally there will be a ruse by which the agent who is lying can be exposed. Solomon's threat to use a sword to divide the baby between the two women each of whom claimed to be the child's mother is an example. Usually, however, additional data is required.

15. The failures fully to specify the rules for determining, on the basis of incomplete information, what the declared state of the world will be and for augmenting the data, by taking additional observations, are manifestations of bounded rationality. Whether transactional problems develop on this account depends on the proclivities of parties to behave opportunistically. The issues are perhaps best illustrated by example (see Section 3.2, below).

information parity. Selective disclosures or distortions are then all the more hazardous for the party who is at an information disadvantage. I emphasize, however, that the problems posed by information asymmetry differ in degree but not in kind from those posed when information sets are identical yet incomplete or, while different, neither party can be said to enjoy a strategic information advantage.

In any event, information impactedness need not impair market exchange if (1) the parties are not opportunistic, (2) an unbounded rationality condition were to obtain, or (3) a large-numbers competition condition prevails — both presently and prospectively. If, however, all of these conditions are violated, a shift of the transaction from market to hierarchy may obtain an account of the above indicated advantages (see Section 2.3) of hierarchy in curbing opportunism.[16]

3.2 Some Examples

3.2.1. THE IDENTICAL BUT INCOMPLETE INFORMATION CASE

Problems can develop under the identical but incomplete information condition if the exchange is made contingent on which state of the world eventuates. Unless the parties have fully stipulated how *ex post* signals are to be mapped into state of the world descriptions, differences in opinion as to which state actually has obtained can be anticipated. That is, even though both parties have identical information with respect to the condition of the environment, they need not agree on what state of the world has actually been realized. To the contrary, if the consideration to be exchanged varies conditionally with which state of the world is agreed (or otherwise declared) to have eventuated, each party can be expected to make opportunistic mappings in support of outcomes favorable to himself.

Thus, suppose that party A agrees to supply party B with $\bar{X}$, on date d, if the mean temperature on date $d-1$ is less than or equal to T_0, and $\bar{X}+\Delta$ otherwise. Suppose also that both parties A and B have free access to temperature readings on date $d-1$ at 4:00 A.M., 12:00 noon, and 8:00 P.M. If on date d the unit-weighted average of the temperatures on the preceding day is well below or well above T_0, the transaction goes through without difficulty. Suppose, however, that the unit-weighted average is slightly less than T_0, while weights of 0.95, 1.10, and 0.95 would increase it above T_0. Party B may now assert that everyone knows that the noon temperature

---

16. The advantages of internal organization in economizing on bounded rationality may reinforce the desire to curb opportunism by shifting the transaction. But it is mainly the incentive, auditing, and dispute settling advantages of internal organization which make information problems of the above described types much less severe within the firm (see Section 3.3, below).

deserves to be assigned a greater weight in computing the daily mean, and that $\bar{X} + \Delta$ should be delivered accordingly. Party A objects, thus haggling and the need to collect additional information ensue.[17] Moreover, in circumstances where the state of the world is multidimensional, the occasion for such disputes to arise naturally increases.[18]

3.2.2. THE INSURANCE EXAMPLE

Recall the insurance example in Section 3 of Chapter 1. Efficient risk-bearing is impeded by information impactedness conditions in both *ex ante* and *ex post* respects. *Ex ante* information impactedness exists if, as is usually the case, insureds know better than insurers what their true risk characteristics are. Moreover, good risks cannot easily distinguish themselves from poor risks because their representations cannot be taken at face value: poor risks can make the same claims. Because it is costly to establish what the true risk attributes of the parties are, information asymmetries and opportunistic proclivities on the part of poor risks combine to yield the adverse selection problem.

The moral hazard problem is also the result of an information impactedness condition, in this instance of the *ex post* variety. Given that a party has been awarded insurance coverage, the question of efficient loss mitigation is posed: Will the insured take the appropriate steps to reduce his exposure to risk, or will he reallocate his assets away from loss mitigation in favor of other activities? The latter is to be expected if insurers are unable easily to determine whether losses are due to negligence or to environmental circumstances. Insureds then can simply disclaim negligence, whether it was a contributing factor or not. Again, information asymmetries and opportunism combine to yield the problem.

3.2.3 FIRST-MOVER ADVANTAGES

First-mover advantages have been referred to above and will appear in several of the chapters which follow. The basic phenomenon is this: Winners of initial contracts acquire, in a learning-by-doing fashion, nontrivial information advantages over nonwinners. Consequently, even though large-numbers competition may have been feasible at the time the initial award was made, parity no longer holds at the contract renewal interval. The information acquired through experience is impacted in the sense that (1) original winners may refuse to disclose it (which is a manifestation of opportunism) or (2) they may be unable, despite best efforts, to disclose it

---

17. Such problems will of course be mitigated if the courts have evolved simple rules for making such declarations when disputes of this kind develop.

18. If the state of the world is described by a vector of n components, each of which can take on only two values, the number of possible states is 2^n. For $n=8$, which hardly constitutes a complex description of the state of the world, the number of possible states is 256.

(because of bounded rationality of the language impeded variety). *Small numbers bargaining situations thus evolve in this way.* Markets frequently give way to hierarchies on this account.

What is sometimes referred to as "knowhow" is an interesting illustration of a first-mover advantage, where knowhow refers to an unpatented and probably unpatentable technology and is to be distinguished from trade secrets in that knowhow "suggests a continuing flow of information and data . . . [whereas trade secret] suggests a single transfer of one secret or a package of secrets with no continuity of flow" (Eckstrom, 1963, p. 127). Knowhow implies a condition of information impactedness, as the following statement by the U.S. Justice Department, in asking relief in the United Shoe Machinery case, suggests (emphasis added):[19]

> Affirmative relief from United's . . . control of the present technology and technicians in the Shoe Machinery field can only be accomplished by releasing to potential customers *United's complete knowhow,* in as current a form as it is possible to do. This means putting United's potential customers in possession of detailed models and blue-prints for the construction of those machines themselves. It means the release of all construction and operating manuals, rules and notices relating to machines, including the general layout plans that United has been in the habit of making available to shoe manufacturers. It envisages the making available of technical personnel to iron out kinks in the production and operating processes and to give to the potential competitors that *intuitive knowledge based upon training and experience that is incapable of translation into written form.* The employees of United's potential competitors need to be given as much and as detailed help as United's own employees, if not more.

Such first-mover advantages play an important role in several of the chapters which follow.

3.3 Internal Organization

Internal organization helps to overcome information impactedness in several respects. Most of the reasons are traceable to the advantages of internal organization over markets in opportunism respects — as developed in Section 2.3, above, Thus, internal organization (of the appropriate kind)[20] serves to attenuate incentives to exploit information impactedness opportunistically. Also, the superior auditing powers of internal organization help to overcome information impactedness conditions.

The language advantages of internal organization also ought to be noted. This is significant in two respects. First, parties that are willing to disclose

19. "Brief for the United States on Relief," U.S. Department of Justice, *United States* v. *United Shoe Machinery Corporation* (1952).

20. This qualification is important. It raises organization form considerations. The relevance of organization form to transactional efficiency is developed in the chapters which follow.

information to which they have selective access will find that this is easier if an efficient internal code has developed which permits idiosyncratic conditions to be communicated with little difficulty. The previously noted coding advantages of internal organization, in relation to markets, thus help to overcome information impactedness.

Second, internal organization is apt to be superior to market organization in experience-rating respects. Parties who might otherwise make opportunistic representations — with regard, for example, to their qualifications to perform a task or supply a component — will be discouraged from so doing if they face the prospect of being experience-rated. Since it is generally considered efficient that well-qualified and poorly qualified types be sorted out quickly and the appropriate discriminating wage or price paid to them, institutional modes that have better experience-rating characteristics are favored, *ceteris paribus.*

This is not to suggest that markets perform no experience-rating functions whatsoever. As Leff (1970, pp. 26-36) and others have urged, business reputation is a valuable resource and firms sometimes share contractual experiences by informally, and sometimes formally, pooling information. The extent to which such information-sharing is efficacious varies between markets: intermediate goods markets, in which transactions take place between firms, are generally more well developed in experience-rating respects than are final goods markets, in which transactions take place between households and firms (Leff, 1970, pp. 29-33).

Although Leff restricts his comparisons to market-mediated exchange, experience-rating differences between market and internal organization also exist and are more germane to our interests here. The communication advantages that Leff imputes to intermediate product markets, in relation to final goods markets, are, I submit, even more well developed within the firm. For one thing, the experience rater and the decision maker will ordinarily be one and the same person — in which event there is no need for an interpersonal, much less interorganizational, communication to occur at all. The decision maker simply consults his own experience with regard to the transaction in question and decides accordingly. Second, because of the previously noted coding advantages of internal organization, subtle nuances within the firm may be impossible to achieve interorganizationally. Again, the volume of communication is reduced, this time on account of language economies.

Third, interfirm experience rating can be risky. Firm A may tell rival firm B that firm X is "possibly O.K.," when in fact it knows firm X to be "slightly substandard." If it relies on these representations, firm B subsequently is put to a rivalry disadvantage. Moreover, inasmuch as the criteria for assignment to one performance category rather than another are not well defined, since firm A cannot be compelled candidly to document its rating, and as firm B's use of X may vary slightly from firm A's, firm B has little basis upon which to register a complaint, much less bring litigation.

Finally, even if firm A accurately reports firm X to be substandard, firm B will lack a depth account of why such an assignment was made. B may then conjecture that A's problems were partly of its own making — for example, that a more carefully drawn contract would have avoided the difficulties. If B's management considers itself to be more clever, the report may be discounted. Since, by contrast, depth accounts are more easily secured with respect to internal transactions, internal disbelief is less likely.

The upshot is that, however well-developed experience-rating is in interfirm contracting respects, intrafirm evaluations are apt to be even more refined. Both horizontal and vertical integration may occur for this reason.

4. Atmosphere

4.1 General

The power of economics, in relation to the other social sciences, is to be traced in no small part to its unremitting emphasis on net benefit analysis. Care must be exercised, however, lest problems be construed too narrowly. This will occur if net benefits are calculated in transaction-specific terms, when in fact there are interaction effects to be taken into account.

This situation is perfectly familiar in the context of technological non-separabilities, where failure to allow for such interaction effects, when in fact they exist, leads to suboptimization. What I wish to emphasize here is that *technological separability does not imply attitudinal separability*. Reference to atmosphere is intended to make allowance for attitudinal interactions and the systems consequences that are associated therewith.

4.2 An Example

Consider the matter of altruism as discussed by Titmuss in his study of blood donors (1971). He compares the British system, which relies entirely on voluntary donors, with the American system, a mixed voluntary-commercial effort, and concludes that the commercialization of blood has had debilitating consequences.

Arrow has reviewed the Titmuss study and observes that "economists typically take for granted that since the creation of a market increases the individual's area of choice, it therefore leads to higher benefits" (1972, pp. 349-350). He then asks: "why should it be that the creation of a market for blood would decrease the altruism embodied in giving blood?" (1972, p. 351).

I submit that an answer to the effect that the standard economists' model is correct and that altruism is unaffected by the creation of markets is glib and inaccurate. The commercialization of blood need not merely expand choices in an instrumental way; it can also transform the nature of the transaction. It seems reasonable to believe that voluntary donors derive satisfaction partly from their sense of indispensability. Knowing that, were their altruism to flag, the system could adjust appropriately by increasing the price a notch impairs their sense of being essential. Also, a dual system raises the question in the mind of the voluntary donor of whether he is being generous or naive.

The standard economic model misses such considerations because it assumes that individuals regard transactions in a strictly neutral, instrumental manner. However, it may be more accurate, and sometimes even essential, to regard the exchange process itself as an object of value. Concern for atmosphere tends to raise such systems issues; supplying a *satisfying exchange relation* is made part of the economic problem, broadly construed.[21]

4.3. Internal Organization

The comparative institutional significance of this discussion is that alternative modes of organization sometimes differ in nontrivial atmospheric respects. Distinctions between calculative and quasimoral "involvements" are relevant. Market exchange tends predominantly to encourage calculative relations of a transaction-specific sort between the parties. Such transactions are carefully metered; unsettled obligations do not carry over from one contract, or related set of transactions, to the next.

Internal organization, by contrast, is often better able to make allowance for quasimoral involvements among the parties. The sociological phenomenon of reciprocity is an example (Gouldner, 1968). While this can and does appear in a market context, it is much more common among members of an internal organization.

Recognition that alternative modes of economic organization give rise to differing exchange relations, and that these relations themselves are valued, requires that organizational effectiveness be viewed more broadly

21. In a related context McKean has observed: "Economics provides no analytical framework for saying anything about the worth of alternative preferences, yet different tastes and consumption patterns may have important spillover effects on us all. Many individuals might be willing to pay something to live in a world where others consumed a different mix of goods, services, and leisure activities" (1973, p. 640). Extend this to read "and a different mix of transactional modes" and the argument in the text is reached.

than the usual efficiency calculus would dictate. Thus, modes of organization or practices which would have superior productivity consequences if implemented within, and thus would be adopted by, a group of expected pecuniary gain maximizers, may be modified or rejected by groups with different values. For one thing, favorable productivity consequences may no longer obtain — which is to say that efficiency and a sense of well-being (that includes, but transcends, equity) are intrinsically (nonseparably) joined. In addition, preferences for atmosphere may induce individuals to forego material gains for nonpecuniary satisfactions if the modes or practices are regarded as oppressive or otherwise repugnant.

A full discussion of atmosphere and its ramifications raises a wider set of sociopolitical issues than can be addressed here.[22] Suffice it to observe that (1) the analysis in subsequent chapters relies principally on the human and environmental factors discussed in the preceding sections; (2) atmosphere is reserved for those transactions for which attitudinal spillovers are thought to be especially strong; and (3) assessing the intensity with which transactions are metered (either between or within modes of organization) is the main occasion to make reference to atmosphere.

5. Summary Remarks

At the risk of oversimplification, the argument of the preceding sections of this chapter can be summarized by the schematic in Figure 3. The main pairings are shown by the heavy double-headed arrows which associate bounded rationality with uncertainty/complexity on the one hand and opportunism with a small-numbers exchange relations on the other. Information impactedness is a derived condition, mainly due to uncertainty and opportunism, which in turn can give rise to a small-numbers result. That exchange takes place within a trading atmosphere is denoted by the broken line that surrounds the human and environmental factors which appear in the organizational failures framework.

To recapitulate, the advantages of internal organization[23] in relation to markets are:

22. In addition to the comparative organizational mode issues that are of interest here, there are also comparative economic systems issues that can be assessed with respect to atmosphere. Arrow conjectures that international productivity differences between countries with, or having access to, common technologies are partly to be explained by trust differences which impair or facilitate exchange. Banfield's study (1958) of the transactional atmosphere in a community of Italian peasants that he observed is to be contrasted with that which prevails in most developed countries. Transactional attitudes are greatly influenced by the sociopolitical system in which exchange takes place.

23. Again, the organization form qualification, discussed in Note 20 above, is critical to the argument.

1. In circumstances where complex, contingent claims contracts are infeasible and sequential spot markets are hazardous, internal organization facilitates adaptive, sequential decision making, thereby to economize on bounded rationality.
2. Faced with present or prospective small-numbers exchange relations, internal organization serves to attenuate opportunism.
3. Convergent expectations are promoted, which reduces uncertainty.
4. Conditions of information impactedness are more easily overcome and, when they appear, are less likely to give rise to strategic behavior.
5. A more satisfying trading atmosphere sometimes obtains.

The shift of a transaction or related set of transactions from market to hierarchy is not all gain, however. Flexibility may be sacrificed in the process and other bureaucratic disabilities may arise as well. The failures of internal organization, in relation to markets, are examined in Chapter 7.

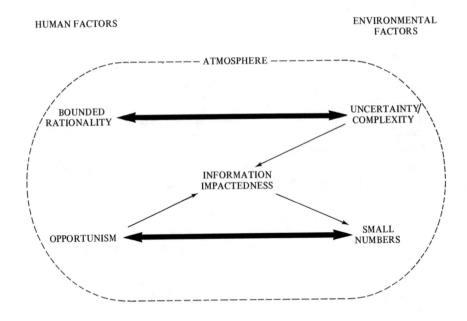

Figure 3. *The Organizational Failures Framework*

3. Peer Groups and Simple Hierarchies

This chapter has the limited purpose of explaining why primary work groups of the peer group and simple hierarchy types arise. I assume, for expositional purposes, that autonomous contracting is initially ubiquitous and ask the question: Why might such contracting be supplanted by nonmarket organization, and what internal forms of organization will first appear?

The simplest nonmarket alternative is the worker peer group. Some of the leading reasons why such groups can be expected to evolve are given in Section 1. As it turns out, peer group organization is itself beset with numerous transactional difficulties. The nature of these difficulties is sketched out in Section 2. A discussion of the ways in which simple hierarchy serves to overcome the transactional problems of peer groups follows in Section 3.

Inasmuch as individuals derive nonpecuniary satisfactions from a wide variety of nonwork group affiliations, while the work group is distinguished by its productivity attributes, the discussion proceeds mainly along productivity lines. But while this delimits the inquiry, it does not imply that workers are schizophrenic with respect to their economic and noneconomic identities. Those social psychologists who have been concerned with the "human side of enterprise" have counseled against this for years. Thus, although an emphasis on productivity will be maintained, an attempt will be made to display sensitivity to the potentially oppressive consequences of alternative modes of organization by reference to on-the-job atmosphere. This problem is briefly considered in Section 4.

1. Peer Group Associations

In order to avoid imputing benefits to hierarchy that can be had, in some degree, by simple nonhierarchical associations of workers, it will be useful to begin with an examination of worker peer groups. These groups involve collective and usually cooperative activity, provide for some type of other-than-marginal productivity and income-sharing arrangement, but do not entail subordination. Such collective organizations offer prospective advantages in indivisibility, risk-bearing, and associational respects.

1.1 Indivisibilities

Indivisibilities of two types can be distinguished. The first type involves scale economies associated with physical assets and is reasonably familiar. Larger scale units, provided they are utilized at design capacity, permit lower average costs to be realized. The group may thus be formed in order to assure that utilization demands will be sufficient.

The second type, somewhat less familiar, are the indivisibilities associated with information. Radner observes that "the acquisition of information often involves a 'set up cost'; i.e., the resources needed to obtain the information may be independent of the scale of the production process in which the information is used" (1970, p. 457). Consequently, groups may also be formed in order to economize on information costs.

The realization of economies of either of these types, however, does not clearly imply, as a technological imperative, collective organization. Thus, technologically speaking, there is nothing that prevents one individual from procuring the physical asset in requisite size to realize the economies in question and contracting to supply the services of this asset to all of the members of the group. Similarly, there is no technological bar that prevents one individual from assuming the information gathering and dissemination function. All parties, suppliers and users of the specialized services alike, could be independent, yet scale economies of both types could also be fully realized. If, therefore, such specialization fails to materialize, it is not because there are technological impediments to monopoly ownership of the physical assets and information services in question. Rather, the problems are to be traced to transactional difficulties that attend market exchange in these circumstances. Accordingly, the incentive to collectivize activities for which indivisibilities are large in relation to the market are transactional in origin.

The arguments here are familiar. They are illustrated in my discussion of Stigler's treatment of vertical integration in Chapter 1 and are developed more extensively in Chapter 5. Briefly, the argument is that market contracting of the complex contingent claims variety is infeasible, on account of bounded rationality, while sequential spot contracting is hazardous where suppliers acquire nontrivial learning-by-doing advantages and an absence of opportunism cannot safely be presumed.[1] The upshot

---

1. To illustrate the hazards of market contracting, consider the case of information specialization. The risk here is that the information specialist will perform creditably until a critical

is that, where indivisibilities of either physical asset or informational types are large and learning-by-doing predictably (albeit uncertainly) obtains, collective organization may arise instead.

The advantage of collective organization, with respect to the exchange of the specialized services in question, is that the incentives of the parties to joint profit maximize is greater. Indivisible physical assets are owned and utilized by the group, rather than privately; associated learning-by-doing advantages thus accrue not to the strategic benefit of the monopolistic supplier but are shared by the membership instead. Information-gathering and dissemination likewise proceed with less concern for strategic nondisclosure or distortion of the data, since individual parties are unable, given the ownership arrangements, to appropriate the private gains to which such opportunistic behavior would otherwise give rise.

1.2 Risk-Bearing Factors

Group affiliation may be sought for insurance purposes if such membership can provide income guarantees to buffer the effects of unanticipated contingencies on terms superior to that which market insurance can provide. Recall in this connection the disabilities of insurance markets discussed in Chapter 1. A group will have an advantage over the market to the extent that it is better able to (1) limit membership in a discriminating way, thus mitigating problems of adverse selection attributable to *ex ante* information impactedness and opportunism on the part of insurance purchasers, and (2) check malingering and other *ex post* manifestations of moral hazard. Advantages of the first kind require that members be able to ascertain the characteristics of applicants in a discerning fashion, while those of the second require that performance be accurately assessed.

Groups of three types can be distinguished: groups engaged in unrelated tasks, groups engaged in a common task, and groups performing an integrated set of tasks. Although the peer group may have little to offer for purposes of membership screening or as a check on malingering if the

---

set of circumstances develop. He then deviates (and appropriates the related gains) by, say, informing all users but one that event e_j has obtained when in fact the state of the world is of type e_k — which is hard to distinguish from e_j ex ante, but for which a very different set of actions is indicated. Thus apprised, firms 1, 2, ..., n zig while firm $n+1$, with which the information specialist is colluding, zags instead.

To be sure, disseminating misinformation and collusion are both apt to be unlawful. But violations of the law have to be proved. Firm $n+1$ claims simply to have "misunderstood" the declaration of e_j to be e_k, thereby to become the lucky beneficiary of his mistake; and the specialist firm confesses "error," while pointing out that discerning the true state of the world, as between e_j and e_k, is difficult. (Note that the example does not require that information specialists acquire learning-by-doing advantages—albeit that such learning seems usual. Opportunism, however, is sufficient for the argument to go through.)

group is of the unrelated task variety, the peer group may have an advantage, in relation to the market, in both of these respects where members are engaged in common or integrated tasks. Members of common or integrated task groups not only know the requisite attributes to look for in admitting a new member but are able, as a by-product of their working relationships, to mutually monitor one another — virtually automatically, at little incremental monitoring expense. Peer group affiliation may thus be sought in part because the group, rather than the individual, is better able to bear risks and because, in relation to the market, the group has superior *ex ante* screening and *ex post* monitoring capabilities.[2]

1.3 Associational Gains

It will be convenient, for the purpose of discussing associational gains, to assume that markets experience no transactional disabilities except as these are explained by the attitudes that individuals have toward completing transactions by one mode of organization rather than another. Again, unrelated, common, and integrated task groups can be distinguished. Since work in an unrelated task group neither requires recurring contacts nor provides a strong basis for communicating common experience, associational gains in such groups are apt to be small.[3] Attention is accordingly focused on common and integrated task groups.

Associational benefits can accrue to peer groups through increased productivity among members of the group who feel a sense of responsibility to do their fair share as members of a group but, left to their own devices, would slack off. Also, and more important, a transformation of "involvement" relations, from a calculative to a more nearly quasimoral mode, obtains. Especially if the metering of transactions among the members of a group is consciously suppressed and kept on an informal basis, which in a peer group is to be expected, involvement relations between the members of a group are less calculative than if the same transactions were to be conducted across a market. A written record of transactions is less fully maintained, and obligations are commonly settled in other than cash or pecuniary equivalent terms. At least some individuals experience a heightened sense of well-being in this way.

I hasten to add, however, that informal involvement relations are not

---

2. That it has such advantages does not establish that it will supplant the market for insurance, however. For this to obtain requires that there be net overall advantages. The risk-pooling properties of common and integrated task groups are relatively inferior because hazards are highly correlated within such groups.
3. The associational benefits of unrelatedly constituted groups can be realized in a social setting. Since the focus here is on the work group, some element of commonality or relatedness would seem to provide the basis for associational gains on the job.

identically valued by all individuals. Other things being equal, peer groups (or other internal modes) will presumably be organized by those individuals who find market transactions less satisfying than a nonmarket relationship, while markets will be favored by those who prefer a more exacting, trans-action-specific correspondence between rewards and deeds. Thus, given diversity of tastes for involvement relations, neither mode need fully displace the other, but both modes will coexist and each will appeal selectively to that part of the population to whose involvement tastes it most nearly corresponds, *ceteris paribus*.

2. Peer Group Limitations

That peer groups may have attractive properties in relation to the market for at least some individuals should be apparent from the above. But they also experience very real limitations. In comparison with both market and hierarchical organization, peer groups, being loose metering structures, are vulnerable to free rider abuses. In addition, collective deci-sion-making processes are often relatively costly, as compared with hier-archical alternatives, by reason of bounded rationality.

2.1 Bounded Rationality

The anarchistic wing of the New Left, according to Lindbeck, holds that "economic decisions should be undertaken in about the same way as they are in a democratic family in a primitive subsistence economy. The ideal seems to be some kind of 'council democracy' in which people are supposed to convince one another or in which decisions are taken by general vote" (1971, p. 36). It may be described as an all-channel network, with everyone connected to everyone else, within which the absence of hierarchy prevails.

Peer group organization can be limited for bounded rationality reasons in both communication and decision-making respects. These are not matters with which the New Left literature has been greatly, or even often casually, concerned.[4] Contrasting the all-channel network with the wheel,[5] as shown in Figure 4, is useful for developing both points.

The feasible group size of a peer group is inherently limited by the

---

4. See the symposium on the "Economics of the New Left" in the November 1972 issue of the *Quarterly Journal of Economics*.
5. The wheel network is topologically equivalent to simple hierarchy. It is useful, however, to reserve hierarchy to a continuing superior-subordinate relationship – which need not obtain if the leadership in the center of the wheel is regularly rotated.

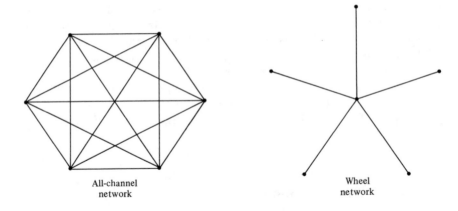

All-channel
network

Wheel
network

Figure 4.

information-processing limits of an all-channel network. Everything cannot be communicated to everyone and joint decisions reached without preempting valuable time that could be productively used for other purposes. Since the number of linkages in all-channel networks goes up as the square of the number of members,[6] peer group size is perforce restricted. If, therefore, economies of scale (of either physical asset or information types) warrant the formation of a larger group than is consistent with an all-channel network, a change in organizational structure may be indicated.

The more severe limitations of the all-channel network can be exposed, however, without requiring that large group size be involved. Thus, suppose that physical asset indivisibilities of only modest proportions obtain—such that everything can feasibly be communicated to every member of the network. It is nevertheless possible that the all-channel network will incur inordinate expense in rule-making and decision-making respects.

To illustrate, consider the problem of devising access rules for an indivisible physical asset which can be utilized by only one or a few members of the group at a time. Although any of a number of access rules may be efficacious, agreement on one must be reached. While a full group discussion may permit one of the efficient rules eventually to be selected, how much simpler if instrumental rules were to be "imposed" authoritatively. Reorganizing from the all-channel to wheel network and assigning the responsibility to specify access rules to whichever member occupies the position at the center avoids the need for full group discussion with little or

6. The number of two-way connections in the all-channel network is given by $N(N-1)/2$, where N is the number of individuals in the group. In the wheel it is given by $N-1$.

no sacrifice in the quality of the decision. Economies of communication are thereby realized.

Similarly, suppose that adaptations to changing market circumstances are needed in order to utilize resources efficiently. While a full group discussion could be held to determine what adaptation is to be made, this is time consuming and may yield little gain if — provided only that everyone pulls in harness — any of a number of adaptations would work. Authoritative assignment of decision-making responsibility to the occupant of the center is again indicated.

Subject to the condition that everyone is given a full turn at the center, the appearance of hierarchy hardly constitutes a violation of the peer group structure. The "leader" is merely a temporary first among equals. Something of this sort seems to be what Mandel had in mind in prescribing "self-management of free communes of producers and consumers, in which everybody will take it in turn to carry out administrative work in which the difference between 'director' and 'directed' will be abolished" (1968, p. 677). And Michels reports that trade union delegates, in the infancy of the English labor movement, "were either appointed in rotation from among all the members, or were chosen by lot" (1966, p. 66).

A problem with such a prescription nevertheless arises if administrative talent is unequally distributed. Unless the job of director is relatively undemanding or the membership is uniformly qualified with respect to administration, where this latter would normally require careful screening as a condition for peer group membership, a tradeoff between performance and peer group democracy must be faced. Either productivity sacrifices must be made, by permitting inferior members to take their turn at administration, or some members of the commune must be denied administrative responsibility.[7] Bounded rationality *differentials* among the membership thus pose peer group strains. The transparent inequality of ability with respect to knowledge and oratorical gifts contributed to the abandonment of delegate selection by rotation or lot in the early trade union movement (Michels, 1966, p. 66).

2.2 Opportunism

Chief among the abuses to which peer group organization is vulnerable are: (1) *ex ante* nondisclosure or disguise of true productivity attributes by new members; (2) joining the peer group in order to acquire knowhow

---

7. This assumes that a comparative advantage among tasks does exist. (Among the possibilities is that anyone can do the administrative tasks but not everyone is an equally good producing agent. It would be a waste of talent in this case to permit superior producers to serve as directors. It is conventional, however, to assume otherwise, which is implicit in the text.)

and to learn trade secrets, thereafter to set up a rival organization; and (3) *ex post* malingering. In all cases, the condition is explained by the conjunction of opportunistic attitudes on the one hand and information impactedness on the other. Correspondingly, the remedy is to be found in either rectifying opportunism or overcoming information impactedness.

It will be convenient to reinterpret the insurance example that was developed in Chapter 1 in productivity terms. Thus, let p in the insurance example now refer to the potential productivity of an individual. If members of the peer group are all rewarded by average group productivity ($\bar{p}$), and if no individual is prepared to accept less than a $p\text{-}\epsilon$ return, the peer group can be viable only if it can successfully screen out low productivity applicants. The peer group, like the insurer, is confronted with an adverse selection problem; low productivity applicants who successfully disguise their true attributes can not only exploit the group but may also render it nonviable.

Suppose, however, that peer groups can somehow screen out such applicants or that high productivity members are fully prepared to subsidize them. Peer group organization is not thereby saved; abuses of the second two types must also be considered. Disincentives must be devised to discourage members from joining for the strategic purpose of acquiring learning-by-doing advantages, and then resigning. Similarly *ex post* malingering, which is the peer group equivalent of moral hazard, constitutes a peer group threat.

Exploitation by members who would join only to be trained, and then resign, could be mitigated by requiring all new members to accept very low (less than $\bar{p}$) compensation during the training period or by demanding that training costs be reimbursed whenever a member voluntarily terminates before a minimum membership period is completed (appropriate health and other exceptions admitted). Although such stipulations are scarcely indications of trustful behavior, and thus might be resisted by "pure" peer group advocates, the spirit of peer group organization essentially survives such covenants and provisions.

By contrast, *ex post* malingering poses more severe difficulties — not that the peer group is entirely lacking in resources in this respect. Informal peer group pressures can be mobilized to check malingering. Hampton, Summer and Webber describe the group disciplinary effects of informal organization in four stages (1968, p. 282). The most casual involves cajoling or ribbing. If this fails, rational appeals to persuade the deviant to conform are employed. The group then resorts to penalties by withdrawing the social benefits that affiliation affords. Finally, overt coercion and ostracism are resorted to. The internal atmosphere is progressively changed to the disadvantage of the malingerer for the purpose of bringing him into line.

That the peer group is able to discourage malingering in this way does not mean that other more effective checks cannot be devised. Whether, however, such additional or alternative controls would be consistent with the peer group structure is seriously to be questioned. Although, as discussed in Section 3, below, recourse to monitoring and the payment of discriminating wages have attractive properties for the purpose of checking free riders, such controls are tantamount to introducing hierarchy.

3. Simple Hierarchy

That peer groups sometimes offer advantages in relation to autonomous contracting is apparent from the discussion in Section 1. But as Section 2 makes clear, peer groups also face limitations in both opportunism and bounded rationality respects. The restricted range of control techniques to which peer groups have access, in seeking to mitigate these conditions, should be appreciated. Realizing more effective control may be possible only if the peer group structure is compromised so severely that it is altered in kind rather than merely in degree.

However, before examining the possible advantages of simple hierarchy over peer groups in bounded rationality and opportunism respects, it will be useful to first consider technological nonseparabilities as a reason for supplanting markets by internal organization. This is interesting for two reasons. For one thing, peer group organization has little to offer as a remedy for defective market exchange when such nonseparabilities appear. Instead, simple hierarchy is apt to obtain immediately. Second, Alchian and Demsetz (1972) rely on such nonseparabilities as the leading reason to explain the origin of firms. I take exception with their view and emphasize transactional factors instead.

3.1 Nonseparabilities

As indicated, Alchian and Demsetz contend that nonseparabilities occasion the shift of economic activities from market-mediated exchange to internal organization. While I concede that this is sometimes the case, I submit that: (1) there are reasons other than nonseparabilities for internal organization to appear; (2) nonseparabilities are much less widespread than is commonly believed; and (3) though nonseparabilities constitute one of the reasons for primary work groups to appear, the argument has little bearing on the joining of simple hierarchies to form complex hierarchies.

The first of these propositions follows from the discussion in Section 1.

The third proposition will be developed in the later chapters where I argue that economizing on the costs of transacting between technologically separable activities occasions the evolution of complex hierarchies.[8] My concern here is accordingly restricted to proposition (2).

The manual freight loading example is used by Alchian and Demsetz to illustrate worker nonseparabilities. The task involves loading heavy cargo into trucks and in order to be done efficiently two men are required to work coordinately. Because of interaction effects between them, the marginal productivity of each worker cannot be determined by observing the total weight loaded during the day. Rather, where "team" production is involved, as it is here, "measuring *marginal* productivity and making payments in accord therewith is more expensive by an order of magnitude than for separable production functions" for which productivity is additive (1972, p. 779). Accordingly, market mediation is supplanted by internal organization in which a "boss" monitors the performance of the team and allocates rewards among members on the basis of observed *input* behavior. Shirking is purportedly attenuated in this way (1972, pp. 779-781).

However familiar the manual freight loading example is among economists and however widespread opinion that such nonseparabilities are ubiquitous, I submit that there are many tasks for which such interaction effects are absent. The issue may be put operationally in the following way. Holding individual task technologies constant, up to but not including the physical transfer of a product from one stage to the next, is it commonly possible to sever the connections between successive workers by placing an intermediate product inventory between them? Many tasks, I submit, are separable in this sense — often between individual workers and almost invariably between small groups of workers. Internal organization thus arises less on account of nonseparabilities than as a means by which to economize on buffer inventories and mitigate costly haggling between technologically separable stages — in most instances because of transactional considerations.

Consider Adam Smith's pin-making example (1937, pp. 4-5). Pin manufacture involved a series of technologically distinct operations (wire straightening, cutting, pointing, grinding, and so forth). In principle, each of these activities could be performed by an independent specialist, and work could be passed from station to station by contract. The introduction of buffer inventories at each station, moreover, would decrease the coordination requirements and thereby reduce contractual complexity. Each worker could then proceed at his own pace, subject only to the condition that he maintain his buffer inventory at some minimum level. A series of independent entrepreneurs rather than a group of employees, each subject to an authority relation, would thus perform the tasks in question.

8. See especially the discussion of the inside contracting system in Chapter 5.

Transaction costs militate against such an organization of tasks, however. For one thing, it may be possible to economize on buffer inventories by having the entire group act as a unit, under common direction, with respect to such matters as work breaks, variable rates of production, etc. Although this could be worked out in advance and made explicit in the contract, or the authority to make such decisions could be rotated among the members of the group, the matter might usefully be assigned to a "boss," who oversees and coordinates the entire operation and can more easily judge the fatigue and related work attitudes in the group.

The more pressing reasons for replacing autonomous contracting by hierarchy, however, turn on adaptability considerations. Suppose one of the individuals becomes ill or injured. Who nominates and chooses a replacement, or otherwise arranges to pick up the slack, and how is compensation determined? Reaching agreement on such matters is apt to be relatively costly in relation to having a boss reassign the work among the members of the group or make other *ad hoc* arrangements on the group's behalf. Similarly, what is to be done if an individual declines to deliver the requisite quantity or quality to the next station? How are penalties determined? Litigation is apt to be costly and time consuming, and to what avail, if the individual lacks the requisite assets to compensate for the losses attributable to his deviant behavior? For the reasons developed more fully in the chapters which follow, hierarchy and an employment relationship commonly yield transactional economies in adaptability and dispute settling respects.[9] By way of anticipating aspects of that argument, it may be useful to observe here that individual workers acquire relatively secure property rights claims to specific job stations under the entrepreneurial organization of tasks described above. These claims are weakened when the set of tasks in question is placed under common ownership and an employment relation is created instead.

3.2 Bounded Rationality

Supplanting the all-channel network in the peer group by a wheel network, in which each member is connected only with the center, can yield savings in both information transmittal and decision-making respects. Such a radial network will be especially efficacious if, once apprised of the relevant data by the various members of the group, the central coordinator is able, with little assistance or consultation, to reach the correct decision and disseminate it among the members of the group.

It is elementary that the advantages of centralization vary with the degree of interdependence among the members — being negligible in an

9. See especially Chapter 4, Section 4 and Chapter 8, Section 3.

unrelated task group, possibly great in a common task group (especially if indivisible physical asset utilization problems are posed), and almost certainly great in an integrated task group. If occasions for adaptation between integrated tasks are unpredictable yet common, coordinated responses may be difficult to secure unless the parties have reference to a common signal.[10]

Arrow summarizes the case for the centralization of information flows and decision-making by setting out a series of four propositions (1974, p. 68):

1. Since the activities of individuals interact with each other, being sometimes substitutes, sometimes complements, and frequently compete for limited resources, joint decision on the choice of individuals' activities will be superior to separate decisions.
2. The optimum joint decision depends on information which is dispersed among the individuals in society.
3. Since transmission of information is costly, in the sense of using resources, especially the time of individuals, it is cheaper and more efficient to transmit all the pieces of information once to a central place than to disseminate each of them to everyone.
4. For the same reasons of efficiency, it may be cheaper for a central individual or office to make the collective decision and transmit it rather than retransmit all the information on which the decision is based.

What is especially relevant to the choice of peer group or simple hierarchy is that, to the extent that the requisite information-processing and decision-making talents are not widely distributed, efficiency will be served by reserving the central information collection and decision-making position to the one or few individuals who have superior information processing capacities and exceptional oratorical and decision-making skills.[11] Something of an elite thereby results, as the select subset bears an asymmetrical relation to everyone else. Not only does the peak coordinator enjoy the power which authority and expertise accord him (Katz and Kahn, 1966,

---

10. This is a version of the convergence of expectation argument that was referred to in Chapter 2, Section 1 and is developed more fully in the discussion of vertical integration in Chapter 5. Observe here that it has a bearing on the choice between peer groups and simple hierarchies as well.

11. Such differences play a prominent role in Frank Knight's rationale for the centralization of decision-making (1965, p. 269):

> [G]roups themselves specialize, finding the individuals with the greatest managerial capacity of the requisite kinds and placing them in charge of the work of the group, submitting the activities of the other members to their direction and control. It need hardly be mentioned explicitly that the organization of industry depends on the fundamental fact that the intelligence of one person can be made to direct in a general way the routine manual and mental operations of others. It will also be taken into account that men differ in their powers of effective control over other men as well as in intellectual capacity to decide what should be done.

Chap. 11), but having more complete information gives him a strategic advantage over everyone else. The peak coordinator has inordinate influence over both the value and factual premises of other members of the group. It is really a fiction, when such an elite develops, to maintain that a peer group any longer exists—even if, in principle, the group can always challenge and even reverse individual decisions. Simple hierarchy effectively obtains.

Lipset, Trow, and Coleman's study of democracy in the International Typographical Union is noteworthy in this regard. They conclude (1956, p. 404):

> The structure of large-scale organization inherently requires the development of bureaucratic patterns of behavior. The conditions making for the institutionalization of bureaucracy and those making for democratic turnover in office are largely incompatible. . . . [Bureaucracy] gives an incumbent administration great power and advantage over the rank and file or even an organized opposition. This advantage takes the form of control over financial resources and internal communications, a large, permanently organized political machine, a claim to legitimacy, and a near monopoly over political skills.

While their remarks apply to the life cycle of bureaucracy in large scale voluntary organizations, similar considerations apply in smaller scale enterprises as well — albeit in attenuated degree.

3.3 Opportunism

As described in Chapter 1, the provision of *ex post* auditing and experience-rating capabilities served to relieve the moral hazard problems besetting the insurance markets. Assuming that the insurance market model generalizes in this respect, the free-rider problems of peer groups should likewise be mitigated in these ways. The peer group, however, is inherently limited as an auditing and experience-rating instrument. Designating a member of the peer group to perform the necessary productivity audits and make corresponding adjustments in the compensation of group members violates both the letter and the spirit of peer groups. Making wages contingent on productivity is really a concession that the peer group form of organization is not viable; whatever it may be called, it is functionally equivalent to introducing hierarchy.[12]

12. Only if any member of the group could perform the auditing and experience-rating functions as well as any other, and if there were little learning involved, so that the position could be turned over regularly, could the peer group engage in auditing and experience-rating as effectively as a hierarchy. Inasmuch, however, as these qualifications are unlikely to be met in many groups (the choice of department heads in academic departments of the university comes as close as I know), a shift to hierarchy in a genuine supervisor-subordinate sense will ordinarily occur when auditing and experience-rating are introduced into a work relationship.

The advantages of hierarchy in which one individual, the supervisor, is expressly assigned the tasks of auditing and experience-rating have been discussed by Alchian and Demsetz (1972). As they point out, auditing serves to overcome information impactedness, while paying compensation in accordance with observed productivity discourages malingering. Admission to the work group, moreover, is made conditional on acceptance by the worker of the supervisor's constitutional authority to perform auditing and experience-rating functions. These constitutional differences between markets and internal organization are central to an understanding of the employment relationship.

Not only does auditing and experience-rating influence the post-admission behavior of members of the work group but it affects the composition of, and standards for, admission to the group as well. Recall in the insurance example that good risks and/or those who were less given to *ex post* opportunism could be induced to join at the mean premium by the prospect that they (and others) would subsequently be experience-rated. The same holds true in the employment context. That productivity potential cannot be accurately discerned *ex ante* and that individuals vary in their sense of responsibility to a job are less critical if the organization is able to discern actual productivity *ex post* and pay the appropriate discriminating wage. High productivity types and/or those who would be prepared to self-enforce covenants not to malinger can thus be induced to affiliate at a low wage by the assurance that this condition will be rectified as information accumulates and more discriminating wage assignments can be made. Moreover, given that those with low productivity and/or high proclivities to malinger will be unable to long exploit the system, easier admission standards can be allowed.[13]

4. Involvement

It would appear, from the above arguments, that simple hierarchy can do everything the peer group can do and more. It can contend better with indivisibilities of both physical and informational types, since it has superior bounded rationality properties. (Not that bounded rationality vanishes; rather, simple hierarchy economizes on the use of scarce bounded rationality resources in both information flow and decision-making respects.) Simple hierarchy also permits auditing and experience-rating effectively to be

---

13. A further advantage of simple hierarchy, in relation to the peer group, is that hierarchy permits risks to be shifted to *particular* subgroups that have superior risk-bearing qualifications. Such individuals or subgroups can become employers and thereby "'assume the risk' or 'insure' the doubtful and timid by guaranteeing the latter a specified income in return for an assignment of the actual results" (Knight, 1965, pp. 269-270). I mention this less because I think it important than for historical perspective.

brought to bear, thereby mitigating the free-rider disabilities to which peer groups are subject. It furthermore offers risk-bearing advantages.

What then prevents the peer group from being fully displaced by simple hierarchy? The main reason,[14] I submit, is that peer groups afford valued involvement relations that are upset, in some degree, by hierarchy. Not only is transparent inequality of rank considered objectionable by some individuals, but auditing and experience-rating may offend their sense of individual and collective well-being. On these accounts, the productivity loss which the peer group form of organization entails is acceptable to some groups — provided, at least, that survival is not threatened.[15]

The more general questions to be addressed, however, are not non-metering (peer group) or full-metering (an exacting *quid pro quo* work relation in which the marginal net benefits of metering, in a transaction-specific sense, are set equal to zero). Rather, given that individuals differ with respect to their preferences for metering, the issues are the following: (1) *to supply the requisite mixture of structures,* which vary in the intensity of metering, thereby to allow individuals to match themselves to organizations in accordance with their involvement-productivity tradeoffs;[16] and (2) to recognize the possibility of attitudinal interaction effects among sets of transactions. Where such interactions exist, a highly transaction-specific approach to metering can be dysfunctional.

Whereas technological interaction effects play a prominant role in economics, attitudinal interactions are commonly neglected. Alchian and Demsetz' discussion of the metering problem of internal organization by reference to faculty appropriation of "office telephones, paper and mail for personal uses beyond strict university productivity" (Alchian and Demsetz, 1972, p. 780) is illustrative. They contend that if these and related practices (what they refer to as "turpitudinal peccadilloes") could be cost-lessly detected, on a faculty-specific basis, such practices would be eliminated, pecuniary rewards could be increased correspondingly, and all could achieve a more preferred position (1972, p. 781). But is this really so? Does it assume, implicitly, that metering intensively, where this is easy

---

14. Another reason, though rather more remote and unusual, is that in some groups the all-channel network is really essential for effective decision-making, and it may be infeasible to wage discriminate – which is to say that hierarchy really serves no purpose.

15. Conceivably the peer group structure will be so satisfying to its members that it will result in greater productivity per unit input than the same group would realize if organized as a hierarchy. This, however, seems doubtful; a productivity loss will generally obtain.

16. Note two things: (1) although, for many individuals, increases in metering have negative effects on involvement at high metering intensities, this does not preclude a positive relation between metering and involvement, for these same individuals, at lower metering intensities; (2) although organizational variety with respect to metering will develop in response to preference differences of the types described, low metering organizations remain vulnerable to free-rider abuses and, accordingly, must take special care, at the admission stage (through pre-admission standards and examination, rigorous trial periods, and so forth), lest their viability be severely tested.

(costless), has no effect on the attitudes of workers with regard to transactions that are costly to meter?

The distinction between perfunctory and consumate cooperation, which is developed more fully in the following chapter, is relevant in this connection. It seems at least plausible that extending metering with respect to such peccadilloes as appear to be of concern to Alchian and Demsetz until the costs and benefits (expressed in transaction-specific terms — that is, without regard for spillover) are equalized at the margin will be regarded as picayune and will elicit resentment. Cooperative attitudes will be impaired with the result that tasks such as teaching effectiveness — which can be metered only with difficulty, because information is deeply impacted, but for which consummate cooperation is important — will be discharged in a more perfunctory way. A less intensive effort to extinguish peccadilloes would thus yield a system gain. The neglect of such interaction effects is encouraged by an insensitivity to atmosphere.[17] The inherent metering limitations which peer groups experience make them less susceptible than hierarchies to such neglect.

5. Concluding Remarks

The simple (or single stage) hierarchies that have been discussed in this chapter will serve as the principal building blocks for the assembly of a complex (multistage) hierarchy in subsequent chapters. As might be anticipated, there are striking parallels between the reasons for workers to be joined in simple hierarchies and the decision to merge simple hierarchies into a multistage hierarchy rather than mediate the transactions between them by market means. In particular, the same transactional factors which impede autonomous contracting between individuals also impede market exchange between technologically separable work groups. Vertical integration is accordingly to be understood mainly as an internal organizational response to the frictions of intermediate product markets, in which bounded rationality and opportunism are again prominently featured, while conglomerate organization is interpreted as a response to (remediable) failures in the capital market, in which these very same human factors appear, albeit that the context differs.

---

17. Moreover, the argument generalizes. Thus ought all externalities to be metered which, taken separately, can be metered with net gains? I think not, since whether an externality is "felt" or not depends partly on whether it is accorded legitimacy. All kinds of grievances may be felt, and demands for compensation made accordingly, if what had hitherto been considered to be harmless by-products of normal social intercourse are suddenly declared to be compensable injuries. It seems not unlikely that the transformation of relationships that will ensue will lead to a lower level of felt satisfaction among the parties – at least transitionally and possibly permanently.

4. Understanding the Employment Relation

This chapter is concerned with the implications of an extreme form of nonhomogeneity—namely, job idiosyncracy—for understanding the employment relation. Although it refers largely to production workers, the argument can be extended, with appropriate modifications, to cover nonproduction workers as well. The purpose is to better assess the employment relation in circumstances where workers *acquire,* during the course of their employment, significant job-specific skills and related task-specific knowledge.[1] What Hayek referred to as knowledge of "particular circumstances of time and place" (1945, p. 521) and what was referred to as first-mover advantages (Section 3.2 of Chapter 2) thus play a prominent role in the analysis.

The principal labor economics studies on which I rely are Becker's work on human capital (1962), the internal labor market literature [especially Doeringer and Piore (1971)], and discussions of collective bargaining by labor law specialists [principally Cox (1958)]. This chapter is not, however, mainly a synthesis. I examine the transactional attributes of alternative contracting modes in a more detailed way than previous treatments and interpret the employment relation in an intertemporal systems context. Also, whereas much of the internal labor market literature emphasizes noneconomic considerations, I interpret evolving institutional practices with respect to idiosyncratic production tasks principally in efficiency terms.

1. As will be apparent, the employment relation is not an isolated case of idiosyncratic exchange conditions. The vertical integration problem turns in no small degree on these same considerations (see the discussion of Stigler's treatment of vertical integration in Section 3.3 of Chapter 1 as well as the more general discussion in Chapter 5, especially Section 4).

Copyright 1975, The American Telephone and Telegraph Company, 195 Broadway, New York, New York 10007. Reprinted with permission from *The Bell Journal of Economics*. This chapter is a variant of a previously published paper on which Michael Wachter and Jeffrey Harris were coauthors.

This is not to suggest, however that extra-economic considerations are thought to be unimportant. To the contrary, the proposition advanced in Chapter 2 that supplying a satisfying exchange relation is part of the economic problem, broadly construed, has special relevance where an employment relation is involved. Indeed, some of the ways in which internal labor markets bear on this proposition are developed in Section 4.3, below. But placing primary reliance on atmosphere to explain internal labor markets poses the following dilemma: Assuming that the same considerations of contractual satisfaction with respect to the nature of the exchange relationship applies to production jobs of all kinds, how is the coexistence of structured (internal) and structureless (recurrent spot) labor markets to be explained? By contrast, rationalizing the absence of structure, where jobs are fungible, and the conscious creation of structure, for idiosyncratic jobs, is relatively straightforward if an efficiency orientation is adopted. Accordingly, the argument runs throughout principally in efficiency terms.

Four alternative labor contracting modes are examined. Two of these, recurrent spot contracting and contingent claims contracting, rely entirely on market-mediated transactions. The other two modes involve a mixture of market-mediated exchange and hierarchy (internal organization). What is commonly referred to as the "authority relation" and the internal labor market mode are of this second kind. These several alternative contracting modes are assessed in cost-economizing terms, where costs include both production and transaction cost elements. Considering that the focus throughout is on contracting, transaction costs naturally receive primary attention.

My purposes, briefly, are as follows:

1. To demonstrate that the interesting problems of labor organization involve the study of transactions and contracting and, except in a rather special idiosyncratic sense, do not turn mainly on technology.
2. To isolate and assess the idiosyncratic job features which characterize internal labor markets with the help of the organizational failures framework.
3. To set out the transactional detail that would attend complex contingent claims contracting in idiosyncratic job circumstances, thereby to disclose why such contracts are prohibitively costly or infeasible.
4. To demonstrate that sequential spot contracting is unsuited to the idiosyncratic tasks in question, whence Alchian and Demsetz' (1972) discussion of the employment relation requires qualification.
5. To examine the authority relation and indicate the limitations associated with Simon's (1957) evaluation of alternative contracting modes.
6. To develop the transactional rationale for internal labor markets (in terms mainly of economizing on bounded rationality and

attenuating opportunism) where jobs are idiosyncratic in nontrivial degree.

A brief discussion of the prior labor economics literature appears in Section 1. Some remarks concerning technology and a description of the job circumstances in which idiosyncratic skills and knowledge are acquired by the labor force are given in Section 2. Three autonomous contracting modes are examined in Section 3. The structural attributes of internal labor markets are then interpreted in Section 4. Concluding remarks follow.

1. Remarks on the
Labor Economics Literature

The internal labor market literature has its roots in the industrial relations-labor economics literature of the 1950's and early 1960's. The important contributions in this area include the work of Dunlop (1957; 1958), Kerr (1954), Livernash (1957), Meij (1963), Raimon (1953), and Ross (1958). This work, which is descriptively oriented, has since been developed and extended by Doeringer and Piore (1971).

The distinction between structured and structureless labor markets is especially notable. Whereas spot market contracting characterizes the latter [as Kerr puts is, the "only nexus is cash" (1954, p. 95)], structured markets are ones for which a large number of institutional restraints have developed. Outside access to jobs in structured markets is limited to specific "ports of entry" into the firm, which are generally lower-level appointments. Higher-level jobs within the firm are filled by the promotion or transfer of employees who have previously secured entry. Training for these jobs involves the acquisition of task-specific and firm-specific skills, occurs in an on-the-job context, and often involves a team element. The internal due process rules, which develop in these internal markets, "are thought to effectuate standards of equity that a competitive market cannot or does not respect" (Doeringer and Piore, 1971, p. 29).

Though coming from a somewhat more theoretical tradition, the study of human capital represents a second and related approach to labor market analysis. It likewise makes the distinction between specific and general training. Incumbent employees who have received specific training become valuable resources to the firm. Turnover is costly, since a similarly qualified but inexperienced employee would have to acquire the requisite task-specific skills before he would reach a level of productivity equivalent to that of an incumbent. A premium is accordingly offered to specifically trained employees to discourage turnover, although in principle a long-term contract would suffice (Becker, 1962, pp. 10-25).

The present analysis is both similar to and different from each of these traditions. It relies extensively on the institutional literature for the purpose of identifying the structural elements associated with internal labor markets. Also, my interpretation of the institutional restraints that have developed in such markets is consonant with much of this literature. What distinguishes my treatment from prior institutional discussions is that it is more micro-analytic — it expressly identifies and evaluates alternative contracting modes and employs the organizational failures framework apparatus throughout.

Like Becker, I am greatly concerned with the organizational implications of task-specific training. But whereas he finds that long-term contracts are vitiated because the courts regard them as a form of involuntary servitude (Becker, 1962, p. 23), I emphasize that the transaction costs of writing, negotiating, and enforcing such contracts are prohibitive.[2]

2. Technology: Conventional and Idiosyncratic Considerations

It is widely felt that technology has an important, if not fully determinative, influence on the employment relationship. I agree, but take exception with the usual view in several respects. First, for the reasons given in the preceding chapter, indivisibilities (of the usual kinds) are neither necessary nor sufficient for market contracting to be supplanted by internal organization. Second, I contend that nonseparabilities at most explain small-group organization. Third, and most important, I argue that the leading reason why an internal labor market supplants spot contracting is because of small-numbers exchange relations. This last turns on task idiosyncrasies as these appear in a moving equilibrium context.

2.1 Conventional Treatments

2.1.1 INDIVISIBILITIES

The implications for economic organization of indivisibilities of both physical capital and informational types were examined in the discussion of peer groups. As indicated there, it is entirely feasible, as a technological matter, for physical assets and informational services for which indivisibilities are significant to be monopoly owned and sold for hire. What

---

2. Becker hints at this in his remark that "any enforceable contract could at best specify the hours required on a job, not the quality of performance" (1962, p. 24). But rather than develop this line of analysis, and address the underlying transactional factors that explain such a condition, he merely notes that workers could always secure a release from long-term contracts by "sabotaging" operations (1962, p. 24). The implications for collective organization are nowhere addressed.

impedes such ownership and exchange arrangements are the transactional difficulties which attend small-numbers trades (see Section 1.1 of Chapter 3). I raise the issue at this time merely to restate my position that conventional arguments which rely on indivisibilities to explain the employment relation do not, without more, go through. Recourse to transactional considerations is ultimately necessary.

2.1.2 NONSEPARABILITIES

More relevant to our purposes here is the allegation that technological nonseparabilities constitute the principal reason for the employment relation, whence hierarchy, to appear (Alchian and Demsetz, 1972). But for such technological conditions, a "normal sales relationship" would purportedly govern the terms under which labor would be made available for hire.

Again, the discussion of the preceding chapter (see Chapter 3, Section 3.1) applies. As indicated there, it is the joining of nonseparability with opportunism and a condition of information impactedness, rather than nonseparability by itself, that occasions the substitution of hierarchy for market exchange. Absent opportunism, free riding problems, of which shirking is one, would never appear. Absent information impactedness, opportunistic inclinations could be checked by paying the appropriate discriminating wage.

Regarded in transactional terms, technological nonseparability represents a case where information impactedness is particularly severe; but I emphasize that this is merely a matter of degree. Lesser degrees of information impactedness plainly exist that do not have these same technological origins but which can and often do occasion the supplanting of markets by hierarchies.[3] (As urged in the preceding chapter, most tasks appear to be separable in a buffer inventory sense — often as between individual workers and almost invariably between small groups of workers — yet hierarchy commonly appears.) Our assessment of the technological nonseparability argument thus comes down to this: Such conditions are *merely symptomatic* of a set of underlying transactional factors which, both here and elsewhere, ultimately explain the organization of economic activity as between markets and hierarchies.

2.2 Small Numbers and Task Idiosyncracies

It is generally agreed that small-numbers exchange conditions are attended by serious market exchange problems (see the discussion of the lighthouse example in Section 2.2 of Chapter 2). The frequency of and

---

3. See the discussion of vertical integration in Section 3.3 of Chapter 1 and Chapter 5; also, see the discussion of indivisibilities in Section 1.1 of Chapter 3; also, see the discussion of small-numbers relations in Section 2.2 below. In each of these cases, hierarchy is substituted for market exchange though nonseparability is not an issue.

manner in which small-numbers labor exchange conditions develop, however, is less widely appreciated. It is the thesis of this chapter that task idiosyncrasies are common, that these give rise to small-numbers exchange conditions, and that market contracting is supplanted by an employment relation principally for this reason.

2.2.1 GENERAL

Doeringer and Piore describe idiosyncratic tasks in the following way (1971, pp. 15-16):

> Almost every job involves some specific skills. Even the simplest custodial tasks are facilitated by familiarity with the physical environment specific to the workplace in which they are being performed. The apparently routine operation of standard machines can be importantly aided by familiarity with the particular piece of operating equipment. . . . In some cases workers are able to anticipate trouble and diagnose its source by subtle changes in the sound or smell of the equipment. Moreover, performance in some production or managerial jobs involves a team element, and a critical skill is the ability to operate effectively with the given members of the team. This ability is dependent upon the interaction skills of the personalities of the members, and the individual's work "skills" are specific in the sense that skills necessary to work on one team are never quite the same as those required on another.

More generally, task idiosyncrasies can arise in at least four ways: (1) equipment idiosyncrasies, due to incompletely standardized, albeit common, equipment, the unique characteristics of which become known through experience; (2) process idiosyncrasies, which are fashioned or "adopted" by the worker and his associates in specific operating contexts; (3) informal team accommodations, attributable to mutual adaptation among parties engaged in recurrent contact but which are upset, to the possible detriment of group performance, when the membership is altered; and (4) communication idiosyncrasies with respect to information channels and codes that are of value only within the firm. Because "technology is [partly] unwritten and that part of the specificity derives from improvements which the work force itself introduces, workers are in a position to perfect their monopoly over the knowledge of the technology should there be an incentive to do so" (Doeringer and Piore, 1971, p. 84).

Training for idiosyncratic jobs ordinarily takes place in an on-the-job context. Classroom training is unsuitable both because the unique attributes associated with particular operations, machines, the work group, and, more generally, the atmosphere of the workplace may be impossible to duplicate in the classroom, and because job incumbents, who are in possession of the requisite skills and knowledge with which the new recruit or candidate must become familiar, may be unable to describe, demonstrate, or otherwise impart this information except in an operational context (Doeringer and Piore, 1971, p. 20). Teaching-by-doing thus facilitates the learning-by-doing process. Where such uniqueness and teaching attributes are at all important, specific exposure in the workplace at some stage becomes essential. Outsiders who lack specific experience can thus achieve parity with insiders only by being hired and incurring the necessary startup costs.

The success of on-the-job training is plainly conditional on the information disclosure attitudes of incumbent employees. Both individually and as a group, incumbents are in possession of a valuable resource (knowledge) and can be expected to fully and candidly reveal it only in exchange for value. The way the employment relation is structured turns out to be important in this connection. The danger is that incumbent employees will hoard information to their personal advantage and engage in a series of bilateral monopolistic exchanges with the management — to the detriment of both the firm and other employees as well.

An additional feature of these tasks not described above but nevertheless important to an understanding of the contractual problems associated with the employment relation is that the activity in question is subject to periodic disturbance by environmental changes. Shifts in demand due to changes in the prices of complements or substitutes or to changes in consumer incomes or tastes occur; relative factor price changes appear; and technological changes of both product design and production technique types take place. Successive adaptations to changes of each of these kinds is typically needed if efficient production performance is to be realized. In addition, life cycle changes in the work force occur which occasion turnover, upgrading, and continuous training. The tasks in question are thus to be regarded in moving equilibrium terms. Put differently, they are not tasks for which a once-for-all adaptation by workers is sufficient, thereafter to remain unchanged.

2.2.2 INTERPRETATION

The production tasks that are of transactional interest in this chapter are ones that are either themselves rather complex or are embedded in a complex set of technological and organizational circumstances. Furthermore, successive adaptations are required to realize efficiency in the face of changing internal and environmental events. A nontrivial degree of uncertainty/complexity may thus be said to characterize the tasks. Training for such tasks occurs in an on-the-job context because of the impossibility, or great cost, of disclosing job nuances in a classroom situation. The relevant job details simply cannot be identified, accurately described, and effectively communicated in a classroom context on account of information processing limitations of both originators (teachers) and receivers (trainees). Sometimes, indeed, the requisite language will not even exist. The pairing of bounded rationality with an uncertainty/

complexity condition thus gives rise to the job-specific training situation. *Teaching-by-doing and learning-by-doing both economize on bounded rationality in these idiosyncratic job circumstances.*[4]

Specialized skills and knowledge accrue to individuals and small groups as a result of their specific training and experience. But while such skills and information accrue naturally, they can be disclosed strategically — in an incomplete or distorted fashion — if the affected parties should choose to. Whether this will obtain depends on the structure of the bargaining relationship. Where job incumbents acquire nontrivial first-mover advantages over outsiders, and, in addition, are opportunistically inclined, what was once a large-numbers bidding situation, at the time original job assignments were made, is converted into a small-numbers bargaining situation if adaptations to unplanned (and perhaps unforeseeable) internal and market changes are subsequently proposed. The reasons for and consequences of this shift from a large-numbers bargaining relationship at the outset to bilateral bargaining subsequently are further developed below.

3. Individualistic Bargaining Models[5]

Four types of individualistic contracting modes can be distinguished: (1) contract now for the specific performance of x in the future; (2) contract now for the delivery of x_i contingent on event e_i obtaining in the future; (3) wait until the future materializes and contract for the appropriate (specific) x at the time; and (4) contract now for the right to select a specific x from within an admissable set X, the determination of the particular x to be deferred until the future. Simon's study of the employment relation

---

4. Doing-while-learning also contributes to the output of the firm. Classroom training is typically at a disadvantage in this respect.

5. Lest the ensuing discussion of autonomous bargaining modes be thought to be contrived and/or unnecessary, since "everyone knows" such bargaining modes are inapposite, I make the following observations: First, though it is widely recognized that complex contingent claims contracting is infeasible [for example, Radner notes that the Arrow-Debreu contracting model "requires that the economic agents possess capabilities of imagination and calculation that exceed reality by many orders of magnitude" (1970, p. 457)], the reasons for this are rarely fully spelled out—either in general or, even less, with respect to labor market contracting. I attempt to rectify this condition in Section 3.1, below. Second, as our discussion of Alchian and Demsetz in Section 3.2 reveals, it is plainly not the case that everyone appreciates that idiosyncratic tasks need to be distinguished from tasks in general and that sequential spot contracting is singularly unsuited for jobs of the idiosyncratic kind. Third, so as to correct the widely held belief that the authority relation represents a well-defined alternative to "normal" market contracting (as recently illustrated by Arrow's (1974, pp. 25, 63-65) reliance on Simon's treatment of the authority relation), I think it important that the ambiguities of the authority relation be exposed.

(1957, pp. 183-195) treats contracts of the first type, which he characterizes as sales contracts, to be the main alternative to the so-called authority relation (type 4). This, however, is unfortunate because type 1 contracts, being rigid, are singularly unsuited to permit adaptation in response to changing internal and market circumstances. By contrast, contingent claims contracts (type 2) and sequential spot sales contracts (type 3) both permit adaptation. If complexity/uncertainty is held to be a central feature of the environment with which we are concerned, which it is, the deck is plainly stacked against contracts of type 1 from the outset. Accordingly, type 1 contracts will hereafter be disregarded.

3.1 Contingent Claims Contracts

Suppose that the efficient choice of x on each date depends on how the future unfolds. Suppose, furthermore, that the parties are instructed to negotiate a once-for-all labor contract in which the obligations of both employer and employee are fully stipulated at the outset. A complex contingent claims contract would then presumably result. The employer would agree to pay a particular wage now in return for which the employee agrees to deliver stipulated future services of a contingent kind, the particular services being dependent upon the circumstances which eventuate.

Contracting problems of several kinds can be anticipated. First, can the complex contract be written? Second, even if it can, is a meaningful agreement between the parties feasible? Third, can such agreements be implemented in a low cost fashion? The issues posed can all usefully be considered in the context of the framework sketched out above.

The feasibility of writing complex contingent claims contracts reduces fundamentally to a bounded rationality issue.

Recall in this connection the conclusion reached by Feldman and Kanter in their assessment of complex decision trees, to wit, "The comprehensive decision model is not feasible for most interesting decision problems" (1956, p. 615). Plainly, the complex labor agreements needed for comprehensive description of the idiosyncratic tasks in question are of this kind. Not only are changing market circumstances (product demand, rivalry, factor prices, technological conditions, and the like) impossibly complex to enumerate, but the appropriate adaptations thereto cannot be established with any degree of confidence *ex ante*. Changing life cycle conditions with respect to the internal labor force compound the complexities.

The enumeration problems referred to are acknowledged by Meade in his discussion of contingent claims contracts. "When environmental uncertainties are so numerous that they cannot all be considered . . . or, what comes perhaps to much the same thing, when any particular environmental risks are so hard to define and to distinguish from each other that it is impossible to base a firm betting or insurance contract upon the occurrence or non-occurrence of any of them, then for this reason alone it is impossible to have a system of contingency . . . markets" (1971, p. 183). Except for bounded rationality, Meade's concerns with excessive numbers, undefinable risks, and indistinguishable events would vanish.

But suppose, *arguendo,* that exhaustive complex contracts could be written at reasonable expense. Would such contracts be acceptable to the parties? I submit that a problem of incomprehensibility will frequently arise and impede reaching agreement. At least one of the parties, probably the worker, will be unable to meaningfully assess the implications of the complex agreement to which he is being asked to accede. Sequential contracting, in which experience permits the implications of various contingent commitments to be better understood, is thus apt to be favored instead.

Assume, however, that *ex ante* understanding poses no bar to contracting. *Ex post* enforcement issues then need to be addressed. First, there is the problem of declaring what state of the world has obtained. Meade's remarks that contingent claims contracts are infeasible in circumstances where it is impossible, on the contract execution date, "to decide precisely enough for the purposes of a firm legal contract" what state of the world has eventuated (1971, p. 183) bear on this. While it is easy to agree with Meade's contentions, I think it noteworthy to observe that, were it not for opportunism and information impactedness, the impediments to contracting which he refers to vanish. Absent these conditions, the responsibility for declaring what state of the world had obtained could simply be assigned to the best informed party. Once he has made the determination, the appropriate choice of x is found by consulting the contract. Execution then follows directly.

It is hazardous, however, to permit the best informed party unilaterally to make state of the world declarations where opportunism can be anticipated. If the worker is not indifferent between supplying services of type x_j rather than x_k, and if the declaration of the state of the world were to be left to him, he will be inclined, when circumstances permit, to represent the state of the world in terms most favorable to him. Similar problems are to be expected for those events for which the employer is thought to be the best informed party and unilaterally declares, from among a plausible set, which e_i has eventuated.[6] Moreover, mediation by

---

6. The issue here is somewhat more subtle, however. The employer, when he assumes the role of the best informed party, will not wish to declare a false state of the world *unless,* at the time he got the worker to agree to a wage w, he represented to the worker that services of type x_i would be called for when event e_i obtained when in fact x_i' services, which the worker dislikes, yield a greater e_i gain. The worker, being assured that he would be called on to perform x_i' services only when the unlikely event e_i' occurred, agreed to a lower wage than he would have if he realized that an x_i' response would be called for in both e_i and e_i' situations—because the employer will falsely declare e_i to be e_i' so as to get x_i' performed.

a third party is no answer since, by assumption, an information impactedness condition prevails with respect to the observations in question.

Finally, even were it that state of the world issues could be settled conclusively at low cost, there is still the problem of execution. Did the worker
really supply x_i in response to condition e_i, as he should, or did he (opportunistically) supply x_j instead? If the latter, how does the employer show
this in a way that entitles him to a remedy? These are likewise information
impactedness issues. Problems akin to moral hazard are posed.

Ordinarily, bounded rationality renders the discription of once-for-all
contingent claims employment contracts strictly infeasible. Occasions to
examine the negotiability and enforcement properties of such contracts
thus rarely develop. It is sufficient for our purposes here, however, merely
to establish that problems of any of these kinds impair contingent claims
contracting. In consideration of these difficulties, alternatives to the once-
for-all supply relations ought presumably to be examined.

3.2 *Sequential Spot Contracts*

Alchian and Demsetz take the position that it is a delusion to characterize the relation between employer and employee by reference to fiat,
authority, or the like. Rather, it is their contention that the relation between
an employer and his employee is identical to that which exists between a
shopper and his grocer in fiat and authority respects (1972, p. 777):

> The single consumer can assign his grocer to the task of obtaining whatever the
> customer can induce the grocer to provide at a price acceptable to both parties.
> That is precisely all that an employer can do to an employee. To speak of
> managing, directing, or assigning workers to various tasks is a deceptive way of
> noting that the employer continually is involved in renegotiation of contracts
> on terms that must be acceptable to both parties .... Long term contracts
> between employer and employee are not the essence of the organization we call
> a firm.

Implicit in their argument, I take it, is an assumption that the transition
costs associated with employee turnover are negligible. Employers, therefore, are able easily to adapt to changing market circumstances by filling
jobs on a spot market basis. Although job incumbents may continue to hold
jobs for a considerable period of time and may claim to be subject to an
authority relationship, all that they are essentially doing is continuously
meeting bids for their jobs in the spot market. This is option number three,
among the contracting alternatives described at the beginning of this
section, done repeatedly.

That adaptive, sequential decision-making can be effectively implemented in sequential spot labor markets which satisfy the low transition

cost assumption (as some apparently do, for example, migrant farm labor) [7] without posing issues that differ in kind from the usual grocer-customer relationship seems uncontestable. I submit, however, that many jobs do not satisfy this assumption. In particular, the tasks of interest here are not of this primitive variety. Where tasks are idiosyncratic, in nontrivial degree, the worker-employer relationship is no longer contractually equivalent to the usual grocer-customer relationship and the feasibility of sequential spot market contracting breaks down.

Whereas the problems of contingent claims contracts were attributed to bounded rationality and opportunism conditions, sequential spot contracts are principally impaired only by the latter. (Bounded rationality poses a less severe problem because no effort is made to describe the complex decision tree from the outset. Instead, adaptations to uncertainty are devised as events unfold.) Wherein does opportunism arise and how is sequential spot contracting impaired?

Recall from the discussion of opportunism in Chapter 2 that opportunism posed a contractual problem only to the extent that it appears in a small-numbers bargaining context. Otherwise, large-numbers bidding effectively checks opportunistic inclinations and competitive outcomes result. The problem with the tasks in question is that while large-numbers bidding conditions obtain at the outset, before jobs are first assigned and the work begun, the idiosyncratic nature of the work experience effectively destroys parity at the contract renewal interval. Incumbents who enjoy nontrivial advantages over similarly qualified but inexperienced bidders are well-situated to demand some fraction of the cost savings which their idiosyncratic experience has generated.

One possible adaptation is for employers to avoid idiosyncratic technologies and techniques in favor of more well-standardized operations. Although least-cost production *technologies* are sacrificed in the process, pecuniary gains may nevertheless result since incumbents realize little strategic advantage over otherwise qualified but inexperienced outsiders. Structuring the initial bidding in such a way as to permit the least-cost technology and techniques to be employed without risking untoward contract renewal outcomes is, however, plainly to be preferred. Two possibilities warrant consideration: (1) extract a promise from each willing bidder at the outset that he will not use his idiosyncratic knowledge and experience in a monopolistic way at the contract renewal interval; or (2) require incumbents to capitalize the prospective monopoly gains that each will accrue and extract corresponding lump sum payments from winning bidders at the outset.

The first of these can be dismissed as utopian. It assumes that promises not to behave opportunistically are either self-enforcing or can be enforced

---

7. See Doeringer and Piore (1971, pp. 4-5); also Kerr (1954, p. 95).

in the courts. Self-enforcement is tantamount to denying that human agents are prone to be opportunists, and fails for want of reality testing. Enforcement of such promises by the courts is likewise unrealistic. Neither case by case litigation nor simple rule-making disposition of the issues is feasible. Litigation on the merits of each case is prohibitively costly, while rules to the effect that "all workers shall receive only competitive wages" fail because courts cannot, for information impactedness reasons, determine whether workers put their energies and inventiveness into the job in a way which permits task-specific cost savings to be fully realized — in which case disaffected workers can counter such rules by withholding effort.

The distinction between consummate and perfunctory cooperation is important in this connection. Consummate cooperation is an affirmative job attitude — to include the use of judgment, filling gaps, and taking initiative in an instrumental way.[8] Perfunctory cooperation, by contrast, involves job performance of a minimally acceptable sort — where minimally acceptable means that incumbents, who through experience have acquired task-specific skills, need merely to maintain a slight-margin over the best available inexperienced candidate (whose job attitude, of necessity, is an unknown quantity). The upshot is that workers, by shifting to a perfunctory performance mode, are in a position to "destroy" idiosyncratic efficiency gains. Reliance on pre-employment promises as a means by which to deny workers from participating in such gains is accordingly self-defeating.

Consider, therefore, the second alternative in which, though worker participation in realized cost savings is assumed to be normal, workers are required to submit lump sum bids for jobs at the outset. Assuming that large numbers of applicants are qualified to bid for these jobs at the outset, will such a scheme permit employers to fully appropriate the expected, discounted value of future cost savings by awarding the job to whichever worker offers to make the highest lump sum payment?

Such a contracting scheme amounts to long-term contracting in which many of the details of the agreement are left unspecified. As might be anticipated, numerous problems are posed. For one thing, it assumes that workers are capable of assessing complex future circumstances in a sophisticated way and making a determination of what the prospective gains are.

8. Consummate cooperation involves working in a fully functional, undistorted mode. Efforts are not purposefully withheld; neither is behavior of a knowingly inapt kind undertaken. Blau and Scott are plainly concerned with the difference between perfunctory and consummate cooperation in the following passage (1962, p. 140):

> the contract obligates employees to perform only a set of duties in accordance with minimum standards and does not assure their striving to achieve optimum performance. . . . [L]egal authority does not and cannot command the employee's willingness to devote his ingenuity and energy to performing his tasks to the best of his ability. . . . It promotes compliance with directives and discipline, but does not encourage employees to exert effort, to accept responsibilities, or to exercise initiative.

Plainly, a serious bounded rationality issue is raised. Second, even if workers had the competence to complete such an exercise, it is seriously to be doubted that they could raise the funds, if their personal assets were deficient, to make the implied full valuation bids. As Malmgren has observed, in a somewhat different but nevertheless related context: " . . . some [individuals] will see opportunities, but be unable to communicate their own information and expectations favorably to bankers, and thus be unable to acquire finance, or need to pay a higher charge for the capital borrowed" (1961, p. 416). The communication difficulties referred to are due to language limitations (attributable to bounded rationality) that the parties experience. That bankers are unwilling to accept the representations of loan-seekers at face value is because of the risks of opportunism.

Third, and crucially, the magnitude of the estimated future gains to be realized by workers often depends not merely on exogenous events and/or activities that each worker fully controls but also on the posture of coworkers and the posture of the employer. Problems with coworkers arise if, despite steady state task separability, the consent or active cooperation of workers who interface with the task in question must be secured each time an adaptation is proposed. This effectively means that related sets of workers must enter bids as teams, which complicates the bidding scheme greatly and offers opportunities for free riding. Problems also arise if gains cannot be realized independently of the decisions taken by management with respect, for example, to the organization of production, complementary new asset acquisitions, equipment repair policy, and so forth. Lump sum bidding is plainly hazardous where workers are entering bids on life cycle earnings streams that are repeatedly exposed to rebargaining.[9]

Finally, but surely of negligible importance in relation to the issues already raised, there is the question of efficient risk-bearing: which party is best situated to bear the risks of future uncertainties—the individual workers or the firm? That individual workers may be poorly suited to bear such risks and, as a group, can pool risks only with difficulty seems evident and further argues against the bidding scheme proposed.

Transactional difficulties thus beset both contingent claims and sequential spot market contracting for the idiosyncratic tasks of interest in this chapter. Consider, therefore, the so-called authority relation as the solution to the contracting problems in question.

---

9. There is the related problem of comparing the bids of workers who have different age, health, and other characteristics. Possibly this could be handled by stipulating that winners have claims to jobs in perpetuity, so that a job can be put up for rebidding by the estate of a worker who dies or retires. Such rebidding, however, is hazardous if the new worker must secure anew the cooperation of his colleagues. Established workers are then in a position strategically to appropriate some of the gains. (This assumes that coalition asymmetries exist which favor old workers in relation to the new.)

3.3   The Authority Relation

Simon has made one of the few attempts to formally assess the employment relation. Letting B designate the employer (or boss), W be the employee (or worker), and x be an element in the set of possible behavior patterns of W, he defines an authority relation as follows (1957, p. 184):

> We will say that B exercises *authority* over W if W permits B to select x. That is, W accepts authority when his behavior is determined by B's decision. In general, W will accept authority only if x_0 the x chosen by B, is restricted to some subset (W's "area of acceptance") of all the possible values.

An employment contract is then said to exist whenever W agrees to accept the authority of B in return for which B agrees to pay W a stated wage (1957, p. 184).

Simon then asks when will such an employment relationship be preferred to a sales contract, and offers the following two conjectures (1957, p. 185):

1. W will be willing to enter into an employment contract with B only if it does not matter to him "very much" which x (within the agreed upon area of acceptance) B will choose, or if W is compensated in some way for the possibility that B will choose x that is not desired by W (i.e., that B will ask W to perform an unpleasant task).
2. It will be advantageous to B to offer W added compensation for entering into an employment contract if B is unable to predict with certainty, at the time the contract is made, which x will be the optimum one, from his standpoint. That is, B will pay for the privilege of postponing, until some time after the contract is made, the selection of x.

He then goes on to develop a formal model in which he demonstrates that the employment contract commonly has attractive properties, under conditions of uncertainty, *provided that the alternatives are* (1) the promise of a particular x in exchange for a given wage w (what he considers to be the sales contract option), or (2) a set of X from which a particular x will subsequently be chosen in exchange for a given wage w' (the employment contract option).

Put differently, the deterministic sales contract is shown to be inferior to an incompletely specified employment relation in which W and B do not agree on all terms *ex ante*, but "agree to agree later" — or better, "agree to tell and be told." But plainly the terms are rigged from the outset. As noted previously, the particular type of sales contract to which Simon refers in attempting to establish the rationale for an authority relation is the only one of the three types of sales contracts described at the beginning of this section that lacks adaptability in response to changing market circumstances. Since employment contracts of both the contingent claims and sequential spot marketing kinds are not similarly flawed, a better test of the authority relation would be to compare it with either of these instead.

Simon's modeling apparatus, unfortunately, does not lend itself to such purposes. It is simply silent with respect to the efficiency properties of alternative contracts in which adaptability is featured. Not only is it unable to discriminate between the authority relation, contingent claims contract, and spot market contracting in adaptability respects, but Simon's model fails to raise transaction cost issues of the types described here.

This is not, however, to suggest that the authority relation has nothing to commend it. To the contrary, such a relation does not require that the complex decision tree be generated in advance, and thus does not pose the severe bounded rationality problems that the contingent claims contracting model is subject to. The authority relation also, presumably, reduces the frequency with which contracts must be negotiated in comparison with the sequential spot contracting mode. Adaptations in the small can be costlessly accomplished under an authority relation because such changes, to the worker, do not matter very much.

Assuming, however, that the parties are prospectively joined in a long-term association and the jobs in question are of the idiosyncratic kind, most of the problems of sequential spot contracting still need to be faced. Thus, how are wage and related terms of employment to be adjusted through time in response to either small, but cumulative, or large, discrete changes in the data? What happens when hitherto unforeseen and unforeseeable contingencies eventuate? How are differences between parties regarding state of the world determinations, the definition of the task, and job performance to be reconciled? Substantially all of the problems that are posed by idiosyncratic tasks in the sequential spot contracting mode appear, I submit, under the authority relation as well.

4. The Efficiency Implications of Internal Labor Market Structures

The upshot is that none of the above contracting schemes has acceptable properties for tasks of the idiosyncratic variety. Contingent claims contracting (Meade, 1971, Chap. 10) fails principally because of bounded rationality. Spot market contracting (Alchian and Demetz, 1972, p. 777) is impaired by first-mover advantages and problems of opportunism. The authority relation (Simon, 1957, pp. 183-195) is excessively vague and, ultimately, is confronted with the same types of problems as is spot market contracting. Faced with this result, the question of alternative contracting schemes naturally arises. Can more effective schemes be designed? Do more efficient contracting modes exist?

The analysis here is restricted to the latter of these questions, which is answered in the affirmative. Although it cannot be said that internal labor market structures are optimally efficient with respect to idiosyncratic tasks, it is nevertheless significant that their efficiency properties have been little noted or understated by predominantly non-neoclassical interpretations of these markets in the past.

My assessment of the efficiency implications of internal labor market structures is in three parts. The occasion for and purposes of collective organization are sketched first. The salient structural attributes of internal labor markets are then described and the efficiency implications of each, expressed in terms of the language of the organizational failures framework, is indicated. Several caveats, including a brief discussion of atmosphere, follow.

4.1 Collective Organization

To observe that the pursuit of perceived individual interests can sometimes lead to defective collective outcomes is scarcely novel. Schelling has treated the issue extensively in the context of the "ecology of micromotives" (1971). The individual in each of his examples is both small in relation to the system — and thus his behavior, by itself, has no decisive influence on the system — and is unable to appropriate the collective gains that would obtain were he voluntarily to forego individual self-interest seeking. Schelling then observes that the remedy involves collective action. An enforceable social contract which imposes a cooperative solution on the system is needed (1971, p. 69).

Although it is common to think of collective action as action by the state, this is plainly too narrow. As Arrow (1969, p. 62) and Schelling (1971, p. 68) emphasize, both private collective action (of which the firm, with its hierarchical controls, is an example) and norms of socialization are also devices for realizing cooperative solutions. The internal labor market is usefully interpreted in this same spirit.

Although it is in the interest of each worker, bargaining individually or as a part of a small team, to acquire and exploit monopoly positions, it is plainly not in the interest of the *system* that employees should behave in this way. Opportunistic bargaining not only in itself absorbs real resources, but efficient adaptations are delayed and possibly foregone altogether. Accordingly, what this suggests is that the employment relation be transformed in such a way that systems concerns are made more fully to prevail and the following objectives are realized: (1) bargaining costs are much lower; (2) the internal wage structure is rationalized in terms of objective task characteristics; (3) consumate rather than perfunctory cooperation is encouraged; and (4) investments of idiosyncratic types, which constitute a potential source of monopoly, are undertaken without risk of exploitation. For the reasons and in the ways developed below, internal labor markets can have, and some do have, the requisite properties to satisfy this prescription.[10]

4.2 Structural Attributes and their Efficiency consequences

4.2.1 WAGE BARGAINING

A leading difficulty with individual contracting schemes where jobs are idiosyncratic is that workers are strategically situated to bargain opportunistically. The internal labor market achieves a fundamental transformation by shifting to a system where wage rates are attached mainly to jobs rather than to workers. Not only is individual wage bargaining thereby discouraged, but it may even be legally foreclosed (Summers, 1969, p. 531). Once wages are expressly removed from individual bargaining, there is really no occasion for the worker to haggle over the incremental gains that are realized when adaptations of degree are proposed by the management. The incentives to behave opportunistically, which infect individual bargaining schemes, are correspondingly attenuated.

Moreover, not only are affirmative incentives lacking, but there are disincentives, of group disciplinary and promotion ladder types, which augur against resistance to authority on matters that come within the range customarily covered by the authority relation.[11] Promotion ladder issues are taken up in conjunction with the discussion of ports of entry in section 4.2.4, below; consider, therefore, group disciplinary effects.

In this connection Barnard observes (1962, p. 169):

> Since the efficiency of organization is affected by the degree to which individuals assent to orders, denying the authority of an organization communication is a threat to the interests of all individuals who derive a net advantage from their connection with the organization, unless the orders are unacceptable

10. Common's discussion with Sidney Hillman concerning the transformation of membership attitudes among the Amalgamated Clothing Workers illustrates some of the systems attributes of collective agreements (1970, p. 130):

> Ten years after World War I, I asked Sidney Hillman . . . why his members were less revolutionary than they had been when I knew them twenty-five years before in the sweatshop. . . . Hillman replied, "They know now that they are citizens of the industry. They know that they must make the corporation a success on account of their own jobs." They were citizens because they had an arbitration system which gave them security against arbitrary foremen. They had an unemployment system by agreement with the firm which gave them security of earnings. This is an illustration of the meaning of part-whole relations.

11. Authority relation is used here in the qualified short run sense suggested in our discussion of Simon in Section 3.3 above.

to them also. Accordingly, at any given time there is among most of the contributors an active personal interest in the maintenance of the authority of all orders which to them are within the zone of indifference. The maintenance of this interest is largely a function of informal organization.

The application of group pressures thus combines with promotional incentives to facilitate adaptations in the small.[12] Even individuals who have exhausted their promotional prospects can thereby be induced to comply. System interests are made more fully to prevail. This concern with viability possibly explains the position taken in labor law that that orders which are ambiguous with respect to, and perhaps even exceed, the scope of authority, are to be fulfilled first and disputed later (Summers, 1969, pp. 538, 573).

4.2.2 Contractual Incompleteness/Arbitration

Internal labor market agreements are commonly reached through collective bargaining. Cox observes in this connection that the collective bargaining agreement should be understood as an instrument of government as well as an instrument of exchange. "The collective agreement governs complex, many-sided relations between large-numbers of people in a going concern for very substantial periods of time" (1958, p. 22). Provision for unforeseeable contingencies is made by writing the contract in general and flexible terms and supplying the parties with a special arbitration machinery. "One simply cannot spell out every detail of life in an industrial establishment, or even of that portion which both management and labor agree is a matter of mutual concern" (Cox, 1958, p. 23). Such contractual incompleteness is an implicit concession to bounded rationality. Rather than attempt to anticipate all bridges that might conceivably be faced, which is impossibly ambitious and excessively costly, bridges are crossed as they appear.

However attractive, in bounded rationality respects, adaptive, sequential decision-making is, admitting gaps into the contract also poses hazards. Where parties are not indifferent with respect to the manner in which gaps are to be filled, fractious bargaining or litigation commonly result. It is for the purpose of forestalling the worst outcomes of this kind that the special arbitration apparatus is devised.

---

12. Of course, informal organization does not operate exclusively in the context of a collectivized wage bargain. Autonomous bargainers, however, are ordinarily expected to behave in autonomous ways. The extent to which group powers serve as a check on challenges to authority is accordingly much weaker where the individual bargaining mode prevails (March and Simon, 1958, pp. 59, 66). By contrast, the individual in the collectivized system who refuses to accede to orders on matters that fall within the customarily define zone of acceptance is apt to be regarded as cantankerous or malevolent, since there is no private pecuniary gain to be appropriated, and will be ostracized by his peers.

Important differences between commercial and labor arbitration are to be noted in this connection. For one thing, ". . . the commercial arbitrator finds facts — did the cloth meet the sample — while the labor arbitrator necessarily pours meaning into the general phrases and interstices of a document" (Cox, 1958, p. 23). In addition, the idiosyncratic practices of the firm and its employees also constitute "shop law" and, to the labor arbitrator, are essential background for purposes of understanding a collective agreement and interpreting its intent (Cox, 1958, p. 24).

In the language of the organizational failures framework, the creation of such a special arbitration apparatus serves to overcome information impactedness because the arbitrator is able to explore the facts in greater depth and with greater sensitivity to idiosyncratic attributes of the enterprise than could normal judicial proceedings. Furthermore, once it becomes recognized that the arbitrator is able to apprise himself of the facts in a discerning and low cost way, opportunistic misrepresentations of the data are discouraged as well.

4.2.3 GRIEVANCES

Also of interest in relation to the above is the matter of who is entitled to activate the arbitration machinery when an individual dispute arises. Cox takes the position that (1958, p. 24)[13]

> . . . giving the union control over all claims arising under the collective agreement comports so much better with the functional nature of a collective bargaining agreement. . . . Allowing an individual to carry a claim to arbitration whenever he is dissatisfied with the adjustment worked out by the company and the union . . . discourages the kind of day-to-day cooperation between company and union which is normally the mark of sound industrial relations — a relationship in which grievances are treated as problems to be solved and contracts are only guideposts in a dynamic human relationship. When . . . the individual's claim endangers group interests, the union's function is to resolve the competition by reaching an accommodation or striking a balance.

13. I am told that this practice is changing and offer three comments in this regard. First, institutional change does not always promote efficiency outcomes; backward steps will sometimes occur — possibly because the efficiency implications are not understood. Second, relegating control to the union on whether a grievance is to be submitted to arbitration can sometimes lead to capricious results. Disfavored workers can be unfairly disadvantaged by those who control the union decision-making machinery. Some form of appeal may therefore be a necessary corrective. Third, that workers are given rights to bring grievances on their own motion does not imply that this will happen frequently. Grievances that fail to secure the support of peers are unlikely to be brought unless they represent egregious conditions on which the grievant feels confidently he will prevail. The bringing of trivial grievances not only elicits the resentment of peers but impairs the grievant's standing when more serious matters are posed.

The practice described by Cox of giving the union control over arbitration claims plainly permits group interests, whence the concern for system viability, to supercede individual interests, thereby curbing small numbers opportunism.

4.2.4 INTERNAL PROMOTION/PORTS OF ENTRY

Acceding to authority on matters that fall within the zone of acceptance[14] merely requires that employees respond in a minimally acceptable, even perfunctory way. This may be sufficient for tasks that are reasonably well-structured. In such circumstances, the zeal with which an instruction is discharged may have little effect on the outcome. As indicated, however, consummate cooperation is valued for the tasks of interest here. But how is cooperation of this more extensive sort to be realized?

A simple answer is to reward cooperative behavior by awarding incentive payments on a transaction-specific basis. The employment relation would then revert to a series of haggling encounters over the nature of the *quid pro quo*, however, and would hardly be distinguishable from a sequential spot contract. Moreover, such payments would plainly violate the nonindividualistic wage bargaining attributes of internal labor markets described in Section 4.2.1, above.

The internal promotion practices in internal labor markets are of special interest in this connection. Access to higher-level positions on internal promotion ladders are not open to all comers on an unrestricted basis. Rather, as part of the internal incentive system, higher-level positions (of the prescribed kinds)[15] are filled by promotion from within whenever this is feasible. This practice, particularly if it is followed by other enterprises to which the workers might otherwise turn for upgrading opportunities, ties the interests of the workers to the firm in a continuing way.[16] Given these ties, the worker looks to internal promotion as the principal means of improving his position.

The practice of restricting entry to lower-level jobs and promoting from within has interesting experience-rating implications. It permits firms to protect themselves against low productivity types, who might otherwise successfully represent themselves to be high productivity applicants, by bringing employees in at low level positions and then upgrading them as experience warrants. Furthermore, employees who may have

---

14. The zone of acceptance is discussed in the quotation from Barnard in Section 4.2.1, above.
15. For a discussion, see Doeringer and Piore (1971, pp. 42-47).
16. Since access to idiosyncratic types of jobs is limited by requiring new employees to accept lower-level jobs at the bottom of promotion ladders, individuals can usually not shift laterally between firms without cost: "Employees in nonentry jobs in one enterprise often have access only to entry-level jobs in other enterprises. The latter will often pay less than those which the employees currently hold" (Doeringer and Piore, 1971, p. 78).

been incorrectly upgraded but later have been "found out," and hence barred from additional internal promotions, are unable to move to a new organization without penalty.[17] Were unpenalized lateral moves possible, workers might, considering the problems of accurately transmitting productivity valuations between firms, be able to disguise their true productivity attributes from their new employers long enough to achieve some additional promotions. Restricting access to low level positions serves to protect the firm against exploitation by opportunistic types who would, if they could, change jobs strategically for the purpose of compounding evaluation errors between successive independent organizations.

Were it, however, that markets could perform equally well these experience-rating functions, the port of entry restrictions described would be unnecessary. The (comparative) limitations of markets in experience-rating respects, which were referred to in Chapter 2, warrant elaboration. The principal impediment to effective interfirm experience-rating is one of communication.[18] By comparison with the firm, markets lack a rich and common rating language. The language problem is particularly severe where the judgments to be made are highly subjective. The advantages of hierarchy in these circumstances are especially great if those persons who are the most familiar with a worker's characteristics, usually his immediate supervisor, also do the experience-rating. The need to rationalize subjective assessments that are confidently held but, by reason of bounded rationality, difficult to articulate is reduced. Put differently, interfirm experience-rating is impeded in information impactedness respects.

Reliance on internal promotion has affirmative incentive properties because workers can anticipate that differential talent and degrees of co-operativeness will be rewarded. Consequently, although the attachment of wages to jobs rather than to individuals may result in an imperfect correspondence between wages and marginal productivity at ports of entry, productivity differentials will be recognized over a time and a more perfect correspondence can be expected for higher-level assignments in the internal labor market job hierarchy.

17. Agents seeking transfer may have gotten ahead in an organization by error. Experience-rating, after all, is a statistical inference process and is vulnerable to "Type II" error. When a mistake has been discovered and additional promotions are not forthcoming, the agent might seek transfer in the hope that he can successfully disguise his true characteristics in the new organization and thereby secure further promotions. Alternatively, the agent may have been promoted correctly, but changed his work attitudes subsequently — in which case further promotion is denied. Again, he might seek transfer in the hope of securing additional promotion in an organization that, because of the difficulty of interfirm communication about agent characteristics, is less able to ascertain his true characteristics initially.

18. Interfirm experience-rating may also suffer in veracity respects, since firms may choose deliberately to mislead rivals. The major impediment, however, is one of communication.

4.3 Three Caveats

The above discussion is incomplete in several respects. For one thing, it does not pretend to be exhaustive in describing the structured aspects of internal labor markets. At most the more prominent features have been identified. Second, the treatment of efficiency effects has not been symmetrical. The focus has been strictly on efficiency gains, while a more complete treatment would be concerned with the *net* gains (and thus would consider efficiency losses as well). However, inasmuch as the efficiency gains of internal labor markets have hitherto been somewhat neglected, an affirmative statement of the ways in which the structure of internal labor markets serves to economize on bounded rationality and attenuate opportunism seems useful.

Third, the contractual atmosphere associated with individualistic and collective contracting modes differs. As compared with individualistic contracting modes, where rewards are usually contingent on performance in a transaction-specific fashion (for example, on a piece rate basis), workers in internal labor markets are metered less intensively. Recall in this connection that compensation rates in internal labor markets are assigned to jobs and that rewards are made contingent on performance through the promotion process. Accordingly, no attempt is made to settle accounts with respect to each transaction as it occurs but workers are experience-rated instead in an overall performance fashion. Also, qualification for advancement on the internal promotion ladder often turns partly on seniority (Doeringer and Piore, 1971, pp. 54-57). The resulting contractual atmosphere not only differs from but is apt to be favored by some workers over that which obtains when each transaction is monitored and the corresponding account is settled separately.

Moreover, Doeringer and Piore's remarks concerning the due process attributes of internal labor markets (1971, p. 29) suggest that there are atmospheric differences between collective and individualistic contracting in this respect as well. The internal due process machinery associated with internal labor markets is apt to be valued not only for the efficiency reasons described in Section 4.2, above, but also because a greater sense of justice (absence of whimsy or prejudice) results.

As pointed out at the outset, however, reference to atmosphere does little to explain the absence of structure for fungible jobs and the appearance of structure where jobs are idiosyncratic. Assuming that atmospheric gains of the types described would be valued for jobs of both kinds, and if it is the case that the structure needed to realize such gains appears only in conjunction with the latter, then the rationale for observed structural differences presumably lies elsewhere. An examination of the efficiency attributes of alternative contracting modes in relation to task characteristics is accordingly warranted. It is the burden of this chapter that the pairing of internal labor markets with idiosyncratic tasks is principally explained in transactional-efficiency terms.

5. Concluding Remarks

Organizational failure and systems considerations appear repeatedly in the foregoing assessment of the properties of alternative contracting modes in relation to idiosyncratic tasks. These highlights are briefly recapitulated here, after which some qualifications are offered.

5.1 Application of the Organizational Failures Framework

But for uncertainty, adaptive sequential decision-making problems would never be posed. Accordingly, the occasion to devise flexible contracts would never develop.

But for bounded rationality, complex contingent claims contracts could be written, and there would be no occasion to investigate other forms of contracting.

But for opportunism, individuals would honestly disclose all information pertinent to the bargain and would self-enforce promises to forego the monopoly powers which accrue to incumbents. Alternatively, were it not for task idiosyncrasies, information impactedness conditions would never develop and outsiders would be on a parity with incumbents in bidding for jobs. In either event, the distortions associated with monopoly advantage would vanish and spot market contracting would suffice. In circumstances, however, where incumbents realize idiosyncratic knowledge and skill advantages over otherwise qualified outsiders, small-numbers conditions evolve. If, additionally, incumbents behave opportunistically, spot market contracting is hazardous.

5.2 The Collective Agreement as a Systems Solution

Frequently more important than the question of whether workers accept authority in the limited sense of "do this" or "do that," at the appointed time and place and in some highly prescribed manner, is their attitude toward cooperation. We have accordingly distinguished between perfunctory and consummate cooperation and have argued that collective organization, in the form of an internal labor market, is well-suited to promote consummate cooperation.

In this respect and others, internal labor markets serve to promote efficiency. Job evaluation attaches wages to jobs, rather than to individuals, thereby foreclosing individual bargaining. The resulting wage structure reflects objective long-term job values rather than current bargaining exigencies. Internal promotion ladders encourage a positive worker attitude toward on-the-job training and enable the firm to reward cooperative behavior. A grievance procedure, with impartial arbitration as the usual final step, allows the firm and the workers to deal with continually changing conditions in a relatively nonlitigious manner. Contract revision and renewal take place in an atmosphere of mutual restraint in which the parties are committed to continuing accommodation. Unionization commonly facilitates the orderly achievement of these results, though it is not strictly necessary, especially in small organizations.

5.3 Qualifications

It should be reemphasized that the argument applies strictly to production tasks of the idiosyncratic kind. Also, as noted in Section 4.3, above, the employment relation and collective agreements are subject to hazards. Only affirmative aspects are dealt with in this chapter.

Finally, there is the organization form issue, to wit, merely to transfer a transaction from the market to the firm does not, by itself, assure that market frictions will be mitigated. To be efficacious, the parties to the transaction must experience different incentives. Although this may partly come about as a result of a deeper appreciation for mutual interdependence, more than this is usually necessary. What internal organization offers is *access to* a distinctive inventory of incentive and control techniques and a related atmosphere within which to operate. For the benefits to be realized requires that the potential be consciously tapped.

Some of the disabilities of internal organization are examined in Chapter 7, while the organization form issue is more fully developed in Chapters 8 and 10.

5. Intermediate Product Markets and Vertical Integration

Assume that production of a final product can be split up into a series of technologically separable stages. Assume, furthermore, that each stage is organized as a simple hierarchy, each of which exhausts scale economies. The questions to be addressed in this chapter are (1) when will the production of components by such technologically separable units be exchanged within a firm rather than across an intermediate product market, and (2) how will such internal transactions be organized? Put differently, given that the final product is to be assembled from a series of separable components, which of these will be bought, which will be made, and how will the latter be organized? This is the vertical integration issue. Both intermode (acquisition) and intramode (organization form) issues are posed.

As it turns out, perhaps not unexpectedly, the reasons for placing technologically separable production units under common direction correspond, in large measure, to the transactional reasons for grouping related tasks within a simple hierarchy. Thus, just as the grouping of tasks under simple hierarchy is efficient in circumstances where the parties are engaged in recurring exchange of a small-numbers sort for which successive adaptations to uncertainty are required, so is the grouping of a set of technologically separable work groups within a complex hierarchy attractive in circumstances where the parties are engaged in recurring small-numbers exchange under conditions of uncertainty. Moreover, the evolution of the small-numbers problem in both internal labor markets and in intermediate product markets is similar. Problems arise mainly in conjunction with contract renegotiation and renewal, rather than at the initial contracting stage, and are to be traced to first-mover advantages.

I begin with a brief review of some of the prior literature that bears, directly or indirectly, on vertical integration and offer a transactional interpretation of what is involved. The make or buy decision in static markets is then examined in Section 2. The economic issues here turn

82

out to be relatively uninteresting. Attention is accordingly shifted in Section 3 to an examination of the properties of intermediate product sales contracts under conditions of uncertainty.

The shift from market to internal transactions is considered in two stages. The effects of common ownership of plant and equipment across successive stages, while otherwise maintaining simple hierarchy, are investigated in Section 4. Such organizational arrangements are shown to experience serious defects, whence the shift to complex hierarchy, in which supervisors assume employment status, in Section 5. The argument is extended from production to include wholesaling functions in Section 6. Concluding remarks follow.

1. Prior Literature:
A Transactional Interpretation

The discussion here does not pretend to be a comprehensive review of the prior literature that deals with vertical integration. It aspires merely to show that the vertical integration of technologically separable production stages ultimately turns on transactional considerations. Although this is sometimes suggested, it is rarely explicit in the literature; indeed, claims to the contrary are common.[1]

1.1 Technological Interdependency

The technological interdependency argument is both the most familiar and the most straightforward: successive processes which, naturally, follow immediately in time and place dictate certain efficient manufacturing configurations; these, in turn, are believed to have common ownership implications. Such technical complementarity is probably more important in flow process operations (chemicals, metals, and so forth) than in separable component manufacture. The standard example is the integration of iron- and steel-making, where thermal economies are said to be available through integration. It is commonly held that where "integration does not have this physical or technical aspect—as it does not, for example, in integrating the production of assorted components with the assembly of those components — the case for cost savings from integration is generally much less clear" (Bain, 1968, p. 381).

I submit, however, that, were it possible to write and enforce a complex contingent claims contract between blast furnace and rolling mill stages,

---

1. Stigler's life cycle explanation for vertical integration has been previously examined in Section 3.3 of Chapter 1. For the reasons given there, the argument turns ultimately on transactional rather than technological factors.

the integration of these activities, for thermal economy reasons, would be unnecessary. The prohibitive cost of such contracting is what explains the decision to integrate. I furthermore contend, for the reasons developed in Section 4, that common ownership, by itself, is not sufficient to realize the potential economies of integration. The type of internal organizational structure that the firm employs also matters. Transaction costs thus both explain the decision to shift a transaction from the market into the firm and, within the firm, what organization form will be chosen.

Finally, I submit that even for transactions that do not involve "physical or technical" aspects of the kind referred to by Bain, integration may nevertheless permit transactional economies to be realized. Flow process economies between otherwise separable production stages are really a special case in which the small-numbers supply condition is particularly evident. Yet, absent thermal economies, or some counterpart physical condition, the opportunities to economize on transaction costs by resorting to vertical integration for exchanges that are conducted under conditions of uncertainty and small-numbers supply still obtain—albeit, perhaps, in less pronounced degree. Put differently, integration of the physical kind described by Bain is merely a special case of the contractual incompleteness issues addressed in Section 3.

1.2 Risk-Bearing and Moral Hazard

The moral hazard problem arises because of the conjoining of inharmonious incentives with uncertainty—or, as Arrow puts it (1969, p. 55), it is due to the "confounding of risks and decisions." To illustrate, consider the problem of contracting for an item whose final cost and/or performance is subject to uncertainty. One possibility is for the supplier to bear the uncertainty. But he will undertake a fixed price contract to deliver a specified result, the costs of which are highly uncertain, only after attaching a risk premium to the price. Assume that the buyer regards this premium as excessive and is prepared on this account to bear the risk himself. The risk can easily be shifted by offering a cost-plus contract. But this impairs the incentives of the supplier to achieve least-cost performance; the supplier may respond opportunistically by running slack (increasing on-the-job leisure) or reallocating his assets in such a way as to favor other work to the disadvantage of the cost-plus contract. (That these are more than mere hypothetical possibilities is revealed by the experience of military contracting on a cost-plus basis.)

Although, if commitments were self-enforcing it might often be institutionally most efficient to divide the functions of risk-bearing and contract execution (that is, cost-plus contracts would have ideal properties), specialization is discouraged by interest disparities. At a minimum, the buyer may insist on monitoring the supplier's work. But he may also decide that integration is more attractive. Not only are the incentives to behave opportunistically thereby attenuated, but monitoring costs are apt to be less as well.[2]

1.3 Variable Proportions Distortions

Consider the case where the assembly stage will support large numbers; fewness appears only in component supply. Whether monopolistic supply prices provide an occasion for vertical integration in these circumstances depends both on production technology and policing expense. Variable proportions at the assembly stage afford opportunities for nonintegrated assemblers to adapt against monopolistically priced components by substituting competitively priced factors (McKenzie, 1951; Vernon and Graham, 1971; Schmalensee, 1973). Although the monopolistic component supplier might conceivably stipulate, as a condition of sale, that fixed proportions in assembly should prevail, the effectiveness of such stipulations is to be questioned — since, ordinarily, such promises will not be self-enforcing and information will be impacted to the disadvantage of the supplier, in which case the implied enforcement costs will be great. Where substitution occurs, inefficient factor proportions, with consequent losses to the system, will result. The private (and social) incentives to integrate, in order to reduce the total costs, by restoring efficient factor combinations, are evident.[3]

It does not follow, however, that a net welfare gain will necessarily obtain. The effect on final price must also be considered. As Warren-Boulton has shown, forward integration into a competitive stage by a monopoly supplier can result in an increase in final price. Whether it will and, if it does, whether a net welfare gain is realized depends in a complex way on the elasticity of substitution, the elasticity of final demand, the condition of entry at the monopolized stage, and input cost relations (Warren-Boulton, 1974).

1.4 Externalities

It is commonplace that failure to make allowance for technological spillover between autonomous agents leads to suboptimization. While

---

2. The reasons for both of these have been developed previously. See especially Chapter 2, Section 2.3.

3. Whether indeed the incentive to restore efficient factor proportions is sufficient to induce integration depends jointly on the magnitude of the monopolistic margins and on the ease of factor substitutions. Since the feasibility of such factor substitutions may be strictly limited, and as monopolistic margins will be restrained by threats of entry (Stigler, 1968, p. 133), threshold sensitivities may not be reached.

taxation is sometimes a feasible way to make such costs evident, integration may also be undertaken for this same reason (Davis and Whinston, 1961).

An alternative suggested by Coase (1960) for dealing with small-numbers externalities is bilateral negotiation. Assuming bargaining costs to be negligible, the assignment of property rights with respect to spillovers to one party or the other can be shown to have no allocative efficiency consequences.[4] But the zero bargaining cost fiction is plainly unrealistic.

As between merger and autonomous market contracting, the question is which mode incurs the lowest transaction costs. In static markets (see Section 2), the two modes would presumably be regarded with indifference. With the introduction of uncertainty, however, successive adaptations to changing market circumstances are needed. A once-and-for-all merger agreement is here apt to entail lower costs than recurrent bilateral bargaining — whence the occasion to integrate again turns on transaction cost considerations.

1.5 Markets for Information

1.5.1 OBSERVATIONAL ECONOMIES[5]

As noted in the discussion of peer groups in Chapter 3, "the acquisition of information often involves a 'set-up cost'; that is, the resources needed to obtain the information may be independent of the scale of the production process in which the information is used" (Radner, 1970, p. 457). Although Radner apparently had horizontal firm-size implications in mind, the argument also has relevance for vertical integration. If a single set of observations can be made that is of relevance to a related series of production stages, vertical integration may be efficient.

Still, the question might be raised, why common ownership? Why not an independent observational agency that sells information to all comers? Or, if the needed information is highly specialized, why not a joint venture? Alternatively, what inhibits efficient information-exchange between successive stages of production according to contract? In relation, certainly, to the range of intermediate options potentially available, common ownership appears to be an extreme response. What are the factors which favor this outcome?

One of the problems with contracts is that of specifying terms. But even if terms could be reached, there is still a problem of policing the agreement.

---

4. This assumes that rents exist in sufficient degree to cover the spillovers in question (Regan, 1972, p. 433).
5. The argument in this subsection repeats issues already covered in Chapters 1 and 3. It is included here in order to make this chapter more self-contained.

To illustrate, suppose that the common information-collection responsibilities are assigned by contract to one of the parties. The purchasing party then runs a veracity risk: information may be filtered and possibly distorted to the advantage of the firm that has assumed the information-collection responsibility. If checks are costly and proof of contractual violation difficult, contractual sharing arrangements manifestly experience short-run limitations. If, in addition, small-numbers conditions prevail, so that options are restricted, contractual sharing is subject to long-run risks as well. On this argument integration for purposes of observational economies is again to be traced ultimately to transaction-cost considerations.

1.5.2 Convergence of Expectations

The issue to which the convergence of expectations argument is addressed is that, if there is a high degree of interdependence among successive stages of production and if occasions for adaptation are unpredictable yet common, coordinated responses may be difficult to secure if the separate stages are operated independently. March and Simon (1958, p. 159) characterize the problem in the following terms:

> Interdependence by itself does not cause difficulty if the pattern of interdependence is stable and fixed. For in this case, each subprogram can be designed to take account of all the subprograms with which it interacts. Difficulties arise only if program execution rests on contingencies that cannot be predicted perfectly in advance. In this case, coordinating activity is required to secure agreement about the estimates that will be used as the bases for action, or to provide information to each subprogram unit about the activities of the others.

This reduces, in some respects, to a contractual incompleteness argument. Were it feasible exhaustively to stipulate the appropriate conditional responses, coordination could proceed by contract. This is ambitious, however; in the face of a highly variable and uncertain environment, the attempt to program responses is apt to be inefficient. To the extent that an unprogrammed (adaptive, sequential) decision-process is employed instead, and in consideration of the severe incentive and control limitations that long-term contracts experience in these circumstances, vertical integration may be indicated.

But what of the possibility of short-term contracts? It is here that the convergence of expectations argument is of special importance. Thus, assume that short-term contracts are defective neither on account of investment disincentives nor first-mover advantages.[6] It is Malmgren's (1961) contention that such contracts may nevertheless be vitiated by the absence of structural constraints; the costs of negotiations and the time required to bring the system into adjustment by exclusive reliance on market (price)

---

6. For a discussion of investment disincentives, see Section 3.3, below. First-mover advantages are also discussed there, as well as in Section 4 and in the preceding chapter.

signals are apt to be great in relation to that which would obtain if successive stages were integrated and administrative processes employed as well or instead.

1.5.3 CAPITAL MARKETS [7]

Richardson poses the problem of interest here by reference to an entrepreneur who was willing to proffer long-term contracts (at normal rates of return, presumably) that others were unprepared to accept because they were not convinced that he had "the ability, as well as the will, to fulfill them. He may have information sufficient to convince himself that this is the case, but others may not" (Richardson, 1960, p. 83). He goes on to observe that the perceived risks of the two parties may be such as to make it difficult to negotiate a contract that offers acceptable risks to each; objective risks are augmented by contractual risks in these circumstances. Integration undertaken for this reason is akin to self-insurance by individuals who know themselves to be good risks but are priced out of the insurance market because of their inability, at low cost, to "reveal" this condition to insurers. (See the discussion of insurance in Section 3, Chapter 1.)

The problem is not that investors are "uninterested" in financing projects of this sort. Rather, it is their inability to discriminate among good risks and poor, coupled with the tendency for poor risks to exaggerate their qualifications, that gives rise to the difficulties. The pairing of information impactedness with opportunism thus again supplies a selective incentive to integrate. [8]

A somewhat special, but nevertheless interesting, occasion to substitute vertical integration for autonomous contracting comes up in conjunction with the management succession problem in service industries. Investment bankers are, or at least have been, apprehensive about taking such businesses public. This may just be partly a matter of unfamiliarity with nonmanufacturing businesses. But bankers are also reluctant to invest in human assets. Unlike the manufacturing business, where a considerable fraction of the value of the firm is represented by durable physical assets, the principal assets of value in many service industries are the human assets of a going concern. The latter can be dissipated relatively quickly, before bankers can be apprised and take remedial action.

---

7. The discussion of capital markets here deals with a relatively narrow issue. Additional discussion of capital markets in relation to vertical integration appears in Section 2 of Chapter 6. Failures of the capital market as these bear on resource allocation more generally are examined in Chapters 7 through 9.

8. Once, of course, the investment has been made and the firm is able to display a successful record of performance, problems of raising additional capital are less severe. Since, however, the prospects for success are worsened for firms that, because of capital market limitations, begin from an undercapitalized state, more failures will occur than would otherwise be the case if entrepreneurs were able easily to display their objective characteristics at the outset.

Faced with such capital market difficulties, many service firms, when confronted with a management succession problem, turn to a manufacturer with which they have already had business dealings to attempt a merger instead.[9] The advantages that the manufacturer has over the banker are (1) his pre-existing familiarity with the business, and (2) the greater control that results from merger, as compared with lending, over both strategic decision-making and operating affairs in the acquired enterprise (see Chapters 6 and 7).

2. Static Markets

Consider an industry that produces a multicomponent product, assume that some of these components are specialized (industry specific), and assume further that among these are components for which the economies of scale in production are large in relation to the market. The market, then, will support only a few efficient-sized producers for certain components.

A monopolistic excess of price-over-cost under market procurement is commonly anticipated in these circumstances — although, as discussed in Section 2 of Chapter 2, this need not obtain if there are large numbers of suppliers willing and able to bid at the initial contract award stage. Assume, however, that large-numbers bidding is not feasible. The postulated conditions then afford an apparent incentive for assemblers to integrate backward or suppliers to integrate forward. Two different cases can be distinguished: bilateral monopoly (oligopoly) and competitive assembly with monopolistic supply. The former is considered here; the latter is treated in Section 1.3, above.

Bilateral monopoly requires that both price and quantity be negotiated. Both parties stand to benefit, naturally, by operating on, rather than off, the contract curve—which here corresponds to the joint-profit maximizing quantity (Fellner, 1947). But this merely establishes the amount to be exchanged. The terms at which this quantity will be traded still need to be determined. Any price consistent with non-negative profits to both parties is feasible. Bargaining can be expected to ensue. Haggling will presumably continue until the marginal private net benefits are perceived by one of the parties to be zero. Although this haggling is jointly (and socially)

9. The acquisition by a manufacturer of his distributors sometimes occurs in this way. An example of this is the acquisition by the Hammermill Paper Company of two paper merchant chains in the 1960's. Both chains were faced with management succession problems and possible liquidation. Hammermill's acquisition of these chains permitted the ownership in both instances to realize something on the human asset values which their organizations had built up, but for which there was not a ready market, and assured an orderly transition. (For details, see the trial transcript of *U.S.* v. *Hammermill Paper Company,* U.S. District Court for the Western District of Pennsylvania, July 1972. The testimonies of Alfred Duval and Courtney Reeves are especially relevant.)

unproductive, it constitutes a source of private pecuniary gain. Nevertheless, being a joint profit drain, an incentive to avoid these costs, if somehow this could be arranged, is set up.

One possible adaptation is to internalize the transaction through vertical integration; but a once-for-all contract might also be negotiated. In a perfectly static environment (one that is free of disturbances of all kinds), these two alternatives may be regarded with indifference: the latter involves settlement on component supply price while a merger requires agreement on asset valuation. Bargaining skills will presumably be equally important in each instance (indeed, a component price can be interpreted in asset valuation terms). Thus, although vertical integration may occur under these conditions, there is nothing in the nature of the problem that requires such an outcome.

A similar argument in these circumstances also applies to adaptation against externalities: joint-profit considerations dictate that the affected parties reach an accommodation, but integration holds no advantage over once-for-all contracts in a perfectly static environment.

Transforming the relationship from one of bilateral monopoly to one of bilateral oligopoly broadens the range of bargaining alternatives, but the case for negotiating a merger agreement in relation to a once-for-all contract is not differentially affected on this account. The static characterization of the problem, apparently, will have to be relaxed if a different result is to be reached.

Consider, therefore, the contractual problem posed at the outset of the chapter: What organizational relations are to be expected if a set of technologically separable work groups (each, say, organized as a simply hierarchy) is engaged in recurring exchange of a small-numbers sort for which successive adaptations to uncertainty are required? Three types of organizational alternatives will be evaluated in the sections which follow: sales contracts, extensions on the model of simple hierarchy, and shifting to a multistage hierarchy in which the transactions in question are completed under an employment relationship.

3. Sales Contracts for Component Supply

Assume that the product in question is technically complex and that it needs to be supplied on a semicontinuous basis.[10] Assume also, unless

10. The continuing supply of an item for which adaptive, sequential decision-making is required is to be distinguished from the one-time supply of a long lived asset. Uncertainty with respect to utilization demands combined with the discrete supply of long lived assets makes it necessary to anticipate flexibility needs from the outset. Adaptability is thus mainly a function of the initial design of these assets. (This assumes that design changes

deterred by reason of contractual disabilities, that periodic redesign and/ or volume changes are made in response to changing environmental conditions. Three alternative supply arrangements can be considered: a once-for-all contingent claims contract, an incomplete long-term contract, and a series of short-term contracts.

3.1 Contingent Claims Contracts

The limitations of complex contingent claims contracts have been set out in previous chapters (see especially Section 3.1 of Chapter 4). Bounded rationality makes it impossible, or prohibitively costly, to attempt to write the comprehensive contract in which contingent supply relations are exhaustively stipulated. Consider, therefore, an intermediate form of contracting — namely, incomplete long-term contracts which include a profit-sharing arrangement[11] — and sequential spot contracts.

3.2 Incomplete Long-Term Contracts

That incomplete contracts, without more, pose trading risks is obvious: the natural posture for each party is to bargain opportunistically when contractual ambiguities develop. But might the hazards of contractual incompleteness be overcome by (1) introducing a general clause into the contract to the effect that the parties agree to be guided during contract execution by joint-profit maximization considerations, and (2) inventing an appropriate sharing rule in order to induce the parties to adhere to the agreement? The purpose of such an arrangement is to encourage the parties to behave cooperatively, in a joint-profit maximizing way, when unforeseen contingencies develop.

The issue is of interest not merely for our purposes here but also because it has a bearing on what Hurwicz refers to as "incentive compatibility" (1972, pp. 320-334; 1973, pp. 23-27). The questions of concern to Hurwicz are (1) whether participants to a nonatomistic market exchange, who do not openly defy the prescribed rules (the rule of principal interest is that they behave as price takers), can successfully cheat, and (2) whether

---

during the asset production process are usually negligible.) Inasmuch as the need to anticipate flexibility demands, and hence specify flexibility properties, is the same whether the item is procured internally or purchased in the market, procurement by sales contract or by internal production can scarcely be distinguished on product adaptability grounds.

11. Such arrangements were not considered in the preceding chapter because it would be arguably too expensive to write and implement such contracts for each individual worker. Here, however, the contractual unit is the simple hierarchy. The contractual costs of sharing rules, as a fraction of the total value added, is accordingly much less. A more complete assessment of the limits of sharing rules is thus indicated.

alternative rules of market exchange can be devised which lead to Pareto optimality. He shows that price-taking rules can be successfully evaded if parties employ false preference maps (1972, pp. 324-332). He also contends that autonomous bilateral trading with a sharing rule sometimes leads to joint profit maximization (1973, pp. 25-26).

This last result crucially depends, however, on an assumption that one of the parties behaves throughout as a fully truthful price taker.[12] I submit that sharing rules will not reliably lead to joint profit maximization if both parties are treated *symmetrically* and are allowed to enter false statements or produce false signals.[13] Consider the following sharing rule arrangements:

1. Faced with an unanticipated change in circumstances, the parties will
    (a) earn π_1 and π_2 respectively if no adaptation is made (that is, present period practices are unchanged from the previous period),
    (b) earn $G > \pi_1 + \pi_2$ if they adapt in such a way as to joint-profit maximize.
2. The rules for dividing G between the parties are as follows (where $0 < a < 1$):
    (a) party 1 will receive
       $a G$ if $a G > \pi_1$ and $(1-a) G > \pi_2$;
       π_1 if $a G < \pi_1$;
       $G - \pi_2$ if $(1-a) G < \pi_2$ (in which case party 2 gets π_2 and $G - \pi_2 > \pi_1$).
    (b) party 2 will receive
       $(1-a)G$ if $(1-a)G > \pi_2$ and $aG > \pi_1$;
       π_2 if $(1-a)G < \pi_2$;
       $G - \pi_1$ if $aG < \pi_1$ (in which case party 1 gets π_1 and $G - \pi_1 > \pi_2$).

Since each party can do no worse and will usually do better by adapting and employing the sharing rule, the incomplete contract does not appear to impede efficiency or occasion costly haggling. Rather, the contrivance of a general clause and sharing rule seems to give the parties to an incom-

---

12. Hurwicz' example involves a farmer and a laborer in bilateral negotiations over the amount of labor to be supplied and the amount of compensation to be paid. Hurwicz assumes that laborers behave honestly as wage takers throughout and argues that farmers who would otherwise be inclined to distort their demand for labor can be induced to act truthfully by introducing a profit-sharing rule. This is correct, but why should the laborer behave as described if by disguising his supply of labor schedule he can do better?

13. Hurwicz disallows the former and permits only the latter: "It is important to understand that . . . [cheating is not done] directly by uttering false statements, but indirectly by behaving inappropriately according to the rules" (1973, p. 23). This emphasis on indirection is because of Hurwicz' reliance on market-mediated exchange, where price signaling is paramount. The distinction between the two types of falsity is artificial, however, and is not maintained here.

plete long-term contract the requisite incentives to adapt efficiently in a joint-profit maximizing way.

But, as might be anticipated, there is a hitch. The foregoing assumes that π_1, π_2, and G are all known or can easily be estimated—while in fact they are unknown and, despite great effort and expense, can ordinarily be estimated only imperfectly. Uncertain revenue streams and, even more, uncertain cost streams must be estimated.[14] To the extent that information sets incompletely overlap — which, given task idiosyncracies and differential exposure to environmental circumstances, they clearly will — each party can be expected to supply incomplete and biased data to the estimators when this suits its purposes. Costly haggling predictably ensues.[15] Hurwicz finesses these issues by assuming that one of the parties to the transaction is continuously truthful, which is plainly heroic.

14. For the skeptics who believe that estimating component costs is a precise science, it is useful to consider the following anecdote concerning the purchase of spark-plugs by the Ford Motor Company. The advantage to the manufacturer of spark-plugs of having his plugs appear as original equipment in Ford cars was apparently considerable, since this improved his sales in the replacement market, where most plugs are sold. This advantage was evident to manufacturer and Ford alike, and Ford was able to purchase plugs at much less cost on this account. The magnitude of this advantage was not, however, fully appreciated by Ford. When the Champion Spark Plug Company went public in 1958 (Champion was the first spark plug firm to go public), Ford's interest in spark-plug manufacture was piqued. The President of Electric Autolite Company testified on deposition as follows with respect to this matter [as reported in Trial Memorandum on Behalf of Defendant Ford Motor Company, filed in the U.S. District Court, Eastern District of Michigan, Southern Division, Civil Action No. 21911 (U.S. *v.* the Ford Motor Company and the Electric Autolite Company) on pages 14-15]:

    . . . Electric Autolite was "concerned" because, when Champion Spark Plug Company "went public" in 1958, "the figures that came out were very large—showing very large profits" and "when Ford saw those figures and saw how much profit there was in it" Electric Autolite "felt" that "the very essence of that much profit going to a supplier would be enough to make Ford think in terms of integration."

    Although Ford's staff of engineers, cost accountants, financial analysts, and so forth, was presumably capable of making a profitability assessment, the costs of such an undertaking were apparently considerable. Once, however, the Champion earnings were revealed, the need to undertake a depth study vanished: the profit disclosure spoke for itself.

15. Suppose, for example, that firm 1 is the buyer and asks that firm 2 decrease his supply of components during the next period by ten percent. In what sense do the sharing rules eliminate the bargaining that would otherwise attend such requests? Firm 2 will presumably ask firm 1 to furnish an estimate of how much G will increase as a result, which firm 1 will be inclined to understate. Firm 1 will ask that firm 2 indicate what π_2 would be in the absence of adaptation, which firm 2 will overstate. Depth studies to develop independent estimates will be costly and to little avail if agreement on basic parameters cannot be reached. Or suppose that the casing for a component can be made of either of two materials, x or y, and assume that type x is initially the least-cost material. A change in factor prices later occurs, however, such that type y now becomes cheaper. The buyer proposes that the seller make the switch. The seller replies that he will, but observes that new tooling will be required and certain machine processes will need to be changed. Also, some retraining expenses and other startup costs will be incurred. By inflating his estimates of

3.3 Sequential Spot Contracts

Both complete and incomplete once-for-all contracts thus experience difficulties. The former are flawed by the great cost of anticipating contingencies and specifying efficient adaptations at the outset. Despite the contrivance of a general clause and sharing rule, the latter is beset by costly haggling. Might then short-term contracts be employed instead? These presumably would permit terms to be redrawn at the contract renewal interval; new information could be appropriately taken into account as events unwind; and only a short-term forecast of the immediate future would be required.

But while short-term contracts have advantages in these respects, they also pose distinctive problems of their own. Thus, if either (1) efficient supply requires investment in special purpose, long-lived equipment, or (2) the winner of the original contract acquires a cost advantage by reason of first-mover advantages (such as a unique location or learning, including the acquisition of undisclosed or proprietary technical and managerial procedures and task-specific labor skills), resort to short-term contracts as a means of filling a semicontinuous supply requirement is unlikely to prove satisfactory.

The difficulty with condition (1) is that optimal investment considerations favor the award of a long-term contract in order to permit the supplier confidently to amortize his investment.[16] But, as just indicated, incomplete long-term contracts pose adaptive, sequential decision-making problems. Consequently, in this instance, optimal investment and optimal sequential adaptation processes are in conflict.

Whether first-mover advantages, assuming that they exist, have any bearing on vertical integration might be disputed on the grounds that initial bidders will capitalize anticipated future gains. While this is surely correct, the argument is hardly dispositive. For one thing, unless the total supply requirements are stipulated, "buying in" strategies are risky. Also, and relatedly, the alternative supply price is not independent of the terms that the buyer may subsequently offer to rivals. Moreover, alternative supply price is merely an upper bound; an aggressive buyer may attempt to obtain a price at the level of current costs on each round. Haggling could be expected to ensue. Short-term contracts thus experience what may be serious limitations in circumstances where nontrivial first-mover advantages obtain.[17]

---

these and other transition costs, the seller attempts to renegotiate the agreement on terms more favorable to him. Since the buyer can only dispute, but cannot easily show, that the seller's cost estimates are exaggerated, the fiction that a sharing rule will suffice to accomplish joint-profit maximization is untenable.

16. The economies of long-term contracts here relate to the Alchian (1960) and Hirschleifer (1962) interpretations of the cost function of the firm.

17. The argument here is substantially identical with that of Section 3.2 in Chapter 4.

It is relevant to note that the technological interdependency condition involving flow process economies between otherwise separable stages of production is really a special case of the contractual incompleteness argument. The contractual dilemma is this: On the one hand, it may be prohibitively costly, if not infeasible, to specify contractually the full range of contingencies and stipulate appropriate responses between stages. On the other hand, if the contract is seriously incomplete in these respects but, once the original negotiations are settled, the contracting parties are locked into a bilateral exchange, the divergent interests between the parties will predictably lead to individually opportunistic behavior and joint losses. The advantages of integration thus are not that technological (flow process) economies are unavailable to nonintegrated firms, but that integration harmonizes interests (or reconciles differences, often by fiat) and permits an efficient (adaptive, sequential) decision-process to be utilized. More generally, arguments favorable to integration that turn on "supply reliability" considerations commonly reduce to the contractual incompleteness issue.[18]

4. Unified Ownership of Plant and Equipment: Simple Hierarchy Extended

Considering the above limitations of autonomous contracting, a shift from market to hierarchy warrants examination. Rather, however, than move immediately to a complex hierarchy, might the unified ownership of plant and equipment between the successive stages suffice? Simple hierarchy would be maintained; only the ownership of physical capital would be changed.

Two variants of the model of simple hierarchy suggest themselves. One entails extending the span of control of a single manager (the owner) over all the workers in the combined facility without an increase in the number of hierarchical levels. The wheel model of Chapter 3 would be maintained, but the number of spokes would greatly increase. However appealing such a suggestion is, it can be dismissed on bounded rationality grounds. Spans of control can be progressively extended only by sacrificing attention to detail. Neither coordination economies nor effective monitoring can be achieved if capacity limits are exceeded.

18. It is sometimes suggested that breach of contract risk affords an additional reason for integration: the small supplier of a critical component whose assets are insufficient to cover a total damage claim leaves the purchaser vulnerable. But this is an argument against small suppliers, not contracting quite generally; the large, diversified supplier might well have superior risk pooling capability to that of the integrated firm. The risks of contractual incompleteness, however, remain and may discourage purchasing from large, diversified organizations. [For a discussion of "ideal" contracts in this connection, see Arrow (1965, pp. 52-53).]

Consider instead, therefore, what Buttrick has described as the "inside contracting system" (1952, pp. 201-202):

> Under the system of inside contracting, the management of a firm provided floor space and machinery, supplied raw material and working capital, and arranged for the sale of the final product. The gap between raw material and finished product, however, was filled not by paid employees arranged in [a] descending hierarchy . . . but by [inside] contractors, to whom the production job was delegated. They hired their own employees, supervised the work process, and received a [negotiated] piece rate from the company.[19]

The system developed among New England manufacturing plants at the time of the Civil War and was continued in many of them until World War I.

The inside contracting system had the attractive attributes that it: (1) provided for the aggregation at a single location of a series of primary work groups that were involved in successive manufacturing processes, thereby reducing transportation expense and assuring that a cheek-by-jowl association would develop with corresponding economies of communication; (2) permitted the capitalist with relatively little technical knowledge to employ his capital productively while limiting his involvement to negotiating contracts with the inside department heads, inspecting and coordinating the output of the various departments, and taking responsibility for final sales; and (3) provided the inside contractors (first-level supervisors) with incentives for efficient labor performance in both supervisory and process innovation respects. In addition, although neither is mentioned by Buttrick, (4) the monopoly powers of the various inside contractors were, in relation to supply by an exclusive outside supplier, presumably limited by the capitalist's ownership of plant and equipment, and (5) problems of information impactedness, which might otherwise inhibit new investment, were avoided. The system nevertheless experienced numerous difficulties (Buttrick, 1952, pp. 210-215):

1. A bilateral monopoly position, albeit restrained, developed between the parties.
2. The periodic renegotiation of rates induced the contractor to hoard information and to delay process innovations.
3. The flow of components was difficult to regulate.
4. Work-in-process inventories were excessive and, since each stage incurred only its own direct labor costs, later stage processes were

---

19. Note two things: (1) inside contracting did bring together, at a single location within a common ownership unit, a series of related technical processes, but vertical integration in this limited sense is not sufficient for transactional efficiency to be realized. Organization form considerations, including especially hierarchical controls, also require attention; (2) the various departments in the inside contracting enterprise each appeared to be technologically separable, at least statically, and thereby constituted an efficient primary work group in the sense of Alchian and Demsetz (1972). Thus, what would appear to be the natural generalization of the Alchian and Demsetz model of manager as monitor is observed to fail the test of the market.

wasteful of components on which early stage work was completed.
5. Contractor incomes were sometimes excessive in relation to those of the capitalist, endangering the status of company officials.

Moreover the system was beset by defective incentives in that:

6. Equipment was not utilized and maintained with appropriate care.
7. Process innovations were biased in favor of labor saving, as against materials saving, innovations.
8. Incentives for product innovation were insufficient.

Buttrick attributes the supplanting of the inside contractor system by a hierarchical control apparatus in the Winchester Repeating Arms Company to the conjunction of internal personnel chages in the late 1800's with external "scientific management" developments in the early 1900's (1952, pp. 213-220). But whatever the immediate explanation for the abandonment of inside contracting at Winchester — or any other firm — might be, it is evident that the inside contractor system possessed serious defects and that, to the extent that a more comprehensive system of hierarchical controls served to mitigate these defects (and did not incur offsetting costs), an eventual change in organization form was to be expected.

Although defects numbered 4 and 7 might have been remedied by making simple changes in the internal pricing system, the other disabilities of inside contracting appear really to be immanent. Given uncertainty, whence the occasion to make coordinated adaptations between successive parts, and bounded rationality, whence the limitations on long-term contracts and the infeasibility of a flat (single stage) hierarchy, the defects listed are manifestations of small-numbers bargaining relations in which opportunism and information impactedness conditions obtain. Thus the disabilities of yet another organizational mode—this time inside contracting—are explained in terms of the markets and hierarchies framework of Chapter 2.

To illustrate, suppose that all of the cost and related data bearing on the exchange were costlessly available to both capitalist and contractor (that is, information impactedness does not obtain). Long-term contracts containing a general clause and sharing rule (of the type described in Section 3) could then be written. Given that a large number of bidders are qualified to compete at the outset, the bilateral monopoly problem (defect number 1) would vanish. Alternatively, if winners of original bids made self-enforcing promises not to exploit first-mover advantages at contract renewal intervals, short-term contracts could be written and the initial large-numbers condition would be sufficient to assure competitive supply relations throughout. Inasmuch, however, as both of these assumptions are a fiction (the necessary information is not costlessly available and promises of the sort described are unreliable), the bilateral monopoly condition emerges.

The information hoarding and strategic delay of process innovations (defect number 2) are manifestations of the gaming behavior which the absence of full information permits. Information relating to costs and technology was asymmetrically distributed to the advantage of the inside contractor. Absent opportunism, this would pose no problem. But the inside contractor was evidently opportunistic; whence defect number 2 resulted.

The disruptions in component flows between the parts (defect number 3) can be attributed in the first instance to contractual incompleteness (bounded rationality). In principle, this could be overcome by relying on the capitalist to coordinate the parts flow in an adaptive, sequential manner. Given, however, that each inside contractor assesses the consequences of intervention by the capitalist in terms of the effect on his individual profit stream (again, promises to be guided by joint profit maximization considerations are unenforceable), this proves unacceptable. The defect, therefore, continues.

The status threat posed by defect number 5 is somewhat special. I conjecture that it arises because the inside contractor was relatively secure against displacement (because of first-mover advantages) and because he was not fully candid in disclosing his true costs to the capitalist. The normal correspondence between hierarchical position and income was sometimes upset as a result, which the capitalist regarded as a status threat. Moreover, adverse efficiency consequences can result if the capitalist attempts to reassert his primacy by converting what could be instrumental contractual relationships into subordination relationships instead. Dysfunctional performance easily obtains when such power contests are waged.

The equipment utilization problems referred to in defect number 6 are akin in their origins to the component flow problems discussed above, while the equipment maintenance problems are a reflection of free-riding behavior.

The defective incentives for product innovation (defect number 8) are due, probably, to appropriability problems. Although the capitalist has an interest in improving the product, he is able, given the first-mover advantages which inside contractors acquire, to introduce such changes only by securing the consent of these contractors. The prospect of having to bargain and the inability to appropriate the full value of product innovations reduces his incentive to undertake research and development efforts. [See Buttrick's discussion of the Winchester Company's experience in this connection (1952, p. 214).]

5. Complex Hierarchy: The Employment Relation Extended

A chronic problem with which economic organization must contend is how to harness opportunism. For the reasons given in Chapter 4, individual workers acquire monopoly powers, in some degree, over jobs. Also, as the above discussion of the inside contracting system reveals, the same holds true for managers of functional departments. While individual interests are promoted by exercising these powers for private gain, the system as a whole incurs additional costs and may be rendered nonviable.

5.1 General

A systems solution that transforms the relation between the parties from one of qualified antagonism to more complete cooperation is clearly indicated. Extending the employment relation, which had the effect of curbing opportunistic behavior among workers in the simple hierarchy, to include department managers serves to promote such an outcome. The firm offers managers job security and an internal equity system, in return for which managers agree to being evaluated in terms of their contribution to the system as a whole — as revealed in part by their attitude of cooperation.

The argument here really parallels that of Chapter 4 in most essential respects. What one wants to devise is a contractual relation that promises fair (competitive) returns, promotes adaptive efficiency, and is relatively satisfying in terms of the involvement experience. Inside contracting is deficient in the first two respects and may pose problems in the third. Shifting inside contractors from a quasi-autonomous bargaining status to an employment relation has advantages in the first two—and in possibly all three—respects.

Several things occur when the inside contractor becomes a manager. First, he no longer has claims on a semi-independent profit stream. Second, his operations become subject to an internal audit. His incentives to engage in opportunistic behavior are attenuated for the first of these reasons, and his information impactedness advantage is reduced by the second.[20] More generally, he becomes a member of a team, and, as a member of the team, becomes subject to a different set of expectations regarding his relation to the whole than is the case when quasi-autonomy is preserved and self-seeking is expected. Informal group influences, of the sorts described in the preceding chapters, are brought more systematically to bear when behavior contrary to the interests of the firm occurs.[21]

20. Conceivably, the capitalist in the inside contracting system could stipulate that all contractors should submit to an audit. The efficacy of an audit varies, however, with the degree of cooperation it receives among the audited work force. The employees in the inside contracting firm, as compared with those in the fully integrated firm where the manager is also an employee, were apt to perceive their relation to the division of which they were a part more strongly than their relation to the whole. Their rewards and loyalties being more firmly attached to the inside contractor, the employees in the inside contracting firm were less inclined to be supportive of an audit.

21. Market cooperation, of course, is also a valuable resource; and informal organization, with infrastructure preserving properties, similarly develops among market participants—

In addition to being audited and evaluated, managers are subject to a relatively refined internal reward and compliance machinery. While a more complete discussion of the operation of the internal compliance system is given in Chapter 8, it is worthwhile to observe here that the expectation that employment terms and prospects are subject to fine tuning adjustments serves to promote functional and check dysfunctional behavior.

5.2. Some Specifics

The general advantages of an employment relation (in contractual incompleteness respects, for dispute settling purposes, and in communication respects) have been examined in earlier chapters. Consider, however, the specific advantages of an employment relation in each of these three respects as they bear expressly on department managers.

5.2.1 PERFORMANCE PROGRAMS

Internal organization encourages investments in organizational infrastructure in ways that permit efficient information-processing. Interfaces can be brought into correspondence by design. Performance programs that provide for assured coordination between the parts may be devised. [As March and Simon observe: "Situations in which a relatively simple stimulus sets off an elaborate program of activity without any apparent interval of search, problem-solving, or choice are not rare. . . . Most behavior, and particularly most behavior in organizations, is governed by performance programs" (1958, pp. 141-142).]

One might argue that, in principle, these very same performance programs might be introduced into a sales contract. Several things discourage this, however. First, the typical performance program is incomplete. Execution requires judgment, which is to say that consummate rather than perfunctory cooperation is expected. The manager and at least some of his subordinates are expected to exercise discretion in a constructive fashion. They are rewarded in turn by performing in a functional manner, though not in a transaction-specific fashion. Were similar gaps to appear in a sales contract, the buyer would be exposed to considerable risk of supplier opportunism. (Attempts, moreover, to negotiate and implement exhaustively complete performance programs that bring the interfaces between two

---

especially in small-numbers situations (Phillips, 1962). Inasmuch, however, as market exchange shifts the tradeoff between an active interest in supporting the system and the pecuniary returns from seeking individual advantage in favor of the latter, the efficacy of informal organization for market maintenance purposes is correspondingly attenuated.

independent organizations into design correspondence are discouraged by all of the factors that make complex contingent sales contracts expensive instruments to write and execute.)

Also, there is a problem of adapting the program (contract) appropriately through time. Internal program elaboration is a natural result of experience and is a manifestation of organizational learning. It occurs costlessly as a by-product of the firm's operations. Such changes are made in a contract, however, only as a result of negotiation. Haggling is commonly to be expected.

5.2.2 FIAT

Pure authority relationships, to be sure, are "analytical abstractions that are rarely found, if at all, in concrete situations. [But] this rarity makes the analytical distinction between them and other forms of influence no less important" (Blau and Scott, 1962, p. 3). Or, as Barnard observes, in referring to the "fiction" of authority: "This fiction merely establishes a presumption among individuals in favor of the acceptability of [hierarchical] orders" (1962, p. 170). He nevertheless insists that "Either as a superior officer or as a subordinate, ... I know nothing more 'real' than authority" (1962, p. 170, n. 5).

Whatever the case, assessing the comparative efficiency of alternative modes of organization requires that the conflict resolution machinery be examined. An authoritative order is usually a more efficient way to settle minor conflicts (for instance, differences of interpretation) than is haggling or litigation. Frequently such differences are not matters of special importance to managers and are therefore resolved administratively without incurring resistance (Whinston, 1964, pp. 410-414). To the extent, however, that interfirm profitability effects would be involved if the transactions in question were to be organized across a market, similar interorganizational conflicts can be settled by fiat only rarely, if at all. For one thing, it would require the parties to agree on an impartial arbitrator, and the agreement itself may be costly to secure.[22] In addition, outside arbitration, as compared with inside conflict resolution, has a less easy (more costly) access to the facts and tends to (1) employ restrictive rules of evidence, (2) consider the issues narrowly, from the point of view of what is actionable rather than in terms of what really is at stake, (3) cast the problem in the context of legal precedent for the class of cases to which it is related rather than in firm-specific terms, and (4) favor equity in relation to efficiency considerations where these goals are in conflict. Altogether one concludes that, in dispute settling respects at least, internal organization is preferred over market mediation for activities for which instrumental disputes frequently arise.

---

22. General clauses with sharing rules fail for the reasons given in Section 3 above.

5.2.3   COMMUNICATION

Among the reasons why hierarchical forms of organization have advantages for communication purposes are that they permit status to be assigned to roles in a determinate way.[23] Arrow contends that authority is viable if it is the focus of convergent expectations: "An individual obeys authority because he expects others will obey it" (1974, p. 72). For functional roles to be influential in this way requires that authority be visible.

Similarly, Barnard observes that "a system of organization communication, in order that it may operate with sufficient accuracy and rapidity, has to be so designed that it may easily and quickly be assured that particular communications are (a) authentic, (b) authoritative, and (c) intelligible" (1946, p. 64). A status system facilitates effective communication in each of these respects (1946, pp. 67, 80). Internal organization, having access to a more finely graded status system than the market, thus may be judged to enjoy a communication advantage, in relation to the market, in the degree to which the needs for authenticity, authoritativeness, and intelligibility are especially great, *ceteris paribus.* The previously described adaptational advantages of internal organization as a response to uncertainty are thus reinforced by considering the importance of status systems to effective communication and by noting that the efficacy of status systems varies by organizational mode.[24]

6.   Forward Integration into Wholesaling

The preceding discussion has been concerned mainly with the vertical integration of successive production stages. But the institutional failures framework applies more generally. Franchising, for example, can usefully be studied in these terms. Forward integration into wholesaling is another illustration. Consider Holton's discussion of the wholesaling issue.

Holton (1968, pp. 151-153) contends that the incentives to integrate manufacturing and wholesaling stages increase as:

1.   The sale of the manufacturer's product becomes more geographically dense.

---

23.   For some of the other advantages of hierarchy for communication purposes, see the discussion of peer group communication and decision-making processes in Chapter 3. Also, see Section 4 of Chapter 4.

24.   A further consequence of status ought to be noted. The finer status grid to which internal organization has access permits it to announce status changes in unequivocal ways which the market cannot — at least in a culture where public announcements of income and wealth or even ostentatious living are regarded as crass. Internal organization is thereby able to economize on pecuniary outlays, by substituting nonpecuniary rewards.

2. The greater the average order size placed by retailers.
3. The greater the proportion of a retail firm's sales accounted for by the product of the manufacturer.
4. The more important the services of the wholesaler are to effective distribution and the promotion of sales.
5. The greater the physical perishability or style obsolescence of the product.
6. The greater the number of efficient-sized wholesaling outlets needed to service the requirements of the manufacturer.
7. The greater the possibility of reducing decision-making to a routine.

Incentives numbered 1, 2, and 3 favor the creation of specialized whole-saling outlets in order to more fully realize economies of distribution — especially if the wholesaling function is important and calls for the training of specialized sales and service personnel. The shift from general to specialized wholesaling reduces the number of wholesale outlets and may result in a small-numbers relation between manufacturer and wholesaler. The small-numbers bargaining indeterminacies, which predictably develop, can be avoided by integrating forward into wholesaling.

Incentive number 4 involves matters of inventory investment, product complexity, and service reliability. If large inventories are required to handle demand uncertainties, a problem of who is to bear the risk in what way is posed. Selling on consignment shifts the risk to the producer but may induce the distributor to carry an excessive inventory. Product complexity and service reliability are apt to favor specialized training. Such product-specific investments easily give rise to small-numbers bargaining problems if the parties are associated in a sales rather than an employment relationship.

Incentive number 5 poses the uncertainty issue in even more explicit terms. The desirability of coordinating decision-making through internal, adaptive, sequential processes rather than by contract is enhanced as physical perishability or style obsolescence increase.

Incentive number 6 is somewhat puzzling. There is no clear transactional advantage that I can discern for this condition — unless, perhaps, there are economies of finance to be realized. Reducing decision-making to a routine (incentive number 7) presumably implies economies of writing performance programs (see Section 4.1, above).

Forward integration into wholesaling would thus appear to be explained largely by the same types of transactional considerations that apply to the vertical integration of successive production stages. This is encouraging in that, to the extent that we have been successful in getting to core issues, one would hope that the approach would have general application.

7. Concluding Remarks

Vertical integration is favored in circumstances where small-numbers bargaining would otherwise obtain — whether this prevails from the very outset or because, once the initial contract is let, the parties to the transaction are effectively "locked in" at the recontracting interval — and where, in the face of uncertainty and on account of bounded rationality, an adaptive, sequential decision-process has optimal properties. Vertical integration economizes on transactions by harmonizing interests and permitting a wider variety of sensitive incentive and control processes to be activated. Thus, the hazards [see Fellner (1949, Chaps. 5-7)] of defection and cheating that are posed when a qualified joint profit maximization agreement is reached between (what continue to be) autonomous or semi-autonomous units are greatly reduced if a comprehensive pooling (that is, merger) agreement is reached instead. For one thing, claims over individual profit streams in the latter case are relinquished — not merely when it suits the purposes of the parties, but on an assuredly continuing basis. Also, as noted in the discussion of group disciplinary effects, the members of a firm generally have stronger infrastructure preserving interests than do the members of more loosely knit associations.

Significant constitutional differences also obtain. Thus, the authorized powers to perform an audit are extended and the degree of cooperation that can be secured from those who are subject to the audit is enhanced if the parties are associated through a merger rather than under a qualified joint-profit maximization agreement. Moreover, the compliance instruments that the firm can bring to bear on its employees to promote favored and discourage disfavored outcomes are more refined and selective than would be admissible under (or for that matter consistent with) a joint-profit maximization agreement in which the parties maintain genuine autonomy.

As a result, instrumental conflicts can be resolved more efficiently; cooperative adjustments to changing market circumstances are promoted. Moral hazards are attenuated, externalities are internalized (which economizes on imputation expenses and overcomes defective property rights assignments), and efficient factor proportions are restored where distortions due to monopolized inputs would otherwise exist. Efficient information exchange, including observational economies, is facilitated, in both accuracy and veracity senses, as well as the convergence of what otherwise would be disparate expectations. Supply reliability that might otherwise be impaired by antagonistic interests, including even malevolence, is better assured.

The discussion of internal organization in this and in previous chapters deals with only elementary forms of hierarchy and relatively simple types of adaptive behavior. The management of a complex firm, however, must deal with such issues as (1) the redeployment of internal resources in response to environmental disturbances in kind, (2) strategic planning, including innovation, and (3) preserving (or not degrading) intrafirm atmosphere as firm size is scaled up. In addition, the eventual limits to internal organization need to be assessed. Aspects of these issues are addressed in the chapters which follow.

6. Vertical Integration, II: Some Qualifications

The affirmative reasons for vertical integration have been developed in the preceding chapter. Qualifications to the argument of three types are taken up in this chapter and the chapter that follows. First, markets often work better than a "legalistic" analysis would suggest because of institutional adaptations by businessmen. Norms of trustworthy behavior sometimes extend to markets and are enforced, in some degree, by group pressures and collective experience-rating systems. Second, certain allegedly anticompetitive consequences of vertical integration are discussed. Third, some of the limitations to which internal organization is subject as the firm grows in size and complexity, organization form held constant, are considered.

The last argument is taken up in Chapter 7, while the first two are addressed here. Some of the reasons why interfirm exchange is less seriously impaired by contractual incompleteness than the discussion in preceding chapters would suggest are examined in Section 1. Possible or purported antisocial consequences of vertical integration are treated in Section 2. Antitrust policy implications are sketched in Section 3.

1. Interfirm Exchange: Some Qualifications

As previously noted (Chapter 2, Section 3.3), business reputation is a valuable resource that is not to be squandered, and firms sometimes develop experience-rating systems in which they pool information with respect to their contractual dealings with common suppliers or customers (Leff, 1970). To describe interfirm exchange in strictly antagonistic terms is accordingly too strong: only a qualified *caveat emptor* relation normally prevails among contracting parties (Kessler and Fine, 1964, p. 441). Businessmen operating in competitive industries in a high trust culture who insist on contractual completeness and exacting execution will find that such transactional attitudes result in excessive costs and render their businesses nonviable.

The differences between business, academic, and legal attitudes toward contracts have been examined by Macaulay (1963). He finds, in general, that interfirm contracts are often much more casual documents and are enforced much less exactingly than is commonly supposed. Also, contractual attitudes differ both as between different management functions within the enterprise and as between businessmen and outsiders.

Within the firm, sales managers and purchasing agents are less concerned with the details and enforceability of contracts than are the financial people and the inside lawyer (or house counsel). Macaulay cites one businessman to the effect that "you can settle any dispute if you keep the lawyers and accountants out of it. They just do not understand the give-and-take needed in business" (1963, p. 61). But even financial types and the house counsel are apt to have a more relaxed attitude about contracting than are outside lawyers or academic economists — who, anxious that the worst of all possible consequences consistent with the terms of the agreement will obtain, are unsettled by informal assurances that "everything will work out."

These differences between outsiders and businessmen partly reflect a common tendency among specialists to interpret issues in terms that complement their particular expertise. This is reinforced by their selective exposure to contracting. (Outside counsel, for example, is apt to be called on only when unusual and difficult contracting issues develop.) But the major difference is that outsiders often have little appreciation either for the costs of transactions or the range of informal sanctions that businessmen have access to.

Just as vertical integration is made attractive by the prospect of economizing on transaction costs, so also may incomplete contracting with informal enforcement serve an economizing purpose. Writing comprehensive contracts (at least those that are specific to a particular item and therefore go beyond what the lawyers refer to as "boiler plate" provisions) is itself expensive. Insisting on exacting contract performance is also costly. Not only can the resulting arbitration and litigating expenses be great, but secondary costs may be generated as well. The contract is apt to be reduced to a minimum-performance document; what could have been a semicooperative venture is turned instead into an "antagonistic horse trade" (Macaulay, 1963, p. 64).

The informal sanctions to which businessmen have access also warrant consideration. Repeated personal contacts across organizational boundaries support some minimum level of courtesy and consideration between the parties (Macaulay, 1963, p. 63). In addition, expectations of repeat business discourage efforts to seek a narrow advantage in any particular transaction. Finally, there is a matter of general business reputation to be concerned with, both at the personal and firm levels. Individual aggressiveness is curbed by the prospect of ostracism among peers, in both trade and social circumstances. The reputation of a firm for fairness is also a business asset not to be dissipated. A poor reputation may require concessions, such as greater price discounts on subsequent deals, for the firm to remain viable (Macaulay, 1963, p. 64).

It cannot be safely concluded, however, that business trust is so great and pervasive that the costs of interfirm contracting are negligible. For one thing, where the item in question is not a list price item (or if *ad hoc* terms are to be arranged) the terms of trade must be negotiated and this can be expensive. Thus, even if contingencies are ignored, haggling over price and terms of delivery may occur. But the contract itself may not be simple. If trading risks are great, the parties to the exchange are commonly prepared to bear additional cost in the form of explicit contingent planning and enforcement expenses. Macaulay notes in this connection that "complexity of the agreed performance over a long period" contributes to "greater contractual expense" (1963, p. 65), and that additional contractual expense is also incurred where the "degree of injury in case of default is thought to be potentially great" (1963, p. 65). More generally, the trading risk problem reduces to one of small-numbers bargaining in the face of uncertainty. As the discussion in earlier chapters reveals, an appreciation for the problems of interfirm contracting requires an understanding of the variety of ways in which a small-numbers condition can develop and a sensitivity to the subtleties of information exchange.

To be sure, trust is important and businessmen rely on it much more extensively than is commonly realized. Interfirm trading nevertheless incurs bargaining costs and trading risks which might be mitigated if instead the transaction were to be integrated, in which case interests are more thoroughly harmonized and a wider variety of sanctions for policing transactions are thereby made available. Thus, although Macaulay's (1963) and Leff's (1970) treatments of quasicontractual relations between firms are important and provide useful perspective, the basic argument of the preceding chapters, which relies merely on systematic incentive and control differences between internal and interfirm organization, is not vitiated on this account.

Richardson's discussion of interfirm cooperation ought also to be cited in this connection. As he puts it: "We must not imagine that reality exhibits a sharp line of distinction; what confronts us is a continuum passing from transactions, such as those on organized commodity markets, where the cooperative element is minimal, through intermediate areas in which there are linkages of traditional connection and good will, and finally to those complex and interlocking clusters, groups and alliances which represent cooperation fully and formally developed" (1972, p. 887). His numerous examples of intermediate forms of cooperative interfirm behavior illustrate the point.

I nevertheless urge that focusing on the significant differences between normal sales and hierarchical relations is useful. For one thing, if the basic differences between these transactional modes can be identified and explicated, terms of reference will emerge that will permit the cooperative properties of intermediate forms of contracting to be more accurately assessed. Furthermore, suppose that all contracts were assigned to the mainly autonomous contracting, mainly hierarchical, or ambiguous categories, and frequency distributions for contracts of each type were drawn with respect to the degree of cooperation. I submit that while the resulting distributions would overlap, the modal degree of cooperation for the hierarchical distribution would surely exceed that for the autonomous distribution. The "relevant" contracts, for the purpose of this book, are those which cluster around these modes.

2. Possible or Purported Antisocial Consequences

Anticompetitive effects of two types are commonly attributed to integration: price discrimination and barriers to entry. The argument has been compactly expressed in the following terms: ". . . vertical integration loses its innocence if there is an appreciable degree of market control at even one stage of the production process. It becomes a possible weapon for the exclusion of rivals by increasing the capital requirements for entry into the combined integrated production processes, or it becomes a possible vehicle of price discrimination" (Stigler, 1968, p. 303).

2.1 Price Discrimination

That even "perfect" price discrimination can lead to allocative efficiency losses, under conventional partial equilibrium assumptions, is evident from the discussion in Section 3.1 of Chapter 1 (though this does not establish that it usually will). My interest here, however, is somewhat different. Attention is restricted to the ways by which vertical integration contributes to the price discrimination result.

Successful price discrimination requires that differential demand elasticities be discovered and sale arranged in such a way as to preclude reselling. Users with highly elastic demands who purchase the item at a low price must not be able to service inelastic demand customers by acting as a middleman; all sales must be final. Although vertical integration may facilitate the discovery of differential elasticities, which is an information advantage, it is mainly with respect to the nonresale condition that it is regarded as especially efficacious.

Thus, let it be assumed that demand elasticity differences are known or easily knowable. Assume also that it is lawful to include a nonresale stipulation in a sales contract. In what respects then can vertical integration help to achieve a price discrimination result? Price discrimination is clearly practiced in some commodities without recourse to vertical integration (witness electricity and telephone service). What are the distinguishing factors? Legality considerations aside, presumably it is the cost of enforcing (policing) terms of the contract that are at issue. Some commodities apparently have self-enforcing properties—which may obtain on account of high storage and resupply costs or because reselling cannot be arranged inconspicuously. The absence of self-enforcing commodity properties is thus what makes vertical integration attractive as a means of accomplishing discrimination. Where promises cannot be believed, the firm may integrate forward into the more elastic market in order to preclude arbitrage between it and another market to which the firm wishes to charge a higher price.

2.2 The Condition of Entry

Stigler observes: "... it is possible that vertical integration increases the difficulty of entry by new firms, by increasing the capital and knowledge necessary to conduct several types of operation rather than depend on rivals for supplies or markets" (1968, p. 138). But why should a simple increase in capital requirements, without more, impede entry? Bork, for example, contends: "In general, if greater than competitive profits are to be made in an industry, entry should occur whether the entrant has to come in at both levels or not. I know of no theory of imperfections in the capital market which would lead suppliers of capital to avoid areas of higher return to seek areas of lower return" (1969, p. 148). Similarly, Bowman observes that "difficulties of access to the capital market that enable X to offer a one dollar inducement (it has a bankroll) and prevent its rivals from responding (they have no bankroll and, though the offering of the inducement is a responsible business tactic, for some reason cannot borrow the money) . . . [have] yet to be demonstrated" (1973, p. 59).

The issue, evidently, is whether an increase of the financial requirements is attended by an *adverse* alteration of the terms under which capital becomes available. A simple explanation is that borrowing by the firm to finance additional plant and equipment is akin to borrowing by the consumer to mortgage a house, but such an analogy is at best imperfect. The firm is borrowing funds in anticipation of realizing a prospective stream of earnings. These prospective earnings, as well as the resale value of the assets in question, are used to support the loan in question. The homeowner, by contrast, is not ordinarily able to augment his earnings by his purchase of a house. Thus, whereas the householder who successively increases the size of his mortgage eventually incurs adverse capital costs, because the risks of default are greater, the firm need not likewise be impeded. Wherein, then, if at all, does vertical integration by established firms disadvantage prospective entrants on account of capital market "defects"?

An assessment of the issues will be facilitated by setting out the specific alternatives. Thus, suppose that two distinct stages can be identified in the industry in question, and let these be designated I and II, respectively. Assume, furthermore, that stage I in the industry is essentially monopolized while stage II may or may not be integrated. The question now is whether a potential entrant, who has developed a technologically satisfactory stage I substitute and has an established reputation in stage I related activity, will be unaffected by the integrated condition of stage II. Consider, in particular, the following conditions: (1) the monopolistic stage I producer is not integrated, in which case the prospective new entrant can enter at stage I only and utilize the facilities of stage II producers (suitably expanded if necessary), and (2) the monopolistic stage I producer is integrated into stage II so that either (a) the new entrant himself comes in at both stages or (b) independent new entrants appear simultaneously at both stages. If Bork and Bowman are correct, the cost of capital ought to be independent of these conditions.

To contend that the terms of finance are the same under 2 (a) as they are under 1 implies that the capital market has equal confidence in the new entrant's qualifications to perform stage II activities as it does in firms that are already experienced in the business. Except in circumstances where experienced firms are plainly inept, this is tantamount to saying that experience counts for nought. This, however, is implausible for transactions that involve large, discrete rather than small, but recurring commitments of funds. Although transactions of the latter type can be monitored reasonably effectively, on the basis of *ex post* experience, this is much less easy for transactions of the large, discrete variety—which are the kind under consideration here. Reputation, which is to say prior experience, is of special importance in establishing the terms of finance for transactions that involve large, discrete commitments of funds.

The reasons for this are to be traced in part to the incompleteness of information regarding the qualifications of applicants for financing. Faced with incomplete information, suppliers of capital are vulnerable to opportunistic representations. Unable to distinguish between those unknown candidates who have the capacity and the will to execute the project successfully from opportunistic types who assert that they are similarly qualified, when objectively (omnisciently) they are not, the terms of finance are adjusted adversely against the entire group. Furthermore, and of special relevance to the issue at hand, if omniscience is lacking, then, as between two candidates for financing who would be judged by an omniscient assessor to have identical capacities and wills to execute the project, but only one of whom has a favourable and widely known performance record, the unknown candidate will find that he is disadvantaged.[1]

Moreover, where both candidates are equally suspect, but one has access to internal sources of financing while the other does not, the candidate requiring outside financing may be unable to proceed. Timing, in this connection, can be of critical significance. If one firm moves to the integrated structure gradually and finances the undertaking out of internal funds, while the second firm perceives the market opportunity later but, to be viable, must move immediately to a comparably integrated structure, the second firm may have to contend with adverse capital market rates.

The learning-by-doing conditions referred to earlier are also germane to an assessment of the earnings opportunities of an integrated versus non-integrated new entrant. By assumption, the prospective entrant is well-qualified in stage I respects. If learning-by-doing yields significant cost advantages and if the prospective entrant has no special qualifications in stage II respects, will his incentive to enter be any the less keen if, by reason of integration, he must now come in at both stages? I submit that if the knowledge gleaned from experience if deeply impacted, which is to say that it is not generally known or easily made knowable to those who lack experience, and if it is very costly to hire away the requisite experienced personnel from the integrated firm (due possibly to the fact that the knowledge advantage which the experienced labor force has acquired is dispersed among a *team* of individuals, negotiating the transfer of which is prohibitively costly), the prospective entrant is plainly at a disadvantage. Information impactedness and imperfect labor markets thus combine to explain the cost disadvantage of the otherwise qualified new entrant in relation to the experienced firm. Were the monopolistic stage I producer not to have integrated into stage II, so that the prospective entrant need come in at stage I only and could rely on already experienced stage II firms to acquire the necessary capital to expand appropriately and service his stage II needs, capital costs would be lower and the prospect of entry thereby enhanced.[2]

The problems, moreover, do not vanish if the new entrant comes in at stage I only and relies on independent entry into stage II to occur. (The comparison here is condition 2(b) in relation to condition 1.) Not only is

1. In a related context, Malmgren has noted: "Some firms will see opportunities, but be unable to communicate their own information and expectations favorably to bankers, and thus be unable to acquire finance, or need to pay a higher charge for the capital borrowed. Bankers and investors of funds in turn will be attracted to those firms which have shown in the past an ability to perceive and exploit effectively new opportunities, as against new firms which can only give their word that what they think is good is in fact good" (1961, p. 417).
2. This assumes that the cost of capital varies directly with the perceived risk of the incremental investment, *ceteris paribus.*

the cost of capital adjusted adversely against would-be new processors here, by reason of the lack of experience referred to above, but simultaneous yet independent entry into both stages may be impeded because of "nonconvergent expectations" — which is to say, there is a risk that interdependent decisions between stages will fail to be made in a compatible way (see Section 1.5 of Chapter 5). Lack of common information among independent stage I and stage II specialists with respect to the market opportunities which they confront and doubts regarding the true investment intentions and contractual reliability of other parties are the apparent impediments to effective coordination. Ultimately, however, the problems are to be attributed to the human and environmental factors described in Chapter 2.

To be sure, the argument has no special monopoly power significance unless the industry in question is already very concentrated[3] or, in less concentrated markets, conditions of effective collusion, which include collective refusal to deal, obtain. In such circumstances, however, actual competition, by itself, cannot be expected to self-police the market in a way that reliably assures the competitive outcome. Accordingly, potential competition has an important role to play. If potential entrants regard imitation of prevailing vertical structures as contributing importantly to the prospect of successful entry (as they may in highly concentrated industries), vertical restrictions that require funds to be raised by less, rather than more, experienced firms can have entry impeding consequences.

The financing issue, thus, is not that capital markets perversely avoid earnings opportunities, which is the test proposed by Bork, or that financing cannot be arranged under any terms whatsoever, to which Bowman refers. Rather, the cost of capital is at issue. If a prospective new entrant has the self-financing to come in at one stage (or can raise the capital at reasonable terms, perhaps because of a proven capability at this stage of operations) but lacks the self-financing and incurs adverse terms should he attempt to raise the capital to come in at the second stage, the condition of entry can clearly be affected by pre-existing vertical restrictions.[4]

2.3 Circumventing Regulation

A third type of antisocial consequence is sometimes imputed to regulation: circumventing regulation. This can occur either at a general level

---

3. Provisionally, I define a very concentrated industry to be one where the four-firm concentration ratio exceeds eighty percent.
4. Economies of scale at stage II can also serve as an impediment to entry if the monopolist has integrated into stage II and new entrants into stage I do not generate the requisite volume to realize stage II scale economies. Although the monopolist's decision to integrate forward may have had a sound basis, in that it economizes on transaction costs, such integration may also be favored by strategic entry impeding considerations.

(often in the context or wartime restrictions) or in connection with public utility regulation. As Coase (1952, pp. 338-339) and Stigler (1968, pp. 136-137) have both pointed out, vertical integration is sometimes employed as a device by which to evade sales taxes, quota schemes, and other methods of nonprice rationing. Since such efforts by the government to interfere with the price mechanism typically apply to market-mediated but not to internal transactions, the shift of such transactions from the market to the firm serves to circumvent these regulatory schemes. This is perfectly straightforward and is derived from received microtheory without appeal to transaction-cost considerations.[5]

Conventional microtheory can also be made to address the following issue: Can a regulated firm that is permitted only a "fair" rate of return in supplying final goods or services effectively evade the regulatory restraint by integrating backward into own-equipment supply? As Dayan (1973) has shown, such backward integration will permit the regulated industry to earn monopoly profits if either equipment transfer prices or the rate of return at the equipment supply stage is unregulated. At least some regulatory commissions appreciate this and have effectively extended regulation to include equipment supply; Michigan Bell is an example (Troxel, 1966, p. 168).

Backward vertical integration in regulated firms can also lead to technical progress distortions. As is generally acknowledged, rate of return regulation introduces a static bias in favor of capital intensive techniques. The intertemporal extension of this bias is to favor technical change of a capital intensive kind.

Of course such intertemporal biases can be transmitted across a market, in a derived demand fashion, as well as between stages of a regulated firm that is integrated backward into own equipment supply. I submit, however, that it is apt to be more pronounced in the latter. Since the integrated firm's equipment business is not really "up for bid," it is less apt to be confronted with the need to choose *publicly* between alternative equipment techniques. The nonintegrated firm, by contrast, does need to make and defend such choices—assuming, of course, that there are at least several alternative sources of supply from which to select. In circumstances where relatively more labor intensive options objectively represent least-cost techniques, this is more likely to be publicly exposed, and hence such techniques adopted, in the context of nonintegrated equipment supply.

The above assumes that competition at the equipment supply stage is feasible. Where it is not, backward vertical integration, for the reasons given in Chapter 5, is arguably efficient. If, however, but for such backward vertical integration, competitive equipment supply at some future time would develop, a tradeoff between monopolistic distortions in present

---

5. Actually, transaction-cost considerations can be introduced indirectly. The reason the government does not attempt to apply sales taxes, quotas, and so forth, to internal transactions as well as to market-mediated transactions is because of the high cost of monitoring the former.

supply and regulatory distortions in future supply needs to be faced. Concerns with backward vertical integration are obviously attenuated to the extent that one has confidence that regulation is or will become effective across both stages.

3. Antitrust Implications

Except for the rather special case where a regulated firm has integrated backward into equipment supply, which needs to be assessed in the context of the regulatory milieu, vertical integration poses antitrust issues of two kinds: price may be adversely affected and the condition entry may be impaired. It needs, however, to be appreciated that adverse effects of neither kind will obtain unless a nontrivial degree of monopoly exists. Accordingly, the enforcement of antitrust with respect to vertical integration ought to be restricted to the monopolistic subset. Elsewhere, the maintained hypothesis ought to be that vertical integration has been undertaken for the purpose of economizing on transaction costs.

Although the price in the downstream market may change as a result of forward integration by a monopolist, the direction of the change cannot be established without knowledge of particular firm and market circumstances (see Section 1.3 of Chapter 5). Likewise, the welfare implications of price discrimination cannot be established without knowledge of underlying demand relations and the transaction costs of effecting differential prices.[6]

By contrast, the condition of entry is less subject to such welfare ambiguities: integration by an established firm into a second stage will rarely make access to a potential entrant into either stage easier; and impeded entry, *ceteris paribus,* generally has disadvantageous welfare consequences.

However, except in dominant firm (or otherwise very concentrated) industries or in moderately concentrated industries where collusion has been successfully effectuated, vertical integration is unlikely to raise entry impediments. Moreover, since, for the reasons given in Chapter 12, collusion in moderately concentrated industries is difficult to achieve, very concentrated industries in which the bulk of production is accounted for by integrated firms constitute the policy-relevant subset of principal concern.

Entry impediments of two types can arise where the leading firms in stage I integrate (backward or forward) into what could otherwise be a competitively organized stage II activity. For one thing, the residual (nonintegrated) sector of the market may be so reduced that only a few

6. Moreover, even if adverse price effects of either type were to exist, transaction cost economies (of the types described in the preceding chapter) need also to be taken into account before a net welfare assessment is reached.

firms of efficient size can service the stage II market. Firms that would otherwise be prepared to enter stage I may be discouraged from coming in by the prospect of having to engage in small-numbers bargaining, with all the hazards that this entails, with these few nonintegrated stage II firms. Additionally, if prospective stage I entrants lack experience in stage II related activity, and thus would incur high capital costs were they to enter both stages themselves, integrated entry may be rendered unattractive. The integration of stages I and II by leading firms is then anticompetitive, in entry aspects at least,[7] if severing the vertical connection would permit a competitive (large-numbers) stage II activity to develop without loss of scale economies.

Vertical integration in industries with low to moderate degrees of concentration does not, however, pose these same problems. Here a firm entering into either stage can expect to strike competitive bargains with firms in the other stage whether they are integrated or nonintegrated.[8] The reasons are that no single integrated firm enjoys a strategic advantage with respect to such transactions and that collusion by the collection of integrated firms (in supply or demand respects) is difficult to effectuate. Vertical integration rarely poses an antitrust issue, therefore, except as the industry in question is highly concentrated or, in less concentrated industries, collective refusals to deal are observed. But for such circumstances, vertical integration is apt to be of the efficiency promoting kind.[9]

7. The net welfare qualification in footnote 6, above, applies here as well. Admittedly, net welfare assessments may be administratively infeasible. It is all the more important, in such circumstances, that antitrust enforcement with respect to vertical integration be delimited to the monopolistic subset; moderately concentrated and unconcentrated industries [as in *Brown Shoe v. United States*, 370 U.S. 294 (1962)] are properly exempted. Again the eighty percent four-firm concentration ratio proposed in note 3, *supra,* is suggested as the criterion for judging high concentration. Possibly this should be adjusted downward (to, say, sixty percent) in an industry where a trend toward vertical integration which has potentially concentrating tendencies is detected — especially if a compelling transactional rationale for integration is absent. As *Brown Shoe* reveals, however, incipiency arguments are easily abused by a zealous antitrust enforcement agency, which counsels that such arguments be invoked with caution.

8. That a firm can expect to strike competitive bargains does not, of course, guarantee that it will earn "normal" profits. This depends on internal efficiency as well as supply and demand conditions. In a growing industry, however, the nonintegrated but otherwise qualified entrant should be able to secure a niche for itself without difficulty — albeit that its profit rate may vary over a business cycle more than do the rates of integrated firms.

9. Actually, there is one further possibility: vertical integration may also be undertaken mistakenly, in the hopes of realizing an anticompetitive advantage in circumstances where original monopoly power is missing. This is not to say that attempts to foreclose markets through forward integration in such circumstances will not disadvantage some competitors, and thus can be dismissed as being of no effect whatsoever. But the effects will at most be transitory; no long-term strategic advantage is to be realized in this way. The role of antitrust here is unclear. It is paternalistic for antitrust to intervene to prevent the integrating firm from making strategic blunders. Whether rival firms should be protected against transient losses is also unclear. For issues in the cement industry, see Allen (1971).

7. Limits of Vertical Integration and Firm Size

Transactional arguments favorable to vertical integration must eventually confront the following dilemma: If firms have such attractive properties for economizing on transaction costs, what prevents the firm from pre-empting the market quite generally? Putting the problem this way raises issues similar to those which have been examined in the context of central planning versus market economies. Unfortunately, however, these planning discussions have been insufficiently specific to be very useful for our purposes here.

In order that the notion of a firm be specified in an operationally engaging way, it will be assumed that some genuine administrative element is involved in the internal organization of an activity. The market, in some transactionally significant way, is pre-empted. (A holding company form of organization in which the component parts enjoy *full* autonomy thus does not constitute internal organization of an administratively interesting kind.) Given this assumption, the argument in this chapter comes down to this: The distinctive powers of internal organization are impaired and transactional diseconomies are incurred as firm size and the degree of vertical integration are progressively extended, *organization form held constant*.

The relevance of the organization form stipulation is developed in Chapters 8 and 9. As will be evident there, certain aspects of the limitations to internal organization that are discussed in this chapter can be attenuated by reorganizing the firm "appropriately." But while such reorganization can shift the point at which the marginal costs of administering the incremental transaction begin to exceed those of completing transactions through the market, the qualitative implications of the present argument are not upset.

From Aubrey Silberston and Francis Seton, *Industrial Management : East and West.* Copyright © 1973 by Praeger Publishers, Inc., New York. Excerpted and reprinted by permission.

More generally, the argument also has relevance for evaluating non-firm forms of internal organization. For the most part, the indicated limits on firms hold *a fortiori* for nonfirm forms of organizing economic activity (Downs, 1967; Drucker, 1973, p. 52). That firms do not fully displace these other forms of internal organization is because nonfirm alternatives have distinctive revenue or performance attributes — including, sometimes, access to a special resource base (attributable, for example, to taxation powers or eleemosynary characteristics). [1] Developing this set of issues is beyond the scope of this treatise.

Some of the leading factors which serve to limit vertical integration, firm size held constant, are given in Section 1, while size related limits are discussed in Section 2. Incentive limits of the employment relation are then considered in Section 3.

1. Internalizing the Incremental Transaction: Some Disabilities

The concern here is less with progressive distortions that occur as the firm grows in size than it is with the types of distortions that are prospectively associated with any transaction which a firm of medium to large size and complexity chooses to discharge. The social psychology and organization theory literatures are the sources for most of the argument. [2] Rather than express the argument in the language of markets and hierarchies from the outset, I first present the issues in the language which the social psychologists and organization theorists have employed. A brief interpretation in terms of the framework is then offered. Although some of the richness of description is lost in the translation, so that reverting to the original language may often be more instructive, I trust that the applicability of the organizational failures framework to the study of internal organizational frictions is made apparent.

1.1 Sources of Transactional Distortion

Among the more severe goal distortions of internal organization are the biases which it experiences that are favorable to the maintenance or

1. These revenue advantages may be coupled with subcontracting restrictions, in which event the recipient organization must complete its operational assignments itself and firms cannot be brought in by indirection.
2. As Arrow has observed: "It is not accidental that economic analysis has been successful only in certain limited areas" (1969, p. 49). Assessing limitations to firm size and complexity is an area where conventional economics, by itself, is at a loss. For a "mainly" economic analysis of the firm-size issue, see Williamson (1970, Chap. 2).

extention of internal operations. Biases of three types are discussed: internal procurement, internal expansion, and program persistence. Communication distortion supports all three. Systems rationality versus subgroup rationality conflicts are posed throughout. The distinction is this: systems rationality entails global optimization whereas rational subgroup behavior is that which enhances the individual and collective objectives of those parties who effectively control the transaction, or related set of transactions, in question.

1.1.1   INTERNAL PROCUREMENT

The internal procurement bias is supported by a number of factors. For one thing, the internal supplier that produces mainly for internal uses may be judged to be at a relative disadvantage in the marketplace. The internal supplier may lack both the large and experienced marketing organization and the established customer connections that nonintegrated external suppliers have access to. In consideration of these conditions, and since fixed costs are sunk, a "preference" for internal procurement might seem appropriate — at least so long as the external price exceeds the variable cost of internal supply.

This may be a specious argument, however, since the fixed costs in question may easily be overstated (there may be a second-hand market for the machinery in question) and individual equipment renewal decisions ought eventually to be made with reference to the long-run viability of the internal facility. Managers are notably reluctant, however, to abolish their own jobs — even in the face of employment guarantees. The problems with such guarantees are that while continued employment may be secure, assurances that status will be maintained, when a position is eliminated, and that promotion prospects will not be upset, upon being romoved from a known promotion ladder, are unenforceable. A preference for internal supply is thus to be expected and may manifest itself by urging that each equipment replacement decision be made serially, in semi-independent fashion. A fundamentally nonviable internal capability may be uncritically preserved in this way. Internal cross-subsidization will then exist.

More generally, the argument is that the existence of an internal source of supply tends to distort procurement decisions. Subgoals of a group or bureaucratic sort are easily given greater weight in relation to objective profitability considerations. This is supported by common membership and the structure of social relations, including a system of shared beliefs and orientations, that emerge.

A norm of reciprocity easily develops. Equivalence of return between the parties, moreover, is inessential to this result.[3] The opportunities for

---

3. For a general discussion of this and related matters, see Gouldner (1960). Gouldner asserts that the norm of reciprocity is as universal and important as the incest taboo.

reciprocity are simply more extensive internally (I buy from your division, you support my project proposal or job promotion, and so forth) than in the market, where reciprocity is mainly limited to commodity trades that are a matter of record. Distinguishing logrolling distortions from "constructive cooperation" between internal parties is thus made difficult by the various and subtle forms that internal reciprocity can take. Exceptions from a systems rationality procurement standard are relatively easy both to self-justify and implement in these circumstances.[4]

1.1.2 INTERNAL EXPANSION

The expansionary biases of internal organization are partly attributable to its dispute settling characteristics. Fiat is efficient for reconciling instrumental differences, but it is poorly suited for mediating disputes that have internal power consequences. A common method of dealing with internal system strain is to adopt a compromise solution by which concessions are made to subsystems rather than require them to give up essential functions or resources (Katz and Kahn, 1966, p. 101). This size preserving tendency is favored by the positive association of both pecuniary and nonpecuniary rewards with size, at least among the functional parts of the enterprise (Williamson, 1970, pp. 51-52). An expansionary bias commonly obtains (Marshall, 1932, pp. 321-322).

Persistent conflict or generalized malfunctioning results frequently in role proliferation: ". . . the creation of specialized roles is a generalized solution for all organizational problems. . . . It is the modal solution for insuring the role requirements of organization are met; a new role (or many) is added to the organization, the requirements of which are solely to see to it that other role occupants are performing in the required manner, at the approved pace, and in the prescribed relation, one to another" (Katz and Kahn, 1966, p. 203). Thus, in addition to the generalized expansionary bias described in Section 2, below, internal organization specifically favors the extension of the compliance machinery. Policing costs easily become a disproportionate share of the total if these tendencies are not checked. Where markets may be said to work well, therefore, the firm might consciously resist the internalizing of incremental transactions for this reason as well.

4. The argument is but a particular illustration of the types of politicking distortions that internal organization is subject to. It is to be contrasted with statements such as Coase's that if reciprocity "leads to inefficiency there is no reason why the [firm] should adopt it (since it would reduce its overall profits)" (1969, p. 39). By implication, either the management of the firm is entirely lacking in opportunities for discretion, or its interests in single-minded profit maximization are presumed. Although such assumptions are characteristic of the usual economic treatments of enterprise behavior, severe difficulties are experienced in attempting to address the limits of internal organization issue if such assumptions are maintained.

1.1.3 PERSISTENCE

Consider the matter of persistence behavior. Partly, this is simply a sunk cost phenomenon (March and Simon, 1958, p. 173; Downs, 1967, p. 195): existing activities embody sunk costs of both organizational and tangible types while new projects require initial investments of both kinds. The sunk costs in programs and facilities of ongoing projects thus insulate existing projects from displacement by alternatives which, were the current program not already in place, might otherwise be preferred. Moreover, unlike plant and equipment, specialized investments in organizational infrastructure may experience little depreciation. Persistence of a wholly objective variety thus can continue over a long interval.

But persistence is also favored by other factors. "If the . . . administrative system has committed itself in advance to the correctness and efficacy of its reforms, it cannot tolerate learning of failure" (Campbell, 1969, p. ⁻10). March and Simon, in their discussion of innovation, suggest that such commitment is common. They distinguish program elaboration, which corresponds roughly to the program proposal and development stages, from program execution, which involves continuing operations, and note that decisions made at the program elaboration stage are rarely re-examined at the execution stage (1958, p. 187).

As a comparative institutional matter, the question is whether firms and markets can be expected to display *differential* attitudes toward or experience *differential* opportunities for persistence. One basis for expecting such differences is that the internal procurement bias referred to above would presumably support project persistence within firms that is unavailable between firms across markets. Information impactedness may also contribute to this result. Thus it may be impossible, at reasonable cost, to easily distinguish between faulty and meritorious internal performance. Responsible parties who are unable to reveal the objective causes of failure and be absolved of fault are thereby induced to press for program extensions beyond objectively rational cut-off limits in the hope that the environment will change and "save" their reputations. The lack of a cross-subsidization base prevents managers of specialized firms, who may be similarly inclined but are more fully subject to the discipline of the market, from effecting such persistence preferences.

Sequential decision-making procedures, designed to permit project review on the merits, if they exist at all, are often overwhelmed by partisan appeals due to the tie-in of advocacy and administration (Campbell, 1969, p. ⁻10).[5] Although this tie-in may have the effect of mobilizing energies that would not otherwise be available, in that individuals will expend super-

---

5. American involvement in Southeast Asia can be partly explained in these terms. (See Sheehan et al. *The Pentagon Papers* (1971).

normal efforts to rectify error, the error admission properties of internal organization would appear to be defective. Fixed costs are not sunk but need to be justified (Wolf, 1973, p. 667); the decision to proceed is transformed into a commitment to "succeed" — whatever the costs. By contrast, interfirm contracts, which separate advocacy from administration, are apt explicitly to provide for periodic review and favor tougher-minded, more calculative assessments if "failure" is objectively indicated.[6]

Drucker contends in this connection that while "[n]o institution likes to abandon anything," budget based institutions are more prone to persist with unproductive or obsolete projects than are revenue based institutions — since the necessary support for the latter will be removed by the market (1973, p. 52). Shifting the incremental transaction from the market to the firm generally results in greater budget based support, whence vertical integration gives rise to persistence tendencies.

1.1.4 COMMUNICATION DISTORTION

One of the serious problems to which market exchange is subject is that the information exchanged between the parties in small-numbers bargaining situations may be manipulated for strategic advantage. Integrating these transactions serves to attenuate these effects. It would be incorrect to conclude, however, that internal communication is not subject to distortion whatsoever. Although incentives are intendedly harmonized by internalization, members of the organization may seek to promote personal goals by diverting the communication system to their own uses (Simon, 1961, p. 171). This is implicit in the discussion of internal reciprocity, expansion, and persistence tendencies discussed above and is explicit in the discussion of idiosyncratic exchange (in employment relation and inside contracting respects) in earlier chapters.

Communication distortions can take either assertive or defensive forms. Defensively, subordinates may tell their supervisor what he wants to hear; assertively, they will report those things they want him to know (Katz and Kahn, 1966, p. 246). Recognition of these assertive tendencies is reflected in the common law of testimony in which demonstrated self-interest on the

---

6. Thus, it may not be possible, at low cost, to demonstrate conclusively to those who are only remotely familiar with the work that a task has been discharged badly. Consequently, at high levels at least: "The removal of an official to whom symbolic attributes have become attached, whether for incompetence or for other more reprehensible causes, unless they are very grave and publicly known, is felt to be derogatory to the office and to be an injury to the organization both internally and often externally as respects its prestige" (Barnard, 1946, p. 82). The pairing of information impactedness with an insistence that internal due process standards be met limit the firm, in relation to the market, in this respect. The agonies associated with the impeachment of President Nixon, prior to his disclosures on August 5, 1974, are illustrative.

part of a witness can lead to discrediting of testimony (Campbell, 1958, p. 350). Distortion to please the receiver is especially likely where the recipient has access to extensive rewards and sanctions in his relations with the transmitter, as in up-the-line communication in an administrative hierarchy (Campbell, 1958, p. 351). The cumulative effects across successive hierarchical levels of these and related adjustments to the data easily result in gross image distortions (Boulding, 1966, p. 8) and contribute to a limitation of firm size (Williamson, 1970, Chap. 2).

Related to this matter of communication distortion for assertive personal or group purposes is the possibility that disaffected members of the organization may, rather than quit the organization, choose to subvert it. Organizational loyalties are imputed to and strategic privileges are accorded to members that are denied to outsiders. (In consideration of the privileges to which members have access, subversion in time of war is commonly punishable by death.) The disaffected employee whose estrangement is unknown may deliberately plant misinformation or disclose sensitive information to outsiders in ways that impair the performance of the firm. To the extent that large, complex organizations are more easily subject to such subversion — which presumably they are — smaller, less complex (hence, nonintegrated) organizations are preferred. [7]

Campbell notes that human links in communication systems are prone to a whole series of biases. Some of these biases are little affected whether transactions are organized through the market or internally.[8] There are circumstances, however, where specialized (hence, nonintegrated) organizations may have a special advantage.

"Evolutionary considerations lead to the expectation that *no* constant errors will be found in an environment ecologically typical. . . . Where constant errors have [an ecologically atypical] origin, they will be found to be part and parcel of psychological processes of general adaptive usefulness" (Campbell, 1958, p. 340).[9] To the extent that organizations are required to deal with ecologically atypical conditions, an isolated organization that trains its personnel to be sensitive to the special characteristics of the atypical environment and faithfully to reproduce observations — without

7. The argument needs to be qualified in that integration may remove a potential entrant (especially where vertical integration is involved) or an actual rival (horizontal integration) and in this respect reduces the risk of disclosure to interested outsiders.

8. Cognitive dissonance, for example, gives rise to perception biases in whatever organizational context it arises. Unless the stress of dissonance is expected to be less severe in one mode rather than another, there is no reason to prefer one over the other in dissonance biasing respects.

9. Arrow notes that there is a general tendency to filter information in accordance with one's preconceptions and indicates: "It is easier to understand and accept information congruent with previous beliefs than to overcome cognitive dissonance" (1974, p. 75). Cognitive dissonance, I would judge, has general adaptive usefulness.

introducing adjustments that, in general, have "adaptive usefulness" but which in the particular case, are dysfunctional — is indicated. [10] Although full structural disassociation between the parts of an integrated enterprise that deal with ecologically atypical conditions and the rest of the firm is possible, integration can scarcely be expected to yield advantages in relations to the market in these circumstances.

1.2   Transactional Disabilities Interpreted

Recall that the joining of bounded rationality with uncertainty makes contractual completeness expensive (if not infeasible) to attain, while incomplete contracts expose market-mediated exchange to the hazards of profit haggling if small-numbers bargaining conditions obtain. Because it is able to suppress or avoid opportunistic profit haggling, internal organization is able to tolerate contractual incompleteness — thereby to economize on bounded rationality, by employing an adaptive, sequential decision-process, without incurring contractual hazards. But internal organization is nevertheless vulnerable to opportunism in other respects.

Again, however, it is not opportunistic inclinations by themselves which explain the problem. Rather, it is opportunism *in conjunction with* both a small numbers and an information impactedness condition that accounts for the transactional disabilities that internal organization experiences. [11]

Shifting a transaction from the market to the firm is significant not because a small-numbers exchange relation is eliminated but rather because the incentives of the parties are transformed. Indeed, the typical internal transaction is really a small-numbers exchange relation writ large. Investment by a firm in fixed plant and organizational infrastructure serves to insulate internal transactions from competition in the product market — with the result that, in the short run at least, there may be no credible alternative source of supply whatsoever. [12] Functional managers, naturally, are not unaware of this condition. Coupled with the information impactedness

---

10. A similar argument holds where the serial reproduction of transmissions across successive levels—which is usually accompanied by gap filling and other "plausibility" adjustments—requires that data be retransmitted in original, unadjusted, and perhaps counterintuitive form.

11. This is not to suggest that bounded rationality and uncertainty are of no importance. Although internal organization economizes on bounded rationality and absorbs uncertainty, it too is limited in these respects. Given these limits, the further question is what factors explain the *distortions* to which internal exchange is subject.

12. The threat to construct a parallel internal supply facility, when a single one will do, falls in the noncredible category. Sometimes, however, replication may be feasible, in which case an internal competition can be set up. To the extent, however, that really effective competition can be realized, market supply is usually even more to be preferred.

advantage that they enjoy, a nontrivial degree of managerial discretion obtains.

Internal opportunism takes the form of subgoal pursuit — where by subgoal pursuit is meant an effort to manipulate the system to promote the individual and collective interests of the affected managers.[13] Such efforts generally involve distorting communications in a strategic manner. Sometimes this may be done by individual managers without the support of others. More often, however, internal distortions are due to the cooperative efforts of two or more managers. (The internal reciprocity phenomenon is a specific manifestation of such collective distortion.)

Although internal auditing and experience-rating serves to check egregious distortions, the general management in the firm is nevertheless severely limited in information impactedness respects. It is simply too expensive (or, for bounded rationality reasons, perhaps infeasible) for the general management to be apprised of everything that is going on at the operating level and adjust compensation accordingly. Moreover, what is of special importance here, these problems become more severe as the firm becomes progressively more complex.

The problem with successively adding related transactions, holding size constant,[14] is that even small degrees of overlap give rise to joint responsibility. Imputations cannot be made with confidence when the nature of the interaction is costly to sort out and the parties enter conflicting claims.

Furthermore, fiat cannot easily be invoked where equity issues are at stake. Norms of internal justice, which support quasimoral involvement, check attempts at vigorously implementing the compliance machinery so long as the "defendant" can establish a reasonable doubt by asserting joint responsibility. The resulting confounding of accountability impairs incentives. Thus, although internal organization is (potentially) better able than the market to distinguish between random events and meritorious performance, and in this respect is superior to the market as a mechanism for assigning rewards to deeds, the inference difficulties that internal auditing experiences *as the firm grows in complexity eventually limit its power in this respect.*

The upshot of this is that distortion-free internal exchange is a fiction and is not to be regarded as the relevant organizational alternative in circumstances where market exchange predictably experiences nontrivial frictions. Implicitly, whenever a transaction is shifted from the market to

13. That managers behave as advocates does not necessarily imply opportunism. Advocacy may be done instrumentally, for the purpose of efficiently getting the issues exposed in a complex system constrained by bounded rationality. Subgoal pursuit involves strategic, not instrumental, behavior.

14. The size constant stipulation requires that the firm be shrunk elsewhere as the incremental transaction is internalized.

the firm, a tradeoff is struck in which it is understood that some irreducible degree of opportunism will continue.

It is significant, moreover, to realize that many of the costs of opportunism will not show up immediately; the firm that is considering shifting from a market to an internal transaction needs to be especially sensitive to future distortions. Thus, the decision to continue a project, once it is begun, the decision to renew or expand the internal facility, once it is in place, and the decision to procure internally, once that capability exists, may not be decisions for which the ordinary profitability calculus will govern. Proposals to internalize a transaction might therefore reasonably be made to "promise" an immediate, nontrivial cost advantage. Required rates of return on new programs should accordingly be set at uncommonly high levels in order to offset predictable, later stage distortion tendencies. (The widely observed practice of stipulating higher marginal rates of return on new programs than the actual rate that the firm realizes on existing programs is consistent with the argument. The same practice should presumably be followed in evaluating government investments, though I suspect that it is not.)

2. Size Considerations

Attention is shifted here from a discussion of the disabilities of vertical integration to consider the general size limits to which the firm is subject. The issue can be put as follows: Holding the degree of vertical integration and organization form constant, are there simple size impediments that radial expansion of the firm eventually incurs? Bounded rationality, bureaucratic insularity, and atmospheric consequences are considered.

2.1 Bounded Rationality

Bounded rationality gives rise to finite spans of control[15] together with the specialization of communication and decision-making functions. It is sufficient for our purposes here, however, merely to emphasize the finite span of control consequence. Faced with this condition, radial expansion of the enterprise requires that additional hierarchical layers be added. The consequence of this for internal communications has been examined elsewhere in conjunction with what I have referred to as the "control loss phenomenon" (1970, Chap. 2).

15. This is a widely noted consequence. For recent discussions, see Marschak (1968, p. 14) and Arrow (1974, p. 39).

Boulding observes in this connection that "almost all organizational structures tend to produce false images in the decision-maker, and that the larger and more authoritarian the organization, the better the chance that its top decision-makers will be operating in purely imaginary worlds" and concludes that image distortion is ultimately responsible for diminishing returns to scale (1966, p. 8). Although some of this image distortion may be done strategically (and thus is attributable to the pairing of opportunism with information impactedness), the main points that I would emphasize here are (1) the extended hierarchy is made necessary by bounded rationality, and (2) even efforts to communicate in a purely instrumental way are subject to serial reproduction losses (Bartlett, 1932). Consequently, unless offset by other factors (of which the acquisition of monopoly power is one possibility), radial expansion of the firm eventually exhibits diminishing returns.

2.2 Bureaucratic Insularity

The issue here is related to what Michels has referred to as the "iron law of oligarchy" — which is a manifestation of bureaucratic opportunism. Although Michels was principally concerned with voluntary organizations, especially labor unions and political parties, his remarks have relevance in other hierarchical contexts as well. Their special significance for present purposes is that bureaucratic insularity varies directly with organizational size (Michels, 1966, p. 71).

> Nominally, and according to the letter of the rules, all acts of the leaders are subject to the ever vigilant criticism of the rank and file. In theory the leader is merely an employee bound by the instruction he receives. . . . But in actual fact, as the organization increases in size, this control becomes purely fictitious.

Given finite spans of control, increasing firm size leads to taller hierarchies in which leaders are less subject to control by lower-level participants. The resulting bureaucratic insularity of the leadership permits it, if it is so inclined, to both entrench and engross itself.

As compared, however, with a voluntary organization, the matter of legitimacy in the business firm is less in relation to lower-level participants than it is to the stockholders.[16] The control problems in each case never-

---

16. The legitimacy of the leadership of the firm in relation to lower-level participants is also relevant, however. This comes up, among other things, in conjunction with the status pathology of large organizations.

Barnard contends that while status systems are "essential to coherence, coordination, and *esprit de corps*," they serve to reduce flexibility and adaptability (1946, p. 82). Status systems predictably lead to distortions by insulating incumbents against displacement and permitting them to be rewarded disproportionately (Barnard, 1946, p. 78).

theless turn on identical considerations, namely, the information impactedness issue. Since problems of stockholder control in this sense typically
become more severe as the firm grows in size and complexity (see Section
3 of Chapter 8), larger size is associated with greater opportunities for discretion. Where the leadership exercises these opportunities by permitting
slack and indulging in corporate personal consumption, size limitations
necessarily follow — especially if lower-level performance varies directly
with higher-level example, which normally is to be expected.

It is noteworthy, however, that business firms differ from other types
of bureaucracies in that voting for the board of directors *can be concentrated* through share ownership (through direct purchase of shares, tender
offers, and the like). This is not possible in most other types of organization where one-man, one-vote rules tend to predominate. This is a basic
distinction between the business firm and bureaucracies more generally.
Incumbent managements can be displaced more easily as a result — though
I would concede that effecting displacement in the large firm is not always
easy (see Chapter 9).

2.3   Cooperation Limits among Lower-Level Participants

Internal organization affords atmospheric advantages of two sorts.
First, it offers associational relations that may be valued. Second, it supports involvements of a continuing sort in which members are more
sensitive to part-whole relations. Increasing size, however, easily upsets
this latter type of systems concern.

As Dahl and Lindblom observe (1963, p. 225), large size and hierarchical structure favor impersonality among the parties, which is more characteristic of a calculative orientation. This is partly attributable to the
specialization of information gathering and the more limited disclosure
of information (on a need-to-know basis) as firm size and hierarchical
structure are extended (organization form held constant). The corresponding assignment of decision-making to what are perceived by lower-level
participants to be remote parts of the enterprise also contributes to this
result. Although efficiency purposes are commonly served in this way,
these must be weighed against the loss of moral involvement. To the extent
that nonknowledgeability and nonparticipation impair moral involvement
and larger-size results in role incompatibility, which it apparently does
(March and Simon, 1958, p. 98), a more calculative orientation is to be
expected. The zone of acceptance of the employment contract is narrowed,
which serves to limit the attractiveness of an employment contract in relation to a sales contract. Put differently, attitudes of voluntary cooperation
are supplanted by a *quid pro quo* orientation. Since, moreover, each
individual in the large organization is small in relation to the whole, so

that the percentage effects of individual behavior are perceived to be insubstantial, the large organization may be thought to be better able to
tolerate perfunctory performance or even deviant conduct.

A reduction in group disciplinary pressures which, in a smaller firm,
operate in the service of enterprise viability (by enforcing norms which
extend the effective influence of supervisors) thus obtains. As Olson puts
it, where "each member . . . is so small in relation to the total that his
actions would not matter much one way or another . . ., it would seem point-
less for one [member] . . . to snub or abuse another for a selfish [antifirm]
action, because the recalcitrant's action would not be decisive in any event"
(Olson, 1968, p. 62). Indeed, should alienation from the enterprise develop
among individual components of the firm, small-group powers may even
be turned against the enterprise in subtle but significant respects. The
disaffected group may allocate rewards and sanctions in a perverse fashion.
Industrial sabotage is an extreme manifestation of this condition.

3. Incentive Limits of the Employment Relation

As indicated in Chapter 4, the employment relation permits long-run
incentives of a promotion ladder sort to be effectuated that are unavailable
in market contracting. The firm consequently enjoys an advantage over
the market in this respect. Firms, however, have very real limitations when
it comes to the award of large bonus payments for entrepreneurial activities. The dilemma here is of two kinds. First, such payments may be
regarded as a status threat by higher-level managers. [Buttrick's discussion
of the problems posed when the incomes of inside contractors occasionally
exceeded that of the capitalist-manager with whom they negotiated terms
(1952, pp. 210, 214) is illustrative.] Second, and more important, awarding
bonuses for exceptional performance introduces transaction-specific elements into the contract. This jeopardizes the integrity of the employment
relation. The long-term systems considerations on which it relies would
give way to a series of *quid pro quo* bargains. Given that the relation between the parties is commonly of a small-numbers sort, on account of task
idiosyncrasies, transaction costs would quickly escalate.

Any organizational imperative to maintain strict correspondence between income and hierarchy naturally serves as a disincentive to entrepreneurial types who might otherwise be prepared to accept a position in the
firm. The special relevance of this condition for firm size and vertical
integration is in connection with new product and process development —
which is the subject of Chapter 10. But for the qualifications given there,
the large firm is frequently at a disadvantage to the small enterprise in

supporting early stages of development — because, among other things, of the bureaucratized reward structure in the large firm which relies on salary and promotion rather than direct participation in the earnings associated with successful innovation.

4. Concluding Remarks

Internal organization ought to be regarded as a *syndrome of characteristics:* distinctive strengths and distinctive weaknesses, in a comparative institutional sense, appear nonseparably — albeit in variable proportions — as a package. Although the existence of market failure constitutes a presumptive basis for internalizing transactions, the "defects" associated with market exchange may need to exceed a nontrivial threshold before internal organization offers a clear cost advantage.

The difficult cases, of course, are those where markets experience defects of intermediate proportions. An examination of the frictions of both market and organizational types is then indicated, but the current state of the art hardly permits a refined net evaluation to be made. An appreciation for the organizational failures to which vertical integration[17] and radial expansion are subject should, at the least, counsel caution in making firm versus market choices.

The distortion propensities of internal organization are especially notable. This holds both with respect to integrating the incremental transactions, where a variety of subgoal related distortions are brought into play, and firm size, where the motivation of both leaders and followers may

17. The discussion does not pretend to be exhaustive, though I would hope that the more important issues have been identified. An additional limitation, not discussed in the text, that integrated forms of organization may experience in relation to nonintegrated is that wage bargains may be insufficiently discriminating in the former— especially in firms that have access to monopoly power. (An example is afforded by seat belt manufacture in the automobile industry. Despite small-numbers supply, with the attendant bargaining problems, as well as indications of supernormal profits among its suppliers, General Motors has not integrated backward into own-supply but rather contracts for these items. A principal reason for this refusal to integrate backward is that General Motors would be required to pay higher labor costs under its labor contract with the United Auto Workers than are its much smaller, independent outside suppliers.)

Also, integration can give rise to wage distortions, especially in cyclical industries. Thus, it is typical, whenever reductions in force are attempted, for senior workers to bump lower-level, junior workers. If senior employees resist wage reductions, "pressure from employees to push the bottom of the wage structure upward" results (Doeringer and Piore, 1971, p. 79). In anticipation of such difficulties, the large firm may defer integration until demands are well-established and, once having integrated, maintain an outside source of supply to buffer output variations. To the extent that smaller, specialized suppliers are less subject to these wage distortions (possibly because intrafirm wage ranges in specialized firms are narrower), incomplete integration is favored.

be impaired. The incentive *and* disincentive properties of the employment relation both have to be considered. As March and Simon have observed, in a related context, the argument for decentralization (markets) has been eviscerated in recent welfare theory by the neglect of motivation (1958, p. 203).

A special qualification mentioned at the outset concerns the matter of organization form. This issue is developed more extensively in Chapters 8 and 9, which follow. Suffice it to observe here that some of the transactional limitations of internal organization can be mitigated if the firm is expanded not in a radial expansion manner but rather along multidivisional lines.

8. The Multidivisional Structure

Starting with the assumption that in the beginning there were markets, progressively more ramified forms of internal organization have successively "evolved." First peer groups, then simple hierarchies, and finally the vertically integrated firm in which a compound hierarchy exists have appeared. As between alternative organizations of the compound hierarchy, the inside contracting system, which preserves considerable autonomy between the several functional parts and the center, was rejected in favor of an employment relation across all stages. What is referred to in Section 1, below, as the "unitary form" enterprise, has emerged.

The question addressed here is how ought the firm be organized as it continues to grow in size and complexity. Issues of both efficiency, with respect to a given goal, and effectiveness, with respect to the choice of goals, are posed. That a simple scaling up of the unitary form enterprise experiences problems that are greatly mitigated by a shift to the "multidivisional structure" illustrates the proposition that "the system cannot be derived from the parts; the system is an independent framework in which the parts are placed" (Angyal, 1969, p. 27) — which is to say once again that internal organization matters.

A discussion of some of the problems of the unitary form enterprise, as it takes on size and complexity, appears in Section 1. The displacement of the unitary form by the multidivisional structure is described and illustrated in Section 2. The distinctive properties of the multidivisional form in miniature capital market respects are examined in Section 3. Optimum divisionalization is discussed in Section 4. The "M-form hypothesis" and concluding remarks follow.

A major problem for testing the M-form hypothesis is that, if all divisionalized firms are classified as M-form firms without regard for the related internal decision-making and control apparatus, an overassignment to the M-form category will result. The internal controls in divisionalized firms

This chapter is a variant of a previously published paper on which Narottam Bhargava was a coauthor.

are quite critical. A scheme for classifying firms according to internal structure is proposed in an Appendix.

1. The Unitary Form Enterprise

1.1 Structural Attributes

As Chandler indicates (1966, Chap. 1), the late 1800's witnessed the emergence of the large, single-product, multifunctioned enterprise — in steel, meatpacking, tobacco, oil, and so forth. These firms were organized along functional lines and will be referred to as unitary form (or U-form) enterprises. The principal operating units in the U-form firm are the functional divisions — sales, finance, manufacturing — as shown in the organization chart in Figure 5. Specialization by function not only was then, but, in organizations of only moderate size at least, is now the "natural" way by which to organize multifunctional activities. In many respects, this is the vertical integration issue. Specialization by function permits both economies of scale and an efficient division of labor to be realized — provided that control over the various parts can also be realized (Ansoff and Brandenburg, 1971, pp. 718-720).

1.2 Consequences of Radial Expansion

The question to be addressed is what problems does the U-form enterprise experience when it expands, if the U-form (functional) basis for decomposing the enterprise remains in effect throughout? An answer that is both compelling and compact is not easy to provide. Mainly, what is involved is that radial expansion of the U-form enterprise (1) experiences cumulative "control loss" effects, which have internal efficiency consequences, and (2) eventually alters the character of the strategic decision-making process in ways that favor attending to other-than-profit objectives[1] Chandler summarizes the defects of the large U-form enterprise in the following way (1966, pp. 382-383):

1. For a more extensive discussion of these effects, see Williamson (1970, Chaps. 2, 3, and 7). The difficulties that the large, U-form enterprise experiences are there summarized in terms of indecomposability, incommensurability, nonoperational goal specification, and the confounding of strategic and operating decisions. Incommensurability makes it difficult to specify the goals of the functional divisions in ways which clearly contribute to higher-level enterprise objectives. Indecomposability makes it necessary to attempt more extensive coordination among the parts; for a given span of control, this naturally results in a high degree of control loss between hierarchical levels. Moreover, to the extent that efforts at coordination break down and the individual parts suboptimize, the intrinsic

The inherent weakness in the centralized, functionally departmentalized operating company . . . became critical only when the administrative load on the senior executives increased to such an extent that they were unable to handle their entrepreneurial responsibilities efficiently. This situation arose when the operations of the enterprise became too complex and the problems of coordination, appraisal, and policy formulation too intricate for a small number of top officers to handle both long-run, entrepreneurial, and short-run, operational administrative activities.

Figure 5. *Unitary Form*

The ability of the management to handle the volume and complexity of the demands placed upon it became strained and even collapsed. Unable meaningfully to identify with or contribute to the realization of global goals, managers in each of the functional parts attended to what they perceived to be operational subgoals instead (Chandler, 1966, p. 156).

These are consequences of bounded rationality, although opportunism, coupled with information impactedness, may also be involved. Bounds on rationality give rise to finite spans of control, which in turn require that additional hierarchical levels be introduced as the U-form enterprise expands — whether the expansion is of the radial or vertical integration variety. Adding hierarchical levels can, if only for serial reproduction reasons, lead to an effective loss of control through incomplete or inaccurate transmittal of data moving up and instructions moving down the organizational hierarchy. Although various decoupling devices may be devised to reduce these transmission needs, these are costly and subject to diminishing returns. Decoupling merely alleviates, but does not overcome, the need for intrafunctional and peak coordination.

Information flows rarely take the form of simple serial reproduction, however. Rather, data are summarized and interpreted as they move forward, and instructions are operationalized as they move down (Arrow, 1974, pp. 53-54; Emery, 1969, p. 114; Beer, 1969, p. 407). Both processes

---

interconnectedness between them virtually assures that spillover costs will be substantial. The confounding of strategic and operating decisions serves further to compromise organizational purpose.

provide additional opportunities for control losses to develop. These can occur in quite unintentional ways.

Continued expansion also eventually overcomes the capacity of the office of the chief executive to provide strategic planning and maintain effective control, which is another manifestation of bounded rationality. The usual means for augmenting this capacity has been to bring the heads of the functional divisions into the peak coordination process. The natural posture for these functional executives to take is one of advocacy in representing the interests of their respective operating units.

This change in the composition of the strategic decision-making unit produces a shift away from preferences characteristic of the office of the chief executive, which tend to be enterprise-wide in scope, in favor of partisan interests more closely associated with the functional divisions. A persistent and collective pressure to provide more and better services is apt to develop; an expansionary bias in favor of staff expenditures easily obtains.

These bounded rationality consequences predictably result from the radial expansion of the U-form enterprise — even one in which the management is fully committed to conducting the affairs of the firm in a steward-ship manner. If, however, managers perceive these stresses on the U-form structure as affording them with opportunities for discretion, because information is impacted to their advantage, and if, in addition, managers are given to behave opportunistically, further consequences obtain. Deliberate distortions will be introduced into the hierarchical information exchange process in support of subgoals. Permissive attitudes toward slack may also develop.

1.3 The Corporate Control Dilemma

In principle, competition in the product market and competition in the capital market will check discretionary outcomes. The resulting distortions and inefficiencies will not be viable where product market competition is extensive. Moreover, competition in the capital market fills the breach where product market competition breaks down: managers who fail to behave as neoclassical profit maximizers will be replaced at stockholder insistence. Two lines of defense thereby exist. If, however, the firms in question enjoy some degree of monopoly in their respective markets, and if, realistically, stockholders have insufficient knowledge or are otherwise indisposed to effect management displacement except where egregious distortions appear, a managerial discretion problem plainly exists.

Although they scarcely expressed the problem in this fashion, the corporate control dilemma perceived by Berle and Means can be inter-preted in these terms. They noted that a separation in ownership from control existed and inquired: "... have we any justification for assuming that those in control of a modern corporation will also choose to operate it in the interests of the stockholders?" (Berle and Means, 1932, p. 121). The universe of firms with which they were concerned in the early 1930's was mainly large U-form enterprises, and many of these firms enjoyed monopoly power in their respective product markets. In consideration of the above-indicated effects on strategic decision-making and corporate goal pursuit that expansion of the U-form firm predictably has, Berle and Means' concern that stockholder objectives were possibly being sacrificed to favor managerial objectives was altogether appropriate.

Students of the large corporation who have succeeded Berle and Means have generally reached the same conclusion; to wit, the separation of ownership from control is extensive, and it is merely a matter of good fortune that the corporate sector performs as well as it does. In the background lurks the suspicion that one day these enclaves of private power will run amok (Mason, 1960, pp. 7-9). A search for substitute *external* controls has been set in motion on this account; solemn supplications on behalf of corporate responsibility have also been advanced. But the possibility that discretionary outcomes might be checked by *reorganizational* changes within the firm has been generally neglected. I submit, however, that organizational innovations, which in the 1930's were just getting underway, have mitigated capital market failures by transferring functions traditionally imputed to the capital market to the firm instead. Not only were the direct effects of substituting internal organization for the capital market beneficial, but the indirect effects served to renew the efficacy of capital market controls as well.

2. Organizational Innovation: The Multidivision Structure

2.1 General

Faced with the types of internal operating problems that emerge as the U-form enterprise increases in size and complexity, the DuPont Company, under the leadership of Pierre S. duPont, and General Motors, under Alfred P. Sloan, Jr., devised what Chandler refers to as the multidivisional (or M-form) structure in the early 1920's. This organizational innovation involved substituting quasi-autonomous operating divisions (organized mainly along product, brand, or geographic lines) for the functional divisions of the U-form structure as the principal basis for dividing up the task and assigning responsibility. Inasmuch as each of these operating divisions is subsequently divided along functional lines (see Figure 6), one might characterize these operating divisions as scaled down, specialized U-form structures. Although this is a considerable oversimplification (for example, operating divisions may be further subdivided by product, geographic, or brand subdivisions before the final U-form structure appears), the observation has at least heuristic merit.

This simple change in the decomposition rules might not, by itself, appear to be all that significant. Indeed, for the reorganization to be fully effective really requires more. The peak coordinator's office (shown in Figure 6 as the general office) also has to undergo transformation and an elite staff needs to be supplied to assist the general office in its strategic decision-making (including control) responsibilities. Chandler characterizes the reasons for the success of the multidivision form as (1966, pp. 382-383):

> The basic reason for its success was simply that it clearly removed the executives responsible for the destiny of the entire enterprise from the more routine operational activities, and so gave them the time, information, and even psychological commitment for long-term planning and appraisal . . . .
>
> [The] new structure left the broad strategic decisions as to the allocation of existing resources and the acquisition of new ones in the hands of a top team of generalists. Relieved of operating duties and tactical decisions, a general executive was less likely to reflect the position of just one part of the whole.

More generally, the characteristics and advantages of the M-form innovation can be summarized in the following way (Williamson, 1970, pp. 120-121):

1. The responsibility for operating decisions is assigned to (essentially self-contained) operating divisions or quasifirms.
2. The elite staff attached to the general office performs both advisory and auditing functions. Both have the effect of securing greater control over operating division behavior.
3. The general office is principally concerned with strategic decisions, involving planning, appraisal, and control, including the allocation of resources among the (competing) operating divisions.
4. The separation of the general office from operations provides general office executives with the psychological commitment to be concerned with the overall performance of the organization rather than become absorbed in the affairs of the functional parts.
5. The resulting structure displays both rationality and synergy: the whole is greater (more effective, more efficient) than the sum of the parts.

In relation to the U-form organization of the same activities, the M-form organization of the large, complex enterprise served both to economize on bounded rationality and attenuate opportunism. Operating decisions were no longer forced to the top but were resolved at the divisional level, which relieved the communication load. Strategic decisions were

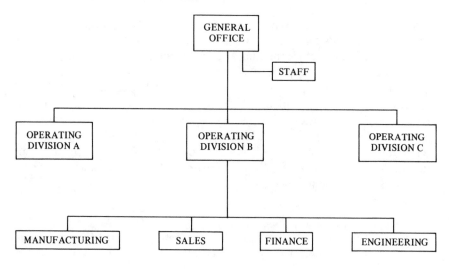

Figure 6. *Multidivision Form*

reserved for the general office, which reduced partisan political input into the resource allocation process. And the internal auditing and control techniques, which the general office had access to, served to overcome information impactedness conditions and permit fine tuning controls to be exercised over the operating parts.

2.2 An Illustration[2]

Suppose there are three activity stages: an early production stage, an intermediate stage in which production is completed, and a marketing stage. Assume that all products originate in a common first stage, that there are four distinct intermediate stage processes, and that there are five distinct final products. That there ought, under these circumstances, to be five divisions, one associated with each final product, is uncertain. For one thing, the economies of scale at the first stage may be sufficient to warrant that all production originate in a single, indecomposable plant. Second, if for some products economies of scale at the second stage are slight in relation to the size of the market, parallel divisionalization may be feasible. Third, even though products may be distinct, there may be interaction effects to consider. (For example, products may be complements.)

Consider the situation shown in Figure 7. Here Q refers to first stage activity, I_i^j refers to intermediate stage processing, P_l^m refers to the final product, and the subscript refers to the process (product) type, while the

---

2. That the exercise is hypothetical and oversimple ought to be emphasized. If, however, it serves to better expose the issues, its purpose will have been realized.

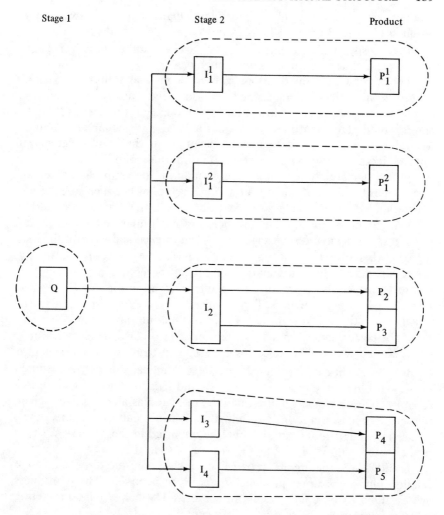

Figure 7

superscript (if any) denotes replication. The proposed divisions are shown by the dotted lines.

That it is generally inefficient for the early stage of a production process to transfer product to a later stage at a price that maximizes the profit of the early stage is well-known. Rather, in order to discourage the use of inefficient factor proportions in the later stages and avoid the restriction of production, product should be transferred at its marginal cost. But then the early stage production divisions cannot, under these circumstances, be evaluated in profit center terms. Rather, Q becomes a cost center and its performance is assessed in least cost rather than net revenue terms.

Plants I_1^1 and I_1^2 are assumed to be identical and produce a common product (designated P_1^1 and P_1^2, respectively). Plant I_2 produces two distinct products, P_2 and P_3, while plants I_3 and I_4 produce the distinct products P_4 and P_5, respectively. Products P_4 and P_5, while manufactured by separate processes, are assumed to be complements.

The rationale for the divisionalization shown is as follows: First, Q is split off as a cost center since, for the reasons given above, it cannot efficiently be operated as a profit center, while to assign it to one of the later stages would place unaffiliated stages at a disadvantage,[3] and to combine several later stages leads to overaggregation (in that such aggregation impairs accountability with the result that internal control is sacrificed in the process) in relation to underlying "natural" decomposability conditions. Rules to insure efficient transactional relations between stages 1 and 2 are assumed to be feasible, whence the divisional standing accorded to Q.

A high degree of coordination between each intermediate stage and its corresponding marketing stage is assumed to exist and warrant the joining of each such pair of stages within a division. As indicated, I_1^1 and I_1^2 are replicated production facilities producing the common product P_1. A territorial market is set up for each plant, with the result that $I_1^1 - P_1^1$ and $I_1^2 - P_1^2$ are both profit centers. Territorialization serves to mitigate interdivisional competition in the product market, but interdivisional "competition," for performance comparison purposes, in other respects is possible.

Technological scale economies are assumed to be such that separate production facilities for P_2 and P_3 are uneconomical. Also, I_2 is assumed to bear a sole source relation to both P_2 and P_3. Since to split I_2 off as a separate division would require that it be operated as a cost center (given the sole source assumption) with the attendant difficulties that this poses, and as interstage coordination would be impaired in the process, a single profit center spanning I_2, P_2, and P_3 is set up instead.

I_3 and I_4 are separate plants between which there is no direct exchange relationship. They supply products P_4 and P_5 respectively. These products are assumed to be complements, however, for which a joint marketing effort is warranted. The resulting profit center spans I_3, I_4, P_4, and P_5.[4]

2.3 Diffusion

Imitation of the M-form innovation was at first rather slow. For one thing, however obvious its superior properties may have been to the innovators, others were naturally skeptical. As Brown puts it (1945, p. 295):

---

3. This assumes that the later stages are about on a parity in terms of the volume and variety of demands placed on the early stage. If one stage were to be much larger than all of the others and to have special needs for coordinating with the early stage, a combination of these two stages might be warranted.

4. This is clearly arbitrary; a divisional separation between marketing and the prior production stage may sometimes be warranted.

> To enterprises that have grown complex within themselves, . . . the resort to [divisionalization] may appear portentious and (since few relinquish without hesitation the accustomed mode of life) uninviting . . . . [The] dissolution of [a firm's] integrated state and the redistribution of responsibilities into multiple organization do present the aspect of a revolutionary rather than an evolutionary change.

Also in industries such as metal refining and forming, the divisionalized structure was not as easy to create as in industries where distinct product or brand lines were readily established. In others, administrative inertia appears to have been substantial. Up through the 1930's, only a handful of other firms had accomplished the transformation (Chandler, Chap. 7). A number of firms, which by 1940 had reorganizational changes in the works postponed these with the onset of World War II. Since 1945, however, the divisionalization of large firms (many of them along M-form lines) has been extensive.

It is of some interest, moreover, to note that the multidivisional structure has more recently been adopted by large European firms. Franko reports that prior to 1968, most large European companies administered their domestic operations through U-form or holding company internal structures (1972, p. 342). With the advent of zero tariffs within the European Economic Community on January 1, 1968, and in the face of continuing penetration of European markets by American firms, however, large European firms have felt compelled to adapt (Franko, 1972, p. 358). A significant number of these firms have been reorganized along multidivisional lines in the past several years.

3. Competition in the Capital Market

3.1 Frictionless Capital Markets

As the remarks of Bork and Bowman cited in Section 2.2 of Chapter 6 make clear, advocates of received microtheory are loath to concede that capital markets may fail to operate frictionlessly. Partly for this reason, the fiction that managers operate firms in fully profit maximizing ways is maintained. Any attempt by managers to opportunistically promote their own goals at the expense of corporate profitability would occasion intervention through the capital market. Effective control of the corporation would be transferred to those parties who perceived the lapse; profit maximizing behavior would then be quickly restored.

Parties responsible for the detection and correction of deviant behavior in the firm would, of course, participate in the greater profits which the reconstituted management thereafter realized. This profit participation would not, however, be large. For one thing, incumbent managements, by assumption, have little opportunity for inefficiency or malfeasance because any tendency toward waywardness would be quickly detected and costlessly extinguished. Accordingly, the incremental profit gain occasioned by takeover is small. In addition, since competition among prospective takeover agents is presumably intensive, the gains mainly redound to the stockholders.

Peterson's sanguine views on corporate behavior are roughly of this kind. He characterizes the latitude of managers to disregard the profit goal as "small" (1965, p. 11) and goes on to observe: "Far from being an ordinary election, a proxy battle is a *catastrophic* event whose mere possibility is a threat, and one not remote when affairs are in *conspicuous* disarray." Indeed, even "stockholder suits . . . may be provoked by evidence of *serious* self-dealing." On the principle that the efficacy of legal prohibitions is to be judged "not by guilt discovered but by guilt discouraged," he concludes that such suits, albeit rare, may have accomplished much in helping to police the corporate system (Peterson, 1965, p. 21; emphasis added).

While I do not mean to suggest that such deterrence has been unimportant, Peterson's observations appear to me to be consistent with the proposition that traditional capital markets are beset by serious problems of information impactedness and incur nontrivial displacement costs if the incumbent management is disposed to resist the takeover effort. Why else the reference to catastrophic events, conspicuous disarray, and serious self-dealing? Systems that are described in these terms are not ones for which a delicately conceived control system can be said to be operating As recent military history makes clear [5] controls that involve a discrete shock to the system are appropriate only when an offense reaches egregious proportions. The limits of opportunism are accordingly wider than Peterson seems prepared to concede.

The reasons, I submit, why traditional capital market controls are relatively crude are because an information impactedness condition exists with respect to internal conditions in the firms and, because of sorting out difficulties, the risk of opportunism on the part of would-be takeover agents is great. Given information impactedness, outsiders can usually make confident judgements that the firm is not adhering to profit maximizing standards only at great expense. The large firm is a complex organization and its performance is jointly a function of exogenous economic events, rival behavior, and internal decisions. Causal inferences are correspondingly difficult to make, and hence, opportunism is costly to detect. Moreover, once detected, convincing interested stockholders that a displacement effort ought to be supported encounters problems. Inasmuch as time and analytical capacity on the part of stockholders are not free goods, which is to say that their information processing limits must be respected, the would-be

---

5. Atomic weapons, with their catastrophic consequences, are ill-suited to support military campaigns involving even half a million men.

takeover agent cannot simply display all of his evidence and expect stock-holders to evaluate it and reach the "appropriate" conclusion. Rather, any appeal to the stockholders must be made in terms of highly digested inter-pretations of the facts. Although this helps to overcome the stockholder's bounded rationality problem, it poses another: How is the interested stock-holder (or his agent) to distinguish between *bona fide* and opportunistic take-over agents.

The upshot of these remarks is that the transaction costs associated with *traditional* capital market processes for policing management, of the sort described by Peterson, are considerable. Correspondingly, the range of discretionary behavior open to incumbent managements is rather wider than Peterson and other supporters of the frictionlessness fiction concede.[6]

3.2   The M-Form Firm as a Miniature Capital Market

In a general sense, the most severe limitation of the capital market is that it is an *external* control instrument. It has limited constitutional powers to conduct audits and has limited access to the firm's incentive and resource allocation machinery. One should not, however, conclude that mere di-visionalization, by itself, is sufficient to correct the inefficiencies and goal distortions that the large U-form firm develops. To emphasize this, the limits of the holding company form of organization are examined below. Attention is thereafter shifted to consider strategic controls of the sort appropriate to an M-form enterprise.

3.2.1 HOLDING COMPANY

What is referred to here as a holding company form of organization is a loosely divisionalized structure in which the controls between the head-quarters unit and the separate operating parts are limited and often unsystem-atic. The divisions thus enjoy a high degree of autonomy under a weak executive structure.[7]

---

6. Smiley concludes his study of tender offers as follows (1973, pp. 124-125):

> Based on our most accurate estimating procedure, per share transaction costs are approximately 14% of the market value of the shares after a successful offer. We feel that this cost level is such as to inspire skepticism about the efficacy of the tender offer in constraining managers to act in the best interests of their shareholders. Another finding was that the equity of firms that have been tendered has lost half of its market value (in the 10 years prior to the tender offer) relative to what the equity would have been worth, had the management operated the firm in an optimal fashion.

7. That this is a somewhat special use of the term-holding company ought to be appreciated. (I considered referring to this as the federal form of organization but decided that that posed at least as many problems.) Essentially what I am after is a category which, for reference purposes, represents divisionalization of a very limited sort.

Perhaps the least ambitious type of divisionalization to consider within the holding company classification is that in which the general office is essentially reduced to a clerical agency for the assembly and aggregation of earnings and other financial reports. The holding company in these circumstances serves as a risk-pooling agency, but in this respect is apt to be inferior to a mutual fund. The transaction costs associated with altering the composition of the portfolio of the holding company, by selling off existing divisions and acquiring new operating companies, will ordinarily exceed the costs that a mutual fund of comparable assets would incur by its trading of common stocks (or other securities) so as to adjust its portfolio. Little wonder that those academics who interpret the conglomerate as being a substitute mutual fund report that it has inferior diversification characteristics to mutual funds themselves (Smith and Schreiner, 1969; Westerfield, 1970).

Moreover, it is not clear that just a little bit of additional control from the general office will lead to results that are superior to those that would obtain were the various divisions of the holding company to be freestanding firms in their own right. Being part of a holding company rather than an independent business entity easily has umbrella effects. If the holding company serves as a collection agency for unabsorbed cash flows and uses these to shore up the ailing parts of the enterprise, the resulting insularity may encourage systematic distortions (of a managerial discretion sort) among the divisional managements. Being shielded from the effects of adversity in their individual product markets, slack behavior sets in.

This is not, of course, a necessary consequence. The general management might consciously refuse to reinvest earnings but mainly pay these out as dividends. Alternatively, it might scrutinize reinvestment decisions every bit as well as the unassisted capital market could. Indeed, because it enjoys an *internal* relationship to the divisions, with all of the constitutional powers that this affords, the general management might be prepared to assume risks that an *external* investor ought properly to decline. (Thus, the general management can ordinarily detect distortions and replace the divisional management at lower cost than can an external control agent similarly detect and change the management of a comparable, free standing business entity. The holding company, in this respect, is less vulnerable to the risks of what might be referred to as managerial moral hazard.) Given, however, that the holding company is *defined* to be a divisionalized firm in which the general office does not involve itself in strategic controls of the sort described below, it is unclear that the holding company form of organization is socially to be preferred to an arrangement in which the various divisions are each set up as fully independent enterprises instead. Holding companies certainly cannot be expected reliably to yield results that compare favorably with those which I impute to the M-form structure.

3.2.2 STRATEGIC CONTROLS IN THE M-FORM FIRM

If indeed the firm is to serve effectively as a miniature capital market, which in many respects is what the M-form structure ought to be regarded,[8] a more extensive internal control apparatus than the holding company form of organization possesses is required. This gets to the core issues. Manipulation of the incentive machinery, internal audits, and cash flow allocation each deserve consideration.

Closer adherence to the goals of the general management can be secured if the special incentive machinery to which internal organization uniquely has access to is consciously exercised to favor operating behavior that is consistent with the general management's objectives. Both pecuniary and nonpecuniary awards may be employed for this purpose.

That salaries and bonuses can be adjusted to reflect differential operating performance, assuming that such differentials exist and can be discerned, is a familiar application of the incentive machinery. That nonpecuniary rewards, especially status, can also be adjusted for this purpose should be evident from the preceding chapter.

Of course, sometimes a change of employment, or at least of position, may be altogether necessary. The division manager may not have the management capacities initially ascribed to him, conditions may change in ways that warrant the appointment of a manager with different qualities, or he may be managerially competent but uncooperative (given, for example, to aggressive subgoal pursuit in ways that impair overall performance). Changes made for either of the first two reasons reflect simple functional assessments of job requirements in relation to managerial skills. By contrast, to replace a division manager for the third reason involves the deliberate manipulation of the incentive machinery to produce more satisfactory results. The occasion to intervene in this way will presumably be rare, however, if the conditional nature of the appointment is recognized from the outset. Rather, the system becomes self-enforcing in this respect once it is clear that the general management is prepared to replace division managers who regularly defect from general management's goals.[9]

Although the general office does not ordinarily become directly involved in the exercise of the incentive machinery within the operating divisions, its indirect influence can be great. The decision to change (replace, rotate) a division manager is often made for the incentive effects this has on lower-level participants. Employment policies — including criteria for selection, internal training procedures, promotions, and so forth — can likewise be specified by the general office in ways that serve to ensure closer

8. The argument is developed more extensively in Williamson (1970, pp. 138-150, 176-177). For somewhat similar views, see Drucker (1970). Heflebower (1960), and Weston (1970).

9. This assumes that there are no property rights (academic tenure, civil service, and so forth) associated with positions.

congruence between higher-level goals and the behavior of the operating parts. A more pervasive incentive impact on lower-level participants who are not directly subject to review by the general office can in these ways be effected.

Adjusting the incentive machinery in any fine tuning sense to achieve reliable results requires that the changes be made in an informed way. A backup internal audit that reviews divisional performance and attempts to attribute effects to the several possible causes — distinguishing especially between those outcomes that are due to changes in the condition of the environment from those that result from managerial decision-making — is useful for this purpose.[10] As Churchill, Cooper, and Sainsbury observe: ". . . to be effective, an audit of historical actions should have, or at least be perceived as having, the power to go beneath the apparent evidence to determine what in fact did happen" (1964, p. 258). Of particular importance in this connection is the recurrent nature of this auditing process. Thus, although current variations of actual from projected may sometimes be "accounted for" in plausible but inaccurate ways, a persistent pattern of performance failure can be explained only with difficulty.

The advantages of the general office over the capital market in auditing respects are of two kinds. First, division managers are subordinates; as such, both their accounting records and backup files are appropriate subjects for review. Stockholders, by contrast, are much more limited in what they can demand in the way of disclosure. Even relatively innocent demands for a list of the stockholders in the corporation, much less the details of internal operating performance, may be resisted by the management and disclosed only after a delay and by court order.

Second, the general office can expect knowledgeable parties to be much more cooperative than can an outsider. Thus, whereas disclosure of sensitive internal information to an outsider is apt to be interpreted as an

---

10. In principle, the superior inference capability of an internal audit, as compared with the relatively crude powers of the capital market in this respect, commends internal organization as a substitute for the capital market not merely because discretionary behavior may thereby be attenuated but also because division managers may be induced to accept risks which in a free-standing firm would be declined. Too often, as Luce and Raiffa observe: ". . . the strategist is evaluated in terms of the outcome of the adopted choice rather than in terms of the strategic desirability of the whole risky situation" (1957, p. 76). This tendency to rely on outcomes rather than assess the complex situation more completely is especially to be expected of systems with low powers of inference. Managers of free-standing firms, realizing that outcomes rather than decision processes will be evaluated, are naturally reluctant to expose themselves to high variance undertakings. *Ceteris paribus,* the low cost access of internal organization to a wider range of sophisticated inference techniques encourages more aggressive risk-taking.

Whether the potential advantages of the divisional structure in auditing respects actually induce more aggressive risk-taking, however, is uncertain. Woods identified a strong conservative bias in the firms that he studied, where the companies were "rewarding the manager whose investment performance exceeds his original forecast and penalizing the one whose performance falls below the forecast" (1966, p. 93).

act of treachery,[11] internal disclosure is unlikely to be regarded opprobriously. Rather, internal disclosure is affirmatively regarded as necessary to the integrity of the organization and is rewarded accordingly. Disclosure to outsiders, by contrast, commonly exposes the informant to penalties[12]— albeit that these may be subtle in nature.

Not only are internal audits useful for ascertaining causality, they also serve as a basis for determining when operating divisions could benefit from assistance. The general management may include on its staff what amounts to an internal management consulting unit — to be loaned or assigned to the operating divisions as the need arises. Partly the occasion for such an assignment may be revealed by the internal audit. Thus, although the general management ought not routinely to become involved in operating affairs,[13] having the capability to intervene prescriptively in an informed way under exceptional circumstances serves to augment its credibility as an internal control agent.[14] Self-regulatory behavior by the operating divisions is thereby encouraged.

In addition to the policing of internal efficiency matters, and thereby securing a higher level of adherence to profit maximization than the unassisted capital market could realize (at comparable cost), the general management and its support staff can perform a further capital market function — assigning cash flows to high yield uses. Thus, cash flows in the M-form firm are not automatically returned to their sources but instead are exposed to an internal competition. Investment proposals from the several divisions are solicited and evaluated by the general management. The usual criterion is the rate of return on invested capital.[15]

Moreover, because the costs of communicating and adapting internally

11. "Kings may vary in the tolerance they show to vices such as incompetence or laziness, but there is no tolerance of treason. Giving damaging information to the press or betraying plans to a rival are the actions of an enemy...; these are unpardonable offenses" (Jay, 1971, p. 266). The disclosure of damaging inside information to the press or to a prospective takeover agent is regarded by the firm's leadership to be of this treacherous kind.

12. The disclosure of cost overruns on the C-5A by an employee of the Pentagon (A. Ernest Fitzgerald) resulted in his being fired. But for subsequent intervention by Senator Proxmire and others, his reemployment was unlikely. [See Mollenhoff (1973).] Such intervention is, of course, unusual and does not assure that the career expectations of the informant will be unimpaired.

13. The reasons for avoiding operating involvement have been given elsewhere. A recent comparative study by Allen of two divisionalized firms broadly supports the general argument. Allen observes that, of the two firms, the high-performing firm had a "fairly simple but highly selective set of organizational devices to maintain control over its divisions," while the management of the low-performing firm became "over-involved," in relation to its capacity, in the affairs of its operating divisions (1970, p. 28).

14. This internal management consulting unit would ordinarily be made available at the request of the operating divisions as well as at the behest of the general management. Such a unit would presumably possess scarce expertise of a high order. It would be uneconomical for each operating division to attempt to replicate such a capability.

15. For a discussion of a sophisticated internal resource allocation model in the International Utilities Corporation, see Hamilton and Moses (1973).

are normally lower than would be incurred in making an investment proposal to the external capital market, it may be practicable to decompose the internal investment process into stages. A sequential decision process (in which additional financing is conditional on prior stage results and developing contingencies) may thus be both feasible and efficient as an internal investment strategy. The transaction costs of effectuating such a process through the capital market, by contrast, are apt to be prohibitive.

In many respects, *this assignment of cash flows to high yield uses is the most fundamental attribute of the M-form enterprise* in the comparison of internal with external control processes, albeit that the divisionalized firm is able to assign cash flows to only a fairly narrow range of alternatives at any one point in time. Even if the firm is actively acquiring new activities and divesting itself of old, its range of choice is circumscribed in relation to that which general investors, who are interested in owning and trading securities rather than managing real assets, have access to. What the M-form firm does is trade off breadth for depth in this respect.[16] In a similar context, Alchian and Demsetz explain: "Efficient production with heterogeneous resources is a result not of having *better* resources but in knowing more *accurately* the relative productive performances of those resources" (1972, p. 29).

4. Optimum Divisionalization

The M-form structure is thoroughly corrupted when the general management involves itself in the operating affairs of the divisions in an extensive and continuing way. The separation between strategic and operating issues is sacrificed in the process; the indicated internalization of capital market functions with net beneficial effects can scarcely be claimed. Accountability is seriously compromised; a substitution of enterprise expansion for profitability goals predictably obtains.

Effective divisionalization thus requires the general management to maintain an appropriate distance. Moreover, this holds for the support staff on which the general management relies for internal auditing and management consulting services. Overinvolvement upsets the rational allocation of responsibilities between short-run operating matters and longer-run planning and resource allocation activities. What March and Simon refer to as Gresham's Law of Planning — to wit, "Daily routine drives

16. For a somewhat similar discussion of the internal resource allocation effects of M-form divisionalization, see Drucker (1970). Also of relevance in this connection are the treatments by Heflebower (1960) and Weston (1970). Certain work at the Harvard Business School also relates to these issues [see Bower (1971) and the references therein; also Allen (1970)].

out planning" (1958, p. 185) — takes effect when operating and strategic functions are mixed. While the arguments here are familiar and their implications for organizational design reasonably clear, maintaining a separation between these two activities apparently poses severe strain on some managements. A desire to be comprehensively involved is evidently difficult to resist.

Optimum divisionalization thus involves: (1) the identification of separable economic activities within the firm; (2) according quasi-autonomous standing (usually of a profit center nature) to each; (3) monitoring the efficiency performance of each division; (4) awarding incentives; (5) allocating cash flows to high yield uses; and (6) performing strategic planning (diversification, acquisition, and related activities) in other respects. The M-form structure is one that *combines* the divisionalization concept with an internal control and strategic decision-making capability. The general management of the M-form usually requires the support of a specialized staff to discharge these functions effectively. It bears repeating, however, that care must be exercise lest the general management and its staff become overinvolved in operating matters and fail to perform the high-level planning and control functions on which the M-form enterprise relies for its continuing success.

Whether and how to divisionalize depends on firm size, functional separability, and the state of information technology (Emery, 1969). Also, it should be pointed out that the reference here to optimum is used in comparative institutional terms. As between otherwise comparable unitary or holding company forms of organization, the M-form structure would appear to possess significant advantages. It cannot, however, be established on the basis of the argument advanced here that the M-form structure is the best of all conceivable structures. Organizational innovations may even now be in the making that will obsolete it in part — but which academics will identify as noteworthy only after several years. A keener sensitivity to organizational innovations and their economic importance than has existed in the past should nevertheless help to avoid the long recognition lags that have transpired before the significance of the M-form structure and its conglomerate variant became apparent.

Lest, however, these remarks lead to an underevaluation of the merits of the M-form structure, I hasten to add that, while evolutionary change is to be expected, the hierarchical decomposition principles on which the M-form is based are very robust. In his discussion of adaptive corporate organization, Beer observes: "The notion of hierarchy is given in cybernetics as a necessary structural attribute of any viable organism. This is not surprising to us, although its theoretical basis is profound, because all viable systems do in fact exhibit hierarchical organizations" (1969, p. 399). Moreover, not only does Simon's review of the properties of complex biological, physical, and social systems reaffirm this, but he emphasizes that hierarchies commonly factor problems in such a way that "higher frequency dynamics are associated with the subsystems, the lower frequency dynamics with the larger systems, . . . [and] intra-component linkages are generally stronger than intercomponent linkages" (1962, p. 477). Hierarchical systems of this sort may be referred to as near-decomposable (Simon, 1962). It is not merely fortuitous that the M-form structure factors problems very much in this way.

5. The "M-Form Hypothesis" and Concluding Remarks

Although the M-form structure was initially devised and imitated as a means by which to correct local conditions of inefficiency and subgoal pursuit, it has subsequently had pervasive systems consequences. These systems effects are partly attributable to competition in the product market; unadapted firms have found it necessary, as a survival measure, to eliminate slack so as to remain viable. But the effects of takeover threats from the capital market are also important. The conglomerate variant on the M-form structure is of particular interest in this connection — which is the subject of the next chapter. Focusing, however, strictly on direct effects, which is sufficient for our purposes here, the argument comes down to this: *The organization and operation of the large enterprise along the lines of the M-form favors goal pursuit and least-cost behavior more nearly associated with the neoclassical profit maximization hypothesis than does the U-form organizational alternative.*[17]

But more than mere divisionalization is needed for these effects to be realized. It is also necessary that a separation of operating from strategic responsibilities be provided. The former are assigned to the operating

17. It will be noted that the argument has been developed in comparative terms. It could, therefore, be as easily expressed instead as a U-form hypothesis; namely, the organization and operation of the large enterprise along the lines of the U-form favors goal pursuit and cost behavior more nearly associated with the managerial discretion hypothesis than does the M-form organizational alternative. This equivalent statement makes evident an underlying symmetry that some may find disconcerning: if one accepts the affirmative argument on behalf of the M-form organization advanced above, a tacit acceptance of managerial discretion theory (in the context of U-form organization) may also be implied. That is, if the M-form organization has, for the reasons given, the superior efficiency, motivational, and control properties that have been imputed to it, then presumably the organization and operation of the large enterprise along the lines of the traditional (U-form) structure contributes to control loss and utility-maximizing behavior of the sort described in Williamson (1964). To the extent, therefore, that the coincidence of large, unitary form structures and nontrivial opportunity sets (mainly by reason of favorable product market conditions) is observed in the economy, utility-maximizing behavior (and its attendant consequences) is to be expected.

divisions while the latter are made the focus of the general management. Moreover, such a partitioning does not, by itself, assure strategic effectiveness; for this to obtain requires that the general management develop an internal control apparatus, to assess the performance of the operating divisions, and an internal resource allocation capability, which favors the assignment of resources to high yield uses.

That divisionalized enterprises sometimes, and perhaps often, fail to meet these stipulations is suggested by Ansoff and Brandenberg, who observe that the performance potential in divisionalized firms frequently goes unrealized because general managements "either continue to be overly responsive to operating problems [that is, nonstrategic but interventionist] or reduce the size of the corporate office to a minimum level at which no capacity exists for strategic and structural decision making" (1971, p. 722). An effort to assess internal controls in divisionalized enterprises and to distinguish among the several types is accordingly indicated if tests of the M-form hypothesis are to be attempted. To facilitate such testing a six-way classification scheme is set out in the appendix.

Appendix: A Classification Scheme[18]

As noted, a major problem is posed for testing the M-form hypothesis in that, if all divisionalized firms are classified as M-form firms, without regard for the related internal decision-making and control apparatus, an overassignment to the M-form category will result. Some divisionalized firms are essentially holding companies, in that they lack the requisite control machinery, while others are only nominally divisionalized, with the general office maintaining extensive involvement in operating affairs. If indeed the M-form designation is to be reserved for those firms that *combine* the appropriate structural and internal operating attributes, information on both aspects is required.

The difficulty with this is threefold. First, information on internal operating procedures is less easy to come by than is that on divisionalization. Second, the appropriate degree of involvement by the general office in the affairs of the operating divisions varies with the nature of the factor or product market interdependencies that exist within the firm and thus need to be "harmonized." Divisions that are involved in the exchange of intermediate products (vertical integration) typically face different control

18. The classification scheme independently proposed by Richard Rumelt [as reported by Scott (1973, pp. 138-139)] is somewhat similar to that suggested here. although he does not make the distinctions among M-form firms (as between M, M', and M̄) that are suggested here and which I believe are important. For an illustrative use of the proposed scheme to a group of eight firms, see Williamson and Bhargava (1972).

needs than those in which such internal, cross-divisional transactions are absent. Similarly, the requisite product market controls are more extensive if operating divisions produce competitive products than when, by reason of product diversification, such interdependencies are absent.

The third problem is that reaching the M-form structure may require the firm to pass through a transitional stage during which the "optimum" control relationship, expressed in equilibrium terms, is violated. An appreciation for the natural life cycle in the M-form enterprise is necessary if these transitional conditions are to be detected and an appropriate classification made.

Although experience with the scheme may disclose certain ambiguities, suggest better definitions, and reveal a need to devise still additional categories, it seems useful to get on with the assignment task and make the subsequent refinements. Surely enough is known about internal organization at this time to begin such an effort. The following classification scheme is accordingly proposed.

1. Unitary (U-form)

This is the traditional functionally organized enterprise. (It is still the appropriate structure in most small- to lower middle-sized firms. Some medium-sized firms, in which interconnections are especially rich, may continue to find this the appropriate structure.) A variant on this structure occasionally appears in which the enterprise is mainly of U-form character but where the firm has become diversified in slight degree and the incidental parts are given semi-autonomous standing. Unless such diversification accounts for at least a third of the firm's value added, such functionally organized firms will be assigned to the U-form category.

2. Holding Company (H-form)

This is the divisionalized enterprise for which the requisite internal control apparatus has not been provided. The divisions are often affiliated with the parent company through a subsidiary relationship.

3. Multidivisional (M-form)

This is the divisionalized enterprise in which a separation of operating from strategic decision-making is provided and for which the requisite internal control apparatus has been assembled and is systematically employed.

Two subcategories should be distinguished: type D_1, which denotes a highly integrated M-form enterprise, possibly with differentiated but otherwise common final products; and type D_2, which denotes the M-form enterprise with diversified final products or services. As between these two, a more extensive internal control apparatus to manage spillover effects is needed in the former.

4. Transitional Multidivisional (M'-Form)

This is the M-form enterprise that is in the process of adjustment. Organizational learning may be involved or newly acquired parts may not yet have been brought into a regular divisionalized relationship to the parent enterprise.[19]

5. Corrupted Multidivisional (M̄-form)

The M̄-form enterprise is a multidivisional structure for which the requisite control apparatus has been provided but in which the general management has become extensively involved in operating affairs. The appropriate distance relation thus is missing, with the result that M-form performance, over the long-run, cannot reliably be expected.[20]

19. Inasmuch as it may take some time for an organization to recognize the need for reorganization, to effect a major structural change, and then become adapted to its operational consequences (which is to say that organizational learning is involved), the period just prior to, during, and immediately following a reorganization along M-form lines is apt to be a disequilibrium interval. Some allowance for the difficulties of adjustment may be needed if the performance consequences of such a change are to be accurately evaluated.

Similarly, the process of effectively integrating new acquisitions within an established M-form enterprise may take time. The incumbent managers of the newly acquired firm may have been able to negotiate, as a condition of support for the acquisition, that their division be accorded special autonomy. Only as this management is redeployed within the parent organization, reaches retirement, or is otherwise induced to accept a more normal divisionalized relationship can the M-form control apparatus be brought fully to bear. Indeed, as a transitional matter to hasten the divisionalization, the general management may, at its first "legitimate" opportunity, involve itself more actively in the operating affairs of the newly acquired parts than would, assessed in equilibrium terms, ordinarily be appropriate. The purpose of this effort, presumably, is to effect a more rapid conditioning of attitudes and transformation of procedures than would otherwise obtain — bringing both more nearly into congruence with those existing elsewhere in the firm. Such apparent overinvolvement ought not to be regarded a contradiction to M-form procedures unless the interference is long continued and widely practiced throughout the enterprise. Otherwise, it is merely a transitional condition and a violation of M-form operations is not implied.

20. It may be necessary to recognize a semicorrupted type of M-form organization. Thus, suppose that several M-form firms are combined and that the general offices of each are

6. *Mixed* (*X-Form*)

Conceivably a divisionalized enterprise will have a mixed form in which some divisions will be essentially of the holding company variety, others will be M-form, and still others will be under the close supervision of the general management. Whether a mixed form is apt to be viable over the long run is perhaps to be doubted. Some exceptions might, however, survive simply as a matter of chance. The X-form classification thus might be included for completeness purposes and as a reminder that organizational survival is jointly a function of rational and chance processes. Over the long pull the rational structures should thrive, but aberrant cases will appear and occasionally persist.

That the X-form lacks for rationality properties, however, is probably too strong. For example, a large U-form firm that enjoys monopoly power in its main market may wish to restrict the reinvestment of cash flows back into this market. At the same time it may discover attractive opportunities to invest some part of these funds in unrelated business activities. Diversification could follow, but not in sufficient degree to warrant disestablishment of the main market from central office control. The diversified parts of the business thus might each be given divisional standing, but the main business retained, for the most part, under its earlier control relationship. Only if the main business itself could be efficiently divided (through product differentiation, geographic territorialization, or other lines), which eventually it may, might divisionalization of this part of the firm's activities be warranted.

---

converted into group headquarters. If, now, the group vice-presidents not only head up their groups but also serve with the president in setting corporate policy, partisan representations are apt to reappear in the strategic decision-making process. Whether this mixed involvement of the group vice-presidents is of sufficient importance to warrant an additional classification is unclear at this time.

9. Conglomerate Organization

The structural phenomenon referred to as the conglomerate form of corporate organization has constituted a public policy anomaly for all of twenty years — and has been a part of the American industrial scene even longer. Only in the past ten years, however, has it begun to take on quantitive significance and receive widespread attention. Although there appears to have been some convergence of views in the past several years, a consensus can hardly be said to have emerged.

The failure on the part of received microtheory to regard the internal organization of the firm as interesting is, I believe, responsible for what Posner has called "the puzzle of the conglomerate corporation" (1972, p. 204). This puzzle has not, however, deterred those who most rely on received microtheory from venturing the opinion that the conglomerate is innocent of anticompetitive purpose or potential and ought not to be an object of antitrust prosecution. But a satisfying affirmative rationale for the conglomerate, based on received microtheory, has yet to appear.[1]

The populist critics of the conglomerate have not allowed this lapse to go unnoticed. Solo's views are perhaps representative. He contends that "when faced with a truly dangerous phenomenon, such as the conglomerate mergers of the 1960's, produced by financial manipulators making grist for their security mills, the professional antitrust economists were

---

1. As discussed in Section 3.1 below, it is sometimes argued that reciprocity has attractive efficiency properties, in that it facilitates price-shading in otherwise rigid price circumstances. While I concede that reciprocity can be used in this way, I do not find it an especially compelling economic rationale for the conglomerate. Surely the entire conglomerate movement is not to be explained in these terms. Also, I think it useful to appreciate that reciprocity can have inefficiency consequences. Once begun, perhaps as a price-shading technique, it may be continued because it suits the bureaucratic preferences of the sales staff.

Adelman (1961) has suggested that the conglomerate has attractive portfolio diversification consequences. Again, however, it is doubtful that the entire conglomerate movement is to be explained in these terms.

155

silent. Like other realities of a modern enterprise, this phenomenon, which will probably subvert management effectiveness and organizational rationale for generations, is outside their conceptual framework." (1972. pp. 47-48).

Several things should be said in this connection. First, in defense of antitrust economists, I would point out that financial manipulation is not their main concern. This is the principal business of the Securities and Exchange Commission rather than the U.S. Antitrust Division. Although Solo might rightfully object that economists are excessively narrow, it is nevertheless the security specialists who, as matters are divided up currently, are presumably at fault. Second, and more important, Solo's sweeping charges leave the particular dangers of the conglomerate phenomenon completely unspecified. Third, I agree that an understanding of the conglomerate requires an extension of the conventional framework. I nevertheless think it noteworthy that populist critics of the conglomerate and mainline microtheorists alike pay little heed to the resource allocation impact, in the form of capital market substitution effects, of internal organization. Finally, conglomerates come in a variety of forms and have a variety of purposes. Accordingly, a selective rather than a broadside attack on conglomerates is indicated.

The emphasis in this chapter is on conglomerates that have attractive rationality properties.[2] The reasons for this emphasis are set out in Section 1. The relation of the conglomerate to competition in the capital market is examined in Section 2. The real and alleged public policy issues posed by conglomerates are addressed in Section 3. Some of the evidence bearing on the performance of conglomerates is reviewed in Section 4. Concluding remarks follow. The basic argument comes down to this: Just as the vertical integration of production is to be explained in large measure by reference to (comparative institutional) failures in the market for intermediate goods, the affirmative aspects of conglomerate organization are to be understood in terms of *failures in the capital market.*

1. The Affirmative Emphasis

An understanding of the conglomerate phenomenon is impeded if all conglomerates are treated as though they were indistinguishable one from another. Some types may pose genuine public policy problems, others have had an invigorating competitive influence, and still others have had essentially neutral effects. Those that combine mixtures of the first two types pose the most troublesome public policy issues.

The main emphasis here is on conglomerates of the revitalizing kind —

2. These are firms which, in terms of the classificatory scheme proposed in the appendix of Chapter 8, are of the M-form, type-D_2 variety.

by which I mean divisionalized firms that are provided with the strategic planning and internal control capability described in Section 3.2 of Chapter 8 and are diversified in sufficient degree to warrant assignment to the conglomerate category.[3] The reasons for delimiting the discussion in this way are two. First, the potentially beneficial consequences of conglomerates have been relatively neglected in the discussions by public agencies of this phenomenon. Although the staff of the U.S. Federal Trade Commission appears to be moderating its position on conglomerates,[4] its earlier position,[5] as well as that expressed by officials in the U.S. Justice Department[6] and developed in congressional staff studies,[7] was to regard the conglomerate as a dubious if not altogether disreputable form of organization. If, however, the conglomerate is a more complex and many sided phenomenon than official statements reveal, a more balanced assessment requires that other aspects of the issue be more fully exposed.

The second reason for focusing on conglomerates that have attractive internal efficiency characteristics is that, over the long pull, their superior viability properties should manifest themselves in terms of differential survival. Those conglomerates that rely on loophole exploitation, "irregular" security issues, follow-the-crowd fadishness, accounting chicanery, and the like for their successes will eventually exhaust the well and be sorted out as loopholes are closed[8] and the test of continuing viability is faced. Although the earnings reported in any one year can be altered greatly by choosing judiciously among a wide variety of "defensible" accounting procedures,[9] the test of earnings over several successive periods is less

---

3. On some of the problems of defining diversification in requisite degree to warrant the conglomerate appellation, see Markham (1973, pp. 7-19).

4. See Staff Report to the Federal Trade Commission, *Conglomerate Merger Performance: An Empirical Analysis of Nine Corporations,* November, 1972.

5. See, for example, the address delivered by former Attorney General John N. Mitchell before the Georgia Bar Association on June 6, 1969. (The text is reprinted in the *BNA Antitrust and Trade Regulation Reporter,* June 10, 1969, No. 413, pp. X-9 to X-11).

   The views of Thomas Kauper, who heads up the Antitrust Division of the U.S. Department of Justice at the time of this writing, are reportedly closer to the tougher position of his predecessor, Richard McLaren, than to those of the Turner administration. See, "Antitrust Strategist," *New York Times,* November 12, 1972, p. F-7.

6. See the Staff Report to the Federal Trade Commission, *Economic Report on Corporate Mergers* (Economic Concentration, Part 8A, Hearings before the Subcommittee on Antitrust and Monopoly, 91st Cong., 1st Sess., Washington, 1969).

7. See, for example *Investigation of Conglomerate Corporations* (a report by the Staff of the Antitrust Subcommittee of the Committee on the Judiciary, House of Representatives, 92nd Cong., 1st Sess., Washington, 1971).

8. The necessary expertise for dealing with loophole closure of these types is possessed by specialists on Internal Revenue and matters related to the Securities and Exchange Commission. Inasmuch as the emphasis here is on antitrust, and since antitrust enforcement is poorly suited to deal with defects in the tax and securities laws, these matters will not be pursued here.

9. For an interesting discussion, see, "What are Earnings? The Growing Credibility Gap," *Forbes,* May 15, 1967, pp. 29-34, 39-41.

subject to cosmetic adjustment in this way. The problems associated with the issue of special debt and equity instruments are likewise revealed over time as maturities become due and/or changes in the condition of the environment require the firm to face adversity. Conglomerate structures that lack financial and structural rationality and want for sound management will — as a group at least, although there will be individual exceptions — decline relatively. If the selection mechanism is working well, they will be required to adapt appropriately, shrink relatively, or face extinction.[10] Accordingly, attention is directed from the outset toward an examination of those types of conglomerates that are believed to have sound structural and management properties.

2. Competition in the Capital Market

Internal organization has an influence on competition in the capital market in three respects. First, divisionalized firms (of the appropriate kind) more assuredly assign cash flows to high yield uses. The arguments here are already familiar from the preceding chapter. Second, the divisionalized firm is well-suited to serve as a takeover agent. Acquired firms that might otherwise run slack are thereby made to operate more efficiently. Third, when the background threat of takeover exceeds threshold probabilities, prospective target firms are induced to take self-corrective measures.

2.1 Internal Resource Allocation

The capital market in an environment of U-form firms was earlier regarded as a less than efficacious surveillance and correction mechanism for three reasons: its external relation to the firm places it at a serious information disadvantage; it is restricted to nonmarginal adjustments; it experiences nontrivial displacement costs. The general office of the M-form organization has superior properties in each of these respects. First, it is an internal rather than external control mechanism with the constitutional

---

10. See Winter (1971). He summarizes the general assumptions needed for the selection argument to go through as follows: (1) firms have decision rules that are adjusted in accordance with the satisficing principle; and (2) profitable firms add to capacity and expand relatively. If, in addition, "persistent search and the innovating remnant serve to eliminate as possible equilibrium positions situations in which possible but untried decision rules would yield higher profits than those currently utilized," long-run profit maximization will obtain (1971, pp. 247-248).

Extinction may, however, take the form of management displacement, through competition in the capital market, if competition in the product market operates slowly.

authority and expertise to make detailed evaluations of the performance of each of its operating parts. Second, it can make fine-tuning as well as discrete adjustments. This permits it both to intervene early in a selective, preventative way (a capability which the capital market lacks altogether), as well as to perform *ex post* corrective adjustments, in response to evidence of performance failure, with a surgical precision that the capital market lacks (the scalpel versus the ax is an appropriate analogy). Finally, the costs of intervention by the general office are relatively low. Altogether, therefore, a profit-oriented general office in an M-form enterprise might be expected to secure superior performance to that which the unassisted capital market can enforce. The M-form organization might thus be viewed as capitalism's creative response to the evident limits which the capital market experiences in its relations to the firm, as well as a means for overcoming the organizational problems which develop in the large U-form enterprise when variety becomes great.[11]

2.2 Takeover

The argument can be carried a step further by considering the effects of the M-form innovation on capital market displacement efforts. *Ceteris paribus,* displacement is more likely the greater the unavailed profit opportunities in the target firm and the lower the costs of effecting displacement. In relation to the U-form enterprise, the M-form innovation enhances the attractiveness of making a displacement efforts in both respects.

The realization of operating economies by reconstituting a large U-form enterprise along M-form lines represents a source of potential profit gain which, in the absence of reorganization, is unavailable. The resulting economies are due to more effective resource allocation (between divisions and in the aggregate), better internal organization (a reduction in technical control loss), and the attenuation of subgoal pursuit. Unitary form organizations for which either (1) divisionalization is difficult (the natural unit is the integrated form)[12] or (2) the prevailing attitudes and distribution of

11. The conjunction of these two consequences in a single organizational innovation should probably be regarded as fortuitous. Thus, the emergence in the late 1800's of large, single-product, multifunctional (vertically integrated) enterprises along U-form lines presumably permitted transactional and possibly technical scale economies to be realized (as well, perhaps, as monopoly power), but the organizational innovation in this instance served to weaken capital market controls. That organizational innovations in the future should favor internal efficiency is reasonably to be expected; that, however, they should also enhance capital market controls is not at all obvious.

12. Even though the natural unit may be integrated, it may be possible to replicate several of these natural units; for example, several parallel product divisions might be created. The long delay in divisionalizing very large steel firms thus is not to be explained entirely in terms of the intrinsic requirements of vertical integration. Vertical integration within operating divisions, but quasi-autonomy between them (subject, probably, to rules

power among the incumbent management make self-reorganization difficult are natural takeover candidates.

Existing M-form enterprises are probably the most effective instruments for achieving displacement. For one thing, they are apt to have superior inference capabilities; the elite staff of the M-form structure may even have as one of its principal assignments the discovery of potential takeover candidates. In addition, such firms are already experienced in the organizational advantages that this structure offers.

2.3 Systems Consequences

Unitary form enterprises that anticipate takeover efforts may attempt to shrink the potential displacement gain by making appropriate internal changes: subgoal pursuit may be reduced or, possibly, self-reorganization along M-form lines may be initiated. Such forestalling efforts are not apt to be common, however, until the probability of a takeover attempt has reached a nontrivial value. Except in U-form enterprises which have been specifically targeted for takeover, this may require that there be a relatively large number of multidivision enterprises actively surveying takeover opportunities. With only a few multidivision firms performing this function, the probability that any one unitary form enterprise will be the object of a takeover attempt is too small to warrant *ex ante* adaptation. Once the number of multidivision firms becomes sufficiently large, however, the effect on unitary form enterprises that are otherwise shielded from product market pressures is equivalent to an increase in competition in so far as subgoal pursuit is concerned. Selection on profits is thereby enhanced; the effects indeed may be pervasive. The argument thus reduces to the following proposition: internal organization and conventional capital market forces are complements as well as substitutes; the two coexist in a symbiotic relationship to each other.

But adaptive responses of a protective rather than a corrective kind might also appear. Although such protective responses serve the interests of incumbent managements, they are apt to be dysfunctional from the standpoint of the system as a whole. Cary (1969) enumerates the corporate devices used to insulate management from attack as follows: (1) amending the certificate of incorporation, including the abolishment of cumulative voting and the specification of super-majority requirements (for example, an eighty percent rule) to approve a merger; (2) acquiring a firm with products similar to those of the takeover agent, in order to produce anti-

---

governing coordinated marketing), is normally feasible in the larger of these firms—which greatly exceed minimum scale requirements for technically efficient production (Bain, 1956).

trust problems; (3) placing additional stock in friendly hands by making a stock acquisition of another firm; (4) restricting loan agreements by including an unacceptable change of management clause; (5) buying off a raider by using corporate funds to purchase his stock; (6) making a tender offer to its own stockholders, so as to drive up the price of its stock above the existing tender offer value; (7) raising the dividend and splitting the shares for a similar purpose; (8) applying for an injunction by claiming that rival tender offers are misleading; and (9) applying to the securities commission of a state to change requirements for tender offers in such a way as to obtain relief. That these tactics are not merely hypotheticals, but in fact have been devised as defenses to the takeover threat posed by the conglomerate, should be noted.[13]

2.4 Special Relevance of the Conglomerate

If the M-form firm is to perform the capital market policing functions described above and if, simultaneously, antimerger policies with respect to horizontal and vertical acquisitions are to remain tough, preserving the conglomerate acquisition option may be essential. Otherwise, the threat of a takeover to firms operated by moribund managements will be rendered effete; bringing every form of market organization — including the conglomerate — under antitrust attack would have the unfortunate and presumably unintended consequence of impairing what Manne (1965) refers to as the "market for corporate control."

But why M-form firms or conglomerates? Under conventional assumptions that more choices are always preferred to fewer, ought not the banking system have superior resource allocation properties? Put differently, why should a miniature capital market ever be preferred to the real thing? Similarly, ought not individual banks, were they so inclined, be able to intervene actively in the internal affairs of firms — even to include the displacement of managements should the need arise?

There are three problems with such arguments: bounded rationality considerations are suppressed; crucial differences between internal and external controls are overlooked; and adaptive responses (given the prevailing institutional rules of the game) are neglected. Thus, were it that decision makers could be easily apprised of an ever wider range of alternatives and choose intelligently among them, there would be little reason to supplant the traditional market. But it is elementary that, where complex

---

13. See the chronology of the Northwest Industries attempt to take over B. F. Goodrich and the defensive responses that this set in motion [as reported in Williamson (1970, pp. 100-102)]. Also, see, the Report by the Staff of the Antitrust Subcommittee describing special protection afforded to regulated industries by their respective regulatory commissions when a takeover was threatened. (Above, note 7, pp. 430-433).

events have to be evaluated, information-processing capacities are quickly reached. As a result, expanding the range of choice may not only be without purpose but can have net detrimental effects. A tradeoff between breadth of information, in which respect the banking system may be presumed to have the advantage, and depth of information, which is the advantage of the specialized firm, is involved. The conglomerate can be regarded as an intermediate form that, ideally, optimizes with respect to the breadth-depth tradeoff.[14]

The failure to distinguish clearly between internal and external control processes is an equally serious defect in the banking argument. The powers of internal organization that are discussed in earlier chapters are, by definition, unavailable to an external control agent — whether he be a purchaser (as in the case of the military services), a supplier (such as a bank), or a regulatory commission. Access to internal information is strictly limited and difficult, without first-hand experience, to evaluate. It is thus unrealistic for the external control agent to attempt to make fine-tuning adjustments in anticipation of prospective market developments; even *ex post* audits are subject to severe limitations. The control instruments that the external agent commands are likewise limited. Control over the screening-selection-promotion process is mainly denied to outsiders; indeed, extensive interference by outsiders in internal personnel matters is apt to be thoroughly disruptive and have demoralizing effects.

Finally, were the banks to attempt aggressively to reallocate resources among sectors, large corporations could be expected to adapt defensively. Greater reliance on internal financing could be expected. Firms might even develop pools that bypassed the banking system.[15]

14. Alchian and Demsetz (1972) interpret internal organization in a somewhat similar fashion. For a study of the use of the computer to extend the firm's capacity to deal effectively with a wider set of investment alternatives, see Hamilton and Moses (1973).

15. In consideration of these disabilities, the banking system would appear to be a poor substitute for the conglomerate. But what explains then the apparent success of the Japanese *Zaibatsu* form of organization? As Bronfenbrenner notes, the *Zaibatsu* has the characteristics of a giant conglomerate in which "there is a commonality of ownership between borrowing firm and its primary lending bank, with *Zaibatsu* banks and their officers investing heavily in the stock of their *Zaibatsu* affiliates" (1970, p. 151). A much more extensive *integration* between banking and the operating affiliates thus constitutes one part of the answer. Funds are not really available for unrestricted investment but are allocated to particular bidders — to the disadvantage of the unaffiliated businesses (Bronfenbrenner, 1970, p. 152). In addition, the Japanese system may be culture-specific in important respects. For one thing, the Japanese Ministry of International Trade and Industry performs a wide range of "extra-legal expansive, regulatory, and protective functions" (Bronfenbrenner, 1970, p. 153) that many Americans would find objectionable. In addition, as Bronfenbrenner puts it, "important for an understanding of the Japanese economy . . . are certain elements of economic sociology" (1970, p. 154) — low mobility, a high degree of paternalism, extensive employment security, and an unusually high propensity to save. The *Zaibatsu* is partly dependent for its success on the continuation of these conditions. That these conditions may not continue is suggested by the recent emergence of labor problems that have hitherto been absent in the Japanese economy.

3. Public Policy Issues

Public policy issues of three kinds are posed by the conglomerate. First, there is the possibility that conglomerates are especially prone to engage in what are thought to be anticompetitive practices. Charges of reciprocity and of predatory cross-subsidization are commonly lodged against conglomerates. Second, conglomerate mergers may impair competition by weakening the threat of potential competition or by giving rise to a condition of conglomerate interdependence. Finally, very large conglomerates may pose social and political issues. Consider these *seriatim*.

3.1 Anticompetitive Conduct

Reciprocal buying involves an informal conditional purchase agreement, such that I buy from you if you buy from me. Though unlawful, it is nevertheless thought to be widely practiced. Since the opportunity to match purchases with sales is more extensive in a multiproduct than in a specialized firm, conglomerates are said to make sales to the possible disadvantage of undiversified but otherwise qualified rivals. Complaints of reciprocity, or reciprocal buying potential, almost always accompany antitrust actions against conglomerate acquisitions.

Three questions arise in connection with the charge of reciprocity. First, are there alternative interpretations of the incentive to engage in reciprocity? Second, what organizational structures are best suited to support reciprocity? And third, what does the evidence show with respect to the proclivity of conglomerates, in relation to other firms, to engage in such practices?

Stigler observes that an affirmative case can be made for reciprocity on the following grounds:[16]

> The case *for* reciprocity arises when prices cannot be freely varied to meet supply and demand conditions. Suppose that a firm is dealing with a colluding industry which is fixing prices. A firm in this collusive industry would be willing to sell at less than the cartel price if it can escape detection. Its price can be reduced in effect by buying from the customer-seller at an inflated price. Here reciprocity restores flexibility of prices.

An assessment of the consequences of reciprocity is thus uncertain: it may be an unfair sales technique, but it may also be an indirect way of evading an oligopolistic price structure. Since there are other ways of shading prices if reciprocity were disallowed, however, and since reciprocity, whatever

16. President's Task Force Report on Productivity and Competition, reprinted in Commerce Clearing House *Trade Regulation Reporter,* 6-24-69, No. 419, p. 39.

its origins, may be continued because it suits the *bureaucratic preferences* of the sales staff, public policy disdain for reciprocity seems to me warranted.

Consider, therefore, whether conglomerate firms are especially given to this practice. Organization form is relevant in this connection. The general proposition is this: M-form enterprises are less given to reciprocity than are U-form firms, *ceteris paribus*. The reason here is that divisionalization concept is corrupted if cross-divisional reciprocity is attempted. Accordingly, it is not sufficient to rest a charge of reciprocity on product mix considerations; proclivity must also be considered. As between conglomerates, those that are organized as M-form firms are poorly suited to engage in such practices. Although failure to make organization form distinctions easily leads to undiscriminating charges that conglomerates quite generally are prone to engage in reciprocity, even the courts appear to recognize the importance of organization form in assessing proclivity charges.[17]

Consider, finally, the evidence. Blake observes in this connection that "empirical research, if it could be carried out, would show that reciprocity is as inevitable a result of widespread conglomerate structure as price rigidity is a consequence of oligopoly structure" (1973, p. 569) —where, apparently, the latter, and hence the former, is believed to be extensive. A recent study by Markham (which was unavailable to Blake), in which the organizational underpinning for reciprocity (in the form of a trade practices department) is examined in relation to the degree of firm diversification,[18] concludes otherwise: ". . . highly diversified companies are no more, and may be even less, given to reciprocity than large corporations generally" (1973, p. 176).

The argument with respect to cross-subsidization is that profits earned in one sector of a business may be used to offset temporary losses in another sector that is engaged in predatory price-cutting. Again this is unlawful. But again it is important to distinguish between predatory cross-subsidization, undertaken for the purpose of damaging rivals, and the rational reallocation of internal resources to support divisions which, if the divisions in question were to be organized instead as free-standing enterprises, would *not* be funded by the capital market. This last need not to be regarded as cross-subsidization in any objectionable sense since, because of the information and incentive advantages of internal in relation to external organization, risks can be efficiently accepted by an M-form enterprise that the unassisted capital market would reject. M-form firms, which have deeper

17. Thus, the Connecticut Court in the ITT-Hartford Insurance case was prepared to dismiss reciprocity arguments by the government because of organization form considerations. (306 F. Supp. 766; 324 F. Supp. 45.)

18. Markham's study combined questionnaire evidence that he developed with diversification evidence developed by Berry (1974).

knowledge of the underlying data, may therefore be prepared to sustain current losses that outside investors would consider unacceptable. (See the reasons given in Chapter 8.)

Whether conglomerate firms are especially given to the practice of predatory cross-subsidization is seriously to be doubted. For one thing, any multimarket organization—including specialized firms operating in geographically dispersed product markets—can engage in such practices. In addition, the organization form distinction is again relevant: the M-form structure is seriously compromised if predatory cross-subsidization is attempted.

While the evidence on predatory price-cutting is incomplete, the examples cited by the U.S. Federal Trade Commission Staff Study of Conglomerates suggest that it is the relatively specialized multimarket firms that are most given to this behavior.[19] Also, Markham's examination of the proclivity to coordinate pricing decisions within each of 204 large manufacturing concerns revealed that pricing decisions were left "almost entirely to division or operating unit managers" in the more diversified of these firms (1973, p. 91).

One concludes that while antitrust vigilance with respect to reciprocity and cross-subsidization is warranted, conglomerate acquisitions ought not to be regarded with special animus on either account.

3.2 Actual and Potential Competition

Actual competition arguments of two kinds are leveled against conglomerates. First, diversification by large corporations is said to result in increasing concentration in individual markets (Shepherd, 1970, pp. 140-141). Berry's subsequent examination of the evidence, however, concludes otherwise: Although the market position of the leading firms of an industry is protected from erosion by the entry of small firms, the "market share of entering large firms is acquired at the expense of the leading four firms" (1974, p. 202).

The second objection to conglomerates in actual competition respects is that a condition of mutual interdependence recognized develops among them, as a result of their multimarket contacts, and that this results in an attenuation of price competition. Blake, moreover, contends that this is not merely a hypothetical possibility but that there is now "hard evidence to support the no longer novel theory — and widely held belief in the business community — that large conglomerates facing each other in several markets tend to be less competitive in price than regional or smaller firms" (1973, p. 570).

---

19. The firms cited by the FTC Staff Study are Safeway, Anheuser-Busch, and National Dairy Products (1969, pp. 406-443).

There are two problems with Blake's argument. First, I would scarcely characterize the evidence on which Blake relies upon as "hard." Part of the evidence cited by Blake is Scherer's discussion of the "spheres of influence hypothesis" (1970, pp. 278-280). But Scherer is very careful to characterize the evidence quite differently — noting that, even with respect to the prewar international chemical industry, which, aside from marine cartels, is his only Western example, the evidence is fragmentary. With respect to other industries he concludes that "there is a dearth of evidence on spheres of influence accords" (1970, p. 279).

Second, the definition of a conglomerate requires attention. Are all specialized firms (such as National Tea, to which Blake earlier refers) that operate similar plants or stores in geographically dispersed locations really to be regarded as conglomerates? By stretching the definition of a conglomerate to include geographically dispersed but otherwise specialized enterprises, is the number of nonconglomerate large firms shrunk to insignificance?

I submit that if the conglomerate is to be defined in product diversification terms, Blake (and the U.S. Federal Trade Commission) ought to be expected to generate examples of conglomerate abuse from the universe of product diversified firms. If all large multimarket firms, whatever their product specialization ratios, are the objectionable subset, it is these, rather than product diversified firms (which is the narrower definition of the conglomerate), that warrant attention. As things stand now, the facts, with respect to conglomerates, have yet to be assembled.

The potential competition argument is that prospective entrants into an industry should be barred from acquiring a large firm already in the industry if, but for such acquisitions, smaller firms (toeholds) in the industry would be acquired, and subsequently expanded, or *de novo* entry would occur instead. The removal of a likely potential entrant from the edge of the market, by permitting it to make a large acquisition, relieves the threat of entry and, arguably, impairs competition.

The anticompetitive potential of conglomerate mergers, in potential competition and other respects, is characterized by Blake as "so widespread that it might appropriately be described as having an effect upon the economic system as a whole — in every line of commerce in every section of the country" (1973, p. 567). He accordingly proposes that conglomerate acquisitions by firms above a specified size [the subset of firms that are to be restricted is not explicitly identified, but Blake makes several references to the top 200 firms (1973, pp. 559-569)] be accompanied by a spinoff of comparable assets (1973, p. 590) and further stipulates that no toehold exception should be permitted (1973, pp. 590-591).

The basis for his refusal to admit a toehold exception is, however, somewhat unclear. For one thing, the acquisition of a very small firm scarcely, by itself, contributes much to the growth of the large firm. Correspondingly, requiring the large firm to release assets in an equivalent amount whenever a toehold acquisition is made is scarcely more than a nuisance.[20] Furthermore, toehold acquisitions made for the purpose of securing a position that will subsequently be expanded *is* internal growth of the sort Blake favors. Either there is little point to Blake's toehold argument,[21] or he regards expansion by small firms as socially to be preferred to similar investments by large firms.

Assuming, *arguendo,* that the same investments will be made whether the small firm is acquired or not, it is easy to agree with Blake. But it is doubtful that the same investments will actually occur. This raises transfer process issues.

The examination of these matters in Chapter 10 suggests that small firms apparently enjoy a comparative advantage at early and developmental stages of the technical innovation process. Large, established firms, by contrast, display comparative advantages at large-scale commercial production and distribution stages.[22] Not only may the management of the small firm lack the financial resources to move to the commercial stage in any but gradualist manner because its credit standing does not permit it to raise significant blocks of capital except at adverse rates,[23] but the management of the small firm may be poorly suited to make the transition. Different management skills and knowledge are required to bring a project successfully to large-scale commercial development than may have been needed at earlier stages. If, because of management experience and team considerations, similar to those described in Section 2.2 of Chapter 6, the talents needed to facilitate internal expansion cannot be costlessly identified and assembled, transferring the project to an established firm that already possesses the requisite talents may be more economical instead. (Again, it is transactions, not technology, which dictate this result.) Put in these terms, it is unclear that the no toehold position survives.

20. For size control purposes, a large firm that engages in a series of toehold acquisitions within a specified time interval might be required to spin off assets comparable to the aggregate of those acquired if some absolute value is exceeded. For that matter, small percentage positions in some industries (for example, petroleum) can represent quite a large absolute asset values. Individual toehold acquisitions in these circumstances might exceed the absolute asset value threshold of, say, $100 million. A spinoff might be indicated.
21. But see the qualification in note 20, above.
22. Though it varies somewhat with organizational structure, projects for which only small-scale commercialization is anticipated are not ones for which large firms are typically well-suited. For a novel organizational solution, see Section 3.5 of Chapter 10.
23. Moving from a prototype to a commercial stage commonly involves a substantial investment in organizational infrastructure, much of which has no value should the enterprise fail. Lacking a known performance record and tangible assets to secure the investment, lenders are apprehensive to invest except on a sequential basis. The risks of opportunism, given information impactedness, are perceived to be too great.

The law with respect to the effects of conglomerate acquisitions on potential competition also appears to be moving away from the broad position ("in every line of commerce, in every section of the country") set out by Blake. Commissioner Dennison, speaking for a unanimous commission in the recent decision by the FTC in *Beatrice Foods,* described the required factual proof that potential competition has been or probably will be reduced as follws:[24]

> Complaint Counsel in essence attempt to rest their case on the existence of concentration ratios alone. The test for finding injury due to elimination of a potential competitor is not simple. Additional factors enter into any analysis of the loss of a potential competitor. Among these are: trends toward concentration in the market; extensive entry barriers; high probability that the lost potential competitor would have actually entered the market; whether the lost potential competitor was one of only a few such potential competitors and whether, if he had entered the market, his new competition would have had a significant impact on price and quality. Although the number of competing firms or trends toward concentration may be enough without more to condemn many horizontal mergers between existing rivals in a market, the *condition of entry by new firms as well as these other factors mentioned above must be considered when dealing with elimination of a potential competitor.*

The reference to the condition of entry in this statement warrants additional development.

As Turner (1965) has forcefully argued, potential competition is apt to be impaired if one of a few most likely potential entrants acquires a firm that exceeds toehold proportions. If the industry in question is highly concentrated, so that, but for the threat of potential competition, competitive results will not reliably obtain, the quality of competition is degraded by the loss of one of a few "most likely potential entrants." I would like to urge that the appellation "most likely potential entrant" has genuine economic significance, as contrasted with transitory business significance, *only* to the

---

24. Docket No. 8814 (FTC, September 28, 1972), 1972-73 Transfer Binder, *Trade Regulation Reporter,* para. 20, 121 at 22, 103, 22, 109 (emphasis added). Dennison's views are usefully contrasted with the first part of the FTC Staff Study of conglomerates — which, like Blake, favors a broad definition of potential competition (1969, p. 15):

> It is difficult, often impossible, to determine the precise identity, or even the number and relative importance of an industry's potential competitors, except to note that the most imminent potential competitors are those (a) engaging in the same industry but serving different geographic markets, (b) bearing a vertical relationship to the industry, or (c) operating in industries that may be currently or potentially related technologically in production or marketing. In the light of American industrial history, the long view of the competitive process argues persuasively for a broad definition of potential competitors; technological and other developments have brought quite unrelated companies into competition at later times.

extent that nontrivial barriers to entry into the industry in question can be said to exist.

The antitrust distinction to be made is between firms which, for transitory reasons, may have demonstrated an acquisition interest in the industry and firms which, in entry barrier respects (which introduces non-transitory considerations), are strategically situated to enter. Because the interest of firms of the first kind is unlikely to persist, being explained by such factors as current interest of the chief executive, temporary cash balances, immediate income statement considerations, and the like, prohibiting entry by acquisition to such firms is of little affirmative economic purpose. No long-term benefit to potential competition is thereby secured. Rather, the principal effect is to shrink the acquisition market, which impairs both the market for corporate control and the incentives for entrepreneurs to invest in new enterprises.

The situation is quite different, however, if the industry in question has nontrivial barriers to entry and the firm evidencing an acquisition interest is one of only a few firms for which *de novo* or toehold entry would be very easy. Consider in this connection the entry barrier conditions identified by Bain (1956), namely, economies of scale that are large in relation to the size of the market, absolute cost advantages, and product differentiation. Although Bain describes these barriers without reference to specific firms, plainly the height of the barrier varies among possible entrants. Those for which the barriers are least are the firms that are usefully designated, in potential competition terms, as most likely potential entrants, *ceteris paribus*.

Thus, though economies of scale may be large in relation to the size of the market, this impediment to entry is apt to be less severe for those few firms which have closely complementary production processes and sales organizations. Similarly, a few firms may be well-situated with respect to absolute cost advantages. Although patents may constitute a severe impediment to entry, high-grade ore deposits may be in limited supply, or specialized labor skills are required, a few firms are apt to stand out from all the rest by reason of a complementary technology, which facilitates inventing around the established patents, because they possess medium grade ore deposits, or because their labor force has acquired, in a learning-by-doing fashion, the requisite specialized skills. Product differentiation advantages are likewise attenuated for those firms that market related types of consumer goods and themselves enjoy brand recognition.

In circumstances, however, where all such barriers to entry are negligible (economies of scale are not great; patents, specialized, or otherwise scarce resources are unimportant; product differentiation is insubstantial), no small subset of firms can be said to enjoy a strategic advantage. Correspondingly, it is fatuous to attempt to identify a group of most likely potential entrants the loss, by acquisition, of any of which would significantly impair the quality of potential competition.[25].

3.3 Giant Size

The above assessment suggests that the conglomerate form poses much less severe public policy issues than Solo, Blake, and others have indicated. Public policy will be served by identifying *specific* instances where conglomerates pose problems rather than by mounting a broadscale attack. Specific abuses (for example, reciprocity) ought to be challenged, but conglomerate acquisitions ought not to be arrested on this account. Similarly, potential competition cases ought to be brought only where nontrivial entry barriers exist and the acquiring firm can be characterized as a most likely potential entrant.

An exception to this case-by-case approach might, however, be warranted where the acquisition of already large firms by other very large firms is contemplated. Such acquisitions might routinely be accompanied by a divestiture of equivalent assets. For one thing, as Hofstadter has observed, the support for antitrust rests less on a consensus among economists as to its efficiency enhancing properties than it does on a political and moral judgment that power in the American economy should be diffused (1964, p. 113). The wisdom of such populist social and political attitudes is illustrated by the misadventures of the ITT Corporation in domestic and foreign affairs (Sampson, 1973). Since much of Blake's disenchantment with conglomerates (1973, pp. 574, 576, 578, 579, 591), appears to be attributable to a concern that giant size and political abuse are positively correlated,[26] I would urge that the case be made expressly in these terms. If giant firms rather than all conglomerates are the objectionable subset, attention ought properly to be restricted to these.

A requirement that very large firms divest themselves of equivalent assets when larger than toehold acquisitions are made is also favored by the prospect that this will serve to curb bureaucratic abuses associated with very large size. Although such divestitures sometimes occur voluntarily (Coase, 1972, p. 67), such efforts predictably encounter bureaucratic resistance. If, however, such divestiture commonly has beneficial effects

25. One might, however, wish to prevent entry by acquisition by "dominant firms," the presence of which discourages rivalry (for long-purse reasons) and otherwise transforms the market in uncertain ways. The Proctor & Gamble acquisition of Clorox was characterized by Justice Marshall in these terms. (*United States v. Falstaff Brewing Corp.*, 410 U.S., 526, 558-559 (1973), Marshall, J., concurring.)

26. That giant size procures political favors does not imply that atomistic organization (for example, farmers) is the favored economic alternative. Often with the latter, however, the favors are more apt to be transparent.

of an organizational self-renewal sort, making divestiture mandatory is scarcely objectionable. It merely strengthens the hand of those in the firm who are anxious to forestall bureaucratization. Absent such a rule, internal agreement on divestiture may be difficult to secure; parties with vested interests will make partisan (opportunistic) representations that will be difficult to reject. Given such a rule, however, the general office can simply plead that it has no choice but to divest (assuming, that is, that a large acquisition is to be made). The preferences of the general office are thus made more fully to prevail.

4. Some Evidence

Despite the intensive attention that has been given to the conglomerate phenomenon over the past twenty years — and especially the past ten years — there has been surprisingly little effort made to evaluate the performance consequences of the conglomerate corporation. Markham's recent study, referred to above, is an exception. Weston and Mansinghka's review of the literature in 1971 turned up only three studies prior to their own, and two of these were concerned with special rather than general performance characteristics. Attention in this section is mainly confined to an examination of the Reid study and Weston and Mansinghka's updated review of the types of performance measures considered by Reid. I conclude with some brief remarks on the second part of the FTC Staff Study.[27]

First, however, it may be useful to consider some "indirect" evidence that is relevant to an assessment of the conglomerate phenomenon. The argument here relies on a combination of *a priori* theorizing and related natural selection considerations. To begin with, there is Chandler's impressive historical survey of the invention and subsequent diffusion of the multidivisional concept. As noted earlier, this organizing approach was originated in the 1920's at Du Pont, under the leadership of Pierre S. du Pont, and General Motors, under Alfred P. Sloan, Jr. Shortly thereafter, but apparently independently, Chandler finds similar organizational

27. Markham's (1973) recent study of conglomerates has been referred to in the text above. He was more concerned with possible conduct abuses of conglomerates than with managerial efficiency effects. Weston, Smith, and Shrieves have studied conglomerate performance using the Capital Asset Pricing Model and conclude: "In the measure which excluded unsystematic risk, ... the performance of conglomerates was approximately twice as high in 'finding securities that were under-priced'" and go on to observe that "unlike mutual funds which do not participate in the management of the firms in which they invest, conglomerate firms may change (for better or worse) the managerial performance of the entities added to their operations" (1972, p. 362). Although Weston et al. do not make organization form distinctions of the sort that I have emphasized, these results are broadly supportive of the general argument advanced in the text.

changes being introduced by Walter C. Teagle at Standard Oil of New Jersey and by Robert E. Wood at Sears and Roebuck. That the new concept was viable is testified to by the persistence of this organizing structure and the resulting success of each of these firms. Even more impressive is the adoption of the multidivisionalization concept among large corporations quite generally,[28] including recent adoptions by large European firms.

Although the timing and nature of structural changes in internal organization are attributable to a variety of causes—including accident, opportunism, faddishness (unthinking imitation)—those structures that prove durable will rarely lack for economic rationality. Chandler's survey suggests that firms which were early to adopt the M-form structure prospered and, in classic natural selection fashion, advanced relatively. Large rivals were eventually induced to adapt, although often this was delayed until a change in the top executive position occurred. For some it became absolutely essential, as a survival measure, to imitate.

That the M-form structure possesses attractive rationality properties (in a comparative-institutional sense) is revealed by the discussion in Chapter 8, which interprets the M-form structure as an internal organizational response to the problem that the U-form firm experienced in the face of large size and complexity. The conglomerate form of organization that adopts the multidivisionalization concept (including a strong general office, supported by an elite staff, which is disposed to give strategic direction to the enterprise and vigorously exercise the compliance machinery in implementing its programs) is less a new form of organization than it is a diversified variant on the basic M-form innovation. This is not, however, to suggest that "mere diversification" is easily accomplished or that its consequences are trivial.

Consider now the evidence reported by Reid (1968) and disputed by Weston and Mansinghka (1971). Reid was interested in determining whether the interests of managers or those of owners could be said to be promoted by mergers, be they conglomerate or otherwise. As indicators of management interests, Reid chose growth rates of sales, assets, and employment, while ownership interest was measured by growth rates of market valuation of shares, net income to total asset ratio, and net income to sales ratio. As Weston and Mansinghka point out, however, the net income to sales ratio lacks significance in periods when the asset mix is changing — as it often is when diversification is occurring. Moreover, Reid's study terminated in 1961, which was still early in the conglomerate movement. Reid nevertheless interpreted his results, judged in terms of the above indicated measures,

28. To repeat, however, divisionalization by itself is not sufficient. The M-form internal control apparatus and its implementation are also needed. Many of the firms that have divisionalized have not gone this further, crucial step.

as mainly revealing that management, rather than ownership interests. were being promoted by conglomerate organization.

Weston and Mansinghka dispute these findings, partly on grounds of internal consistency and partly because more recent data (through 1968) contradict them. Thus, they observe that Reid's "measures of performance were either not significant or significant in the wrong direction for ten or more of the 14 industries for each of each of his six measures" (1971, p. 929) , and that while conglomerates did not compare well with nonmerging firms they compared favorably with those that did merge (1971, p. 930) . Also, they note that Reid's principal measure of profitability (net income available to stockholders divided by total assets) is defective. Unless interest charges are added to the numerator or debt financing subtracted from the denominator, firms employing financial leverage (as conglomerates have been prone to) are unfairly penalized.[29]

Be that as it may, Weston and Mansinghka studied the comparative performance of large conglomerates in relation to other large firms over the interval of from 1958 to 1968 for each of the following five growth rate dimensions, which roughly parallel those used by Reid: total assets, sales, net income, earnings per share, and market price. They found that the mean growth rates for conglomerates were significantly higher on all counts. They then turned to an examination of earnings performance — measured mainly as before or after tax earnings before interest to total assets — and found that while conglomerates in 1958 had inferior earnings records, they had achieved parity or better by 1968. Altogether they concluded that "an important economic function of conglomerate firms has been raising the profitability of firms with depressed earnings to the average for industry generally" (1971, p. 934).

Although additional studies of conglomerate performance need to be made, including an effort to make the organization form distinctions proposed in Chapter 8, the provisional judgments that one reaches are that, in principle, the M-form conglomerate is not without real (as opposed to merely pecuniary) economic purpose and that, in fact, even when none of the organization form distinctions set out in the previous chapter are made, conglomerates as a group appear to have some commendable properties — which properties, presumably, would be all the more apparent among conglomerate firms of the M-form kind.

Consider now Part Two of the FTC Staff Study on conglomerates.[30]

---

29. This last is a valid point but really should be explored further. Leveraging may well lead to higher average returns to equity, but simultaneously increases the variance. Although this can be offset by "homemade diversification" under ideal assumptions, these are rarely fully satisfied in practice. As a result, in some degree at least, measuring mean returns to equity gives an incomplete measure of earnings performance.
30. See note 4, above.

The study reviews alleged anticompetitive consequences of large conglomerate firms (mainly predatory pricing supported by "deep-pocket" resources, mutual forebearance, and reciprocal buying) as well as possible procompetitive effects of conglomerate mergers (such as expanding toehold positions, economizing on certain administrative functions, and facilitating efficient resource allocation). The FTC Staff Study found these various arguments to be conjectural and, in an effort to resolve the issues, undertook a study of nine large conglomerates.

The Staff Study produced an essentially neutral verdict: neither anticompetitive nor procompetitive results are systematically associated with conglomerate merger activity. The main objection which the FTC Staff Study raises concerns financial reporting by conglomerates. Public assessment of conglomerate performance is made difficult by the failure to report on a divisional basis.

While greater disclosure of divisional performance seems to me feasible and has merit, I question whether the multidivisional model of conglomerate organization on which the Staff Study relies (1972, pp. 44-46) is correctly interpreted. Thus, the study notes that while changes in auditing were usually made after acquisition (1972, p. 50) and that new financing was usually arranged through conglomerate headquarters (1972, p. 53), both of which have a bearing on corporate control and overall resource allocation processes, few efforts were made to centralize the R & D, advertising, purchasing, and so forth, of the operating divisions (1972, p. 57). The FTC Staff Study concludes, correctly I think, that refusal to centralize this last group of functions is consistent with the multidivisional model of organization. But it then contends that, absent intervention in the operating affairs of the divisions, the possibility of efficiency improvements is seriously to be doubted (1972, p. 85). Indeed, they appear to be of the opinion that conglomerate synergism requires active involvement by the general management in operating affairs; accordingly, the multidivisional structure is held to be in "conflict with the synergism argument" (1972, p. 192).

Their discussion of new investment likewise warrants scrutiny. The FTC Staff Study takes the position that "really substantial improvements in productive efficiency would probably have to be accompanied by expenditures for new plant and equipment" (1972, p. 68). An attempt is therefore made to establish whether investments in acquired firms increased or decreased following the acquisition. While no significant pattern is detected, investment declines outnumbered increases (1972, pp. 69-72).

I submit that both the treatment of new investment and the discussion of the relations between operating involvement, synergy, and organization form are mistaken. With respect to investment, the question is not whether additional resources are invested in the acquired divisions, but rather whether resources are allocated among the divisions in favor of high yield activities. If some of the acquired firms are generating excessive cash flows, in relation to their investment opportunities, while others are not generating enough, a mixture of increases and decreases is to be expected — which is what they report.

The discussion of operating involvement, synergy, and organization form seems to miss entirely the proposition that the conglomerate is to be regarded as a miniature capital market. Synergy in a conglomerate is not mainly attributable to the headquarters supply of consulting services to the divisions. More important are the internal incentive and resource allocation changes that the M-form conglomerate is able to effectuate. Operating involvement is emphatically *not* the device by which synergy is mainly realized.[31]

5. Concluding Remarks

A transactional interpretation of the conglomerate, in which the limitations of capital markets in corporate control respects are emphasized, reveals that conglomerate firms (of the appropriate kind) are not altogether lacking in social purpose. If maintaining the market for corporate control is thought generally to be beneficial, if reallocating resources away from lower to favor projects with higher net private returns also generally yields social net benefits as well, and if the antitrust enforcement agencies are to maintain a tough policy with respect to horizontal and vertical mergers, a policy of moderation with respect to conglomerate mergers is indicated. In particular, public policy with respect to conglomerate acquisitions should be focused on (1) mergers where potential competition is meaningfully impaired, and (2) mergers by giant firms not accompanied by a spinoff (or other means of disposing) of comparable assets.

Maintaining a market for mergers also has a bearing on the incentives of individual inventors and small firms to engage in early stage research and development activity. The argument here is elaborated in the chapter which follows.

31. Since the FTC Staff Study explicitly relies on my treatment of the multidivisional structure and of conglomerate organization [Williamson (1970)] for their discussion of internal organization, their treatment of conglomerate synergy is somewhat curious.

10. Market Structure in Relation to Technical and Organizational Innovation

The present chapter differs from the earlier ones in two respects. First, although efficiency and progressiveness are by no means independent, there is a difference in the emphasis of each — particularly when new product (as contrasted with new process) considerations are introduced. Earlier chapters are mainly cost oriented; progressiveness is featured here. Second, unlike previous chapters, an effort is made to survey an extensive empirical literature and to put it in perspective.

But there are also strong connections between this chapter and the earlier ones. The internal organizational failures orientation of Chapter 7 is maintained, only here the emphasis is on innovative performance. Also, the notion that firms and markets coexist in symbiotic equilibrium, with internal and market modes being both alternative and complementary means for organizing technologically separable activities, is further developed. Third, the notion of organizational innovation that was introduced in Chapter 8 is extended here. Finally, the organizational failures framework is brought to bear on still another industrial organization issue.

The literature on technical innovation and market structure[1] is surveyed in Sections 1 and 2. While it would simplify policy issues greatly if it could be shown that market structure and technical innovation were tightly linked, this appears not to be the case. An "optimum" degree of competition, which holds across all industries and all times, for promoting technical progress

1. Scherer's excellent treatment of technical innovation (1970, Chap. 15) covers much of the same material and comes to many of the same conclusions that are reached here. The present chapter differs from most prior works in that it includes a discussion of organizational innovation and attempts to develop a systems view that embraces both technical and organizational innovation.

This chapter is a variant of a previously published paper which Donald Turner coauthored.

cannot be established by appeal to either theoretical argument or empirical analysis. Organizational innovation, which is a relatively neglected aspect of the innovation question, is examined in Section 3. An attempt to draw organizational and technical aspects together in a systems framework is made in Section 4.

1. Technical Innovation and Market Structure: The Conventional Dichotomy

The discussion of technical innovation begins with an examination of the conventional dichotomy. Although this requires that a good deal of old material be covered, it seems essential that this matter be put to rest at the outset. This completed, a series of recent refinements to the technical innovation-market structure issue are then considered in Section 2.

However complex the subject matter under consideration may appear to be, there is always a possibility that the underlying structure is fundamentally simple. The trick is to cut through to the heart of the matter. Once this is discovered, all else falls easily into place. What I characterize here as the conventional dichotomy — that, depending on one's lights, the market structure most conducive to technical progress involves large size and monopoly power or, alternatively, small size and competition — aspires to do this. Unfortunately, the effort in this instance must be judged a failure.

1.1 The Arguments

Relations between market structure and economic performance are rarely simple, albeit that straightforward applications of price theory sometimes suggest otherwise. This is especially true when the performance measure in question is technological progress. Although Arrow has shown that the incentive to innovate is greater under competition than under monopoly (1962, pp. 619-622), this assumes that the appropriability of the potential gains attributable to the innovation is not significantly greater under monopoly. Also, Demsetz argues that Arrow's demonstrated incentive differential fails when appropriate standardization techniques are employed (1969, pp. 16-19). Scherer's more recent study (1967) of the effects of rivalry on R & D, mainly in the context of a duopoly model, concludes that rivalry generally favors R & D—but even this is qualified and, considering the special nature of the model, scarcely dispositive. Kamien and Schwartz (1974) are intrigued by the possibility that there exists an optimum degree of rivalry. They show that an intermediate degree of competition appears often to promote a faster development rate, but the relation between their competition variable and market structure is unclear and the assumptions of the model are rather restrictive in any case.

The upshot is that there does not appear to be a great deal of useful policy advice to be gleaned from existing theoretical studies of the relations linking market structure with technical progress.[2] Consider, therefore, the conjectures offered by interested observers.

I count here as potentially relevant those observations relating market structure to technical progress that have occurred since antitrust first became a social issue. Consider in this connection the statement of Marshall who, speaking in 1890, expressed the view that differential progressiveness was "the main reason for regarding with some uneasiness any tendency . . . towards [the] consolidations of business" (Pigou, 1956, p. 279). He went on to observe that while the employment of scientific specialists may occasionally place the large firm at a technical advantage, "these advantages count for little in the long run in comparison with the superior inventive force of a multitude of small undertakers" (Pigou, 1956, p. 280). In 1897 Hadley took a similar position (1897, p. 383) :

> The tendency of monopoly to retard the introduction of industrial improvement is . . . a more serious thing than its tendency to allow unfair rates. This aspect of the matter has hardly received proper attention. We have been so accustomed to think of competition as a regulator of prices that we have lost sight of its equally important function as a stimulus to efficiency. Wherever competition is absent, there is a disposition to rest content with old methods, not to say slack ones. In spite of notable exceptions this is clearly the rule.

Subsequent developments in competitive theory were, as Stigler points out, much concerned with the refinement of static efficiency analysis (1956, pp. 270-271). Attention to the progressiveness dimension correspondingly wanted. Partly as a reaction to this almost exclusive focus on static resource allocation, and partly as a result of his own interest in economic development, Schumpeter countered with what might be characterized as the alternative hypothesis. Like Hadley, he took the position that the kind of competition that counts is attributable to "the new commodity, the new technology, the new source of supply, the new type of organization (the largest-scale unit of control for instance) — competition which commands a decisive cost or quality advantage and which strikes not at the margins of the profits and the outputs of the existing firms but at their foundations and their very lives" (1942, p. 84). Unlike Hadley, however, this emphasis on dynamics led Schumpeter to conclude that it is *transient* monopoly, not competition, that is a prerequisite to progress (1942, Chap. 8).[3]

---

2. An earlier treatment is that of Fellner's (1951). Usher (1964) considers the new product innovation issue but draws no implications on the effect of market structure (other than to note that the private incentives of monopolists to innovate are less than the social).

3. For a more sophisticated interpretation of Schumpeter, including a contrast between the earlier Schumpeter of *The Theory of Economic Development* with *Capitalism, Socialism and Democracy*, see Phillips (1971, pp. 4-15).

Neither Hadley nor Schumpeter was especially precise regarding a specification of the monopolistic condition; Schumpeter was especially ambiguous in this respect. As Stigler notes, Schumpeter regards "every departure from perfect competition in a stationary economy . . . [as] monopoly, and this is why it is so easy to show that monopoly is necessary to progress" (1956, p. 272). Thus, while restoring attention to the progressiveness dimension in a useful way, Schumpeter left the matter of the optimum organization of industry somewhat unclear.

In what might be characterized as the neo-Schumpeterian position, this structural ambiguity is largely overcome: large size and structural monopoly are said to be most conducive to technical progress. Galbraith expresses it as follows (1952, p. 91; emphasis added):

> . . . a benign Providence*. . . has made the modern industry of a *few large firms* an almost perfect instrument for inducing technical change. It is admirably equipped for financing technical development. Its organization provides strong incentives for undertaking development and putting it into effect . . . .
>
> There is no more pleasant fiction than that technical change is the product of the matchless ingenuity of the small man forced by competition to employ his wits to better his neighbor. Unhappily, it is a fiction. Technical development has long since become the preserve of the scientist and the engineer. Most of the cheap and simple inventions have, to put it bluntly, been made.

This view, hereinafter referred to as the Galbraithian hypothesis, has been expressed (both before and since) in a variety of ways [see the citations in Jewkes, Sawers, and Stillerman (1959, pp. 29-31)]. It is, in my experience, the one that prevailed among most undergraduates in the 1960's. One might characterize it as a truth that every schoolboy knows; it may even qualify as the conventional wisdom. But this may be attributable more to the effectiveness of the media ("progress is our most important product"; "better things for better living. . . through chemistry," and so forth) than to the empirical (nonfictional) accuracy of the argument.

1.2 The Evidence

I deal here strictly with the matters of how R & D expenditures vary in relation to large size and with the influence of industrial concentration on innovative performance. Large size does not necessarily imply monopoly power, and in this sense might be distinguished from a pure monopoly theory of innovation. There is, however, a tendency for large absolute size to be associated with large relative size, and the Galbraithian position seems to be that large absolute and relative size,[4] individually and in combination, can be expected to yield greater innovative performance. Consider the

4. Although relative size is an incomplete measure of market power, it is surely one of the more important structural dimensions. It is, at once, the structural measure most commonly

evidence on absolute size as it bears on the conventional dichotomy first.

Based on data reported by the National Science Foundation, which considers three size classes of firms (below 1,000 employees, 1,000-5,000 employees, and over 5,000 employees), there is a clear tendency for firms in the largest of these three-size classes to spend more on R & D as a percentage of sales (Nelson, Peck, and Kalachek, 1967, p. 67). This is, however, an insufficiently fine basis for classification: virtually all the firms in the *Fortune* 500 largest industrials series had over 5,000 employees in 1968; General Motors numbered its employees at 750,000 in that year. A breakdown within the over 5,000 category is thus indicated if the absolute size question is to be dealt with in policy relevant terms. Hamberg's investigation of the relation between R & D intensity and firm size among 387 firms selected from the *Fortune* list of the 500 largest industrials in 1960 is useful for this purpose. Taking these corporations as a group and correlating the ratio of R & D employment/total employment against size measured as total employment, a positive, significant correlation was obtained. When total assets are used to measure size, however, a negative, insignificant result was reported (1966, p. 58).

A major problem in interpreting these results nevertheless arises in that the technological potential to innovate differs greatly across industries. Therefore, Hamberg distributed these firms across seventeen two- and three-digit industry groups. He then investigated the elasticity of R & D employment in relation to size (measured as total employment or total assets in each industry) by obtaining least-squares estimates to the regression equation $Y_{ij} = a_j X_{ij}^{B_j}$ (where the subscripts i, j refer to the firm and industry respectively, Y is R & D employment, X measures size, and the estimated value of B_j is the relevant elasticity). Elasticity values greater than unity favor the Galbraithian hypothesis, while values less than unity favor the competitive version. Hamberg generally obtained elasticity values greater than one, although often these were not statistically significant (1966, pp. 60-63). Overall, he concluded, "a case can be made for the hypothesis that research intensity . . . increases with size among the larger firms in but three industries" (1966, p. 61).

Comanor performed a roughly parallel set of tests using a somewhat finer industry classification than Hamberg (1967, pp. 640-643). Among the twenty-one industries in his sample, six had elasticities that exceeded unity (but none was statistically significant) while fifteen had elasticities less than unity (of which seven were statistically significant). He attributed the

---

referred to in the literature, the most widely available in the statistics, and the most often considered by the antitrust agencies and the courts. Any decisive tendency for either the competitive or the Galbraithian hypothesis to be supported by the data should, presumably, be detected with a simple concentration ratio characterization of market power. I therefore consider successively the large size and concentration ratio relations.

differences in his results and Hamberg's mainly to the broader industry classifications used by Hamberg (1967, p. 641). The true relation, apparently, is sufficiently close on this issue that modest changes in industry definitions yield different results.

Mansfield approached the matter by posing a somewhat different question. He examined R & D expenditures (expressed as a percent of sales) of the very largest firms in relation to their large but not giant-sized rivals in the chemical, petroleum, drug, steel, and glass industries. "Except for the chemical industry, the results provide no evidence that the largest firms in these industries spent more on R & D, relative to sales, than did somewhat smaller firms. In the petroleum, drug, and glass industries, the largest firms spent significantly less; in the steel industry, they spent less but the difference was not statistically significant" (1968, pp. 94-95). Scherer also found that, among a wider class of industries, the R & D intensity of the largest firms did not usually exceed that of their upper middle-sized rivals. He observed that the data do not support the contention that "gigantic scale is . . . an essential condition for vigorous industrial research and development activity: . . . bigness may indeed be a stifling factor" (1965, p. 265).

Roughly, these results are displayed graphically in Figure 8, where R & D intensity is plotted on the ordinate and relative (not absolute, since the comparisons are strictly intra-industry) firm size on the abscissa. Assuming that R & D expenditures experience constant returns to scale, one could, based on the relations shown in Figure 8, make a case for the proposition that the relative contribution to progressiveness is greatest among upper middle-sized firms. Giant size, however, is not obviously warranted on this criterion and might instead be actively resisted. [5]

Consider now the influence of industrial concentration, expressed generally as a four-firm concentration ratio, on R & D expenditures. Hamberg (1966, Chap. 4) and Horowitz (1962) reported a positive correlation between R & D expenditures and industrial concentration. Scherer discovered a much weaker but slightly positive association (1965, pp. 1119-1121). Kendrick concluded from an examination of Terleckyj's data that there is no significant correlation between productivity changes and industrial concentration (1961, p. 170). Stigler detected "hints that industries with lower concentration had higher rates of technological progress" (1956, p. 278),

---

5. Scherer concluded his survey of the evidence with the remark that "among the largest 500 or so U.S. industrial corporations, increases in size do not as a rule contribute positively to the intensification of R & D inputs or inventive outputs, and in more cases than not, giant scale has a slight to moderate stultifying effect. The most technically progressive American firms appear, with the possible exception of chemicals and petroleum producers, to be those with sales of less than $ 200 million at 1955 price levels" (1970, p. 361). Adams's study of the French R & D experience concludes that "bigness is not a prerequisite for progressiveness" (1970, p. 408).

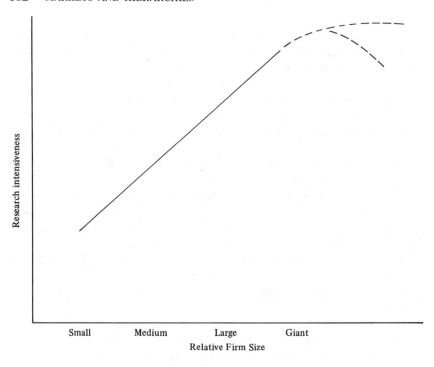

Figure 8

while I, using Mansfield's data, found a negative correlation between the proportion of innovations introduced by the four largest firms and industrial concentration (1965). (The last is strictly a small-numbers result and allows for productivity as well as expenditure effects.)

Mansfield's is probably the best balanced view of this matter. He considered diffusion (the rate at which an innovation, once introduced, is adopted by other firms in the industry) as well as the proclivity to innovate. He fould that while greater concentration may be associated with a lower rate of diffusion (1968, p. 217), overall — except, possibly, for innovations that require a large amount of capital — "there is no statistically significant relationship between an industry's concentration and its estimated rate of technological change" (1968, p. 245).

I conclude, as did Nelson, Peck, and Kalachek, that the Galbraithian position "is somewhat exaggerated" (1967, p. 67), or as Mansfield put it, the "available evidence does not seem to support this hypothesis" (1968, p. 245). This does not, however, imply that the competitive alternative is endorsed. Progressiveness performance is too complex to be adequately characterized by either of these polar extremes. At the very least, important exceptions to the proposition that competitive market structures favor progressiveness need to be admitted.

2. Technical Innovation and Market Structure: Refinements

Some of the major qualifications and refinements that have emerged from recent research on the technical progress question are considered here. Essentially the argument comes down to this: Research and development is not one large, undifferentiated whole. Distinctions with respect to productivity, major versus minor inventions, other market structure dimensions, research responsiveness, basic versus applied research, large, complex versus "normal" R & D, and invention versus development would appear to be especially relevant.

It goes without saying that if one chooses among the data virtually anything can be "proven." But however useful conspicuous observations may be as a basis for formulating hypotheses, they constitute a hazardous basis for claiming generality. Bell Labs, General Electric, and Du Pont each possess impressive research facilities and personnel, but they do not, apparently, represent average tendencies. (For studies in contrast, consider Western Union and U.S. Steel.) Only a second glance at the statistics is sufficient to dispel any initial impression that the concentration and progressiveness conditions observed in a few glamorous industries are representative (Jewkes et at., 1959, pp. 167-73). The studies reported above reinforce this judgement. Possibly, however, a more refined treatment of the data will better support the Galbraithian position.

2.1 Productivity

If, over some range, there are scale economies (or diseconomies) associated with R & D, the productivity of R & D will vary with expenditures accordingly. Recall in this connection the intra-industry results which show that absolute firm size and absolute R & D spending move together. As shown in Figure 8, however, R & D *intensity* (expressed as a percentage of sales) is observed to level off, if not turn down, as firm size increases. But might the productivity of R & D programs in very large firms be greater than are those of their smaller rivals, in which case this latter relation is explained by scale economies associated with R & D?

The evidence, though not extensive, does not support this proposition. If productivity can be judged by patents issued per dollar R & D expenditure, the performance of the very largest firms in most industries is somewhat below that of their large but somewhat smaller rivals (Scherer, 1965b). Similar results, using a somewhat more refined measure of productivity, albeit for a smaller sample of industries, are reported by Mansfield. "When the size of R & D expenditures is held constant, increases in the size of firm are [usually] associated with decreases in inventive output" (1968, p. 216). Comanor found that diseconomies of scale in the pharmaceutical industry were encountered at even moderate firm size (1965, p. 190). The Galbraithian hypothesis, regarded as a statement of average tendencies, evidently derives little comfort from productivity considerations.

2.2 Major Versus Minor Inventions

Just as the productivity of R & D is a relevant distinction, so is the economic importance of inventions. If the importance varies systematically by the source of the invention, the weight to be assigned to the several sources of invention needs appropriately to be adjusted.

Hamberg has set forth and evaluated the hypothesis that large, industrial laboratories are apt to account for a larger proportion of minor than they are of major inventions (1963). As he observes, the hypothesis is not altogether original. Some of the reasons why such a relation might be expected, however, had previously been neglected. Both economic and organizational factors are adduced in favor of the hypothesis.

Basic to the argument is the proposition that major new inventions are usually high-risk activities. The large corporation may be structurally and/or constitutionally ill-suited to bear these. But then a firm need not itself be the source of major, new inventions in order to participate in the commercial development of such items: it may be able to buy into successful new developments originated elsewhere — an aspect of the argument developed in Section 4, below. That it is not especially well-suited to perform high-risk inventive research is, necessarily, a comparative rather than an absolute proposition. It relies mainly on the contention that large organizations, business or otherwise, experience internal organizational failures. Moreover, while claims that the large firm possesses offsetting financial advantages in relation to small firms have merit, the argument requires, at least with respect to high-risk activities, certain qualifications.

Hamberg takes the position that "The one feature of large business size and monopoly power that appears to carry potential weight is associated with the usually large — absolute — profits of the big monopolistic firms as a source of funds to finance research and innovation" (1966, p. 43). Small firms, perhaps especially successful ones, tend often to find that internal resources are simply inadequate to meet their growing financing needs. These internal financing advantages of large, established firms are apt to be reinforced by their superior access to debt financing. Thus, whereas the established firm has tangible assets and a demonstrated operating capability to offer as security, the small firm requiring research funding has only an uncertain prospect of success to offer. Debt financing for the small firm in these circumstances is not apt even to be feasible.

Internal and debt financing do not, however, exhaust the sources of possible funding for inventive activity. The equity capital market, and in particular that part of the equity capital market that is referred to as venture capital (to emphasize its high-risk character), needs also be considered. Here small enterprises may actually enjoy a structural advantage. Investors in tax brackets for which high-risk capital gains investments are attractive may, because of inability to select among the investment projects in a large firm and appropriate the undiluted gains of risky activities, direct their funds to small, specialized enterprises instead. The financing disadvantages of the small firm for venture capital purposes may thus be less substantial than is often suggested.[6]

The organizational limitations of the large firm as a source of major, new inventions are attributable to its bureaucratic character. This matter is treated more extensively in the discussion of organizational failure in Section 4. Here a simple sketch of the argument is provided as it applies to inventive research. It relies in large part on the proposition that "in the large firm, the team system and an 'average man' mentality generally prevail" (Hamberg, 1963, p. 107). Hamberg cites the research views of the research coordinator of Standard Oil of Indiana, Daniel P. Barnard: "We find the self-directed individual being largely replaced by highly organized team attack in which we employ many people who, if left entirely to their own devices, might not be research-minded. In other words, we hire people to be curious as a group. . . . We are undertaking to *create* research capability by the sheer pressure of money" (1963, p. 107).

Such an approach to research places a high premium on harmony. An emphasis on research results develops which tends to favor support for short-reach programs (Hamberg, 1963, pp. 109-110). As Jewkes, Sawers, and Stillerman point out, such attempts at organization may threaten the spontaneity which is often regarded as vital to a successful research atmosphere (1959, pp. 132, 182-183). Creative scientists and inventors may be driven to locate elsewhere.

So much for the arguments, what does the evidence support? What, historically, have been the sources of invention? What is the professional standing of corporation scientists? What types of research are most commonly undertaken in the large corporation?

---

6. For a somewhat casual but nevertheless interesting discussion of the venture capital market, see Main (1973). He distinguishes between adventure capital and venture capital, and indicates that the former consists essentially of the entrepreneur's own savings and the support of family and friends. Venture capitalists, by contrast, come in at the next stage, "when the entrepreneur has something to show" (Main, 1973, p. 72).

For a discussion of the venture capital sources for a series of recent new ventures, see the *Fortune* magazine series during 1973 on "The Innovators." An interesting variant is brought out in the sixth article of this series, in which General Electric spins off and retains partial ownership in new ventures which originate in G.E. laboratories (Sabin, 1973). This is discussed further in Section 4.

Hamberg's survey of the sources of invention makes it evident that major new developments have historically (and, although perhaps in somewhat reduced degree, continue to) come preponderately from sources outside the large corporation. Grosvenor, in a study published in 1929, found that only twelve of seventy-two major inventions made since 1889 had originated in industrial laboratories. Jewkes, Sawers, and Stillerman traced the origins of sixty-one major inventions of the twentieth century, most of which occurred between 1930 and 1950. Of these, twelve could be attributed to the laboratories of large corporations, thirty-three were the work of independent inventors, five were from laboratories of small firms, and the remainder were unclassifiable. Hamberg examined twenty-seven inventions made during the period 1946-1955. Seven were the products of large industrial laboratories, twelve were from independent inventors, and the remaining were from small firms, universities, and an agricultural experiment station (1963, p. 96; 1966, p. 16). Schmookler's (1957) study of patent statistics over the period 1950-1957 disclosed that between fifty to sixty percent of the recent inventions were from inventors working outside the organized research groups of the corporate industrial laboratories. Although the relative and possibly absolute importance of the independents has been gradually declining (Nelson et al., 1967, p. 57), the base is too large and the rate of decline too slow for the inventive influence of this group to pass quickly to extinction.[7]

The suggestion that the corporate research atmosphere is not calculated to attract eminent scientists also finds support (Hamberg, 1963, p. 108; Scherer, 1970, p. 354). This is not necessarily a particularly surprising or even undesirable result—especially in view of the systems approach to the innovation question that is advanced in Section 4. It suffices here to point out that, as a matter of perspective, industrial scientists in the large corporation are not, typically, ten feet tall. Again, there are occasional exceptions, but the focus here is on average tendencies. If smaller firms are able merely to attract competent engineers and scientists, they are not at a serious talent disadvantage.

7. It has been suggested that the relations between large and small firms with respect to major, new inventions is a statistical artifact: The large firms tends to decompose the invention process into a series of stages and, as a result, reports numerous small developments. Cumulatively these are properly considered major developments, but the records fail to report this activity as such.

I am somewhat at a loss as to how adequately to respond to this argument. To some extent it may be correct. To the degree that it attempts to restore improvement innovations to a position of importance, I am sympathetic but believe that this can be handled separately (see below). For the most part, however, the procedures employed by Grosvenor, Jewkes et al., and Hamberg do not appear to be seriously biased in the fashion suggested. These investigators took what were generally recognized to be major inventions and traced their origins. Internal decomposition processes should not seriously influence these results. The same cannot be said, however, of Schmookler's treatment of patent statistics. Here the argument has more potential bite.

Consider finally the research emphasis of industrial laboratories. Nelson, Peck, and Kalachek conclude: "Outside defense and space-related R & D . . . and possibly some segments of the civilian electronics and chemical industries, the bulk of corporate R & D is modest design improvement work not reaching very far—the type of work that results in yearly changes in automobile design, gradual improvements in the automaticity, speed, and capacity of machine tools, rather than radically new products and processes" (1967, p. 54). It might not be unfair to characterize industrial R & D as mainly mundane rather than exotic, contrary to the conventional wisdom. Indeed, the majority of what gets reported as R & D expenditure is concentrated in the production process—including design, engineering, and tooling, as well as manufacturing and marketing startup costs (Mansfield, 1968, p. 106). A study by Mansfield and Hamberger concluded that "the bulk of R & D carried out by large corporations is relatively safe and aimed at fairly modest advances in the state of the art" (Mansfield, 1969, p. 66). Even in a corporation as large and competent as Du Pont, of the major inventions that it implemented from 1920 to 1949, many more, proportionately, of the improvement inventions than of the new product inventions were originated in Du Pont's laboratories (Mueller, 1962, pp. 342-343).

Although this may appear to relegate the large corporations to a position of secondary importance, this is not intended. For one thing, an improvement emphasis by the large firms may represent a rational allocation of resources in a systems sense. For another, while there may be a "good deal of truth" in the improvement hypothesis, "technical change in many industries may be due in considerable measure to the cumulative effect of many 'improvement' inventions" (Mansfield, 1968, p. 93). Put differently, technical change in some industries *is* mainly of the improvement sort. Finally, in some industries and for certain types of research, the reported average tendencies between new product and improvement innovations do not hold. This is discussed, below.

That, in principle, the distinction between major and minor inventions is important would be freely conceded by most of those who have been involved in the industrial R & D controversy. That, in most industries, the large industrial research laboratory appears mainly to be a source of improvement inventions and that other sources play so substantial a role in the major new development aspects of research comes as some surprise to many—including myself. Not that small firms and inventors would be expected to play no role in this activity, but that they are so important is almost astonishing.

2.3 Other Dimensions of Market Structure

With the exception of concentration, the above discussion runs exclusively in terms of absolute size. The focus, thus, is mainly on the bigness rather than the monopoly claims of the neo-Schumpeterian hypothesis. If, however, the latter is also to be addressed, the frame of reference needs to be expanded. Relevant to a judgment of the influence of monopoly on innovation would be the condition of entry and changes in relative shares. These in turn may be influenced by such matters as product differentiation, extent of vertical integration, and the degree to which parallel action is observed.

Scherer concludes that the evidence from case studies supports the view that actual and potential competition, present at least in moderate degree, stimulate technical progress, "both as direct sources of innovation and as spurs to existing industry members" (1970, p. 377). This appears to be a majority opinion. Studies by Comanor (1967) and Phillips (1966) address other aspects of market structure, but the results have not been wholly conclusive or the welfare implications obvious. Perhaps for the present it is sufficient to rest on the observation that, on the average, concentration does not appear to have a significant influence on innovation and that, in a systems sense, an active market in inventions favors progressiveness. The latter is considered further in Section 3.

2.4 Research Responsiveness

Two questions are raised by the matter of research responsiveness. First, are oligopolistically organized industries more adept at exploiting their technological potential? Second, are there science related industries which, by reason of the opportunities for commercial development afforded by their close connections with a sophisticated external science base, stand apart as exceptions from the general argument? Consider the oligopoly argument first.

Ideally, one would like to test whether there is any systematic relation between market structure and the proclivity of an industry to take advantage of its technological opportunities. This would require that realized achievement be compared with technological potential. Characterizing the latter in a sufficiently precise way to make meaningful comparisons does not, however, appear to be feasible. Nevertheless, those who espouse the case for oligopoly on account of its superior progressiveness properties appear to rely in large part on the proposition that oligopoly—by reason of the rich network of interfirm relations among the member firms (in which both offensive and defensive research considerations play a role)—induces more complete exhaustion of an industry's innovative potential. Even if only indirect evidence can be brought to bear on the argument, this presumably would be useful.

If, as seems plausible, the richness of oligopolistic interaction should usually be strongest among the largest firms in the industry, then oligopolistically induced proclivities to innovate ought to be evident by comparing the relative research performance of the largest firms in less concentrated industries with those with greater concentration. The largest firms in the more concentrated industries ought to perform relatively better. The data, though limited, contradict the argument (Williamson, 1965). Scherer contends that there is "considerable evidence" that dominant firms are "slow innovators but aggressive followers" (1970, p. 371). For the present it would appear to be judicious to regard the oligopolistic interaction hypothesis at best to be unproven and probably doubtful.

Consider now the possibility that in certain science based industries, market structure is the outcome of at least partly exogenous technological change. Phillips is the leading exponent of this view. He argues that the adaptations by firms which operate in an environment in which a "related science creates more or less continuous opportunities for innovation" can alter market structure, with the result that only a few successful firms survive (1970, p. 15). He makes a compelling case for this in the commercial airline industry (1970). Default and stochastic market failure considerations not unlike those discussed in Chapter 11, below, help to explain his results.[8]

There is, more generally, broad agreement that the technological opportunities in the chemical and electrical industries are greater than in the mechanically based industries (Scherer, 1965b, pp. 1100, 1121; Nelson et al., 1967, pp. 40-43). Also, Nelson, Peck, and Kalachek observe that "science-based inventions have been the major factor differentiating the products and processes of the twentieth from the nineteenth centuries" (1970, p. 40). This subset of industries is thus of special significance in assessing the market structure-innovation issues. Do such industries display quite different innovation in relation to firm size characteristics than come through from the average tendencies reported earlier?

The matter, unfortunately, has not been extensively studied. Casual references to what is often referred to as the "chemical exception" seem to suggest that certain industries do violate the usual rules, and it will be recalled that Mansfield did find that the largest firms in the chemical industry spent more on R & D, relative to sales, than did somewhat smaller firms (1968, p. 94). Judging from patent statistics, however, Scherer reports: "For both chemicals (with stone, clay, and glass) and electrical equipment, there may be slightly increasing returns up to sales of roughly $500 million, but beyond that point a definite flattening out of the patenting function is evident" (1965b, p. 1110). What would seem to be required really, is a series of intensive industry studies — such as Phillips' study of the commercial airline

8. Thus, Phillips concludes: "The risks that firms face in a rapidly changing technological environment have been illustrated. Some of the manufacturers erred by failing to develop new aircraft types which technological changes were making possible. Others erred by attempting types which, except with enormous development costs, were not techically feasible. A few — and only a few — succeeded in avoiding these mistakes and, thus, in maintaining a position in the market" (1970, p. 127).

industry—of the potentially exceptional cases. Which industries genuinely display exceptional tendencies, and what are the limits of the argument?

2.5 Basic Versus Applied Research

While rarely explicit, the suggestion is often made that much of industrial research, especially the research conducted by the larger companies, can appropriately be designated as basic research. In a gross sense at least, this view must be rejected. Industrial R & D in 1961 was predominantly development (seventy-eight percent) and applied research (eighteen percent), with basic research accounting for only four percent of the total (Nelson et al., 1967, p. 55). Although large firms are more apt to sponsor basic research than their smaller rivals, major in-house basic research occurs in only a few industries: eighty-three percent was attributable to six industries, with four of these (chemicals, electrical equipment and electronics, aerospace, and petroleum) accounting for over seventy percent (Nelson et al., 1967, p. 56). This raises again the science based exception question considered above.

Lest the tail wag the dog, one should, presumably, regard arguments that favor big business on account of differential basic research propensities with caution. This is not to say that the argument lacks merit in certain of the science based industries which, as pointed out above, have had a disproportionate impact on twentieth-century life styles. But the argument does not appear to warrant great weight when applied across the board; a discriminating attitude with respect to basic research is thus indicated. Even within the science based subset, giant size is not clearly required.

The study by Mansfield and Hamburger of the R & D programs of twenty-two major firms in the chemical and petroleum industries bears on this matter. They found that although the "largest firms in the sample devote a larger proportion of their R & D budget to more basic. more risky, and longer term projects than their smaller competitors . . . the differences between the largest firms and firms one-half their size are seldom large, if they exist at all" (Mansfield, 1969, p. 71).[9] Thus, even in industries which, in a comparative sense, are known to direct a high percentage of R & D expenditures to basic research, giant size does not appear to favor basic research support of unusual proportions.

---

9. Lest the argument be interpreted as a strong contradiction to the suggestion advanced earlier that large firms may not be especially well-suited to perform high-risk inventive research, note that: (1) the firms in the Mansfield-Hamberger study were all established enterprises of at least moderate size, so that the comparison is strictly limited; (2) the results refer to inputs rather than outputs; and (3) the chemical and petroleum industries may, by reason of their science based nature, qualify for inclusion in the exceptional subject.

2.6 Large, Complex Versus "Normal" R & D

The romantic notion that the large industrial research laboratory is typically engaged in basic research on major new product developments is frequently buttressed by claims that the imperatives of modern technology are such as to leave little opportunity for any but the very large firms to conduct research on the requisite scale.[10] The argument, apparently, is that the so-called chemical exception is becoming the rule. Although there may be some tendencies in this direction, these appear to be limited rather than general and, even where observed, are gradual. For those who take the position that the near term future is apt to be a simple extrapolation of the past, there appears to be little reason to expect that the relations reported above will soon be drastically upset.

There are, nevertheless, projects the size and complexity of which require unusual research resources. Examination of military and space R & D suggests that great absolute size may be necessary to support much of this research (Nelson et al., 1967, p. 53) — although a case can be made that some of this bigness is attributable to the choice of inferior research and contracting practices by the military services (Kaysen, 1963; Williamson, 1967). If, however, the prevailing approach to military R & D is taken as given, great size may be necessary adequately to support military R & D efforts. Private R & D also, occasionally, involves "complex multi-component systems or complicated chemical processes" for which great size is important (Nelson et al., 1967, p. 53).[11]

One should take care, however, lest the argument be inappropriately generalized. Atomic energy and Apollo programs are exotic and conspicuous, but they are not really typical. It is, moreover, interesting to note that the Apollo program was conducted not by a single, integrated contractor but by a series of independent corporations coordinated by NASA.[12] Although this may have been dictated partly by reasons of time pressure, the strategy can also be supplied with an underlying contractual rationale (Williamson, 1967). In any event, projects that require a large, complex R & D capability are less common in the private sector and would appear to constitute an identifiable subset — for which exceptions to the main

10. See the citation to Galbraith in the text above. Also his restatement in (1967); for other similar views see the citations in Jewkes et al. (1959, pp. 29-31).
11. As Jewkes, Sawers, and Stillerman note, large size is more apt to be an advantage for "empirical" inventions, which are common in the chemical process industries, than for "systematic" inventions, which are conceived as a system and are more characteristic in mechanical engineering (1959, pp. 164-165).
12. For a recent discussion of the task force approach to complex projects, illustrated by reference to the Apollo program, see Alexander (1969).

argument may be necessary — rather than the general case (current or prospective).

2.7 Invention Versus Development

The distinction between invention and development in the treatment of innovation will be considered in greater detail in Section 4. Suffice it here to point out that while modest resources are frequently sufficient to support invention and even early stage development work (Jewkes et al., 1959, pp. 210-212), later stage development often incurs much greater expense (Scherer, 1970, p. 356). Although giant size is rarely indicated on this account, large size may be. Individuals and small firms that engage in inventive and early stage development work may, therefore, eventually have to face the prospect of achieving large size if the innovation is to be brought successfully to completion. Firms that are already large and possess extensive research laboratories and supporting facilities presumably enjoy an advantage in the later stages. Thus, unless smaller firms can efficiently secure access — on their own or through market processes — to an equivalent capability, they may be deemed to experience serious innovative weaknesses.

3. Organizational Innovation and Market Structure

3.1 Economic Importance of Organizational Innovations

As the study of innovation goes, organizational innovation, by comparison with technical innovation, is a relatively neglected subject. Conceivably this is because, judged at least in economic terms, it is much less important. This is contradicted, however, by views such as Arrow's, who contends: "Truly among man's innovations, the use of organization to accomplish his ends is among both his greatest and his earliest" (1971, p. 224). In a similar vein, Cole has observed that "if changes in business procedures and practices were patentable, the contributions of business change to the economic growth of the nation would be as widely recognized as the influence of mechanical inventions or the inflow of capital from abroad" (1968, pp. 61-62). The organizational innovations to which Cole refers to include, in addition to the organization form changes treated in earlier chapters, refinements in cost accounting, work scheduling, personnel, collective bargaining procedures, and so forth. The patenting of such innovations would, at a minimum, have announcement effects. If, in addition, such patents could be enforced, their profitability potential could be better established.

That property rights, in the form of patents, on organizational innovations are not awarded is less attributable to problems of describing the patented organizational form or procedure, although this, too, can pose difficulties, than it is to problems of imitation and enforcement. Since it is impossible to tell, by monitoring output streams, what types of administrative procedures have been followed, detection would probably require on-site inspection. Also, inventing around such patents would be easy. Once the new structure or procedure has been disclosed and its merits proved, variants would be easy to devise. Lacking enforceability, the rights would be quite illusory.

In addition to these "defects" common to organizational innovations in general, the economic significance of organization form changes — which are of special interest to the study of firm and market structures — are especially difficult to assess. The initial response of rival firms and financial analysts to an organization form innovation is typically to disregard it. Partly this is because reorganization is a common reaction by firms that are experiencing adversity. Discerning whether the response is intended to eliminate accumulated bureaucratic deadwood, to buy time from the stockholders by giving the impression that corrective action has been taken, or, instead, represents a really fundamental change in structure that warrants more widespread attention is initially unclear. (It is noteworthy that the General Motors executives went to considerable effort in the 1920's to apprise the business community at large of the character and importance of the multidivisional structure which they had devised — but to little avail.)

Expressed in transaction cost terms, the problem is that opportunistic structural changes cannot easily be distinguished from fundamental ones because of information impactedness and bounded rationality. Given the incapacity (or high cost) of communicating about and abstractly assessing the importance of organizational changes, due partly to the fact that the language for characterizing organization form changes is rather primitive, the tendency is to wait and see how organizational changes manifest themselves in performance consequences. Inasmuch as performance is a function of many factors other than organizational structure alone, sorting this out is difficult. Accordingly, a long recognition lag between fundamental innovation and widespread imitation is common. Being conceptually less tractable, organization form innovations have received much less in the way of formal analysis than have technical innovations.

3.2 Market and Economy-wide Concentration Effects of Form Organization Form Changes

But while changes in the internal structure and control procedures in the firm have not received much quantitative analysis, it is not as though the implications of such developments have been altogether neglected by academics and other policy analysts. Changes in organization form are frequently associated with increases in the breadth and depth of economic activity performed within the firm and, where such effects obtain, often give rise to expressions of dismay.

Dismay is registered because such innovations are regarded as devices for realizing monopoly power. Schumpeter's early work on economic development suggested that organization form and monopoly were associated (1961, p. 66) —although the effect was not unidirectional; organizational innovations could either create or destroy monopoly. The connection between organization form and monopoly is somewhat less evident in his later work (1942, pp. 84-85), but the impression that organization form changes have competitive effects has persisted while recognition of their bidirectional nature has been supplanted by a tendency to regard such changes as mainly anticompetitive.

As the discussion in earlier chapters makes evident, vertical integration and multidivisionalization plainly can and sometimes do have anticompetitive purpose and effect. The principal motivation for and consequence of these innovations, however, has been to enhance efficiency. Although future organizational innovations may represent an effort to achieve monopoly power in a novel and subtle fashion, really fundamental organization form changes are apt to signal beneficial efficiency effects as well or instead.[13]

As had been indicated repeatedly, internal organization and market exchange can be usefully regarded as substitutes. Integration and diversification, viewed in this way, are usually matters of degree; pure cases of firms that are fully integrated or completely specialized, although possibly interesting, generally fall in the null set.

3.2.1 VERTICAL INTEGRATION AND CONCENTRATION

Partly the incentive for vertical integration is traceable to such institutional rules of the game as the practice of collecting sales taxes on market-mediated but not internal transactions. But vertical integration is mainly explained by the costs of writing and enforcing interfirm contracts that are avoidable, in large measure, by resorting to internal organization. That firms do not fully displace intermediate product markets is because internal organization, mainly for bureaucratic reasons, is also costly.[14] The arguments on both sides of this issue are already familiar from preceding chapters.

Vertical integration, by itself, has no immediate effect on market concentration at any stage. It may, however, be a means of mobilizing latent

---

13. Coase's remarks on the propensity of economists to impute monopoly properties to business practices which they do not understand are relevant in this regard (1972, p. 67).

14. As note 17 in Chapter 7 suggests, unionization sometimes discourages vertical integration. But the main limits to internal organization are of the bureaucratic distortion kind.

monopoly power (for example, by facilitating price discrimination) and can have eventual concentrating effects as well. The latter might obtain if, by foreclosing markets, entry were inhibited to any but a fully integrated supplier, thereby raising capital requirements.

Concentration can also result if vertical integration is used against rivals in a predatory manner. The circumstances in which vertical integration can be successfully used in these ways, however, are rather special. Except where vertical integration involves the combination of stages with nontrivial market shares in already concentrated industries, monopoly purpose is apt to be lacking or ineffectual. The integration of successive stages by already very large firms can, of course, lead to an increase in economy-wide concentration — but this raises large-size rather than market power issues.

3.2.2 MULTIDIVISIONALIZATION

Given the evident inability of the unitary form organization to deal with large size and complexity, it seems safe to predict that, but for the development of the multidivisional structure (or some comparable corporate form innovation), firms that had attained large size would have had their growth arrested. Smaller rivals that did not experience as severe coordination and control problems would, presumably, have grown relatively.[15] Diseconomies of large scale attributable to control loss experience would in this way have placed a limit on firm size; concentration of production would have been checked.

The multidivision form of organization, by overcoming many of these control loss conditions, permitted already large firms that adopted this structure to continue their growth — at least absolutely and, for many of them, relatively as well. In classical natural selection fashion (Friedman, 1953, p. 22), those that adopted the new form and realized the economies which it permitted prospered and acquired resources with which to expand. The initial impact of the multidivision structure can thus be judged to have increased industry concentration above what it otherwise would have been.

That its eventual effect has been to increase concentration (expressed in an industry rather than economy-wide basis) is less clear. A related and frequently more important consequence of divisionalization than mere magnification has been that it has facilitated diversification. Thus, although some of the firms that have adopted the multidivision structure have indeed maintained high product specialization ratios, many others have not. Hence, while the overall effect of the multidivision form innovation has been to increase feasible firm size, and in this way has permitted *economy-wide*

---

15. Thus, while Du Pont was unable in 1919 to make some of its new ventures break even, many of its smaller rivals were prospering (Chandler, 1966, p. 112). Had Du Pont been unable to solve its coordination and control problems, a relative decline in its market position could have been expected.

concentration to increase, its diversification consequences leave the effect on *industry* concentration uncertain.

There are, of course, important concentration influencing factors other than organization form to consider (Bain, 1968, Chap. 6). It is, nevertheless, interesting to note in this connection that adoption of the multidivision form of organization has been particularly common among large firms since World War II (Chandler, 1966), and that from 1945 to the present the major concentration increases have occurred on an economy-wide but not on an industry basis (Subcommittee on Antitrust and Monopoly, 1966, pp. 2-3; Bain, 1968, Chap. 5). This may be strictly coincidental, but the progressive adoption of the multidivision structure would appear to have been a contributing factor. Of greater relevance to the purposes of this chapter, however, is the systems impact (which, generally, has hitherto been neglected) of organization form changes as these relate to technical innovation.

4.   A Systems Approach

While there are important exceptions, the literature relating technical innovation to firm size and industry structure yields the following average tendencies: R & D expenditures (expressed in relation to firm size) are not usually greater and are often lower for the very largest firms in an industry by comparison with its large but somewhat smaller rivals; the productivity of research expenditures follows roughly the same pattern; industrial R & D is, preponderately, applied in nature, with a few large firms and a few industries offering partial exceptions; research conducted in most large industrial laboratories favors minor improvement inventions rather than major new inventions; the short-reach nature of most industrial research (military and space research and some chemical or other continuous process research constituting principal exceptions) does not require large-scale support.

Suppose, as a policy matter, that one is instructed to select a program that will enhance technical progressiveness and that the alternatives are either to encourage or discourage increases in the absolute and relative size of the largest firms in every industry. If the foregoing review is an accurate assessment of the situation (which assumes that the studies are unbiased), a preference for the giant-size discouragement program would not seem injudicious.

One might object that the policy options postulated are unnecessarily constrained. The survey of the evidence in Sections 1 and 2 describes central tendencies, but there are notable exceptions. In particular, the science based industries may warrant individual treatment. Considering that half of the research and development in the United States is publicly financed and that much of it goes to this science based subset, using budget money rather than antitrust policy as a means by which to achieve technical objectives in science based firms is both more direct and, arguably, more effective.[16]

Suppose that science based exceptions were made. One might then object that the policy options are underspecified with respect to other industries. What kinds of size encouragement and discouragement programs are contemplated? Since radical changes can be seriously disruptive, assume that only gradualist measures are intended; side effects attributable to extreme changes are thereby avoided. A more subtle objection might then be registered: the above review tends to regard the technical innovation question as a matter of optimum firm size, while in fact the innovation process ought to be more broadly conceived.

The last point is developed below with the assistance of a rudimentary statement of a systems approach to technical innovation. Possible breakdowns in the system are also considered. The argument is an application of market and organizational failures analysis to the special problems that technical innovation poses.

4.1 General

An efficient innovation system (for devising, developing, producing, and distributing new products and services) is the assigned objective. Although it is possible that innovation is an indecomposable process, it seems not implausible that a piecewise development by stages is feasible. The tendency in the technical innovation literature to focus on inputs and early stages of the innovation process has perhaps discouraged the development of a broader viewpoint. As Stigler has emphasized, however, invention is merely the first in a series of uncertain stages in the innovation process,[17] and the necessary expertise in bringing the process to completion (which includes not merely invention but also experimental development, market testing, and commercial production and distribution) may differ between stages

16. Indeed, some of the specialists in the technical progress area who commented on earlier versions of the manuscript questioned whether antitrust is an appropriate instrument to bring to bear on the technical change problem in any sector whatsoever.

17. A related, but somewhat more extreme, view is that invention is a largely autonomous activity and that the first stage of innovation is the perception of a latent market demand. Once this has been discovered, it is usually possible to find a hitherto unutilized invention that can be made, with appropriate development, to fill the need. Although occasionally this may be true, it does not seem typical. There is always in some sense a latent "need," say, for new, low cost materials to be substituted against extant, high cost items. But searching the new materials universe does not, by itself, yield nylon or polyester. To the extent, therefore, that the argument has merit, it almost certainly has to be delimited. I will proceed on the assumption that inventions themselves are usually the result of perceived market demands, which makes them an active or integral rather than passive aspect of the innovation process.

(Stigler, 1956, pp. 281-82). The necessary judgment, frequently, is not how to proceed but whether to proceed. A critical rejection mechanism for developments that lack essential marketability is needed as well as a capacity to bring feasible projects efficiently to completion.

The innovation process can conveniently, if arbitrarily, be divided into three stages: invention, development, and final supply.[18] Corresponding to each is a decision process that may be designated, respectively, as proposal, selection, and a composite process involving coordinated production and distribution. Assuming that innovation can meaningfully be decomposed in this way, the question to be addressed is whether, despite decomposability of the process, a single size or form of organization has optimum properties with respect to all stages. Alternatively, is there a *transfer process* that permits individual firms to specialize according to characteristic strengths, thereby to realize a larger total yield than would be possible were each required to take the process unassisted to completion? More generally, are there circumstances in which transfer is both feasible and advantageous but others which favor internal—that is, administrative (intrafirm) rather than market (interfirm) —processes instead?

The frequency with which transfer is observed to occur (Hamberg, 1966, p. 162, Jewkes et al., 1959, pp. 168, 186, Mansfield, 1968, p. 58) is, presumably, evidence favorable to the interfirm specialization argument. This raises the possibility that an optimum system need not include among its part any firms which, when the R & D process is regarded strictly in *intrafirm* terms (as is common, if not prevailing), would be considered individually optimal. Yet, many innovations do not go the transfer process route. This raises the question of what factors explain the coexistence of these two processes.

Among the conventional explanations for internal development are the following:

1. Efficient final supply for many innovations does not require great size. If small firms can easily bring innovations to completion unassisted, transfer is unnecessary.

2. The need for improvement, especially process improvement, innovations is apt to be more evident in firms that are already engaged in final supply. In many cases these will be the larger firms. To the extent that close cooperation with production and/or marketing personnel facilitates the accomplishment of such innovation activity, large firms will tend naturally to perform in-house research and development on these items.

3. Large firms may be induced for defensive purposes to support some minimum internal R & D effort; reliance on transfer is too risky.

---

18. For a somewhat different but nevertheless similar decomposition, see Scherer (1970, p. 350).

Often, it is alleged, these defensive incentives are greatest among large firms in oligopolistic industries.

So much for internal innovation. What explains transfer? If large firms can do everything that small firms can do and more, why should *any* innovations go the transfer process route? Probably the simplest explanation consistent with the "replication plus" argument is that small firms may, occasionally, strictly as a matter of chance, stumble upon an innovation for which they lack the capability to bring to completion. Transfer is dictated on this account.

But while such considerations permit the coexistence of internal and transfer processes to be qualitatively reconciled, the reported volume of transfer activity is too large to be accounted for so easily. Also, other reasons can be advanced for expecting innovation to follow the internal development route. Both organizational and market failures need to be examined in these connections.

Consider the three stage innovation process described (invention, development, efficient final supply) and isolate the stage at which the greatest size requirements are experienced. Assume, as is usually the case, that efficient final supply is the critical stage for determining minimum efficient scale. Does a firm of requisite final supply-size experience any disabilities in attempting itself to perform early stage functions as well?

Approaching the problem in this way focuses on what may be characterized as organizational failures. If these exist, additional reasons to expect the transfer process to operate may be discovered. A symmetrical treatment of these matters would also recognize the possibility of market failures. Are there factors that inhibit the transfer process from operating efficiently?

4.2 Organizational Limits of the Large Firm

As noted, economies of scale in production and distribution will, frequently, make large (but not often giant) size the preferred structure for efficient final supply. Large size may not, however, be necessary at either of the two earlier stages. The question that is addressed here is whether there are diseconomies attributable to defective decision-making and/or incentive processes that operate at the proposal and selection stages. Put differently, what prevents the large firm from replicating everything a series of small firms could perform and more?

The organizational limits of the large firm that are described below serve as affirmative incentives for the transfer process to operate. The argument assumes that there are no intermediate forms of organization in which large firms become part owners of small firms and in other respects provide management or technical assistance to small ventures. This not only simplifies the exposition but, for the most part, seems roughly to correspond with prevailing practices. (A recent organizational innovation at General Electric, called the "Technical Ventures Operation," represents a radical departure from this norm. It is discussed separately in Section 4.5, below. For the purposes of this section and the two sections which follow, I restrict the discussion to autonomous large- and small-firm operations.)

4.2.1 LIFE CYCLE CONSIDERATIONS

A general discussion of size-related and intrinsic limitational factors of internal organization is given in Chapter 7 and need not be repeated here. There are, however, particular limitations of internal organization that bear on technical innovation that are not included in the earlier discussion. Of special interest is the history dependency of a firm, which constrains the options available to it at any point in time. Among the "life-cycle" attributes of large organizations noted by Downs in his study of bureaucracy[19] are the following aging phenomena (1967, pp. 18-20, 96-101):

1. As bureaus grow older they encounter more situations and develop institutionalized rules for dealing with them when these recur. Although this may have desirable efficiency consequences in many circumstances, in others it serves to limit the bureau's range of response and, hence, its innovativeness.
2. When a bureau is first created, it is usually dominated by zealots. Zealots, however, tend not to be good administrators. As the bureau grows older and the need for efficient administration increases relatively, the zealots (who tend to be innovators) are displaced by administrators with more conservative orientations.[20]
3. Rapid rates of growth are difficult to sustain as absolute size becomes great. Thus, while successful small organizations in which growth is rapid offer numerous opportunities for individual advancement, promotion is less easy in the large bureaucracy. The more enterprising members of the large bureaucracy may thus be induced to locate elsewhere.

These effects are summarized in Downs' Law of Increasing Conservatism: *"All organizations tend to become more conservative as they get older, unless they experience periods of very rapid growth or internal turnover"* (1967, p. 20). Since innovation, in relation to production, tends to be untidy, innovation — which is a poorly structured, high-risk activity — may

---

19. Downs is mainly concerned with government bureaucracies, but large organizations of whatever sort can be expected to display the same characteristics, albeit, in the case of the business firm, in somewhat lesser degree.
20. The life cycle tendency of bureaucracies towards conservatism has also been remarked by Michels (1966).

not be an activity which the large, mature bureaucracy is constitutionally well-suited to handle.

4.2.2 VENTURE CAPITAL

The limitations of the large firm with respect to venture capital noted in Section 1, above might also be mentioned in this respect. Although these limitations may be more than offset by capital access advantages from more conventional sources, the point is that outside venture capital may be specifically earmarked for investment in high-risk inventive activities for which investor appropriability is substantial. Large firms, as usually constituted, are not calculated to attract such sources of funds. In circumstances where high mean-variance outcomes are favored, the risk pooling which the large (and particularly the diversified) corporation provides can simultaneously impair the investment attractiveness of these firms to venture capital suppliers.

4.2.3 BUREAUCRATIC COMMITMENT

In addition to the reasons given above, which relate mainly to the limitations of the large firm in relation to the proposal process, the large firm may also experience shortcomings with respect to its selection properties. Its error admission characteristics may be defective. From the standpoint of the career prospects of a bureaucrat, fixed costs are not sunk but need to be justified. As noted in Chapter 7, the decision to proceed frequently becomes a commitment to succeed, whatever the costs. Sequential decision-making procedures designed to permit project review on the merits may be overwhelmed by partisan appeals. A tendency to persist beyond judicious cutoff limits easily results.

4.2.4 ENTREPRENEURIAL INCENTIVES

Bureaucracies generally maintain close correspondence between hierarchical position and compensation. Such a relation can be predicted on sociological grounds (Simon, 1957) and, where the management of proven resources is involved, on economic grounds as well (Mayer, 1960). This may even suffice for some types of innovation, as the views of Daniel P. Barnard (research coordinator at Standard Oil of Indiana) cited in Section 2.2, above appear to suggest. But such incentives are poorly suited to satisfy the entrepreneurial appetites of individuals who are prepared to risk their personal savings and careers in pursuit of big stakes.

Were it that large firms could compensate internal entrepreneurial activity in ways approximating that of the market, the large firm need experience no disadvantage in entrepreneurial respects. Violating the congruency between hierarchical position and compensation appears to generate bureaucratic strains,[21] however, and is greatly complicated by the problem of accurately imputing causality. Where did the idea originate who discerned its commercial importance, who refined it, and so forth? Since sorting this out is inordinately difficult,[22] distributing rewards among those who participated will have highly arbitrary and possibly counter-productive qualities (in that it may elicit resentment and noncooperation on future ventures). Where, instead, innovations are successfully developed by small firms, the rewards accrue to those who have expressly assumed monetary risks and who have removed their careers from bureaucratic promotion ladders. Although the resulting imputations may sometimes be arbitrary,[23] they do not occasion bureaucratic dysfunctions of the types described above.

4.2.5   PARALLEL R & D

In principle, the large firm should constitute a superior instrument with which to conduct parallel R & D in comparison with a series of small firms. The reason for this is that it affords an opportunity to realize efficient information exchange and thereby eliminate inferior projects and wasteful duplication at an early point in time (Arrow, 1962b, p. 356). Markets would be vulnerable to opportunism were they to be used for such information exchange purposes. The difficulty is this: The value of information to a purchaser (or group of purchasers) is not known until he has the information, but once it is disclosed he has acquired it without cost (Arrow, 1962a, p. 615). Were it possible to extract self-enforcing commitments to the effect that "I promise to pay full valuation for all information disclosed," no problem would exist. But such promises are idly made. The seller, by reason of information impactedness (he does not know the true value to the buyer and can develop this only at great expense, if at all), is unable to enforce such terms.

Often, however, and perhaps usually, the large firm appears not to be able to support a genuine parallel R & D effort (Peck, 1962, p. 294). Its planning propensities may preclude this; however attractive adaptive, sequential decision-making may be in principle, bureaucrats frequently display a preference for comprehensive planning instead (Schlesinger, 1967, p. 189). Partly, this may reflect a lack of appreciation for the experi-

21. See the discussion of inside contracting in Chapter 6 and the discussion of incentive limits in Section 3 of Chapter 7.
22. Even if it were feasible, it would be very costly. Bounded rationality, opportunism, and information impactedness are all involved.
23. Stealing the ideas of others and commercializing on them is a chronic problem. Large firms often complain and sometimes sue former employees on the grounds that the basic idea belongs to and initial development costs were borne by the large firm from which the employee has opportunistically defected.

mental approach. But it may also be that it is difficult to assess internal competition on the mertis in a fully dispassionate way. Groups that are associated with projects that are to be phased out in favor of others are prone to press for project continuation and marshall political support on their behalf. (The discussions of project persistence biases and internal reciprocity arrangements in Chapter 7 are relevant in these connections.)

An organizational dilemma is thereby posed. The internal distortion biases of large firms which themselves sponsor parallel R & D projects are avoided by going to the market, but efficient information-sharing can hardly be expected among a series of small autonomous firms, each pushing its own R & D approach. An uncertain verdict is thus reached in assessing alternative modes of organization in parallel R & D respects.

4.3 Market Impediments to Transfer

Some of the leading reasons why large firms are poorly suited to sponsor early stage entrepreneurial activity have been sketched above. Some of the principal market impediments to transfer are considered here.

4.3.1 MORAL HAZARD

Stigler has observed: "It is only to be expected that, when a new kind of research develops, at first it will be conducted chiefly as an ancillary activity by existing firms . . . [but eventually] we may expect the rapid expansion of the specialized research laboratory, selling its services generally. These specialized laboratories need not be in the least inferior to 'captive' laboratories" (1956, p. 281). But parity in the technical sense to which Stigler refers does not assure parity in a contractual sense. Assigning R & D to outside research organizations may, because of inherent task uncertainty, pose risk-sharing problems which, contractually, are not easily resolved. The cost-plus contract is an example.

The moral hazard problems posed by cost-plus contracts are akin to those discussed in conjuction with the insurance illustration in Chapter 1; the pairing of opportunism with information impactedness again presents the difficulty. Suffice it to observe that where such problems exist there is no "clean" market solution: a cost-plus contract assigns the risk to the sponsoring agency (which may be well-suited to bear it) but undermines least-cost incentives, while a fixed price contract maintains incentives but shifts the risk in what may be an inefficient (high cost) way.

At least occasionally, vertical integration backward into research is the most attractive way to overcome the dilemma posed when high-risk programs are to be performed: the sponsoring firm (agency) assumes the risk itself and assigns the task to an internal research group. It essentially writes a cost-plus contract for *internal* development. That this does not have the debilitating incentive consequences that often result when similar contracts are given to outside developers is attributable to differences in the incentive and compliance machinery: managers are employees, rather than "inside contractors" (of the sort described in Chapter 6), and thus are unable to appropriate individual profit streams; also the internal compliance machinery to which the firm (agency) has access is vastly superior to and more delicately conceived than the policing machinery that prevails between organizations. Internal organization thus arises in part because of its superior properties in moral hazard respects.

4.3.2 SMALL NUMBERS

Considerations of market thinness reinforce the need to be sensitive to tradeoff considerations. If the market to which innovations can be sold is, by reason of high concentration, thin, it may be essential, in order to maintain the bargaining position and hence the incentives of the innovators, that new entry and subsequent expansion be a feasible route by which to bring the process to completion. Lacking the prospect of entering independently into the industry to which the innovation applies, the innovator runs the risk that bids will fail to reflect full valuations — perhaps significantly.

Established firms face a tradeoff between the gains of inhibiting entry, in order to increase current profits and maintain their respective market positions, and the advantages of participating (in a systems sense) in maintaining the flow of new product developments. Inasmuch as the latter involves both uncertainty and future rather than immediate returns, established firms may sometimes opt for an entry inhibiting policy. The social interest, however, would appear generally to be served by preserving easy access.[24]

Access difficulties into industries such as automobiles and basic metals illustrate these difficulties. In the former case, refusal by the assemblers to adopt an innovation can, whatever its merits, stand as a bar to acceptance. In the latter, innovations are apt to involve process changes, the adoption of which requires incorporation into a continuous process operation. If entry is not a feasible route by which to achieve adoption and if resistance to change is contemplated, outside parties will have less incentive to support as much inventive activity as they otherwise would. Relevant in this connection is Arrow's expressed concern over why patent royalties in the aluminum, petroleum, and chemical industries are so low. "It really calls for some explanation, why the firm that has developed the knowledge cannot demand a greater share of the resulting profits — ideally all except a competitive return on the capital invested" (1962b, p. 355).

---

24. For a somewhat similar appraisal, see Nelson et al., 1967, pp. 71-72; also Scherer, 1970, p. 377.

I submit that first-mover advantages, including an established market position, in conjunction with market thinness provides a partial explanation for this condition. Scherer notes that "speed of penetration . . . is perhaps the most important single advantage enjoyed by large firms in developing new products" (1970, p. 353). The innovating firm that does not already have an established market position is thus at a relative disadvantage in this respect. Its fallback, and hence its bargaining position, is thereby weakened; a refusal to sell to less credible. If, in addition, the industry to which it would sell the innovation is one of small numbers, elicited bids may fail to reflect full valuation. [25] As a consequence, the inventive incentives among independents and small firms are predictably impaired, with the result that more of the burden of conducting research is shifted onto the large established firms — which, for reasons given earlier, may be constitutionally less well-suited to perform inventive activity.

4.3.3 UNIQUENESS

Consider finally the possibility that certain high-talent, scientific personnel possess a degree of monopoly power in bargaining over their employment conditions. As Marschak has forcefully observed, such uniqueness conditions plainly exist and sometimes have interesting economic consequences (1968, p. 14). Its relevance here is that such researchers may sometimes insist, as part of the inducements-contribution package, that some fraction of their time be available for "undirected" research activity. The large firm that accedes to such stipulations will occasionally find itself originating projects that it would otherwise leave for others to develop.

None of this is to deny that the prospect of appropriating the monopoly gains associated with a patentable invention provides an incentive for firms of any size to sponsor early stage R & D. Presumably, however, the risk adjusted rates of return to R & D are brought into correspondence at the margin with other types of investments, and the question is what firms in what market circumstances enjoy a relative advantage and why. An evaluation of market failures on the one hand and organizational failures on the other is necessary for this purpose.

4.4 Systems Solution by Classical Specialization

I am inclined to regard the early stage innovative disabilities of large size as serious and propose the following hypothesis: An efficient procedure by which to introduce new products is for the initial development and market

---

25. Undervaluation bidding by buyers is more likely if a stream of such innovations are to be auctioned over time rather than if only one or a few appear. The risk among buyers of undervaluation bidding is that tacit agreements will be opportunistically violated — with the firm that puts in a higher than normal bid realizing an advantage.

testing to be performed by independent inventors and small firms (perhaps new entrants) in an industry, the successful developments then to be acquired, possibly through licensing or merger, for subsequent marketing by a large multidivision enterprise. I do not, however, mean to suggest that this is the only efficient process. As indicated above (perhaps especially with respect to improvement innovations), there are others; also, market failures, in particular instances, discourage stagewise specialization.

The argument is a simple extension of classical specialization arguments to include technical progress within the framework of systems analysis. In consideration of the disabilities that different forms of organization experience at different stages of the innovation process, and in view of the empirical results regarding research proclivities of large firms reported in Sections 1 and 2, the established multidivision form organization that follows a conscious policy of imitation or acquisition as an important part of its new product strategy (supplemented, perhaps, by a set of internal operating rules designed to check its worst tendencies to persist with own-projects for which merit is objectively lacking) may be judged to display rationality of a high order in its allocation of resources to R & D. Put differently, a division of effort between the new product innovation process on the one hand, and the management of proven resources on the other may well be efficient. The frequency with which transfer is observed to occur (Hamberg, 1966, p. 21; Jewkes et al., 1959, pp. 168, 186; Mansfield, 1968, p. 58) plainly adds credence to the hypothesis.

4.5 Systems Solution by Organizational Innovation

Conceivably the perceptive large firm can attempt to debureaucratize itself and overcome certain of its worst tendencies. Replicating the characteristics of the small firm is not, however, apt to be easy. (The task force approach to projects may have distinct advantages for this purpose, but it is unlikely to be a perfect substitute. Truly entrepreneurial types find neither the latitude nor the rewards of this approach to innovation sufficient.) In comparison with the costs of going to the market and utilizing the transfer process, intensive efforts at debureaucratization are apt to be relatively expensive. If, naturally, organizations experience certain (mainly irreversible) life-cycle changes, it may be more economical simply to acknowledge these and permit specialization by stages to occur rather than force innovation through the internal development route.

The recent development by General Electric of what it refers to as its "Technical Ventures Operation" (TVO) is sufficiently interesting to warrant separate attention. This organizational innovation was originated in 1970 and can hardly be said to be proven. It is furthermore limited to a small subset of G.E.'s new project ventures. Nevertheless, TVO represents an imaginative effort to join the advantage of large and small firms.

The problem for which the TVO was devised to handle is that G.E. found itself developing technologies that were potentially viable but the markets for which were too small in relation to G.E.'s "immense size and method of operating" (Sabin, 1973, p. 145). G.E. sometimes attempted to sell the unwanted technologies, but frequently found no "suitable" buyers, while the sale of other developments prevented it from "keeping abreast of a business in which it [had] a scientific interest" (Sabin, 1973, p. 145) and for which knowhow was evidently important.

The possibility of setting up separate but wholly owned new ventures was rejected in favor of a scheme in which G.E. sets up a new entity to which the physical assets as well as the patents or a license to use the technology are transferred. G.E. then "takes about a one-third interest in the new business, and the ramaining two-thirds are split between the scientists and managers who help launch the new company, on the one hand, and outside investors on the other" (Sabin, 1973, p. 147). The rationale for this is, especially in view of the discussion in earlier sections of this chapter, altogether fascinating. According to David J. BenDaniel, who heads the TVO (Sabin, 1973, p. 147):

> A subsidiary arrangement would still leave the managers bogged down in the hierarchical reporting procedures required by large corporations. Even more important, by giving the new company's managers a direct ownership stake, G.E. supplies an incentive for performance that can't be equaled within a large corporation. The managers must invest in the venture themselves. . . .
>
> The rationale for raising outside capital has several aspects. For one thing, any such venture generally needs more financial backing than the entrepreneurs can give it (and G.E. doesn't want to pour more capital into it). BenDaniel also considers the raising of outside capital a test of the managers' entrepreneurial mettle (though he usually helps them). And, finally, the whole capital-raising procedure subjects the venture to independent scrutiny by outside businessmen who are unlikely to have their judgment swayed by sentimental attachment to the technology.

The advantages of TVO in relation to G.E. for the projects in question thus reduce to the following: hierarchical communications are reduced; entrepreneurial incentives unavailable within the large corporation are introduced; and commitment biases which would otherwise appear are checked. Plainly TVO and related organizational innovations that are designed to mitigate the bureaucratic distortions to which large firms are subject bears watching.

11. Dominant Firms and the Monopoly Problem

Both this and the following chapter examine structural monopoly issues from a transactional point of view. The evolution of dominant firm industries is considered here; problems of effecting oligopolistic collusion are dealt with in Chapter 12. Whereas a more assertive antitrust policy with respect to the dominant firm industries is encouraged, I am highly skeptical of "shared monopoly" approaches to the oligopoly problem.

The transactional approach to the dominant firm condition that is emphasized here may be contrasted with the more conventional conduct explanation. The implicit assumption of the conduct approach to violations of section 2 of the Sherman Act is that persistent monopoly is not to be expected unless supported by anticompetitive practices, patent protection, or unusual scale economies. This position is challenged here. Not that anticompetitive practices, patents, or unusual scale economies cannot contribute to dominance. But this construes the dominant firm outcome too narrowly. An expanded market failures interpretation of dominance is proposed.

In particular, I argue that dominant firm outcomes are (at least sometimes, perhaps usually) less to be attributed to conduct, patents, or technology than they are to a breakdown of the self-policing properties of markets. Chance events (uncertainty), unusual business acumen (management idiosyncracies), and default failures (ineptitude on the part of actual and potential rivals) are the main causative factors which have previously been neglected that can give rise to such breakdowns. Whether dominant firm outcomes resulting from market failures of chance event and default types occasion public policy intervention depends in large measure on whether or not unassisted market processes are likely to undo such condi-

Chapter based on O. E. Williamson, "Dominant Firms and the Monopoly Problem: Market Failure Considerations," 85 *Harvard Law Review* 1512-31 (1972), Copyright 1972 by the Harvard Law Review Association.

tions in any short period of time. Assessing this requires that first-mover advantages, if any, be evaluated.

The chapter proceeds as follows: The current approach to unlawful monopolization is described in Section 1. The proposed market failures interpretation is developed in Section 2. The basis for government intervention under the proposed approach is given in Section 3. The question of remedy is addressed in Section 4, and the structure-conduct controversy is reassessed in the light of this argument in Section 5. The argument is expressly reinterpreted in organizational failures terms in Section 6.

1. The Current Approach to Unlawful Monopolization

Antitrust policy has long been plagued by the problem of continued dominance[1] of an industry by a single firm which has obtained its position by lawful means. Traditional judicial interpretations of the offense of monopolization under section 2 of the Sherman Act[2] have focused on the presence or absence of predatory or exclusionary tactics in obtaining or retaining monopoly power.[3] To be sure, it has been argued that Judge Hand's opinion in Alcoa[4] comes very close to suggesting that a firm may be found to have monopolized unlawfully a market simply by maintaining monopoly power for a period of time substantial enough to indicate that market forces by themselves will be unable to undo the firm's dominant position.[5] But the most recent U.S. Supreme Court definition of the offense appears to reject

1. For the purpose of this chapter dominant firm industries will be defined to be industries for which the output of a single firm has persistently exceeded sixty percent of the relevant market and entry barriers are great. Much higher market shares are required if entry barriers are insubstantial. [If entry can occur frictionlessly, even one hundred percent market share does not imply market power. Cf. Stigler (1968, p. 133).] To be sure, the sixty percent, entry impeded condition is somewhat arbitrary. It has the advantage, however, of focusing attention on a relatively narrow group of industries. If the approach proposed in this chapter can successfully be applied to industries in which the largest firm has consistently maintained a sixty per cent market share, consideration can then be given to reducing the cutoff limit. It would seem injudicious, however, to apply the argument immediately to dominant firms with much lower market shares.

2. 15 U.S.C. Sec. 2 (1970). Section 2 provides in part: "Every person who shall monopolize, or attempt to monopolize, or combine or conspire with any other person or persons, to monopolize any part of the trade or commerce among the several States, or with foreign nations, shall be deemed guilty of a misdemeanor . . . . "

3. See, for example, *United States* v. *Grinnell Corporation.*, 384 U.S. 563, 570-571 (1966); *Standard Oil Company.* v. *United States*, 221 U.S., 1, 62 (1911).

4. *United States* v. *Aluminum Company of America*, 148 F.2d 416 (2d Cir. 1945).

5. Turner has recently come out in favor of such an approach (Turner, 1969, p. 1217).

this purely structural approach and to continue to require the presence of abusive conduct before finding unlawful monopolization.[6]

As the law is currently interpreted, dominance does not constitute a section 2 violation if the structure of the industry is attributable to "a superior product, business acumen, or historic accident."[7] A superior product presumably implies a patent monopoly or a cost advantage attributable to scale economies. These are not matters of principal concern here. That dominance due to business acumen or historic accidents should be outside the ambit of section 2 is, however, open to dispute. Indeed, it will be argued that to regard these cases as exempt from section 2 scrutiny is not only unwarranted, but has had the effect of obfuscating legitimate issues and perversely constraining the enforcement agencies to rely on conduct offenses in dealing with the dominant firm industries. Since it is widely felt that dominance ought not to be permitted to continue indefinitely,[8] this has frequently resulted in antitrust suits being brought against these firms on grounds which bear little relation to the structural condition in question.

The implicit assumption in the conduct approach to unlawful monopolization is that competition works — at least in the limited sense that, absent deliberate impairment of competition, actual and potential business competitors can be relied upon to perform self-policing functions by responding appropriately to opportunities for private gain. Except for circumstances in which economies of scale are large in relation to the market (the "natural monopoly" situation) or where the government itself protects a monopoly through the patent system, persistent dominance of an industry by a single firm is not to be expected.[9]

The position taken here is that while considerations of fair play are not to be neglected, the conclusion that structure will take care of itself relies

6. "The offense of monopoly under section 2 of the Sherman Act has two elements: (1) the possession of monopoly power in the relevant market and (2) the willful acquisition or maintenance of that power as distinguished from growth or development as a consequence of a superior product, business acumen, or historic accident." *United States* v. *Grinnell Corporation.*, 384 U.S. 563, 570-571 (1966).

7. Id. at 571.

8. That this is the prevailing attitude is revealed by the positions of the antitrust enforcement agencies and the courts. The Antitrust Division of the U.S. Justice Department regularly scrutinizes dominant firm industries for indications of anticompetitive conduct. Cases are occasionally brought on what appear to be contrived grounds and sympathetic hearings are accorded these in the courts. Since there is no great public outcry against these efforts, the acceptance if not the support of the public, might also be presumed.

9. *Standard Oil Company* v. *United States*, 221 U.S. 1,62 (1911) ("monopoly would be inevitably prevented if no extraneous or sovereign power imposed it and no right to make unlawful contracts having a monopolistic tendency were permitted"). Except for allowing for the possibility of scale economies, this is approximately Posner's view also (Posner, 1969, pp. 1596-1597).

too greatly on average tendencies. That strong competitive instincts normally obtain and that concatenations of chance events do not ordinarily result in dominance are both conceded. But aberrations can and will appear and the implied time horizon for self-policing to be efficacious may be unacceptably long.[10] Indeed, the concession by the Court that business acumen and historic accident may contribute to dominance suggests that competition may not operate smoothly and reveals a possible contradiction between the actual market factors responsible for dominance and the alleged conduct offenses on which dominant firm complaints rest.

2. A Market Failure Interpretation of Dominance

The existence of dominant firms which, but for anticompetitive conduct, are apparently immune from the antitrust laws has several undesirable consequences. First, the existence of a dominant firm, whatever its origins, commonly results in resource misallocation — including, but not limited to monopolistic output restriction.[11] Second, as Turner has cogently argued, the inability to deal effectively with established monopoly results in what may sometimes be an excessive expansion of antimerger enforcement (1969, p. 1213). Were the enforcement agencies and courts better able to "correct undue concentration as it appears, there would be less need to prevent mergers which present only remote possibilities of anti-competitive consequences" (Turner, 1969, p. 1214). Third, for structural dominance to

10. Posner relies on Brozen's recent finding that a "high-level of concentration in an industry tends to dissipate by natural forces within an average period of ten years," together with the fact that "the average length of a divestiture proceeding in a monopolization case involving a major regional or national market is 8 years" to support his conclusion that "it seems unlikely that administrative methods of deconcentration will work significantly more rapidly than the market" (Posner, 1970, p. 417, n. 50). The Brozen analysis, however, is disputable. See MacAvoy, McKie & Preston (1971). Moreover, even if Brozen's results were to be accepted, Posner relies heavily on average market tendencies which, in the particular cases of high concentration involved here, may be inapposite. Finally, Posner takes prevailing judicial practices as given, despite the fact that various reform proposals are directed to eliminating the delay in antitrust actions. See, for example, the Neal Task Force Report (1969, p. 7).

11. Resource misallocation can take several forms. The usual objection to monopoly is that it results in output restriction with a consequent loss of consumers' and possibly producers' surplus. This may be extended to include losses due to inefficient operations or general lack of aggressive management, but this strand of the argument is not well-developed. Monopoly also gives rise to income distribution effects. These, however, are commonly of a much more mixed nature than is usually appreciated. See Caves (1967, pp. 99-100); also Posner (1969, pp. 564-568). Objections to monopoly can also be raised on the grounds that it provides an incentive to distort the durability of goods. See Barro (1972).

remain beyond the reach of section 2 produces charges that antitrust enforcement is a charade (Galbraith, 1966, p. 794; Miller, 1968, p. 136). Whatever its merits in other respects, confidence that an American-style antitrust apparatus can monitor an enterprise system is impaired. Conspicuous, if limited, failures easily become the basis for captious contempt. Finally, dominance in business may be used as an excuse for bigness in other spheres of economic and political activity — to the possible detriment of the public (Stigler, 1952, p.123).

The antitrust enforcement agencies are not unaware of these difficulties. Substantial enforcement resources are accordingly invested in the study of dominant firm industries. Since, however, the admissible grounds for filing a complaint are limited, the main effort is to scrutinize the behavior of dominant firms to discover evidence of offensive business conduct. Considerations of reciprocity, leasing practices, and the like are seized upon to support claims that dominance has resulted from unfair business practices. That, objectively, the conduct in question could not reasonably lead to the dominance result is simply disregarded. Attention is focused instead on whether certain practices were employed and, if so, whether they may have had some, however slight, anticompetitive effect. That the process is regarded by outsiders, and even some insiders, as artificial and contrived is only to be expected.

This chapter advances the proposition that the Court's instincts are correct in that dominance is often to be attributed to "business acumen" or "historic accident." However, rather than treat such dominance as exempt from the coverage of section 2, it is argued that frequently it should be regarded as an actionable manifestation of market failure. Under such an interpretation, government intervention to upset this condition seems reasonable, provided only that (1) the dominant firm's market position can be judged to be relatively secure and hence unlikely to be undone by the operation of unassisted market processes, and (2) an efficacious remedy can be devised. Contrived proof of anticompetitive conduct would thereby be made unnecessary in order to obtain relief.

2.1 Business Acumen

The usual position on business acumen is that scarcity of decision-making skills is not responsible for dominance. One way of putting this is to state that requisite talent is available in elastic supply. The view expressed by Kaysen and Turner is typical. They assume that not only is there a sufficient supply of first-grade managerial talent to run a few hundred companies, but that such talent is relatively transferable as well. Thus, should any particular firm develop an "advantage in men and methods, rivals can and will copy the methods and hire the men away" (1959, p. 9).

Only recently has this position come under scrutiny. Marschak, in expressing concern over the ready tendency of economists to accept or employ assumptions of fungibility, has offered the following observation on the distribution of talent: "There exist almost unique, irreplaceable research workers, teachers, administrators; just as there exist unique choice locations for plants and harbors. The problem of unique or imperfectly standardized goods . . . has been indeed neglected in the textbooks" (1968, p. 14). Studies in entrepreneurial history would seem to bear him out: unusual men with exceptional personal force and organizing talent occasionally appear, and their influence has pervasive industry consequences (Chandler, 1966; Chandler and Salisbury, 1971).

Were superlative management the only factor responsible for differential business acumen between firms, the dominant firm that made such a showing might reasonably be exempted from divestiture. If the talent in question is not divisible, much as a scale economy of a technological sort is not, then the firm should be permitted to maintain its size because to do otherwise would result in a nontrivial loss of efficiency. The resulting monopoly power is simply an unhappy by-product of this condition.

Even in light of these considerations, however, the business acumen doctrine may sweep too broadly. For one thing, the management superiority that gave rise to dominance may refer to an earlier period in the firm's history. Often it will have manifested itself through an organizational innovation of a significant sort. The firm may then remain dominant despite the lack of any continuing superior acuity. Displays of unusual organizing ability early in a firm's development that have since lapsed do not obviously support the same policy conclusion reached above. The advisability of placing a time limit on a defense for dominance that relies on management excellence during an earlier period at least warrants consideration.

An even more serious difficulty with the business acumen doctrine is the relative nature of the argument.[12] Dominance does not necessarily imply superiority on any absolute scale. The dominant firm may have displayed no special management expertise but extant and potential rivals, on which the responsibility for self-policing functions devolves, may have been uncommonly inept. Persistent ineptitude of this sort is an indication that the self-policing functions of rivalry have disintegrated. Such discreditable performance on the part of principal rivals during critical formative stages of an industry's development will be referred to as *default failure*.

Management superiority (business acumen) may therefore take either of two forms. First, absolute superiority may have contributed to dominance — although this may have been associated with an early period in the firm's history and may since have lapsed. And second, the advantage of the

12. As Alchian explains in his discussion of natural selection: "The crucial element is one's aggregate position relative to some actual competitors.... As in a race, the award goes to the relatively fastest, even if all the competitors loaf" (Alchian, 1950, p. 213).

dominant firm may be attributable to the ineptitude of actual and potential rivals. If, for the reasons given below, unassisted market processes cannot be expected to rectify such dominant firm outcomes in any short period of time, the possibility of eventual government intervention to relieve these conditions ought seriously to be entertained in the second situation, and in the first when the absolute superiority is not both contemporaneous and indivisible.

2.2 Historic Accident

Although all of the firms in an industry may have been performing in a fully creditable, but unexceptional, manner, the dominant firm may be thrust ahead of its competitors by an unusual sequence of fortuitous events. Such an outcome will be referred to as *chance event failure.*

It is relevant in this connection to distinguish between defects in the competitive process and dissatisfaction with a stochastic outcome. In order to focus strictly on accidental outcomes, the stochastic generating mechanism will be assumed to operate without defect. Unwanted outcomes thus are to be attributed strictly to the laws of chance intrinsic to the probabilistic process and not to systematic distortions in the mechanism.[13] Even under these conditions, however, probabilistic processes can be expected to generate, with statistical regularity, occasional outcomes that may be deemed to have "undesirable" properties.[14] The argument is illustrated by the simulation experiment reported by Scherer.

Scherer began with industry of fifty equally sized firms and, for each firm, obtained a series of annual growth rates by sampling repeatedly from a common distribution of growth rates. The growth path of each firm was determined in this way; and industry concentration ratios, at ten-year intervals, were computed. The resulting firm size distributions often revealed high concentration, since "[s]ome firms will inevitably enjoy a run of luck, experiencing several years of very rapid growth in close succession" (1970, p. 127).[15]

13. The absence of predatory or exclusionary conduct or of default failure may thus be presumed.
14. Consider the following fair coin-tossing experiment described by Alchian (1950, p. 215):

> Suppose two million Parisians were paired off and set to tossing coins in a game of matching. Each pair plays until the winner on the first toss is again brought to equality with the other player. Assuming one toss per second for each eight-hour day, at the end of ten years there would still be, on the average, about a hundred-odd players. . . . The implications are obvious. . . . Should one rule out luck and chance as the essence of the factors producing the long-term survival of the enterprise?

The relevance of this argument for our purposes is that luck can contribute not merely to survival but also to dominance.

15. If, in addition, growth rates are serially correlated, as Mansifield's evidence suggests (1962, pp. 1036-1038), concentration outcomes are all the more likely.

Moreover, what is relevant for our purposes, concentration once achieved was not easily undone. "Once the most fortunate firms climb well ahead of the pack, it is difficult for laggards to rally and rectify the imbalance, for by definition, each firm — large or small — has an equal chance of [continuing to grow] by a given percentage amount" (Scherer, 1970, p. 127). Thus, repeated application of the same stochastic mechanism that, within a relatively brief interval, gave rise in some industries to concentration cannot reliably be expected to undo this result in any short period of time.[16] If, during the course of their development, industries typically undergo changes that progressively reduce the frequency and intensity of the random disturbances to which they are exposed, dominant firm outcomes will be all the more secure.

Three stages in an industry's development are commonly recognized: an early exploratory stage, an intermediate development stage, and a mature stage. The first or early formative stage involves the supply of a new product of relatively primitive design, manufactured on comparatively unspecialized machinery, and marketed through a variety of exploratory techniques. Volume is typically low. A high degree of uncertainty characterizes business experience at this stage. The second stage is the intermediate development stage in which manufacturing techniques are more refined and market definition is sharpened; output grows rapidly in response to newly recognized applications and unsatisfied market demands. A high but somewhat lesser degree of uncertainty characterizes market outcomes at this stage. The third stage is that of a mature industry. Management, manufacturing, and marketing techniques all reach a relatively advanced degree of refinement. Markets may continue to grow, but do so at a more regular and predictable rate. More accurate and complete information regarding market developments becomes available. Unanticipated system breakdowns are progressively eliminated as experience accumulates and statistical inference techniques are improved. Plant and equipment are in place;

---

16. The argument in the text is illustrated in yet another (if somewhat more artificial) way by the following example. Suppose, as in note 14 above, that the experience of a firm in the marketplace is likened to the repeated toss of a coin in which heads denote success and tails denote a setback. Assume that the probability of heads on each trial is 0.49 and the probability of tails is 0.51. Suppose further that (1) the title of dominance is conferred on every firm which, from the outset, flips ten or more consecutive heads and (2) once conferred the dominance status is retained so long as the difference between the total number of heads flipped less the total number of tails exceeds eight.

Dominance, thus interpreted, will occur infrequently: only eight firms out of 10,000 can expect to achieve dominant firm status. But dominance, once achieved, is also resistant to undoing by the repeated application of the same stochastic mechanism that was responsible for the dominant firm outcome. The expected number of additional trials that will be required for dominance to be "undone" under these circumstances is 100. Cf. Feller (1957, pp. 311-318). Although the system displays self-correcting tendencies (since, as the number of trials increases without limit, dominance will always be undone under the conditions stated), these proceed rather slowly.

employees with firm-specific experience and attachments are on hand; established connections with customers and suppliers (including capital market access) all operate to buffer changes and thereby to limit large shifts in market shares. Significant innovations tend to be fewer and are mainly of an improvement variety (Kuznets, 1953, pp. 258-267). Circumstances which, at an early stage in an industry's development, would have given rise to considerable dislocation now are attenuated.

Relevant in this connection is Kaysen and Turner's discussion of barriers to entry as a function of the stage of development of an industry (1959, pp. 73-75). As they point out, new entry into a mature industry is impeded by the lack of knowhow, by the difficulty of upsetting established customer connections, and by the absence among would-be entrants of a known performance record to be assessed by factor suppliers (including the capital market). What this argument comes down to, essentially, is this: The potential entrant into a mature industry must not only raise capital sufficient to finance plant and equipment at an efficient scale but must, in addition, have resources sufficient to cover the startup costs which, in a mature industry, may be considerable. Unlike entry at an early stage in an industry's development, where differential experience and reputation effects are, perforce, negligible, cost differences between established firms and new entrants at a mature stage are to be anticipated precisely because these factors now may be considerable. First-mover advantages may be said to favor those firms which, for whatever reason, were there early.[17]

Among the first-mover advantages that warrant special attention are those that are associated with the market for management talent. As noted earlier, Kaysen and Turner assume the management talent issue away. The argument goes through if the stock of talent is sufficient to staff prospective

---

17. The argument may be put somewhat more formally as follows: Suppose price at time t is given by $P(t) = k\,AC^L$ where $k > 1$ and AC^L is the average cost incurred by the lowest cost supplier in the industry at time t. Suppose, also, that there is learning-by-doing, but this accrues only through own-experience (there is no interfirm transfer of learning); in particular, assume that the average cost of firm i at time t is given by $AC_i^t = \overline{AC}$ $f\,(t\text{-}t_i)$, where $\overline{AC}$ is initial average cost of a new entrant, t_i is the time at which firm i enters, $f(0) = 1$, and $f' < 0, f'' > 0$. Although early entrants into the industry have no cost advantage over later entrants, in the sense that the profile of average costs is any different, the margin profile, $P(t) - AC_i^t$, will differ between early and late entrants— with early entrants having the advantage. Thus, let firms be listed by order of entry, in which case $AC_1^t < AC_n^t$. Depending on the magnitude of k and the time lapse between the entry of firm 1 and firm n, it may well be that at the time at which firm n contemplates entry (say t'), $P(t') - AC_n^{t'} < 0$—in which case firm n will not, at least initially, be able to break even (albeit that $P(t') - AC_1^{t'} > 0$).

The argument is plainly oversimple in that both the pricing strategy is arbitrarily imposed and the assumption of no interfirm transfer of learning is too strong (late entrants can ordinarily imitate successes and avoid failures of their predecessors). Also, scale economies are assumed away. Despite these limitations, the model has heuristic merit.

rivals of the dominant firm, if this talent can be easily identified, and if problems of transferability and interpersonal compatibility are not severe. Of these assumptions, the first two are probably the most plausible. But for the occasional exception of truly gifted entrepreneurs, talent in sufficient numbers and its easy identification will accordingly be taken as given. Problems of interpersonnal compatibility and transferability, however, are more formidable.

That managers are imperfectly mobile resources — partly because of personal (including family) preferences and partly because employment contracts commonly include such deterrents to mobility as nonvesting — [18] is obvious. Less evident, but nonetheless important, is the matter of who works well with whom under what circumstances. This is the compatibility issue. Barnard expresses it succinctly as follows: "...the question of personal compatibility or incompatibility is much more far-reaching in limiting cooperative effort than is recognized" (1962, p. 146). Efficient adaptation to changing circumstances is impaired "when there is incompatibility or even mere lack of compatibility, [since] both formal communication and especially communication through informal organization become difficult and sometimes impossible" (1962, p. 147). Although team considerations might be overcome by raiding the dominant firm to accomplish the transfer of a coherent group, executing such a transfer poses much more formidable problems than does the hiring of a few key individuals.

The relevance of this condition to the present argument is a temporal one. Thus, it is not that early entrants somehow avoid the costs of assembling the necessary talent but that, given that their cost experience is symmetrical and contemporaneous, none could be said to experience a disadvantage. As between established firms and would-be entrants, however, a contemporaneous cost difference in this respect does exist. To the extent that the prospective entrant's initial costs exceed the steady-state costs of established firms in the industry, a higher price to (steady-state) cost margin will be required to induce entry. *Ceteris paribus*, nontrivial transaction costs in the market for management talent inhibit entry.

Although the industry life cycle stability properties referred to above might be offset if the industry in question is one with a dominant firm, dominance seems more likely to reinforce stability. This obtains for two reasons: the dominant firm is able often to manage variety, and rivalry is apt to be attenuated.[19] The management of variety can take several forms.

18. Although nonvesting serves as a deterrent to mobility, it need not be regarded as an imperfection in the market for managerial talent. Nonvesting may be stipulated by *fully knowledgeable* parties to a labor contract because it encourages investment in firm-specific human capital.
19. Moreover, if dominance is coupled with vertical integration and large absolute size, still further uncertainty absorption may occur. See Malmgren (1961, pp. 402-403).

One of the more important is the supplanting of market tests by engineering and administrative processes. The dominant firm employs an internal selection mechanism to choose among alternative proposals and thereby avoids the unsettling effects of competitive market tests such as would obtain naturally among a group of independently acting firms in a competitive market. Thus, whereas in a fully competitive market the independently acting firm is a variety generator in relation to its rivals, the dominant firm absorbs potential variety through internal decision-making processes. In a similar way, the dominant firm may be able to follow a program of contrived depreciation (Barro, 1972).

Rivalry will be further attenuated if extant and potential rivals behave more discreetly in a dominant firm industry than they would otherwise. Potential entrants in particular may recognize that where any significant market share can be secured only at the expense of the dominant firm, there is an especially high risk of economic reprisal. Although extant rivals sometimes enjoy umbrella effects, they may also forego aggressive initiatives, which would be freely undertaken in a less concentrated industry, if these threaten to upset established relationships.

In short, the degree of uncertainty in a mature industry with a dominant firm can be expected to be less than both (1) what the same industry experienced in its intermediate development stage, and (2) what the industry would have experienced in its mature stage but for the presence of a dominant firm. The argument leads to the following proposition: In consideration of the indicated attenuation in the shocks that the system experiences, a position of dominance (achieved by whatever means—including a fortuitous combination of chance events during an industry's intermediate stage of development) is resistant to undoing once the industry has reached an advanced stage of development. To the extent, therefore, that the Court's exemption from section 2 scrutiny of dominance acquired through business acumen or historic accident relies implicitly on the assumption that such dominance will soon be upset by the operation of the market, the doctrine is of dubious merit. The combination of first-mover advantages together with normal variety attenuation and absorption processes in a dominant firm market suggest instead that a doctrine which relies on this line of reasoning ought to be regarded warily.[20]

---

20. This position may be contrasted with that expressed by Posner, who argues that, predatory practices and natural monopoly conditions aside, dominance will be secured and maintained only if dominant firms either (1) forego monopoly gains or (2) possess superior skill (1969, p. 1597). Foregone monopoly gain presumably implies that dominant firms earn only competitive returns—which may have been the case with Alcoa but appears not to be the case with IBM. Although the superior skills referred to are presumably of an absolute variety, these may be attributable instead to first-mover advantages that arise from discontinued acumen, historic accident, or default failure — in which case the affirmative defense for monopoly that Posner evidently intends does not obviously obtain.

3. Government Intervention and Market Failure

3.1 The Problem of Equity and Economic Disincentive

Even if it is conceded that market failures of the types described can lead to dominant firm outcomes which unassisted market forces are unlikely to erode, it might still be argued that government intervention through the antitrust laws is inappropriate in instances where dominance has been achieved through innocent conduct. Antitrust action in these cases might produce severe disincentive effects in the economy as a whole, where the possibilities of outdistancing rivals through superior skill, more consistent, albeit unexceptional, performance, or pure luck operate to induce new entry and to spur existing competitors on to greater efforts. A recent argument to this effect has been made by Marris (1972, p. 113):

> ... trust busting effectively contradicts the most fundamental principle of capitalism. Whatever may be said of the liberty of the individual, capitalism insists on the liberty of the organization. That liberty includes the right to grow, and the system rewards, with growth, the fruits of both good luck and good guidance. I cannot conceive how any political or other mechanism can sustain that principle if it is modified to read "You shall continue to be rewarded for success, but for successive success you shall be punished." I can conceive of some kind of society based on organizational devolution with some effective and inviolable resistance to concentration, but it would not be capitalism, and it certainly could not permit private ownership of the means of production.

Whether considerations of default failure, which are omitted from this statement, would lead Marris and others who adopt this position to conclude otherwise is uncertain. Default failures might, after all, be defended on the grounds that, subject only to rules of fairness, the victor deserves the spoils. The principle is commonly extended to include the proposition that it is even right to reward the tortoise for the indiscretions of the hare; persistence, even though some contestants perform discreditably, nevertheless has merit. But even setting default failure aside, the assertion that the imperatives of capitalism are as described might reasonably be questioned.

A somewhat more flexible position is taken by Turner, who suggests that, insofar as the arguments against intervention in a consolidated dominant firm situation are based on fears that such intervention will either produce a disincentive to future competition or result in an inequitable denial of earned rewards, the real issue is not whether a dominant firm deserves indefinite antitrust immunity, but rather for *how long* such antitrust insularity should be granted (1969, pp. 1220-1221):

[D]issolution of a monopoly that has patent monopolies are limited to seventeen years. There is no apparent reason why any firm should have a right to enjoy indefinitely, or even for seventeen years, the fruits of monopoly from sources other than original unexpired patents or economies of scale.

The notion that the government should intervene to upset dominant firms after they have enjoyed their dominance for a certain number of years[21] need not be regarded as a new doctrine, but rather as a simple extension of market failure analysis to embrace a set of issues that has previously been misconstrued — by the courts and economists alike. As interpreted here, dominance attributable to default failure, chance events, or the management excellence of an earlier era constitutes an outcome for which relief, if it can be efficaciously devised, is appropriate. That there is a *prima facie* case for the government to intervene when markets fail is scarcely novel.[22] The reluctance of the government to address the dominant firm outcome in the market failure terms suggested here is not because the dominant firm condition is thought to be innocent — otherwise, the effort to contrive conduct offenses would not be made — but because differential expertise (business acumen) has been misinterpreted and chance events (historic accidents) have been accepted acquiescently.[23] The interpretation proposed here, however, suggests that these can properly be brought within the ambit of market failure analysis and that the usual presumption of government intervention where remediable market failures occur is warranted. Thus, although special problems would be posed were the government to intervene in markets that fail to display self-correcting tendencies by upsetting dominant firm outcomes attributable to chance events, default failures, or discontinued acumen, the underlying rationale for the intervention is not really unfamiliar.

Consequently, section 2 of the Sherman Act should be interpreted by the courts to require a finding that persistent dominance is presumptively unlawful, provided only that the industry can be judged to have reached an advanced stage of development.[24] The latter requirement reflects a judgment that the dominance outcome is unlikely to be undone by unassisted market forces in any short period of time once the industry has reached

---

21. Whatever period is allowed for enjoyment of dominance must be long enough to provide sufficient incentives to entrepreneurs in incipient dominant firms throughout the economy.
22. Market failure is not, however, a sufficient condition for intervention to occur. The efficacy of any attempt to intervene needs also to be assessed. That governments often fail in such attempts needs to be appreciated.
23. Thus, considerations of differential expertise seem tacitly to have been taken to imply the absolute and continuing superiority of the dominant firm's management, so that default failure and lapsed expertise were disregarded, while unfavorable stochastic market outcomes were simply to be endured.
24. This requires that a judgment be made with respect to an industry's stage of development. Expert opinion together with statistical tests, for example fitting the industry's development history to a logistic curve, could probably be combined for the purpose of making an overall evaluation.

maturity. The dominant firm charged with a violation would be able to rebut the presumption of unlawful monopolization by demonstrating that its dominance was the result of economies of scale leading to a natural monopoly, of the exercise of an unexpired patent,[25] or of continuing indivisible, absolute management superiority. But dominance attributable to market failures of the types described in Section 2, above, would provide the occasion for government intervention.

3.2 Distinguishing Absolute and Relative Superiority

Whether a default failure outcome is more than a hypothetical possibility — to be conceded in principle but not observed in practice — is perhaps to be doubted. Relevant in this connection is the experience of the diesel locomotive industry, where an argument not only can be but has been advanced that the dominance by General Motors of diesel locomotive manufacture is to be explained by default failure among the steam locomotive firms.[26] Although this record needs to be developed and documented more thoroughly, I find the evidence more than suggestive that the dominance of General Motors in this industry was the result of ineptitude on the part of the steam locomotive manufacturers and imperceptiveness among potential rivals.[27] Though more conjectural, IBM's dominance of the electronic computer industry appears in part to be attributable to default failure — first, on the part of Sperry-Rand, in the early 1950's, followed by General Electric a few years thereafter.[28]

An examination of the sequential decision processes of both the dominant firm and its rivals is indicated if default failure is reasonably to be established in a given period. What major options with what expected payoffs were available to each firm during the interval in question? Rather than evaluate firms in terms of realized outcomes, an assessment of the merits of each firm's strategic posture is called for. A reconstruction of

25. Turner has argued that once a firm's patents expire it should be subject to divestiture if it has attained a position of dominance that is impervious to market forces (1969, pp. 1220-1221). Having allowed the firm to enjoy the fruits of its invention for seventeen years, he sees little reason to allow it to continue to extract monopoly profits on the basis of a position of dominance established during the years of patent protection.

26. See *Hearings Pursuant to S. Res. 61 Before the Subcom. on Antitrust and Monopoly of the Senate Comm. on the Judiciary*, 84th Cong., 1st Sess., pt. 8, at 3948-3997 (1955) (testimony of C. R. Osborne).

27. The steam locomotive manufacturers appear to have been severely disadvantaged by their limited manufacturing experience: no two steam locomotives were ever built exactly alike. Id. at 3957. This job shop tradition must be compared with the approach of General Motors, which involved extensive standardization in the manufacture of diesels. Implementing an organizational innovation of this sort may have been beyond the competence of the management of the steam locomotive firms.

28. For suggestive discussions of defective decision-making in each of these firms, see, "Sperry-Rand: Still Merging," *Fortune,* March 1960, vol. 61, pp. 125-132, 160-166, and *Forbes,* "GE's Edsel," April 1, 1967, pp. 21-26.

ex ante opportunities, rather than a recitation of *ex post* realizations, is accordingly needed. While this requires more intensive examination of individual business practices than antitrust specialists have conducted in the past, will frequently require access to internal documents not publicly available, and may sometimes come to naught, dominant firm outcomes would appear to be sufficiently rare, distinctive, and important to warrant an exploratory effort along these lines. The only problem is that academics, who might be prepared to do the studies, may not have access to the necessary data; while enforcement agencies, as currently constituted, lack the staff and resources to make such an assessment.[29]

An indirect test for absolute management superiority is whether the dominant firm has been a leader in developing new management practices, as revealed especially by organizational innovations. Again, General Motors, under the leadership of Alfred P. Sloan, Jr., illustrates a management that appears to have displayed unusual ability in this respect (Chandler, 1966).

From an enforcement point of view, however, the distinction between absolute and relative superiority may often be inessential. What is significant is that if either or both have contributed to a dominant firm outcome for which dissolution will bring efficacious relief, a section 2 suit is warranted. Dissolution would, however, pose problems if (1) the existing management possesses absolute superiority that will be wastefully dissipated were dissolution to be attempted, or (2) the disincentives that the managements of incipient dominant firms would experience would be substantial. Where the superiority in question is that of past, rather than current, management, the first of these problems does not appear. Whether the second is more than conjectural is uncertain.[30] The issue appears in the discussion of remedy below.

Assuming, as indicated, that management superiority will normally be manifested through organizational innovation, the first test of a contemporaneous absolute superiority claim is whether the dominant firm — whatever the original occasion for dominance — has *recently* distinguished itself as an organizational innovator. Absent a showing that established dominant firms are especially fecund sources of organizational innovations of a surpassing sort, for which there is no evidence, few firms can expect to qualify at this stage as exceptions. Among those that do, there is a further test of whether dissolution will impair innovative performance. Since the

29. The recent expansion of the economics staff in the Antitrust Division of the U.S. Department of Justice together with the increased budget of the Division may soon overcome this indicated disability.

30. To contend that firms will be greatly discouraged from taking initiatives that might subsequently lead to dominance seems dubious. Unless prospective rewards are mainly very distant, truncating a stream of earnings after fifteen years does not much impair incentives. With a twenty percent discount rate, the present value of a dollar earned in the fifteenth year is .065.

diffusion of important organizational innovations is ordinarily to be encouraged, and as this will commonly be promoted by dissolution, net losses in this respect will presumably be incurred only infrequently. Indeed, considering the difficulties of making a determinative assessment and the indicated low *a priori* probabilities of obtaining an affirmative result, claims of absolute, contemporaneous superiority might be disallowed altogether.

4. Remedies for Structural Dominance

The objective of a remedial decree in cases of structural monopoly should be to induce the dominant firm that is found guilty of a section 2 violation to divide itself into competitive parts within some reasonably short period of time after the first finding by a court that a violation has occurred.[31] Unless the dominant firm voluntarily divides itself into two or more viably competitive parts within a stipulated interval, say five years, the government would be entitled to court-ordered divestiture.

Although this proposal is not problem free, it does have several attractive attributes. First, the management itself, which presumably has the requisite expertise, has the incentive to redistribute the firm's assets into coherent, internally efficient and hopefully competitive parts. Only failure by the firm to exercise this option would require the government to intervene—although the proposed division by the firm would be subject to judicial review to determine whether competitive requirements had been met.

Second, a gradual procedure is provided by this method of divestiture. No immediate interruption of activity need occur; the transition can be performed as expansion and plant renewal decisions come up for consideration. The high transition costs that an immediate dissolution order might impose are thereby mitigated.

Finally, both physical and human assets will be reassigned. Often the expertise of a firm's personnel may constitute its most significant resource. While the duplication of physical assets by existing and potential rivals may be relatively easy, the acquisition of management and technical groups possessing the requisite experience can be much more difficult. The discussion of knowhow in Section 3.2 of Chapter 2, in connection with the United Shoe Machinery case, is relevant in this connection. Recall that it was the U.S. Justice Department's contention that affirmative relief required that United Shoe's potential competitors be given "consulting"

31. The relief proposals advanced in this section are a variant of those devised by the White House Task Force on Antitrust Policy. A major difference is that the Neal Report (1969) dealt with both industries dominated by a single firm and those dominated by several firms.

assistance so that they might acquire "that intuitive knowledge based upon training and experience that is incapable of translation into written form. The employees of United's potential competitors need to be given as much and as detailed help as United's own employees, if not more,"[32] Such consulting assistance would be unnecessary if dominant firms were to divide themselves into viable parts, since the requisite expertise and experience (knowhow) would presumably be distributed among the parts in the process.

Requiring dominant firms to undergo divestiture may, however, have undesirable side effects. First, the dominant firm may engage in aggressive monopolistic pricing, thereby encouraging new entry and the eventual erosion of its dominant market position (Turner, 1969, p. 1221). The emerging dominant firm faces a choice between alternative profit streams. It can choose the profit stream associated with continuing dominance and accept the prospect of eventual dissolution; or it can, during the latter part of the industry's intermediate development stage, increase its prices in order to realize greater short-run profits and effect a decline in market share below threshold levels. Although this second course of action would result in transitional welfare losses, these may not be great. I [like Turner (1969, p. 1221)] would be inclined to accept them — in the expectation that, even in these circumstances, a net social gain would commonly obtain from the early dissolution of the emerging dominant position.[33]

Pre-existing dominant firms, however, would not pose these same difficulties. A firm that already qualifies as dominant at the time the proposed policy is adopted should automatically face a dissolution proceeding. Changes in market share during the period of the proceeding would presumably be small and in any event could be disallowed as a basis for release. Indeed, were an increase in price to cost margin to be attempted, an injunction might reasonably be granted to prevent its implementation.

32. See note 19, Chapter 2, above.

33. This assumes that the industry in question will thereafter perform in a more competitive manner and thus realize allocative efficiency gains. There are several reasons to expect that this will occur. For one thing, technical progress is unlikely to be impaired and may well be improved as a result of greater competition. See Turner and Williamson (1971, p. 135). Also, price competition may be enhanced. Weiss, relying on Stigler's treatment of oligopoly, notes that oligopolistic collusion depends for its success on the individual seller's ability to detect nonrandom sales losses due to chiseling; and this "means that we should be very much concerned about the shares of the top one or two firms and that the shares of any firm beyond about the fourth cannot make much difference" (Weiss, 1971, p. 374). But whether or not such effects are realized in each individual instance, the more general social gains described at the outset of the chapter favor the policy in question.

There is, nevertheless, one especially troublesome possibility to be considered: where default failure has occurred and new entry is not induced by the monopolistic pricing policy adopted by the prospective dominant firm, the firms that are benefited by the shift of the dominant firm to a high price mode are those hypothetical hares whose discreditable performance is responsible for the prospective dominance condition in question.

Second, the dominant firm may, in anticipation of a section 2 complaint, undertake programs designed to make the cost of divestiture exceedingly great. Kaysen and Turner, for example, stipulate that "the court shall not approve a plan involving division of the assets of a single plant" (1959, p. 269).[34] Dominant firms that are anxious to forestall a dissolution order may be induced on this account to engage in excessive equipment specialization and plant size concentration.[35] A satisfactory deterrent to such behavior is not easy to devise. Perhaps the only realistic policy is to reject the single plant exception unless nontrivial economies of scale can be clearly shown — in which case the relief issue would not be faced since dominance here is permitted.[36]

If this approach is adopted, however, problems in evaluating claims of single plant economies must be anticipated. To the extent that these economies are said to be attributable to technological factors, objective engineering evidence could be required. Since, beyond a certain size, plant replication typically affords economies, for example, by permitting better access to factor markets and by reducing the transportation expense of servicing customers,[37] the demands for a clear showing of technological economies can be relatively strict. In the absence of such a showing, divestiture, despite high transition costs, could be required. Advance announcement of this policy ought to discourage "strategic" investment in single plants.

Third, allowing a firm to produce its own plan of divestiture may lead to a division that creates noncompeting parts, for example, splitting into an industrial division and a consumer products division. Although such a separation would be consistent with stockholder interests, the government would presumably object if alternatives involving active, contemporaneous competition between parts of the firm could be arranged. Where contemporaneous rivalry cannot be obtained, but the nonoverlapping divisions are both viable and enjoy reasonable parity with respect to size, relief may still be partly efficacious: divisions operating in nonoverlapping markets but sharing common knowledge will, when given independent standing, increase the potential for future competition.

Finally, the dominant firm may allow itself to be run inefficiently. Managers and employees may indulge themselves in on-the-job leisure or in other "corporate personal consumption" activities. In these circumstances, rivals presumably can easily overtake the dominant firm. The

34. See, also, *United States* v. *United Shoe Machinery Corporation*, 110 F. Supp. 295, 348 (D. Mass. 1953) (Wyzanski, J.), *aff'd per curim*, 347 U.S. 521 (1954).

35. There have been suggestions that General Motors has recentralized certain of its manufacturing activities for this reason. Wall St. J, Nov. 5, 1968, at p. 8, col. 3.

36. The stipulation of nontrivial economies is essential. Otherwise, the misallocative effects of the resulting market power may well exceed the efficiency gains — in which case the economies defense should be disallowed.

37. See Georgescu-Roegen (1967, pp. 56-62).

industry would thus restructure itself, but with considerable transition costs. Uncertainty with respect to the time that the government will file a section 2 complaint, however, should tend to discourage this behavior. Moreover, competition in the capital market, operating primarily through the takeover mechanism,[38] might be regarded more sympathetically as it applies to the dominant firm industries, since this serves as a check on inefficient practices.[39]

5. Application to the Structure-Conduct Controversy

Baldwin, in a recent survey of the structure versus conduct controversy, distinguishes strong from qualified structuralist positions and contrasts these with a conduct approach to enforcement. The strong structuralist position, which he associates with Bain, Caves, and Stigler, is that structure determines conduct, for the most part, and that tinkering with conduct is unlikely to have significant consequences so long as the underlying structural defect remains. The essential distinction is between symptoms and causes, where conduct reflects the former and structure the latter.[40]

The conduct approach relies on the assumptions that competitive instincts in the U.S. economy are strong and that large numbers competition is usually feasible. Given these, advocates of the conduct approach, of which Baldwin appears to be one, contend that (1) the traditional and appropriate concern of the law has been with conduct, and (2) effective competition will obtain if the law prevents the "deliberate impairment, misdirection, or suppression of competition" (Dirlam and Kahn, 1954, p. 28). Structure will take care of itself if fair play is maintained.

Nothing in the argument developed in earlier sections of this chapter suggests that vigilance with respect to fair play ought to be relaxed. But I am apprehensive that an exclusive emphasis on fair play will suffice. It fails to allow for market failure of the chance event variety and dismisses the possibility of dominance by default. Also, it assumes that relief which is restricted to a few conduct practices (such as lease-only contracts in *United Shoe*) will be efficacious. This imputes high potency to a few practices and assumes, implicitly, that alternative means to accomplish the same end, while conforming to the letter of the law, are unavailable. As Bain points out,

38. See Chapters 8 and 9 for a development of this part of the argument.
39. Any successful takeover agent would be expected not merely to reduce slack but also revert to the high price, short-run profit maximization mode described above.
40. As Baldwin points out (1969, p. 127), Bain and Caves qualify this position to acknowledge that predatory and exclusionary practices can influence the condition of entry. Conduct can in these respects affect structure, but this aspect of the argument has never been extensively developed or its empirical significance assessed.

however, "as soon as one specific set of collusive practices is found illegal and enjoined, another set may be invented (not nominally violating the first injunction) to accomplish the original purpose" (1959, p. 495).

Moreover, with few notable exceptions, such as perhaps the franchise system in automobiles,[41] it seems unlikely that individual business practices, taken by themselves, are apt to have sufficiently decisive consequences to support the conduct approach. More often, probably, conduct that has exclusionary consequences will rest not on any particular practice but is the result of a systematic strategy employed by the dominant firm or industry in question — which is to say that it is a pervasive set of interrelated practices, rather than any one or a few, that has the anticompetitive effect.

The prospect that narrow conduct remedies taken by themselves will subsequently produce nontrivial structural changes must, on this line of argument, be regarded as dubious. However, this raises the question of why, in the cases cited by Baldwin (*United Shoe, Eastman Kodak,* and *IBM*),[42] mainly conduct remedies were, on subsequent review by the courts, reported to be relatively efficacious in producing the intended structural correction.

Baldwin, in selecting these three cases for consideration, expresses the view that (1969, p. 128):

> ... for the purpose of analyzing the appropriateness and effectiveness of remedies seeking modification of structure indirectly through restraints on conduct, the most helpful cases are those in which the court handing down or approving the decree and jurisdiction also accepted a provision that the effectiveness of the original remedy would be examined after a specified length of time.

If, after an eight- or ten-year period, the court were to find that significant structural change had occurred, Baldwin is of the opinion, apparently, that the success of the conduct remedy is to be presumed.

Two alternative explanations are neglected, however. For one thing, the courts may have employed weak standards of judging efficacy.[43] For another, the prospect of a mandated structural remedy may be so ominous as to induce the dominant firm subject to review to take measures which, collectively, will reduce its market share to acceptable proportions. Thus, power to produce the intended effect is not to be imputed to the conduct remedy *per se;* indeed, any conduct remedy, however trivial, *coupled with* a contingent structural review stipulation may be sufficient. On this argument, the economic significance of the decree resides in the latent or

41. See Bain (1956, pp. 300, 301, 307) for an argument on the effects of auto franchising.
42. *United States* v. *United Shoe Machinery Corporation*, 110 F. Supp. 295 (D. Mass 1953); *United States* v. *Eastman Kodak Company*, 1954 Trade Cas. #67, 920 (W.D.N.Y. 1954); *United States* v. *International Business Machines Corporation* 1956 Trade Cas. #68, 245 (S.D.N.Y. 1956).
43. This is supported by the government's appeal of the United Shoe outcome.

expressed threat of subsequent structural change if the weaker (conduct) remedy is ineffective.

This last view is consistent with the position advanced above (and expressed previously by others) that, ordinarily, conduct remedies *by themselves* cannot be expected to produce significant structural consequences.[44] What is more interesting, perhaps, is that, as interpreted here, the contingent review procedure that the courts have fashioned is not all that different from the relief policy proposed in Section 4 above. The advantage of the approach proposed in this chapter is that it addresses the issues in a relatively unconvoluted way.

6. Dominant Firms and the Organizational Failures Framework

The implicit reliance on the organizational failures framework in preceding sections of this chapter will be made explicit here. That chance event and default failures directly relate to the framework is reasonably obvious; the interpretation of business acumen, by contrast, is somewhat more involved. The conduct approach to the enforcement of section 2 of the Sherman Act and the feasibility of fashioning structural remedies can also be interpreted in organizational failure terms. Consider these *seriatim*.

6.1 Chance Event Failure

By definition, chance events are attributable to uncertainty. But the mere fact that decisions are made in the face of uncertainty does not establish that failure obtains. Rather, it is chance outcomes which involve a considerable element of "surprise" or are due to an unusual sequence of chance events that pose the problem.

Surprise outcomes are attributable to the conjunction of bounded rationality with uncertainty. Thus, it is not that low probability outcomes with high payoffs carrying only fair (risk adjusted) expected returns have eventuated. The outcomes in question, rather, are those which, in a conscious commitment sense, were completely unanticipated. It is unrealistic and even disingenuous to impute rational choice to participants who

---

44. *Eastman Kodak*, which involved a tie between color film purchase and processing, may be an exception. The product acceptability of actual and potential film producers could have been impaired for lack of sufficient processing outlets. If the threshold expenses of putting a viable, independent processing program into effect were considerable, the tie would tend to inhibit color film competition. See the discussion of vertical integration in relation to the condition of entry in Section 2.2 of Chapter 6.

plainly lack the capacity to assess and position themselves strategically with respect to the complex situation of which they are a part:[45] where all the participants are severely limited in bounded rationality respects, differential outcomes are explained, to a large extent, by luck.

6.2 Default Failure

The assumption that markets have self-policing properties rests implicitly on a large numbers assumption. Where instead the responsibility for effective rivalry falls on a very few actual and potential rivals, the performance of each becomes critical. Should these firms fail to perform in a creditable way and should this failure persist, what might otherwise have been a relatively competitive oligopoly may become a dominant firm industry instead. A small-numbers condition at the outset thus places the assumption of self-policing markets in jeopardy.

What is essential for default failure, however, is not that one or a few firms fail to grasp a single opportunity, but that this failure occurs repeatedly. Persistent failure to discern and/or realize its profit opportunities is involved. That this should ever occur is a reflection of internal ineptitude and failures in the capital market. With respect to the latter, interested outsiders either fail to perceive the foregone opportunities (on account of information impactedness) or are unable to effect takeover except at great cost (because stockholders cannot take representations of ineptitude on the part of the incumbent at face value, on account of the risk of opportunism; because displaying the evidence in a compelling way and getting stockholders or their agents to evaluate it is costly, given bounded rationality; and because incumbent managements may opportunistically throw up a series of obstacles to takeover). Issues of these kinds are familiar from treatments of competition in the capital market in preceding chapters.

6.3 Business Acumen

The existence of a business acumen advantage implies a differential distribution of strategic decision-making or organizational talents. Presumably, however, the marginal productivity of high talent experiences diminishing returns. Except, therefore, as these talents may be associated

---

45. Tests of two sorts are germane. First, the chance events themselves may be of a sort which are really decisive and of a quite unanticipated sort. (The onset of World War II in the diesel locomotive industry is an example.) Second, it may be possible by examining file documents and interviewing executives to establish that the outcomes in question were never really within the domain of those which the firm anticipated.

with a single, unique individual, what is it that explains the failure of the market to redistribute this talent among rival firms? Put differently, will the market process on which Kaysen and Turner rely for reallocating management talent operate smoothly?

At least two factors impede this. First, there is the problem of discerning who the really talented managers are. Business performance is the result of collective decision-making in what is commonly a complex system. Who is responsible for what? Information incompleteness conditions obtain. Many managers are involved, but the exceptional ones can be discerned only with difficulty.[46] Moreover, this cannot be easily overcome by asking the high talent managers to come forward. For one thing, they may not really know. Also, the less talented can make the same representations (opportunistically) and the market cannot confidently distinguish between them.

Second, there is the problem of team considerations. This is a manifestation of idiosyncratic group experience, as discussed earlier in connection with the employment relationship in Chapter 4 and in Section 2.2 above. Although recognition that team factors can be important goes back some two hundred years,[47] the issue has been widely disregarded among academic economists.

6.4   The Conduct Approach

Whether the reliance by the enforcement agencies on conduct complaints to bring suits against dominant firms should be regarded as opportunistic might be disputed. Given that chance event and default failures are apparently inadmissible grounds upon which to base a section 2

---

46. Witness the frequency with which efforts to revitalize a moribund firm by hiring an executive in a successful firm come to naught.

47. Though he put the argument in terms of craftsmen rather than executives, Benjamin Franklin expressed the team organization issue in the following terms in the 1800's:

> Manufactures, where they are in perfection, are carried on by a multiplicity of hands, each of which is expert only in his own part, no one of them a master of the whole; and if by any means spirited away to a foreign country, he is lost without his fellows. Then it is a matter of extremest difficulty to persuade a complete set of workmen, skilled in all parts of a manufactory, to leave their country together and settle in a foreign land. Some of the idle and drunken may be enticed away, but these only disappoint their employers, and serve to discourage the undertaking. If by royal munificence, and an expense that the profits of the trade alone would not bear, a complete set of good and skillful hands are collected and carried over, they find so much of the system imperfect, so many things wanting to carry on the trade to advantage, so many difficulties to overcome, and the knot of hands so easily broken by death, dissatisfaction, and desertion, that they and their employers are discouraged altogether, and the project vanishes in smoke.[Cited by Stigler (1951, p. 190).]

complaint, the enforcement agencies face a dilemma: either the domi-nant firm condition is outside the reach of the antitrust laws or they must proceed in a contrived way by attributing the dominance condition to unlawful conduct. Following the latter course may then be regarded as simply maximizing enforcement effectiveness subject to constraint. The failure is not one of enforcement; the interpretation by the judiciary of the law is at fault.

This, however, implicitly assigns a narrow and passive role to the enforcement agencies. A more ambitious interpretation of their responsi-bility is to correct judicial failures by bringing good cases supported with good arguments. The court is there to be convinced. At least, therefore, until such an effort has been made and failed, reliance by the enforcement agencies on contrived conduct offenses seems opportunistic.

However, a further question is raised: Why have the agencies been successful in employing the conduct strategy? I submit that bounded rationality and information impactedness are the critical factors. None of the parties — complainant, defendant, or court — has a sufficiently rich model to sort out the quantitative consequences of the conduct in ques-tion (which is a manifestation of bounded rationality), and the requisite data in any event are apt to be deeply impacted. Given that the courts regard dominant firm outcomes apprehensively, a showing that certain conduct practices were engaged in and could have had some, however slight, structural effect has been sufficient to prevail.

6.5 Remedy

Remedy issues of two types arise in connection with the dominant firm condition. First, will unassisted market processes reliably undo dominant firm outcomes in any short period of time? Second, what prob-lems are presented if the grounds for bringing a dominant firm complaint are expanded in the manner suggested?

That unassisted market processes may not suffice is due in large measure to first-mover advantages. Dominance conditions, once achiev-ed, are for this reason resistant to undoing. But it does not follow that an effort to achieve remedy by dissolution is warranted. This depends on the capacity of the judicial system to address the dominant firm condition in a timely and competent fashion.

As presently constituted, neither the enforcement agencies nor the courts have the manpower and the necessary expertise to assess the issues in a determinative fashion. Institutional reform designed to mitigate these bounded rationality limits ought thus to accompany any effort by the judi-ciary to address the dominant firm issue along the lines of the suggested market failures argument.

7. Conclusion

Although expanding section 2 enforcement to include dominance acquired by discontinued acumen, chance event, and default failure poses numerous difficulties,[48] the approach proposed has the advantage over existing policy of addressing the issue of single-firm dominance in a direct and candid manner. Assigning residual responsibility to the government to intervene in a dominant firm industry that has reached an advanced stage of development (within which self-correcting market processes operate only slowly) relieves the need to rely on claims that anticompetitive conduct is the culprit. It thereby allows enforcement to proceed in a more assertive, less contrived way.[49] Dominant firm industries in which a conduct offense was tenuously associated with dominance could be attacked expressly in terms of structural monopoly (or mixed structural-conduct monopoly). Equally important, the reach of antitrust enforcement could be extended to include industries in which dominance cannot be attributed even remotely to predatory or exclusionary business tactics. Industries in which dominance has manifestly resulted from chance event or default failures, and which now enjoy apparent insularity, would thus come within the ambit of section 2 enforcement without strain.

That notions of stochastic and default failures serve to relieve the strain under which conventional analysis labors in treating the dominant firm condition is hopefully evident. That the proposed enforcement policy follows directly, however, might be disputed. Thus, others might be prepared to accept the argument that dominant firm outcomes are commonly explained by chance event and default failures, but then conclude that such dominance is sufficiently rare that it be tolerated as one of the costs that is associated with what, ordinarily, is a well-working, self-policing enterprise system.

48. Other problems in implementing this proposal not noted in the text might also be anticipated. For example, the Sherman Act carries criminal, as well as civil, sanctions. However, as Turner has observed: "It would appear wholly inappropriate to impose criminal sanctions for . . . the mere retention of monopoly power for a substantial period of time without objectionable conduct of any kind" (1969, p. 1222). Turner also suggests that dissolution suits of the sort described should be brought only by the government, since monopoly cases should not be undertaken lightly and "private suits are much less likely . . . to reflect a thorough assessment and dispassionate conclusions regarding the public interest" (1969, p. 1224).

49. Mason characterizes the conduct approach as follows: "There is a school of thought that . . . believes that all undesirable market situations can, in fact, be reached by a rule on restrictive conduct. . . . But if the undesirability lies primarily in the situation . . . this procedure somewhat resembles an attack on kidnapping by prosecuting kidnappers for income tax violation" (1959, p. xiv).

Indeed, for those industries in which the degree of dominance falls below the suggested threshold level, toleration is what is proposed here. But rather than accept all monopolistic outcomes, however egregious, with the same degree of equanimity, the more severe cases are put through a dissolution proceeding. Mainly this is because (1) unassisted market processes are least likely to upset the dominance condition in these industries in any short 'period of time, (2) uncontested dominance runs contrary to prevailing social norms and undermines confidence in an enterprise system, and (3) the side effects of a delimited policy are not judged to be sufficiently serious to offset the prospective economic and social gains.

12. Oligopoly:Interfirm versus Intrafirm Organization

The treatment of oligopoly in this chapter is less an analysis of oligopoly as such than it is an explanation of why oligopoly can be expected to differ in nontrivial ways from monopoly. Although this difference may seem obvious, it has not always been so; the view that dissolution into oligopoly is no remedy for monopoly is widely held.[1] Patinkin expresses it as follows: Unless there are "enough independent firms resulting from the dissolution to make the operation of competition possible . . . we will replace monopoly with some oligopolistic situation, and it is quite possible that we would be as badly off as under monopoly" (1947, p. 184).

I take exception to this position here. It fails to make allowance for the advantages of internal organization as compared with interfirm contracting in adaptational respects, and it gives insufficient standing to the differential incentives and the related propensity to cheat that distinguish internal from interfirm organization.

Some of the leading treatments of oligopoly are reviewed below, after which I examine oligopoly as a problem of "contracting." I then contrast dominant firm behavior with oligopolistic interdependence and conclude with a statement of the policy implications.

1. Some Antecedents

1.1 Economic Antecedents[2]

1.1.1 FELLNER ON QUALIFIED JOINT-PROFIT MAXIMIZATION

Fellner contends that it is impossible to deduce determinate prices and outputs for oligopoly markets on the basis of demand and supply functions

---

1. See, for example, Galbraith (1952, p. 58). The view that tight oligopoly and monopoly are equivalent is especially prevalent among nonindustrial organization specialists.
2. Two important treatments of the oligopoly problem to which I would call attention, but do not discuss here, are Telser (1972) and Shubik (1973). Both are somewhat in the spirit

that are derived from technological data and utility functions (1949, pp. 9-11). Rather, fewness carries with it a range of indeterminacy. Thus, although received price theory is useful for establishing the region of indeterminacy, notions of conjectural interdependence are needed to ascertain how choice is made within these limits. As he sees it, ". . . all problems of conjectural interdependence are essentially problems of bargaining — provided we interpret bargaining in the broader sense, including the 'implicit' variety" (1949, p. 16).

Within the range of indeterminacy, Fellner identifies four factors which determine relative bargaining power. The first two are concerned with social and political limits on bargaining and need not detain us here. The second two are more situation-specific: the ability of the parties to take and to inflict losses during stalemates; and toughness, in the sense of unwillingness to yield (1949, pp. 27-28).

He notes that quasi-agreements (bargains) will change in response to shifts in relative strength among the parties, and that changing market circumstances make it necessary for oligopolistic rivals to adapt their behavior appropriately (1949, p. 34). Such quasi-agreements, moreover, "do not usually handle *all* economic variables entering into the determination of aggregate gains" (1949, p. 34). Although this is partly due to "administrative circumstances," where these are left undefined, "it is largely a consequence also of uncertainty due to which various persons and organizations discount their own future possibilities. . . . This is especially true of those variables that require skill and ingenuity in handling (such as those directly connected with advertising, product variation, technological change, and so forth)" (1949, pp. 34-35). Later, he indicates that the use of strategic variables of these kinds requires inventiveness (1949, pp. 183-184), and that "the present value of this future flow of inventiveness cannot be calculated with sufficient accuracy" for the relative strength of the parties to be established (1949, p. 185). This in turn prevents the corresponding quasi-agreement from being reached. As an industry "matures," however, and particularly if new entrants do not appear, the degree of competition with respect to nonprice variables may be attenuated (1949, pp. 188-189).

Fellner indicates that profit pooling would not be necessary to reach a full-blown, joint-profit maximization result in those oligopolies where (1) the product is undifferentiated and (2) all firms have identical horizontal cost curves (1949, p. 129). In these circumstances, a simple market sharing agreement will suffice to achieve this result. Such conditions, however, represent a very special case. Even here, moreover, there is the need to reach agreement on what adjustments to make to changing demand conditions: who decides? how are differences reconciled?

---

of the transactional approach that I propose, and both develop a useful modeling apparatus to help evaluate the issues.

In the more usual case where cost differences and/or product differentiation exist, joint-profit maximization requires interfirm cash flows. Complete pooling under these conditions implies that "no attention is paid to how much profit each participant earns directly on the market but only to how much the aggregate of the participants earns. Each participant is compensated from the pool of earnings according to his share" (1949, p. 135). This, however, is held to be hazardous both for antitrust reasons and, even more, because some firms will be at a "substantial disadvantage if the agreement is terminated and aggressive competition is resumed" (1949, p. 133). Consequently, only qualified joint-profit maximization among oligopolists is to be expected.

1.1.2 STIGLER ON OLIGOPOLY

Stigler takes as given that oligopolists wish, through collusion, to maximize joint profits (1964, p. 44) and attempts to establish the factors which affect the efficacy of such aspirations. While he admits that "colluding firms must agree upon the price structure appropriate to the transaction classes which they are prepared to recognize" (1964, p. 45), his analysis is focused entirely on the problem of policing such a collusive agreement. "A price structure of some complexity" (1964, p. 48), one which makes "appropriate" provision for heterogeneity among products and buyers and for the condition of entry, is simply imputed to oligopolists.[3]

Stigler notes that since secret violations of such agreements commonly permit individual members of an oligopoly to gain larger profits (where these are expressed as expected, discounted values) than would their adherence, a mechanism to enforce agreements is needed. Enforcement for Stigler "consists basically of detecting significant deviations from the agreed-upon prices. Once detected, the deviations will tend to disappear because they are no longer secret and will be matched by fellow conspirators if they are not withdrawn" (1964, p. 46). Accordingly, a weak conspiracy is one in which "price cutting is detected only slowly and incompletely" (1964, p. 46).

Since an audit of transaction prices reported by sellers is unlawful, and in any event may be unreliable (1964, p. 47), transaction prices paid by buyers are needed to detect secret price cutting. Stigler contends, in this connection, that statistical inference techniques are the usual way in which such price cutting is discovered. In particular, the basic method of detecting a price cutter is that he is getting business that he would not otherwise obtain (1964, p. 48). Among the implications of this statistical inference approach to oligopoly are that (1) collusion is more effective in markets where buyers correctly report prices tendered (as in government bidding), (2) collusion is limited if the identity of buyers is continuously changing

---

3. Stigler assumes "that the collusion has been effected, and a price structure agreed upon" (1964, p. 46).

(as in the construction industries), and (3) elsewhere the efficacy of collusion varies inversely with the number of sellers, the number of buyers, and the proportion of new buyers, but directly with the degree of inequality of seller firm size (1964, pp. 48-56).

1.2 Legal Antecedents

1.2.1 TURNER ON CONSCIOUS PARALLELISM

Turner contends that conscious parallelism, by itself, does not imply agreement. Additional evidence that the observed parallelism is not simply "identical but unrelated responses by a group of similarly situated competitors to the same set of economic facts" is needed before agreement can be inferred (1962, p. 658). He illustrates the argument by posing an "extreme hypothetical" in which there are only two or three suppliers — each of identical size, producing an identical product at identical costs — and markets are static (1962, p. 663). He contends, in these circumstances, that "the 'best' price for each seller would be precisely the same, would be known to be the same by all, and would be charged without hesitation in absolute certainty that the others would price likewise" (1962, pp. 663-664). Although he is not explicit on this, the price that he appears to have in mind is the joint-profit maximizing (monopoly) price.[4]

Turner then goes on to note that the hypothetical is rather unrealistic. Products are rarely fully homogeneous, cost differences will ordinarily exist, and adaptations will need to be made to changing market circumstances (1962, p. 664). He accordingly holds that "for a pattern of noncompetitive pricing to emerge ... requires something which we could, not unreasonably, call a 'meeting of the minds'" (1962, p. 664).[5] He declines, however, to regard this as unlawful. Absent explicit collusion, this is merely rational price making in the light of all market facts (1962, p. 666). "If monopoly and monopoly pricing are not unlawful per se, neither should oligopoly and oligopoly pricing, absent agreement of the usual sort, be unlawful per se" (1962, pp. 667-668).

4. If this interpretation is correct, Turner does not believe such a price to be collusive. Plainly, however, it is—at least in the sense that it is *not* the price that independently acting Cournot duopolists (or triopolists) would charge. Given linear demands and constant marginal costs, the Cournot equilibrium output, for each firm, where price interdependence is not taken into account (that is, the conjectural variation term is zero), is $q = [1/(n+1)]\ \bar{Q}$, where n is the number of firms in the industry and $\bar{Q}$ is the competitive output. The joint-profit maximizing output for each such firm, by contrast, is $q^* = \frac{1}{2n}\bar{Q}$. Plainly, $q^* < q$ for $n > 1$. (For $n = 1$, both yield the monopoly output.)

5. Note again, as pointed out in note 4, above, that independently operating Cournot duopolists do not charge competitive prices yet are not colluding in any usual sense either. Turner seems implicitly to hold that independent pricing will yield the competitive solution. Hence, any price that exceeds the competitive price is regarded as an indication of interdependence realized. Posner appears also to be of this view. (See below.)

Because the behavior in question cannot be rectified by injunction ["What specifically is to be enjoined?" (1962, p. 669)], relief would presumably have to take the form of dissolution or divestiture (1962, p. 671). This however, is to admit that the fundamental issue is structure, not remediable conduct. Unless structural monopoly is to be subject to dissolution. structural oligopoly ought presumably to be permitted to stand. Although Turner declined in 1962 to propose a structural remedy for either condition, he has since altered his position on both (1969).

1.2.2 POSNER ON OLIGOPOLY

Posner takes exception to Turner's position that oligopolistic interdependence of a natural and noncollusive sort explains the price excesses in oligopolistic industries. Rather, a small-numbers condition is held to be merely a necessary but not a sufficient condition for such price excesses to appear (1969, p. 1571). Because "interdependence theory does not explain ... how oligopolistic sellers establish a supracompetitive price" (1969. p. 1568), including adjustment to changing market conditions, Posner suggests that the study of oligopoly proceed in terms of cartel theory instead (1969, pp. 1568-1569).

The basic argument here is that "voluntary actions by the sellers are necessary to translate the rare condition of an oligopoly market into a situation of noncompetitive pricing" (1969, p. 1575). Effective cartel behavior is, moreover, costly to effectuate; costs of bargaining, adaptation, and enforcement must all be incurred (1969, p. 1570). The upshot is that since "tacit collusion or noncompetitive pricing is *not inherent* in an oligopolistic market structure but, like conventional cartelizing, requires additional, voluntary behavior by sellers" (1969, p. 1570; emphasis added), a conduct remedy under section 1 of the Sherman Act is held to be appropriate (1969, pp. 1578-1593). Once the oligopolist is faced with the prospect of severe penalties for collusion, tacit or otherwise, Posner concludes that the rational oligopolist will commonly decide not to collude but will expand his output until competitive returns are realized (1969, p. 1591).[6] Self-correcting performance is thus induced in this way.

2. Oligopoly Regarded as a Problem of Contracting

In order to focus attention on what I believe to be the critical issues, I will assume, initially, that oligopolistic agreements are lawful, so that there is no legal bar to collusion, but that oligopolists cannot appeal to the

---

6. This conclusion appears, however, to be unwarranted — for the reasons given in note 4, above.

courts for assistance in enforcing the terms of an oligopolistic agreement. The oligopolists can, however, themselves take punitive actions to bring deviant members into line, provided only that laws prohibiting the destruction of property, libel, and so forth are respected. Entry is assumed to be difficult; also, I assume that profit pooling is permitted but that horizontal mergers between the firms are disallowed.[7]

I will argue that oligopolists will commonly have difficulty in reaching, implementing, and enforcing agreements under these circumstances, but this argument does not mean that laws regarding oligopoly are of no account. The stipulations that horizontal mergers are disallowed and that collusive agreements are unenforceable in the courts are both important in this connection. If, however, it can be shown that monopolistic outcomes are difficult to effectuate even when the laws permit collusion, then the performance differences between dominant firms (monopoly) and oligopolistic firms are not principally to be attributed to the unlawfulness of collusion among the latter.[8] It follows, of course, that if express and lawful agreements (contracts) are difficult for oligopolists to reach and implement, tacit agreements are even less reliable instruments for achieving collusion.

A contract between two or more parties will be attractive in the degree to which: (1) the good, service, or behavior in question is amenable to unambiguous written specification; (2) joint gains from collective action (agreement) are potentially available; (3) implementation in the face of uncertainty does not occasion costly haggling; (4) monitoring the agreement is not costly; and (5) detected noncompliance carries commensurate penalties at low enforcement expense. Consider the oligopoly problem with respect to each of these.

2.1 Contract Specification

Recall that express oligopolistic collusion is assumed to be lawful. The parties to the collusive arrangement can therefore negotiate openly and express the details of the agreement in writing without exposing themselves to prosecution. The question to be assessed here is whether the latitude thus afforded will permit a comprehensive collusive agreement to be specified.

I submit that, except in rather special and unlikely circumstances, a comprehensive joint-profit maximizing statement (which does not entail merger) will usually be infeasible. The reason for this is that a comprehensive statement of such a kind requires an inordinate amount of knowledge

---

7. Telser (1972) does not make this last assumption. His analysis differs from mine partly for this reason.
8. I do not, however, mean by this to suggest that the antitrust statutes prohibiting collusion are without purpose. They certainly compound the typical oligopolist's problems.

about the cost and product characteristics of each firm, the interaction effects between the decision variables within each firm, and the interaction effects of decision variables between firms. Not only is the relevant information costly to come by, to say nothing of digesting it and devising the appropriate adaptation for each of the firms to make, but this needs to be done *ex ante*, for a whole series of contingent future events, most of which will never materialize, if anything approximating a complete contract is to be written.

The point is that joint-profit maximization, even as an abstract exercise, is very difficult to accomplish once one departs from the simplest sort of textbook exercise. Homogeneous products, identical linear and horizontal cost curves, and static markets constitute the "ideal." Maintaining these product and cost assumptions in the face of changing demand does not greatly complicate the abstract analysis, in that the conditions of joint-profit maximization are easy to display, but the operational problems become somewhat more difficult in the face of uncertainty, for the reasons given in Section 2.3, below.

In circumstances, moreover, where differentiated products are involved, product and process innovations are occurring, organization form changes are taking place, selling expense and financial strategies are open to determination, and the like, the resulting complexity becomes impossibly great in relation to the bounded rationality capacities of planners. When, in addition, the optimization problem is cast in a multiperiod framework under conditions of uncertainty, abstract analysis breaks down.

The recent study by Hamilton and Moses (1973) of intrafirm profit maximization in a multidivisional enterprise is of some interest in this connection. They attempt operationally to address the problem of joint-profit maximization in a multiproduct firm where (1) product lines are *independent*, (2) only heuristic rather than full-blown optimization methods are attempted, and (3) only the *financial* decision is considered. Their model, which has since been implemented by the International Utilities Corporation, contains approximately 1,000 variables and 750 constraints and tests not one but various configurations of the strategic variables. Replicating such an arrangement by interfirm agreement boggles the mind. Complicating the analysis further to include interdependent products (which, of course, is the case in oligopoly) and the full range of decision variables referred to above reveals the manifest impossibility of attempting to comprehensively joint-profit maximize — even by heuristic simulation methods, much less by determinant contractual agreements. One concludes, accordingly, that the absence of legal prohibitions to collusive contracting is not what prevents comprehensive collusive contracts from being reached.[9] Rather, elementary bounded rationality considerations explain this condition.

9. Again, however, the view expressed in note 8, above applies.

2.2 Joint Gain Agreement

Suppose, *arguendo*, that it were possible to specify the joint-profit maximizing strategy contractually. Would the parties then be prepared to make such an agreement? I submit that, but for the simple textbook cases referred to above, they would commonly decline to accept comprehensive joint-profit maximization of the profit pooling kind.

Partly disagreement might arise, as Fellner suggests, on account of differences between the parties concerning the appropriate discount rates to be used in evaluating future prospects. Surely more fundamental, however, are the risks and monitoring expenses that profit pooling entails. As Fellner notes, some of the parties must accede to reductions in relative output and to contractions in relative firm size if the joint-profit maximizing result is to be realized. This, however, is hazardous. Firms which are authorized to expand relatively as a result of the agreement will be powerfully situated to demand a renegotiated settlement at a later date. Wary of such opportunism, firms for which retrenchment is indicated will decline from the outset to accept a full-blown profit pooling arrangement. Moreover, even setting such concerns aside, monitoring the profit pooling agreement will be costly because of the pairing of opportunism with information impactedness. These issues are best addressed in the context of the moral hazard discussion in Section 2.4, below.

2.3 Implementation Under Uncertainty[10]

Implementing an agreement under conditions of uncertainty requires the parties to agree, when changes in the environment occur, on what new state of the world obtains. Problems can arise if, for any true state of the world description, (1) some parties would realize benefits if a false state were to be declared, and either (2a) information regarding the state of the world is dispersed among the parties and must be pooled, or (2b) despite the possession of identical information by all the parties, definitive agreement must still be reached. The issues are those discussed in Section 3 of Chapter 2 and need not be repeated here. I merely point out that implementing an oligopolistic agreement under conditions of uncertainty can occasion costly haggling if the parties are given to making opportunistic representations with respect to the data and an outside arbiter can be apprised of true conditions only at great cost.

10. Unlike the preceding and succeeding subsections, the argument here assumes that joint-profit maximization is not attempted.

2.4 Monitoring Contract Execution

As Stigler points out, and as is widely recognized, oligopolists have an incentive to cheat on price fixing agreements if they believe that cheating will go, for a time at least, undetected. Given that information about individual sales is impacted, in that the seller knows exactly what the terms were but, given uncertainty, his rivals do not and can establish the terms only at some cost, the individual seller can often cut prices below the agreed level to the disadvantage of the other parties to the conspiracy. The pairing of opportunism (which is here manifested as cheating) with information impactedness explains this condition.

The argument, moreover, applies to oligopolistic collusion with respect to nonprice decision variables as well. If anything, agreeing to collude with respect to marketing expense, R & D efforts, and the like is even more hazardous for nonopportunistic parties, who are prepared to abide by the agreements, than is price collusion. Although it is easy to establish after the fact that a rival has made significant design changes or introduced a new product in violation of the agreement, such information may come too late. If recovery from a large shift in market share, attributable, say, to an "illicit" innovation is inordinately expensive, the detection of such a violation is to little avail. Although firms can mitigate these risks by maintaining a defensive posture against such contingencies, comprehensive collusion in nonprice respects can scarcely be said, in that event, any longer to be operative.

The matter of profit pooling, referred to in Section 2.2, above, needs also to be examined in monitoring respects. Even if firms were prepared to enter into profit pooling agreements, in which all profits are pooled and each participant is assigned his share of the total, there is still the problem of determining what the contribution of each firm to the pool should be. Individual firms have an incentive to understate true profits in these circumstances.

Moreover, merely to audit the earnings of each firm, even to the extent that *all* sources of revenue and cost are fully disclosed, is not sufficient to avoid distortion. An assessment of individual expense items must also be made. The problems facing the auditor here are akin to those that face the defense agencies in monitoring cost-plus (or, more generally, cost-sharing) defense contracts.[11] Unless it can be established that certain types or amounts of actual costs are unwarranted, and hence will be disallowed, each firm has an incentive to incur excessive costs.

Expense excesses can take any of several forms. Perhaps the simplest is to allow some operations to run slack, which is to say that the manage-

---

11. For discussions of defense contracting, see Scherer (1964) and Williamson (1967).

ment and workers in the firm take part of their rewards as on-the-job leisure. A second way is to allow emoluments to escalate, in which case corporate personal consumption expenditures exceed levels which, from a profit maximizing standpoint, would be incurred. Third, and most important, firms may incur current costs which place them at a strategic advantage in future periods. Developing new and improved technology, training the work force, and so forth are examples of the latter. Evaluating individual firm performance in these several respects is at least an order of magnitude more difficult than simple audits of revenue and cost streams. Conformably, profit pooling, even were it legal, poses severe contract enforcement problems.

2.5 Penalizing Contract Violations

Recall that it was assumed that while collusive agreements are not unlawful, the participants in such agreements cannot call upon the courts to help enforce the agreement. Instead, violators must be determined and penalties must be administered by the parties to the contract. Problems of two types arise in this latter connection. First, there is the problem of whether the penalties imposed will be efficacious. Put differently, do the penalties, if implemented, constitute an effective deterrent to the would-be violator? Second, even if penalties can be devised that would be efficacious, will the parties to the conspiracy be prepared to impose them?

Because the conspirators lack legal standing, conventional penalties such as fines and jail sentences are presumably unavailable. Rather, penalties are *exacted in the marketplace* by confronting the violator with unusually adverse circumstances. Price reductions are matched and perhaps even undercut. Normal types of interfirm cooperation (for example, supply of components) is suspended. Key employees may be raided, and the like. Except, however, as deviant firms are highly dependent on rivals for vital supplies, such market reactions may well be ones that the deviant is prepared to risk.

For one thing, the contract violator is not the only firm to be adversely affected by exacting these penalties in the marketplace. The firms meting out the penalties also incur costs.[12] Second, and related, securing the collective action needed to punish the violator may be difficult. Thus, although all firms may agree both that a violation has taken place and that the violator deserves to be punished, not all may be prepared to participate in administering it. Defectors (for example, those willing to supply the deviant with the essential component, perhaps at a premium price), which

---

12. Punitive market responses require firms to incur short run profit sacrifices in the hope of discouraging future chiselers and returning the current chiseler to the fold.

is to say opportunists, who refuse to incur the costs of punishing the violator, naturally reduce the prospective costs of being detected in violation of the agreement. Where such defection is deemed likely, collusive contracts are all the less likely.[13]

3. The Contracting Approach and Prior Treatments Contrasted

Like Fellner, the problem of oligopoly under the contracting approach is treated as one of interdependence recognized. Also, as Fellner does, the multidimensional nature of the interdependence issue is emphasized; price coordination is only a part of the problem, especially in differentiated product industries. But whereas Fellner attributes the problems of interdependence to the complexities of discounting uncertain future values and in pooling risks, I put the issue in contingent claims contracting terms. While these are not unrelated, the latter highlights the contracting issues and permits us to draw expressly on the organizational failures framework of Chapter 2. A more complete assessment of the problems of oligopolistic collusion is thereby afforded.

Stigler's analysis runs almost entirely in terms of prices. Moreover, he takes as given that the collusive agreement has already been reached. Attention is focused instead on cheating and on statistical inference techniques for detecting cheaters. While this last is very useful and calls attention in an interesting way to aspects of the oligopoly problem that others have rather neglected, it is also incomplete. The discussion in Section 2 reveals that monitoring is only one of a series of contracting steps, and not plainly the one that warrants priority attention.

Both Turner and Posner also give primary attention to prices in their discussions of oligopoly. But the similarity ends there. Thus, whereas Turner emphasizes tacit collusion of the interdependence recognized

13. Although the opportunistic behavior described mainly reflects an effort to realize short run individual gains, to the disadvantage of the group, in an aggressive way, firms may also engage in such behavior for defensive reasons. Defensively it reflects a lack of confidence in the trustworthiness of other members of the group and an unwillingness to risk being put to a strategic disadvantage.

While aggressive or assertive opportunism is to be expected whenever the viability of any particular firm is threatened, whatever the degree of "maturity" of the firms in an industry, defensive opportunism will vary inversely with maturity. Since defensive opportunism, if widely practiced, is mutually disadvantageous, and as this is self-evident to the parties, organizational learning is normally to be expected. Among other things, ways of announcing or signaling intentions in ways that will not be misinterpreted as aggressive, when no such intention exists, are apt to develop. Unless, therefore, the industry is one for which new entrants regularly appear, which easily has disruptive interfirm learning or accommodation consequences, occasions for defensive opportunism are apt to decline as an industry matures.

sort and finds injunctive relief to be inefficacious, Posner regards the interdependence theory unsatisfactory, discusses oligopoly instead as a cartel
problem, and concludes that injunctive relief is appropriate.

The spirit of my discussion is somewhat akin to Posner's cartel analysis,
but the specifics plainly differ. For one thing, I restate the problem in terms
of what a *lawful* cartel could accomplish. Also, I am much more concerned
than Posner with the details and impediments to successful interfirm contracting. Finally, as will be apparent below, I agree with Turner that
injunctive relief in highly concentrated, homogeneous product, entry
impeded, mature industries is unlikely to be effective. Structural relief is
here indicated instead.

4. Policy Implications: Dominant Firms versus Oligopolistic Interdependence

The monopolist (or dominant firm) enjoys an advantage over oligopolists in adaptational respects since he does not have to write a contract
in which future contingencies are identified and appropriate adaptation
thereto are devised. Rather, he can face the contingencies when they arise;
each bridge can be crossed when it is reached, rather than having to decide
ex ante how to cross all bridges that one might conceivably face. Put differently, the monopolist can employ an adaptive, sequential decision-
making procedure, which greatly economizes on bounded rationality
demands, without exposing himself to the risks of contractual incompleteness which face a group of conspiring oligopolists. Adaptation within a
firm (as compared with between firms) is furthermore promoted by the
development of efficient, albeit often informal, communication codes
and an associated trust relationship between the parties. Thus, while I do
not mean to suggest that there are no costs whatsoever to dissolution, and,
accordingly, do not propose it as an automatic remedy (see Sections 3 and
4 of Chapter 11), to suggest that oligopolists will be able easily to replicate
the intrafirm join-profit maximization strategy of a monopolist is simply
unwarranted.[14] Even if cheating on a specific agreement were not a problem, there is still the need among oligopolists to reach the specific agreement. The high cost of exhaustively complete contracting discourages
efforts toward comprehensiveness — in which case, because actual oligopolistic contracts are of the incomplete coordination kind, competition
of a nonprice sort predictably obtains.

14. The dominant firm must contend with both actual and potential rivals in devising its
strategy, and in this respect differs from the monopolist, which only faces potential competition. Although the dominant firm's maximizing problem is somewhat more complicated
on this account, it can nevertheless develop and implement a policy for dealing with actual
and potential rivals much more easily and effectively than can a group of oligopolists the
collective market shares of which equal that of the dominant firm.

To assume, moreover, that oligopolists will self-enforce whatever limited agreements they reach is plainly unreasonable. Rather, cheating is a predictable consequence of oligopolistic conspiracy; the record is replete with examples.[15] The pairing of opportunism with information impactedness explains this condition.

The monopolist, by contrast, does not face the same need to attenuate opportunism. Even within the monopoly firm in which semi-autonomous operating divisions have been created, with each operated as a profit center, interdivisional cheating on agreements will be less than interfirm cheating because (1) the gains can be less fully appropriated by the defector division, (2) the difficulty of detecting cheating is much less, and (3) the penalties to which internal organization has access (including dismissing division managers who behave opportunistically) are more efficacious. Unlike independently owned oligopoly firms, the operating divisions do not have fully pre-emptive claims on their profit streams (whence, the inclination to cheat is less) and, unlike oligopolies, they are subject to detailed audits, including an assessment of internal efficiency performance. Also, while oligopolists can usually penalize defectors only by incurring losses themselves (for example, by matching or overmatching price cuts), the monopoly firm has access to a powerful and delicately conceived internal incentive system that does not require it to incur market penalties of a price-cutting sort. It can mete out penalties to groups and individuals in the firm *in a quasijudicial fashion* —which is to say that it assumes some of the functions of a legal system. Altogether, one concludes that the cheating (price-cutting) which characterizes oligopoly is a less severe problem for the dominant firm.

More generally, the argument comes down to this: it is naive to regard oligopolists as shared monopolists *in any comprehensive sense* —especially if they have differentiated products, have different cost experiences, are differently situated with respect to the market in terms of size, and plainly lack a machinery by which oligopolistic coordination, except of the most primitive sort, is accomplished and enforced. Except, therefore, in highly concentrated industries producing homogeneous products, with nontrivial barriers to entry, and at a mature stage of development, oligopolistic interdependence is unlikely to pose antitrust issues for which dissolution is an appropriate remedy. In the usual oligopoly situation, efforts to achieve collusion are unlikely to be successful or, if they are, will require sufficient explicit communication that *normal remedies* against price fixing, including injunctions not to collude, will suffice.

Where, however, the industry is of the special sort just described, recognized interdependency may be sufficiently extensive to permit tacit

15. For some discussions and examples of cheating and the breakdown of oligopolistic collusion, see Patinkin (1947, pp. 200-204), Posner (1969, p. 1570), and Smith (1966, pp. 113-166).

collusion to succeed. Injunctive remedies, as Turner noted, are in such circumstances unsatisfactory (1962, p. 669). Accordingly, dissolution ought actively to be considered. The recent case brought by the Antitrust Division against the major firms in the gypsum industry affords a current example of where, assuming the charges can be proved, dissolution would appear to be warranted.[16] By contrast, the cereal case brought by the Federal Trade Commission is not one for which comprehensive collusion seems likely.[17]

This does not, however, imply that the cereal industry poses no public policy problems whatsoever. Simply because the shared monopoly model does not fit well does not mean that public policy concerns vanish. But I would urge that attention be focused on those specific practices in the industry which are thought to be objectionable. If, for example, excessive advertising in the cereal industry can be reasonably established, this can be dealt with directly. Selective attention to specific wasteful practices, rather than grand conspiracy theories, are thus called for.

A related implication of the argument is that *dissolution of dominant firms is not an idle economic exercise*, done to reduce large aggregations of corporate power for political or social purposes alone but unlikely to have significant economic performance consequences. For all the reasons developed above, several independent entities cannot realize the same degree of coordination between their policies in price and nonprice respects as can a single firm. Moreover, the price and nonprice differences that predictably arise (Kaysen and Turner, 1959, pp. 114-115) will typically redound to the consumer's benefit.[18] Accordingly, a more assertive antitrust policy with regard to the dissolution of dominant firms is indicated.

16. *United States* v. *United States Gypsum Company*, Crim. No. 73-347 (W.D. Pa., Filed Dec. 27, 1973); cf. *United States v. United States Gypsum Company*, Crim. No. 1042-1073 (D.D.C., filed Dec. 27, 1973).
17. In re Kellogg Company, Dkt. No. 8893 (FTC, filed Jan. 24, 1972).
18. Wasteful selling or product development expenditures among differentiated product oligopolists are sometimes, however, observed. Specific steps might properly be taken to restrict this were a dominant firm to be split into independent, differentiated parts.

13. Conclusions

The foregoing treatment of markets, hierarchies, and related antitrust issues is more microanalytic than previous economic studies of these matters. Whether such an approach qualifies as economics is problematical. If, however, an examination of the transactional details that are associated with the organization of economic activity by alternative modes is to be declared outside the scope while simultaneously the analysis of markets, hierarchies, and antitrust issues in preceding chapters is thought to be fruitful, significant features of the economic problem will fall beyond the range of economic analysis, narrowly construed. Much that has relevance to industrial organization as well as aspects of labor economics and the study of comparative systems would evidently be excluded.

The organizational failures approach to economic organization emphasizes that it is transactions rather than technology that mainly determine the efficacy of exchange by one mode of organization as compared with another. This is not to say that technology is unimportant, however. Rather, the argument is that increasing returns and technological nonseparabilities are rarely decisive. Appeal to such considerations ordinarily explains only relatively small and specialized organizational structures. Were it that complex, contingent claims contracts could be written, negotiated, and enforced at low cost or that incomplete or short-term contracts did not pose hazards, market mediated exchange among relatively small and specialized autonomous traders would be pervasive. The shift of transactions from autonomous market contracting to hierarchy is principally explained by the transactional economies that attend such assignments.

Two things bear noting in this connection. First, the parties to the exchanges in question are assumed to be engaged in recurrent contracting. One-time or occasional exchanges are not matters for which the organizational failures framework is especially germane. Second, the choice between market and hierarchy needs to be addressed in terms of particular types of markets and particular internal organizing modes. That market modes display considerable variety — with respect, for example, to the condition of entry, the size distribution of firms, and so forth—is altogether

248

familiar. That the internal organizational principles of hierarchies also matter is less familiar but nevertheless apparent from preceding chapters. These considerations should be borne in mind continuously.

Some remarks concerning the proposed paradigm are offered in Section 1. The organizational failures framework is then reviewed in Section 2. Antitrust implications of the argument are summarized in Section 3. Possible directions for future research are sketched in Section 4.

1. Toward a Transactional Paradigm

It is elementary that analysis influences the way the world is perceived, including the power to delude and misguide as well as to illuminate and instruct (Nelson, 1974, p. 3). It is also widely agreed that if mechanism B, not mechanism A, is thought to be generating the phenomena of interest, the intellectually respectable thing to do is to build theory B (Koopmans, 1957, p. 140). The heavy emphasis on the development of mathematical economics during the past thirty years, however, has often favored theory A constructions. Transactional frictions, which do not yield easily to formal analysis, have been relatively neglected in the process.[1] Although this may have been necessary, as a transitional measure, to reach the present level of refinement of economic theory, it has sometimes been at the expense of being artificial.

Inasmuch, however, as high theory is necessarily entitled to extreme abstractions, whence the occasion for concern? The test of "relevance," for theorists, is frequently obscure. But the commitment of theory to frictionless systems has encouraged a limited or selective sensitivity to frictions by applied types as well. To the extent that public policy prescriptions have suffered as a result — which I believe has sometimes been the case — this, plainly, has been unfortunate.

I attempt here to set out some of the differences between the proposed approach and alternative ways of addressing applied microeconomic issues. For those who, like myself, are inclined to be eclectic, no comprehensive commitment to one approach rather than another needs to be made. What is involved, rather, is the selection of the approach best suited to deal with the problems at hand. Although the matching of models to problems is not always easy, I find the alternative of forcing one model to handle all the issues to be even less satisfactory — for the reasons given by Nelson and Koopmans at the outset.[2]

1. A number of high theorists have been attracted to the study of transaction costs in the past few years. Recent efforts to introduce transaction costs into mathematical models of markets are as yet tentative and exploratory, however.
2. Eclecticism, like other scientific attitudes, can be learned — provided that the scientific atmosphere is conducive. That scientific understanding turns on atmosphere is widely

1.1 Some Alternative Modeling Approaches

The following review of alternative models is brief and, perforce, incomplete. In some respects it is even a caricature. While regrettable, rectifying this would require a much more expansive discussion. The purposes of the exercise will be realized if the major differences between existing approaches to the study of firm and market structures and that proposed in this book are made evident.

1.1.1 RECEIVED MICROTHEORY

It is widely felt that "the economic background required for understanding antitrust issues seldom requires detailed mastery of economic refinements" (Areeda, 1967, p. 4) — by which is meant, presumably, that the standard economic models of firms and markets that are found in intermediate microtheory textbooks will normally be sufficient for antitrust purposes. I doubt that this is the case. Conventional analysis needs sometimes to be augmented and at other times supplanted by expressly considering transactional problems.

Demand curves (average revenue curves), average cost curves, and the marginal curves of revenue and cost drawn to each of these constitute the basic modeling apparatus for most antitrust treatments of firms and markets. Implicit in most of these models are efficiency assumptions of two kinds. First, it is assumed that the firm operates on its production function, which shows the maximum output of product that can be realized from each feasible combination of factor inputs (mainly labor and capital). Failure to operate on the production function would imply wasteful use of inputs; this is assumed away. Second, given factor prices, it is assumed that the firm chooses the least-cost factor combinations for each possible level of output. The total cost curve, from which average and marginal cost curves are derived, is constructed in this way.

Whether the competitive or monopolistic model of the firm is most appropriate depends on whether economies of scale are large in relation to the market. But whichever model is employed, the prevailing behavioral assumption is one of profit maximization. The nature of the firm with respect to what it will make and what it will buy is normally taken as given; matters of internal organization (hierarchical structure, internal control processes) are likewise ignored. Conformably, competition in the capital market issues rarely surface, much less are probed in depth. That many interesting problems of firms and markets are suppressed or bypassed by

---

conceded. Consider the following statement by Friedman concerning the use of competitive and monopoly models: "The capacity to judge . . . [which model to use] is something that cannot be taught; it can be learned but only by experience and exposure in the 'right' scientific atmosphere, not by rote" (1953, p. 25).

reducing the firm to a production function to which a profit maximization objective has been assigned should come, perhaps, as no surprise.

1.1.2 THE STRUCTURE-CONDUCT-PERFORMANCE PARADIGM

The industrial organization tradition that has developed around the structure-conduct-performance paradigm employs the received micro-theory model of the firm as a building block, but the principal unit of analysis is the industry. The influence of market structure and of interfirm conduct on economic performance occupies the center stage.

The resulting study of firm and market activities is even less micro-analytic than are the models of received microtheory referred to above. However useful this approach has been for many purposes, it is necessarily limited in others. Policy analysts of this tradition, including especially many economists at the Federal Trade Commission, often impute anticompetitive purposes to complex or unfamiliar business practices when instead the principal object of the practices is transactional efficiency. A hostility to complex business organization — be it vertical integration, conglomerate organization, novel credit or leasing arrangements, and the like — commonly obtains.

1.1.3 THE PROPERTY RIGHTS TRADITION

The property rights approach to economic organization is much more recent. Furubotn and Pejovich (1974) trace its origins to the work of Armen Alchian in the 1950's. Several different strands of this approach can be identified.

The frictionlessness variant is a rather extreme, albeit provocative and often instructive, member of the property rights family. The strong version of the "Coase theorem," namely, that allocative efficiency will obtain, whatever the assignment of proeperty rights, if bargaining costs are negligible, is illustrative.[3] That this may now be obvious or even trivial is one thing.[4] But it was scarcely obvious when Coase first advanced the proposition in 1960 and has since spawned a huge literature. It sensitized many to the proposition that the existence of spillover need not occasion intervention by the state.

The assumption of frictionlessness is severely at odds with the approach taken herein. Instead of being omniscient,[5] contractual participants in my scheme are limited in bounded rationality respects. Instead of costless

---

3. Alchian and Kessel's discussion of frictionless capital markets is another example (1962, p. 160).
4. See, however, the qualifications in Regan (1972).
5. Omniscience is a strong variety of unbounded rationality. It is rarely explicitly assumed by anyone, but it is fully consistent with the assumption of frictionlessness and might as well be introduced explicitly.

bargaining, my negotiations are characterized by information impactedness, opportunism, and the sacrifice of valuable resources as parties seek strategic advantage and thereafter engage in haggling.

A second strand of the property rights argument is that institutions evolve in the service of efficiency (Alchian, 1969; Demsetz, 1967). This is closer to the approach taken here, in that transaction costs are admitted and efficiency considerations are emphasized, but the human and environmental factors, and particularly the interactions that exist between these factors, which are responsible for transaction costs are incompletely developed.

My analysis differs in that transaction costs are expressly traced to the human and enviornmental factors that appear in the organizational failures framework. It also differs in that I am inclined to be somewhat more interventionist than are many of those who are associated with this second tradition. Rather than regard all noncollusive private sector economic outcomes to be "good," if only the government would permit the private sector to function,[6] I am plainly prepared to upset some of them—as my treatment of vertical and conglomerate organization and of the dominant firm problem illustrates.

A third approach that comes out of the property rights literature is that it is "effective control" that matters. My initial work on managerial discretion (Williamson, 1964) is an example. A managerial utility function is postulated and the implications of information impactedness, which prevents stockholders from exercising comprehensive controls, are explored. Attempts to generalize the approach to universities and hospitals (Newhouse, 1970) have since been made.

While this approach moves usefully in the direction of "realism in motivation," it pays scant attention to "realism in process."[7] It simply employs too high a level of aggregation to address transaction-specific issues of the kinds that I have been concerned with in this book — and which I feel are of greater economic importance.

1.2 Distinctive Features of the Markets and Hierarchies Approach

The principal features of the markets and hierarchies analysis developed in this book are:

6. Examples are Coase on the Federal Communications Commission (1959) and Demsetz on public utility regulation (1968).

7. For a brief discussion of realism in motivation, which entails reformulating the objective function, versus realism in process, of which the *Behavioral Theory of the Firm* is an example (Cyert and March, 1963), see Williamson (1964, pp. 10-17). The realism in process that concerns me in this book is more microanalytic than is the Cyert and March approach, which focuses on the implications of simple decision rules and simple adaptation rules for firm behavior. My unit of analysis is the transaction and, unlike Cyert and March, a comparative institutional (market or hierarchy) orientation is maintained.

1. It makes evident that it is transactions rather than technology that underlie the interesting issues of microeconomic organization.
2. A comparative institutional attitude is maintained: markets and hierarchies are regarded as alternative contracting modes.
3. It makes explicit provision for rudimentary attributes of human nature (bounded rationality and opportunism) and relates these to a set of environmental factors (complexity/uncertainty and small numbers) in the context of an organizational failures framework.
4. It is much more microanalytic than previous treatments, focusing as it does on the transactional details of recurrent contracting under alternative modes of organization. Reducing, as it does, to a study of contracting means that the contracting expertise of lawyers developed in other contexts can be drawn upon.[8]
5. However useful the fiction of frictionless is for some purposes, it is an impediment to the study of the efficiency properties of alternative modes of economic organization. The frictionless fiction is accordingly abandoned.
6. Organization form, which is concerned with the decomposition principles of hierarchy, is introduced as an internal organizational counterpart to the familiar market structure measures of industrial organization.
7. New questions or a different slant on old questions is afforded across a wide range of issues — including peer group organization, the employment relation, vertical integration, conglomerate organization, technological progress, dominant firms, and oligopoly.
8. The approach is comparatively value-free — it is biased neither for nor against unfettered market modes of organization.
9. Supplying a satisfying exchange relation is made part of the economic problem by introducing the notion of atmosphere. The disregard for attitudinal interaction effects, among transactions and within groups, that is associated with *quid pro quo* modes of analysis in which separability is implicitly assumed is thereby avoided.

2. The Organizational Failures Framework and Hierarchy

The organizational failures framework applies to the study of a variety of exchange relations that are not *prima facie* associated and applies symmetrically to market and nonmarket forms of organization alike. It attempts

---

8. See Macaulay (1963) and Leff (1970).

to identify ultimate, as contrasted with immediate, sources of transactional friction. As compared with previous efforts to explain market and organizational failures, it relies on a relatively small set of explanatory factors.

The emphasis on transactions favored here bears a similarity, which is sometimes quite close, to John R. Commons' study of institutional economics in the 1930's. Thus I, like Commons, regard the transaction as "the ultimate unit of economic investigation" (1934, p. 6). Also, Commons addressed himself to what he referred to as the "going concern" and the "working rules" that appertain thereto (1934, p. 69), with special emphasis on contracting for future events. In the language favored here, Commons was concerned with the development of efficient modes for completing transactions which involved recurrent contracting under conditions of uncertainty. The significant differences between the working rules (which include the incentive and control instruments and associated constitutional powers) of markets and internal organizations are plainly germane for comparative institutional choice-making purposes. Thus, although there is no simple correspondence between the rather elaborate quasi-judicial vocabulary developed by Commons for evaluating transactions and the language of the organizational failures framework, his general approach and many of the institutional phenomena which were of concern to Commons are the same as those dealt with here.

The organizational failures framework consists of a set of human factors on the one hand, and a related set of environmental factors on the other, which together explain the efficacy of contracting. The environmental factors are uncertainty/complexity and small numbers, which are familiar to economists from the prominent role they play in the market failure literature. The human factors are bounded rationality and opportunism, which are somewhat less familiar. Not that discussions of these human attributes have never appeared previously in the economics literature, but an effort to identify these as key human factors and to relate these to the environmental factors mentioned above has not previously been attempted. In addition, there is a derived condition, referred to as information impactedness, and a systems related influence, referred to as atmosphere, that completes the framework. My remarks here focus on these less familiar categories, with emphasis on the way in which each is affected by internal organization.

Bounded rationality can take either computational or language forms. The pairing of limited computational capacity with uncertainty is what makes a complete set of contingent claims contracts infeasible or very costly to write. In circumstances where incomplete contracting exposes the agents to the negotiations to considerable risk of opportunistic behavior, alternatives to market forms of organization may be favored instead. Internal organization can thus arise on this account.

Internal organization not only serves to curb such opportunism (see below), thereby relaxing the need for complete contracts, but hierarchy also has advantages in computational and planning respects, in that it facilitates the specialization of decision-making and economizes on communication expense. Economies of communication are realized in part through specialization of information collection and dissemination, partly through idiosyncratic coding economies, and partly by promoting the convergence of expectations [in the sense of Malmgren (1961)].

As indicated, bounded rationality is manifested not merely as a computational constraint but is also the result of language limitations. This latter, when paired with an information impactedness condition, can also occasion internal organization. Here the bounded rationality problem is that participants to a transaction sometimes lack the ability to communicate successfully about the nature of the transaction through the use of words or symbols that are contractually meaningful. The requisite language may not exist or the individuals concerned may not have access to it — possibly because they are intrinsically limited in their ability to acquire it.

But while the individuals in question may be language-limited in contractual respects, they may nevertheless be able in other respects successfully to communicate about the phenomena in question. It is merely the failure, or prohibitive cost, of formal language that impedes the exchange. A picture, according to a Chinese proverb, is said to be worth ten thousand words. A demonstration may be worth ten million. Apprenticeship systems, which involve learning- and teaching-by-doing, are often the most efficient means of communication for this reason.

The assumption that individuals behave in a self-interested way is so commonplace to economics that it would seem scarcely to warrant separate attention. Opportunism, however, is more than simple self-interest seeking. It is self-interest seeking with guile: agents who are skilled at dissembling realize transactional advantages. Economic man, assessed with respect to his transactional characteristics, is thus a more subtle and devious creature than the usual self-interest seeking assumption reveals.

Opportunism can involve either data distortion or the making of self-disbelieved promises. Data distortion is possible, of course, only if an information impactedness condition obtains. Symmetrically, information impactedness by itself would pose no transactional problem if individuals could be relied on candidly to reveal the information to which they have selective (low cost) access. It is the proclivity of individuals to distort to their advantage the data to which they have preferred access which poses the contractual problem. *Ceteris paribus,* forms of organization which serve to check these distortion tendencies, possibly by reducing the information disparities between the parties through auditing, will be favored. Internal organization may obtain for this reason.[9]

9. This is not, however, to say that internal organization does not have to contend with distortion problems of its own. It does. For the reasons given in Chapter 7, internal supply is beset by reciprocity, expansion, and persistence biases. The decision to procure internally, once that capability exists, the decision to continue a project, once it is begun, and

Atmosphere is a concept which noneconomists are apt to find less objectionable than economists. Indeed, much of what economists do is to rationalize how human behavior is to be understood in familiar net gain terms, and to debunk such relatively loose concepts as atmosphere. Scratch an economist and you find a deeply committed rationalist.[10]

That the rationality approach has powerful advantages is beyond dispute. But there is a risk that it will be employed with excessive zeal. There is a tendency to focus on the parts, which often lend themselves to rationalization, sometimes at the expense of the whole.[11] Reference to atmosphere has the advantage that it expressly raises systems considerations. What are the prevailing attitudes, how are these influenced by the nature of the transactions, and with what spillover consequences?

The usual assumption in economics, implicit if not explicit, is that individuals regard their relation to the system in a strictly neutral, dispassionate manner. Subject only to the condition that transactions are technologically separable, each transaction can be priced separately and metered independently. I submit, however, that technological separability is merely a necessary and not a sufficient condition for transactions to be regarded independently. Attitudinal separability must also be established. To process transactions which are technologically separable but attitudinally interrelated, in either individual or group respects,[12] as though they were independent necessarily misses spillover effects in the pricing and metering of these transactions. Suboptimality will result if the fiction of independence is maintained when in fact attitudinal spillover exists at the margin.

The problem in all of this is to identify when such attitudinal considerations operate strongly and when they can be safely neglected. I conjecture that transactions which affect conceptions of self-esteem and/or perceptions of collective well-being are those for which attitudinal considerations are especially important. The employment relation is the leading instance of a market exchange where the influence of metering intensity on work attitudes needs to be assessed with care. More specifically, efforts to divide the employment relation into parts and assess each separately in strictly

---

the decision to renew or expand an internal facility, once it is in place, are each subject to subversion by the bureaucratic process. Consequently, where effective (large numbers) competition exists, both presently and prospectively, market supply is apt to be favored. In circumstances, however, where parity among suppliers is upset by nontrivial first-mover advantages, reliance on market supply is no longer clearly to be preferred.

10. Arrow describes an economist as one who "by training thinks of himself as the guardian of rationality, the ascriber of rationality to others, and the prescriber of rationality to the social world" (1974, p. 16).

11 Halberstam (1973) describes President Kennedy and his team of top advisors, especially McNamara and McGeorge Bundy, as committed rationalists, and attributes the misadventure of the United States foreign and military policies in Vietnam to these qualities. Eisenhower, by contrast, was much more of a political animal.

12. Individual spillovers are apt to be intertemporal. Group spillovers occur within sets of mutually sympathetic individuals.

calculative, instrumental terms can have, for some individuals at least, counterproductive consequences.

It is interesting to speculate why individuals do not regard all market transactions neutrally. Though I do not pretend that it is a complete explanation, I submit that one of the reasons for this is that individuals are generally not schizophrenic with respect to their economic and noneconomic identities. Individuals who experience nonmetered externalities in noneconomic contexts and reach nonmarket accommodations thereto bring the attitudes and experiences which evolve in these nonmarket circumstances to the workplace as well. Rather than regard transactions in strictly *quid pro quo* terms, with each account to be settled separately, they look instead for a favorable balance among a related set of transactions.[13]

The above discussion of the affirmative ways in which hierarchy affects each of the factors that appears in the organizational failures framework may be summarized compactly as follows:

> *Bounded rationality.* Hierarchy extends the bounds on rationality by permitting the specialization of decision-making and economizing on communication expense.

> *Opportunism.* Hierarchy permits additional incentive and control techniques to be brought to bear in a more selective manner, thereby serving to curb small-numbers opportunism.

> *Uncertainty.* Hierarchy permits interdependent units to adapt to unforeseen contingencies in a coordinated way and furthermore serves to "absorb" uncertainty.[14]

> *Small numbers.* Hierarchy permits small-numbers bargaining indeterminacies to be resolved by fiat.

> *Information impactedness.* Hierarchy extends the constitutional powers to perform an audit, thereby narrowing (prospectively at least) the information gap that obtains between autonomous agents.

13. Also, and relatedly, individuals resist being "used" in an entirely instrumental way. Poets and philosophers refer to the dignity of man. A strict *quid pro quo* exchange relation with respect to something as central to one's dignity as his employment denigrates this image. For jobs that are idiosyncratic, productive losses easily obtain if an effort is made continuously to settle current accounts.

    The economics of the New Left is relevant in this regard. The New Left rejects conventional economics in part because the implied exchange relations are regarded as oppressive. But the New Left is both unselective in its critique and naive in prescribing the peer group as the preferred form of organization. It is unselective in that it makes little effort to identify those transactions for which extra economic considerations are most important. It is naive in disregarding both bounded rationality and opportunism as factors which severely limit the efficacy of peer group organization.

    The viewpoint urged here is that, whether one regards market systems as liberating or exploitative, none of the factors in the organizational failures framework can be safely neglected in assessing alternative modes. To do so runs the risk that organizational extremes will be favored which will be found lacking in viability.

14. For discussions of uncertainty absorption, see Cyert and March (1963) and Malmgren (1961).

Atmosphere. As compared with market modes of exchange, hierarchy provides, for some purposes at least, a less calculative exchange atmosphere.[15]

These are the advantages of hierarchy. In circumstances where market exchange would occur between small numbers of traders under conditions of uncertainty, hierarchical exchange is apt to be favored. But two caveats should be noted. First, hierarchy experiences both size and transactional limits — for the reasons given in Chapter 7. Second, the advantages indicated are merely potential. For this potential to be realized requires that appropriate principles for decomposing hierarchies be followed and the requisite incentive and control apparatus supplied. This is the organization form issue, as developed in Chapters 8 and 9.

3.   Antitrust Implications

The policy implications of the argument that are of principal concern are those having to do with antitrust. Dewey has described the role of economists in antitrust as follows (1959, p. i):

> The important issues in the control of monopoly are "economic" in the sense that judges and administrators are compelled to make decisions in the light of what they think the business world is "really" like, and it is the task of economists through research and reflections to provide them with an increasingly accurate picture.

While this book does not aspire to describe business reality, it is an effort to provide a more accurate picture. To the extent that it both succeeds in this objective and has a policy impact, antitrust enforcement will proceed more selectively in the future.

A brief summary of the antitrust implications of the argument with respect to vertical integration, conglomerate organization, dominant firms, and oligopoly is set out here. This by no means exhausts the applications of the organizational failures framework to antitrust, but these are the main issues with which I have been concerned in this book.

3.1   Vertical Integration

My examination of vertical integration in transactional terms leads to a mixed verdict. The more strident claims of those who proclaim vertical integration (and, more generally, vertical market restrictions of all kinds)

---

15. Note, however, that the peer group may be preferred to hierarchy in this respect — at least in small organizations.

to be altogether innocent of anticompetitive potential are shown to be exaggerated. For one thing, it may be a means of mobilizing latent monopoly power (for example, by facilitating price discrimination — which may or may not yield efficiency gains). In addition, although vertical integration, by itself, has no immediate effect on market concentration at any stage, it can have entry impeding consequences in highly concentrated industries if, by foreclosing a market, entry were to be inhibited to any but a fully integrated supplier, and if labor and capital markets do not operate frictionlessly. Where, however, the industry in question is not highly concentrated, this same anticompetitive potential is much less severe. Absent collusion, the presumption that vertical integration is innocent or beneficial is generally appropriate. Vertical merger guidelines,[16] which currently advise that acquisitions will be challenged where a ten percent firm at one stage of an industry acquires a six percent firm at another stage, are plainly overrestrictive.[17]

Of course, vertical integration, once accomplished, does not commit the firm to continuing the integrated relationship indefinitely — although there are often strong bureaucratic incentives to do so. When, however, competitive supply becomes feasible, internal supply, as a public policy matter, becomes relatively disfavored — because it is not apt to be the least cost mode.[18] In consideration of the bureaucratic proclivities to maintain an integrated relationship, more attention ought probably to be given to the matter of supplying firms with incentives for voluntary divestiture.

3.2 Conglomerate Organization

The broadside attack that some lawyers and economists have leveled against conglomerates appears to be overdrawn. Again, frictions in the capital market turn out to be of fundamental importance. Absent takeover frictions or the incomplete congruence between the preference function of incumbent managements and the firm's stockholders, the conglomerate appears to lack a compelling economic purpose of a socially redeeming kind. In an economy, however, where returning funds to and reallocating funds by the capital market incurs nontrivial transaction costs and/or managers of specialized firms opportunistically display positive earnings retention preferences, the internal reallocation of resources to higher yield uses is what most commends the conglomerate as compared with similarly constituted specialized firms. The conglomerate in these circumstances assumes miniature capital market responsibilities of an energizing

16. U.S. Department of Justice, *Merger Guidelines*, May 30, 1968 (mimeographed).
17. Donald Turner, who headed the Antitrust Division at the time that the merger guidelines were issued, informs me that he shares the view that the vertical merger guidelines are too restrictive.
18. See note 9, above.

kind. That some antitrust specialists are unimpressed with such consequences is explained by their assessment that only economies having technological origins are deserving of consideration — coupled perhaps with a conviction that the supplanting of "competitive market forces," however feeble these forces may be, by internal organization is anticompetitive.[19]

Once it is conceded, however, that the capital market incurs nontrivial transaction costs in resource allocation and management surveillance respects, there is plainly a case for encouraging, or at least not impeding, organizational innovations which have the potential to attenuate internal organizational distortions. Subject to the organization form qualifications which I have repeatedly emphasized, the conglomerate has attractive properties in that it both makes the market for corporate control more credible, thereby inducing self-policing among otherwise opportunistic managements, and promotes the reallocation of resources to high yield uses. Except, therefore, among giant-sized firms, where the risk of offsetting social and political distortions is seriously posed, a more sympathetic posture by the antitrust enforcement agencies toward conglomerates would seem warranted.

3.3 Dominant Firms

The transactional approach to the dominant firm condition may be contrasted with more conventional explanations, which typically attribute dominant firm outcomes to economies of scale in production or to unlawful conduct. I contend that many of these allegations of anticompetitive conduct are contrived — at least in the sense that, even if the conduct in question occurred, it could not plausibly produce a dominant firm condition. Also, although I believe that economies of scale should be admitted as a defense for dominance, I expect that technological economies will commonly be exhausted at a size that falls well short of dominance in a mature industry.

My position is that dominance is often to be attributed to default failure on the part of rivals and to stochastic market failure. *Persistent* failure by actual and potential rivals to grasp economic opportunities at critical formative stages of an industry's development can strap society with a dominant firm for many years thereafter. Chance events during this early

---

19. See, for example, Blake (1973, pp. 566, 574, 578, 579). Blake's views on technology are shared by many economists. Thus, Adams contends: "The unit of technological efficiency is the plant not the firm. This means that there are undisputed advantages of large-scale integrated operations at a single steel plant, for example, but there is little technological justification for combining these functionally separate plants into a single administrative unit" (1970, p. 229). The statement is correct as far as it goes, but it does not go far enough. Transactional as well as technological factors need to be considered in assessing overall efficiency.

development period can also contribute to dominance — which outcomes, moreover, are unlikely to be undone by unassisted market processes if, at the mature stage of an industry's development, stochastic disturbances are attenuated. Rather than accede passively to such monopolistic outcomes or proceed against dominant firms along (contrived) conduct lines, structural relief, if default or.stochastic market failure can be shown, is urged.

3.4 Oligopoly

The principal implication of the argument with respect to oligopolistic industries is that oligopoly ought not uncritically to be equated with a dominant firm condition. It is much more difficult to negotiate a comprehensive collusive agreement, and there are many more problems of effecting a joint-profit maximizing outcome, than are commonly suggested. Theories of "shared monopoly" ought accordingly to be regarded with skepticism. A rational antitrust policy would presumably first address the dominant firm industries and, where feasible, effect dissolution there before going on to attack oligopolies. Contrary to what is sometimes said, there *are* prospective benefits from converting a dominant firm industry into an oligopolistic one.

The foregoing assessments may be contrasted with more usual attitudes toward structural monopoly. Absent unlawful conduct, dominant firm outcomes are rarely challenged. By contrast oligopolistic industries have recently been made the special target of attack by both the Neal Task Force[20] and the Hart Bill.[21] The differences, I conjecture, between the recommendations made here and those reached elsewhere are attributable to the fact that the transactional factors which are emphasized here have, for the most part, been neglected previously.[22]

4. Some Directions for Future Research

4.1 Theoretical

A leading theoretical need is for additional work on the properties of hierarchy. The mathematical theory of hierarchical forms is not, unfortu-

---

20. Neal et al., "White House Task Force on Antitrust Policy" *BNA Antitrust and Trade Regulation Report*, No. 411, May 27, 1968, Special Supplement, Part II.

21. "Industrial Reorganization Act," *Congressional Record of the 92nd Congress*, 2d., sess., July 24, 1972, vol. 118, S11494.

22. Although dominant firm industries are not excluded from the oligopoly subset of concern in the Neal Report and the Hart Bill, neither are dominant firm industries selected out for special attention, which is the position taken here.

nately, well-developed (Varaiya, 1972, p. 497). Simon's (1962) interdisciplinary review of the evolution of hierarchy and his heuristic discussion of its advantages provides useful background for such an effort.[23]

The economic properties of hierarchical modes of organization can be fully established only after additional work is done on bounded rationality and on the efficacy of internal control processes. Lest, however, internal controls be unduely emphasized and pressed with excessive zeal, more attention to the economics of atmosphere is simultaneously required.

The importance of organizational innovation to economic efficiency is poorly understood. Arrow contends in this connection that "the prime need in organizational design is increasing capacity to handle a large agenda. . . . Shortrun efficiency and even flexibility within a narrow framework of alternatives may be less important in the long run than a wide compass of potential activities" (1974, p. 59). This is a provocative and intuitively appealing statement, but plainly needs to be explained. Both historical and theoretical studies can contribute to our understanding of these issues. The diffusion of organizational innovations — within industries, across industries, and across cultures — both in terms of the mechanics of the diffusion process and the economic consequences associated with organizational innovations of various kinds, of which I would nominate the multidivisional structure as the leading example, warrants investigation.

4.2   Empirical

Assuming that measures of organizational structure can be worked up for a large number of corporations over a significant period of years, both cross sectional and time series studies of the influence of organization form on enterprise performance can be performed. Although individual instances of improved performance are easy to cite, the extent to which performance trends in individual firms are affected by organization form changes can be established only by more systematic study of the time series data. Among the types of cross section studies that might usefully be repeated by introducing organization form as an explanatory variable are studies of rates of return to alternative sources of funds (Baumol et al., 1970; Grabowski and Mueller, 1974), industry studies of comparative firm efficiency (Gordon, 1965), as well as more general studies of financial and economic performance (Meyer, 1967). The recent work of Weston and his associates (1970; 1972) on conglomerate performance could also be refined by making organization form distinctions.

Historical studies of vertical integration, such as Buttrick's (1952), would contribute to an understanding of the reasons for and properties of

---

23. See Alexander (1964) and Ashby (1960).

vertical structures. In conformity with the basic thrust of this book, an emphasis on transactional rather than technological conditions is urged. Studies of quasi-integrated modes of organization (for example, franchising) could also usefully be undertaken. A sensitivity to the tradeoff between the incentives of autonomous enterprises and the controls of integrated structures is apt to be important in this connection.

Addressing the dominant firm issue could proceed along either of two main lines. The ambitious approach would involve a reconstruction of the history of the industry, especially during its intermediate development stage, for the purpose of assessing default and/or chance event failure. This would require that major events be reconstructed and critical decisions made by rivals and prospective entrants be evaluated. A less demanding approach would be simply to assume that dominance has resulted from market failures of the types described and check against the possibility that the dominant firm outcome is attributable, instead, to economies of scale or original unexpired patents.

The latter approach is intellectually less satisfying than an attempt to reconstruct the history of the industry during the period when dominance emerged. Inasmuch as the number of dominant firm industries is relatively small, it may be feasible to take the more ambitious approach by having such studies done by academics. The active interest and support of the antitrust enforcement agencies would nevertheless facilitate such an effort. Collaboration between academics and antitrust enforcement officials with respect to the dominant firm industries would seem altogether warranted.

4.3 Public Policy Toward Regulation

The plausibility of arguments that large-numbers bidding at the outset reasonably guarantees that a good or service will thereafter be supplied on efficient terms (Demsetz, 1968) ought to be reexamined with more self-conscious attention to the details of the contracting process. Can "irrelevant complications," such as equipment durability and uncertainty, be assumed away without stripping the argument of all policy significance? When these are introduced and the limits of short- and long-term contracts are acknowledged, is the case for the private sector "solution" still compelling? If not, an assessment of the transactional properties of alternative modes of organizing the activity in question is plainly required before an assignment to the most efficient mode can be made.[24]

24. I have since had occasion to follow up this line of investigation. The results confirm my conjecture that the Demsetz franchise bidding scheme is insufficiently microanalytic and is beset with severe operational limitations. See my "Franchise Bidding for Natural Monopolies — in General and with Respect to CATV," forthcoming.

Bibliography

Adams, Walter, "Galbraith Wrong in Fact and Policy," *Hearings Before the Subcommittee of the Select Committee on Small Business*, U.S. Senate, 90th Cong., 1st Sess., June 29, 1967. Repr. in P. A. Samuelson, ed., *Readings in Economics*, 6th ed., New York: McGraw-Hill Book Company, 1970, pp. 227-230.

Adams, William J., "Firm Size and Research Activity: France and the United States," *Quarterly Journal of Economics. 84:* 386-409, August 1970.

Adelman, M. A., "The Antimerger Act, 1950-1960," *American Economic Review, 51;* 236-244, May 1961.

Akerlof, G. A. "The Markets for 'Lemons': Qualitative Uncertainty and the Market Mechanism," *Quarterly Journal of Economics, 84*: 488-500, August 1970.

Alchian, A. A., "Uncertainty, Evolution and Economic Theory," *Journal of Political Economy, 58:* 211-221, June 1950.

_____."Costs and Outputs," in M. Abramovitz et al., *The Allocation of Economic Resources: Essays in Honor of Bernard Francis Haley.* Stanford: Stanford University Press, 1959, pp. 23-40.

_____ , "Corporate Management and Property Rights," in H. G. Manne, ed., *Economic Policy and Regulation of Corporate Securities.* Washington: American Enterprise Institute for Public Policy Research, 1969, pp. 337-360.

_____ and H. Demsetz, "Production, Information Costs, and Economic Organization," *American Economic Review, 62:* 777-795, December 1972.

_____ , and H. Demsetz, "The Property Rights Paradigm," *Journal of Economic History, 33*: 16-27, March 1973.

_____ and R. A. Kessel, "Competition, Monopoly, and the Pursuit of Pecuniary Gain," *Aspects of Labor Economics.* Princeton: Princeton University Press, 1962.

Alexander, C., *Notes on the Synthesis of Form.* Cambridge: Harvard University Press, 1964.

Alexander, T., "The Unexpected Payoff of Project Apollo," *Fortune. 80:* 114-117 ff., June 1969.

Allen, Bruce T., "Vertical Integration and Market Foreclosure: The Case of Cement and Concrete," *The Journal of Law and Economics. 14:* 251-274. April 1971.

Allen, Stephen A., III, "Corporate Divisional Relationships in Highly Diversified Firms," in Jay W. Lorsch and Paul R. Lawrence, eds., *Studies in Organization Design.* Homewood, Ill,: Richard D. Irwin, Inc., 1970, pp. 16-35.

Angyal, A., "A Logic of Systems," in F. E. Emery, ed., *Systems Thinking.* Middlesex, England: Penguin Books Ltd., 1969, pp. 17-29.

Areeda, Philip, *Antitrust Analysis.* Boston: Little, Brown and Company, 1967.

Arrow, K. J., "Economic Welfare and the Allocation of Resources for Invention," in *The Rate and Direction of Inventive Activity*. Princeton: Princeton University Press, 1962, pp. 609-625.

———, "Comment," *The Rate and Direction of Inventive Activity*. Princeton: Princeton University Press, 1962, pp. 353-358.

———, *Aspects of the Theory of Risk Bearing*. Helsinki: Yrjo Jahnssonin Saatio, 1965.

———, "The Organization of Economic Activity," *The Analysis and Evaluation of Public Expenditure: The PPB System*. Joint Economic Committee, 91st Cong., 1st Sess., 1969, pp. 59-73.

———, *Essays in the Theory of Risk-Bearing*. Chicago: Markham, 1971.

———, "Gifts and Exchanges," *Philosophy and Public Affairs*, Summer 1972, 343-362.

———, *Limits of Organization*. New York: W. W. Norton & Company, Inc., 1974.

Ashby, W. R., *Design for a Brain*. New York: John Wiley & Sons, Inc., 1960.

Bain, J. S., *Barriers to New Competition*. Cambridge: Harvard University Press, 1956.

———, *Industrial Organization*. New York: John Wiley & Sons, Inc., 1968.

Baldwin, W.L., "The Feedback Effect of Business Conduct on Industry Structure," *Journal of Law and Economics, 12:* 123-153, April 1969.

Banfield, E. C., *The Moral Basis of a Backward Society*. New York: The Free Press, 1958.

Barnard, C. I., *The Functions of the Executive*, 2d ed., Cambridge: Harvard University Press, 1962.

———, "Functions and Pathology of Status Systems in Formal Organizations," in W. F. Whyte, ed., *Industry and Society*. New York: McGraw-Hill Book Company, Inc., 1946, pp. 46-83.

Barro, R. J., "Monopoly and Contrived Depreciation," *Journal of Political Economy*, March/April 1972, *81:* 598-602.

Bartlett, F. C., *Remembering*. Cambridge, England: The University Press, 1932.

Baumol, W. J., *The Stock Market and Economic Efficiency*. New York: Fordham University Press, 1965.

———, P. Heim, B. Malkiel and R. Quandt, "Earnings Retention, New Capital, and the Growth of the Firm," *Review of Economics and Statistics 52:* 345-355, November 1970.

Baxter, William F., "Legal Restrictions on Exploitation of the Patent Monopoly: An Economic Analysis," *Yale Law Journal 76:* 267-370, December 1966.

Becker, G., "Investment in Human Capital: A Theoretical Analysis," *Journal of Political Economy*, Supplement. *70:* 9-44, October 1962.

Beer, S., "The Aborting Corporate Plan: A Cybernetic Account of the Interface Between Planning and Action," in E. Jantsch, ed., *Perspectives of Planning*. Paris, 1969, pp. 397-422.

Berle, A. A. and G. C. Means, *The Modern Corporation and Private Property*. New York: Commerce Clearing House, Inc., 1932.

Berry, C. H., "Corporate Diversification and Market Structure," *The Bell Journal of Economics and Management Science*, 196-204, Spring 1974.

Bhargava, Narottam, *The Impact of Organization Form on the Firm: Experience of 1920-1970*. Unpublished Ph.D. dissertation, University of Pennsylvania, 1972.

Blair, John M., "The Conglomerate Merger in Law and Economics," *Georgetown Law Review, 43:* 79-92, Summer 1958.

Blake, H. M. "Conglomerate Mergers and the Antitrust Laws," *Columbia Law Review*, 73: 555-592, March, 1973.

Blau, P. M. and R. W. Scott, *Formal Organizations.* San Francisco: Chandler Publishing Company, 1962.

Bork, Robert H., "The Rule of Reason and the Per Se Concept: Price Fixing and Market Division, I," *Yale Law Journal, 74:* 775-847, April 1965.

_____, "The Rule of Reason and the Per Se Concept: Price Fixing and Market Division, I," *Yale Law Journal, 74:* 775-847, April 1965.

_____, "The Rule of Reason and the Per Se Concept: Price Fixing and Market Division, II," *Yale Law Journal, 75:* 375-475, January 1966.

_____, "Vertical Integration and Competitive Processes," in J. Fred Weston and S. Peltzman, eds., *Public Policy Towards Mergers.* Pacific Palisades, Calif.: Goodyear Publishing Company, 1969, pp. 139-149.

Boulding, K. E., "The Economics of Knowledge and the Knowledge of Economics," *American Economic Review, 58:* 1-13, May 1966.

Bower, Joseph L., "Management Decision Making in Large Diversified Firms," draft, October 1, 1971.

Bowman, Ward S., *Patents and Antitrust Law: A Legal and Economic Appraisal.* Chicago: University of Chicago Press, 1973.

Bronfenbrenner, Martin, "Japan's Galbraithian Economy," *Public Interest, 21:* 149-157, Fall 1970.

Brown, Alvin, *Organization, A Formulation of Principles.* New York: Hibbert Printing Company, 1945.

Brown, Donaldson, "Pricing Policy in Relation to Financial Control," *Management and Administration, 1:* 195-258, February 1924.

Buttrick, J., "The Inside Contracting System," *Journal of Economic History, 12:* 205-221, Summer 1952.

Campbell, Donald T., "Systematic Error on the Part of Human Links in Communication Systems," *Information and Control,* Vol. 1, 1958. pp. 334-369.

_____, "Reforms as Experiments," *American Psychologist. 24:* 409-429, April 1969.

Cary, William, "Corporate Devices Used to Insulate Management from Attack," *Antitrust Law Journal,* (1) *39:* 318-333, 1969-1970.

Caves, R., *American Industry: Structure, Conduct, Performance,* 2d ed., Englewood Cliffs, N.J.: Prentice-Hall, Inc., 1967.

Chandler, Alfred D. Jr., *Strategy and Structure.* New York: Doubleday &Company, Inc., Anchor Books Edition, 1966.

_____, and S. Salisbury, *Pierre du Pont and the Making of the Modern Corporation.* New York: Harper & Row, Publishers, Incorporated, 1971.

Chernoff, H. and L. E. Moses, *Elementary Decision Theory.* New York: John Wiley & Sons, Inc., 1959.

Churchill, N. C., W. W. Cooper and T. Sainsbury, "Laboratory and Field Studies of the Behavioral Effects of Audits," in C. P. Bonini et al., eds., *Management Controls: New Directions in Basic Research.* New York: McGraw-Hill Book Company, 1964, pp. 253-267.

Cicchetti, C. J. and M. A. Freeman, "Option Demand and Consumer Surplus: Further Comment," *Quarterly Journal of Economics, 85:* 528-539, August 1971.

Coase, R. H., "The Nature of the Firm," *Economica N. S.* 1937, *4:* 386-405, repr. in G. J. Stigler and K. E. Boulding, eds., *Readings in Price Theory.* Homewood, Ill.: Richard D. Irwin, Inc., 1952.

_____ , "The Federal Communications Commission," *The Journal of Law and Economics. 2:* 1-40, October 1959.

_____ , "The Problem of Social Cost," *Journal of Law and Economics, 3:* 1-44, October 1960.

_____ , "The Regulated Industries: Discussion," *American Economic Review. 54:* 194-197, May 1964.

_____ , "The Conglomerate Merger," working paper for the Task Force on Productivity and Competition, *Report of the Task Force on Productivity and Competition* (the Stigler Report), February 18, 1969, repr. in *B.N.A. Antitrust and Trade Regulation Reporter,* No. 415, X-1 — X-2, June 24, 1969.

_____ , "Industrial Organization: A Proposal for Research," in V.R. Fuchs, ed., *Policy Issues and Research Opportunities in Industrial Organization.* New York: National Bureau of Economic Research, 1972, pp. 59-73.

Cole. A. H., "The Entrepreneur: Introductory Remarks," *American Economic Review, 63:* 60-63, May 1968.

Comanor, W. S., "Research and Technical Change in the Pharmaceutical Industry," *Review of Economics and Statistics, 47:* 182-190, May 1965.

_____ , "Market Structure, Product Differentiation, and Industrial Research," *Quarterly Journal of Economics, 81:* 639-657, November 1967.

Commons, John R., *Institutional Economics.* Madison: University of Wisconsin Press, 1934.

_____ , *The Economics of Collective Action.* Madison: University of Wisconsin Press, 1970.

Cox, A., "The Legal Nature of Collective Bargaining Agreements," *Michigan Law Review, 57:* 1-36, November 1958.

Cyert, R. M., and J. G. March, *A Behavioral Theory of the Firm.* Englewood Cliffs, N. J. : Prentice-Hall, Inc., 1963.

Dahl, R. G. and C. E. Lindblom, *Politics, Economics and Welfare.* New York: Harper & Row, Publishers, Incorporated, 1963.

Davis, L. E., and D. C. North, *Institutional Change and American Economic Growth.* Cambridge, England: Cambridge University Press, 1971.

Davis, Otto A. and Andrew Whinston, "Externalities, Welfare, and the Theory of Games," *Journal of Political Economy, 70:* 241-262, 1962.

Dayan, David, *Vertical Integration and Monopoly Regulation.* Unpublished Ph.D. dissertation, Princeton University, 1972.

Demsetz, H., "Toward a Theory of Property Rights," *American Economic Review, 57:* 347-359, May 1967.

_____ , "The Cost of Transacting," *Quarterly Journal of Economics, 82:* 33-53, February 1968.

_____ , "Why Regulate Utilities?" *Journal of Law and Economics, 11:* 55-66, April 1968.

_____ , "Information and Efficiency: Another Viewpoint," *Journal of Law and Economics, 12:* 1-22, April 1969.

Dewey, D., *Monopoly in Economics and Law.* Chicago: Rand McNally & Company, 1959.

Diamond, P., "Political and Economic Evaluation of Social Effects and External-ities: Comment," in M. Intrilligator, ed., *Frontiers of Quantitative Economics.* Amsterdam: North-Holland Publishing Company, 1971, pp. 30-32.

Dirlam, J., and A. Kahn, *Fair Competition, The Law and Economics of Antitrust Policy.* Ithaca, N. Y.: Cornell University Press, 1954.

Doeringer, P. and M. Piore, *Internal Labor Markets and Manpower Analysis.* Boston: D. C. Heath and Company, 1971.

Downs, Anthony, *Inside Bureaucracy.* Boston: Little, Brown and Company, 1967.

Drucker, Peter F., "The New Markets and the New Capitalism," *The Public Interest*, No. 21: 44-79, Fall 1970.

_____, "On Managing the Public Service Institution," *The Public Interest*, No. 33: 43-60, Fall 1973.

Dunlop, J., "The Task of Contemporary Wage Theory," in G. W. Taylor and F. C. Pierson, eds., *New Concepts in Wage Determination.* New York: McGraw-Hill Book Company, 1957, pp. 117-139.

_____, *Industrial Relation Systems.* New York: Holt, Rinehart and Winston, Inc., 1958.

Eckstrom, L. J., "Industrial Foreign Licensing Arrangements," in W. S. Surrey and C. Shaw, eds., *A Lawyers Guide to International Business Transactions.* Philadelphia: Committee on Continuing Legal Education of the American Law Institute and the American Bar Association, 1963.

Edgeworth, F. Y., *Mathematical Psychics.* London: Kegan Paul, 1881, repr. New York: Kelley and Millman, 1954.

Edwards, C. D., "Economic Concentration, Part 1: Overall and Conglomerate Aspects," *Hearings before the Subcommittee on Antitrust and Monopoly,* Committee on the Judiciary, U.S. Senate, 82nd Cong. 1964, pp. 36-47.

Emery, J. C., *Organizational Planning and Control Systems: Theory and Technology.* New York: The Macmillan Company, 1969.

Etzioni, A., *A Comparative Analysis of Complex Organizations.* New York: The Free Press, 1961.

Feldman, J. and H. Kanter, "Organizational Decision Making," in J. March, ed., *Handbook of Organizations.* Chicago: Rand McNally & Company, 1965, pp. 614-649.

Feldman, Paul, "Efficiency, Distribution and the Role of Government in a Market Economy," *Journal of Political Economy*, 79: 508-526, May/June 1971.

Feller, W., *An Introduction to Probability Theory and Its Application.* New York: John Wiley & Sons, Inc., 1957.

Fellner, William, "Prices and Wages under Bilateral Oligopoly," *Quarterly Journal of Economics, 61:* 503-532, August 1947.

_____, *Competition Among the Few.* New York: Alfred A. Knopf, Inc., 1949.

_____, "The Influence of Market Structure on Technological Progress," *Quarterly Journal of Economics, 65:* 560-567, November 1951.

Fisher, F. M. and P. Temin, "Returns to Scale in Research and Development: What Does the Schumpeterian Hypothesis Imply?" *Journal of Political Economy, 81:* 56-70, January/February 1973.

Franko, Lawrence G., "The Growth, Organizational Efficiency of European Multi-national Firms: Some Emerging Hypotheses," *Colloques International Aux C.N.R.S., 1972,* No. 549: 335-366.

Friedman, M., *Essays in Positive Economics.* Chicago: University of Chicago Press, 1953.

Galbraith, J. K., *American Capitalism: The Concept of Countervailing Power,* Boston: Houghton Mifflin Company, 1952.

———, "Control of Prices and People," *The Listener, 76 :* 793-795, December 8, 1966.

———, *The New Industrial State.* Boston: Houghton Mifflin Company, 1967.

Gardner, John W., *Self Renewal: The Individual and the Innovative Society.* New York: Harper & Row, Publishers, Incorporated, 1964.

Georgescu-Roegen, N., "Chamberlin's New Economics and the Unit of Production," in R. E. Kuenne, ed., *Monopolistic Competition Theory: Studies in Impact.* New York: John Wiley and Sons, Inc., 1967, pp. 31-62.

Goffman, I., *Strategic Interaction.* Philadelphia: University of Pennsylvania Press, 1969.

Gordon, R. J., "Airline Costs and Managerial Efficiency," *Transportation Economics.* New York: Columbia University Press, 1965, pp. 61-92.

Gouldner, A. W., "The Norm of Reciprocity," *American Sociological Review, 25:* 161-179, 1961.

Grabowski, Henry G. and Dennis C. Mueller, "Life Cycle Effects on Corporate Returns on Retentions," *Review of Economics and Statistics,* forthcoming.

Green, H. A. J., *Consumer Theory.* Middlesex, England: Penguin Books Ltd., 1971.

Grosvenor, W. M., "The Seeds of Progress," *Chemical Markets,* 1929, pp. 23, 24, 26.

Guetzkow, H., "Communication in Organizations," in J. G. March, ed., *Handbook of Organizations.* Chicago: Rand McNally & Company, 1965, pp. 534-573.

Hadley, A. T., "The Good and Evil of Industrial Combination," *Atlantic Monthly, 79:* 377-385, March 1897.

Halberstam, David, *The Best and the Brightest.* New York: Random House, Inc., 1973.

Hamberg, D., "Invention in the Industrial Laboratory," *Journal of Political Economy, 71:* 95-116, April 1963.

———. *R & D: Essays on the Economics of Research and Development.* New York: Random House, Inc., 1966.

Hamilton, W. F. and M. A. Moses, "An Optimization Model for Corporate Financial Planning," *Operations Research, 21:* 677-692, May/June 1973.

Hampton, D., C. Summer and R. Webber, *Organizational Behavior and the Practice of Management.* Glenview, Ill.: Scott, Foresman and Company, 1968.

Handler, M., "Twenty Fourth Annual Antitrust Review," *Columbia Law Review, 72:* 1-63, January 1972.

Harberger, A. C., "Three Basic Postulates for Applied Welfare Economics: An Interpretative Essay," *Journal of Economic Literature, 2:* 785-797, September 1971.

Harrison, B., *Education, Training, and the Urban Ghetto.* Baltimore: The Johns Hopkins Press, 1972.

Hayek, F., "The Use of Knowledge in Society," *American Economic Review, 35:* 519-530, September 1945.

Heflebower, R. B., "Observations on Decentralization in Large Enterprises," *Journal of Industrial Economics, 9:* 7-22, November 1960.

Hicks, J. R., "Annual Survey of Economic Theory: The Theory of Monopoly," *Econometrica, 3:* 1-20, January, 1935.

_____ "The Rehabilitation of Consumer Surplus," *Review of Economic Studies,* *7:* 108-116, February 1941.

Hirschman, A. O., *Exit, Voice and Loyalty.* Cambridge: Harvard University Press, 1970.

Hirshleifer, J., "The Firm's Cost Function: A Successful Reconstruction," *Journal of Business. 35:* 235-255, July 1962.

_____, *Investment, Interest and Capital.* Englewood Cliffs, N.J.: Prentice-Hall Inc., 1970.

Hofstadter, Richard, "What Happened to the Antitrust Movement," in Earl F. Cheit, ed., *The Business Establishment.* New York: John Wiley & Sons, Inc., 1964, pp. 123-151.

Holton, Richard H., "The Role of Competition and Monopoly in Distribution: The Experience in the United States," in J. P. Miller, ed., *Competition, Cartels and Regulation.* Amsterdam: North-Holland Publishing Company, 1962, pp. 263-307, repr. in Lee E. Preston, ed., *Social Issues in Marketing.* Glenview, Ill.: Scott, Foresman and Company, 1968, pp. 137-167.

Horowitz, Ira, "Firm Size and Research Activity," *Southern Economic Journal, 28:* 298-301, January 1962.

Hurwicz, Leonid, "On Informationally Decentralized Systems," in C. B. McGuire and R. Radner, eds., *Decision and Organization.* Amsterdam: North-Holland Publishing Company, 1972, pp. 297-336.

_____ , "The Design of Mechanisms for Resource Allocation," *American Economic Review, 63,* 1-30, May 1973.

Jay, A., *Corporation Man.* New York: Random House, Inc., 1971.

Jewkes, J., D. Sawers and R. Stillerman, *The Sources of Invention.* New York: St. Martin's Press, 1959.

Kamien, Morton and Nancy Schwartz, "On the Degree of Rivalry for Maximum Innovative Activity," Discussion Paper No. 64, The Center for Mathematical Studies in Economics and Management Science, Northwestern University, January 1974.

Katz, D. and R. L. Kahn, *The Social Psychology of Organizations.* New York: John Wiley & Sons, Inc., 1966.

Kaysen, Carl, "Improving the Efficiency of Military Research and Development," in C. J. Friedrich and S. E. Harris, eds., *Public Policy.* Cambridge: Harvard University Press, 1963, pp. 230-268.

_____, "The Present War on Bigness: I," in *The Impact of Antitrust on Economic Growth,* Fourth National Industrial Conference Board Conference on Antitrust in an Expanding Economy, New York, 1965, pp. 31-38.

_____, "Models and Decision Makers: Economists and the Policy Process," *Public Interest,* No. 12: 80-95, Summer 1968.

_____, and D. F. Turner, *Antitrust Policy.* Cambridge: Harvard University Press, 1959.

Kendrick, J. W., *Productivity Trends in the United States.* Princeton: Princeton University Press, 1961.

Kerr, C., "The Balkanization of Labor Markets," in E. Wight Bakke et. al., *Labor Mobility and Economic Opportunity.* Cambridge and New York: The Technology Press of the Massachusetts Institute of Technology, and John Wiley & Sons, Inc., 1954, pp. 92-110.

Kessler, F. and E. Fine, "Culpa in Contrahendo, Bargaining in Good Faith, and

Freedom of Contract: A Comparative Study," *Harvard Law Review, 77:* 401-449, January 1964.

Knight, F. H., *Risk, Uncertainty and Profit.* New York: Harper and Row, Publishers, Incorporated, 1965.

Koopmans, T., *Three Essays on the State of Economic Science.* New York: McGraw-Hill Book Company, 1957.

Kornai, J., *Anti-equilibrium.* Amsterdam: North-Holland Publishing Company, 1971.

Kuhn, Thomas S., *The Structure of Scientific Revolutions.* Chicago: University of Chicago Press, 1962.

Kuznets, Simon, *Economic Change.* New York: W. W. Norton & Co., Inc., 1953.

Leff, A., "Injury, Ignorance and Spite—The Dynamics of Coercive Collection," *Yale Law Journal. 80:* 1-46, November 1970.

Leibenstein, H.. "Allocative Efficiency vs 'X-Efficiency'," *American Economic Review, 56:* 392-415, June 1966.

Levhari, D. and T. N. Srinivasan, "Durability of Consumption Goods: Competition versus Monopoly," *American Economic Review, 59:* 102-107, March 1969.

Lindbeck, A., *Political Economy of the New Left: An Outsiders View.* New York: Harper & Row, Publishers, Incorporated, 1971.

Lipset, S. M., M. A. Trow and J. S. Coleman, *Union Democracy: The Internal Politics of the International Typographical Union.* Chicago: The Free Press of Glencoe, Ill, 1956.

Livernash, E., "The Internal Wage Structure," in G. W. Taylor and F. C. Peirson, eds., *New Concepts in Wage Determination.* New York: McGraw-Hill Book Company, 1957, pp. 140-173.

Luce, R. D. and H. Raiffa, *Games and Decisions.* New York: John Wiley & Sons, Inc., 1957.

MacAvoy, P. S., J. W. McKie and L. E. Preston, "High and Stable Concentration Levels, Profitability, and Public Policy: A Response," *Journal of Law and Economics, 14:* 493-500, October 1971.

McKean, Roland W., "Discussion," *American Economic Review. 61:* 124-225, May 1971.

———, "Symposium: Time in Economic Life: Comment," *Quarterly Journal of Economics. 87:* 638-640, November 1973.

McKenzie, L.. "Ideal Output and the Interdependence of Firms," *Economic Journal, 61:* 785-803, December 1951.

Macaulay, S., "Non-Contractual Relations in Business," *American Sociological Review, 28,* 55-70, 1963.

Main, Jeremy, "Finding Funds to Start Your Own Business," *Money, 2:* 70-73, March 1973.

Malmgren, H., "Information, Expectations and the Theory of the Firm," *Quarterly Journal of Economics, 75:* 399-421, August 1961.

Mandel, Earnest, *Marxist Economic Theory.* (Translated by B. Pearce), vol. 2, Rev. Ed. New York: Monthly Review Press, 1968.

Manne, Henry G., "Mergers and the Market for Corporate Control," *Journal of Political Economy, 73:* 110-120, April 1965.

Mansfield, Edwin, "Comments on Inventive Activity and Industrial R and D Expenditure," *The Rate and Direction of Inventive Activity.* Princeton: Princeton University Press, 1962.

———, *The Economics of Technological Change.* New York: W. W. Norton and Company, Inc., 1968.

———, "Industrial Research and Development: Characteristics, Costs and Diffusion of Results," *American Economic Review. 59:* 65-71. May 1969.

March, J. G. and H. A. Simon, *Organizations.* New York: John Wiley & Sons, Inc., 1958.

Markham, J., *Conglomerate Enterprise and Public Policy.* Boston: Division of Research, Harvard Graduate School of Business Administration, 1973.

Marris, Robin, "Is the Corporate Economy a Corporate State?" *American Economic Review, 62:* 103-115, May 1972.

Marschak, Jacob, "Economics of Inquiring, Communicating, Deciding," *American Economic Review, 58:* 1-18, May 1968.

Marshall, A., *Industry and Trade.* London: The Macmillan Company, 1932.

Mason, E. S., "Preface," to C. Kaysen and D. Turner, *Antitrust Policy.* Cambridge: Harvard University Press, 1959, pp. xi-xxiii.

———, ed., *The Corporation in Modern Society.* Cambridge: Harvard University Press, 1960.

Masson, R. T., "Executive Motivations, Earnings, and Consequent Equity Performance," *The Journal of Political Economy. 79:* 1278-1292, 1971.

Mayer, T., "The Distribution of Ability and Earnings," *Review of Economics and Statistics, 52:* 189-195, May 1960.

Meade, J. E., *The Controlled Economy.* London: George Allen & Unwin, Ltd., 1971.

Meij, J., *Internal Wage Structure.* Amsterdam: North-Holland Publishing Company, 1963.

Meyer, J. R., "An Experiment in the Measurement of Business Motivation," *Review of Economics and Statistics. 49:* 304-318, August 1967.

Michaelman, Frank, "Property, Utility and Fairness: Comments on the Ethical Foundations of 'Just Compensation' Law," *Harvard Law Review. 80:* 1165-1257, April 1967.

Michels, Robert, *Political Parties.* New York: The Free Press, 1966.

Miller, Arthur S., *The Supreme Court and American Capitalism.* New York: The Free Press, 1968.

Modigliani, F., "New Developments on the Oligopoly Front," *Journal of Political Economy. 66:* 215-232, June 1958.

——— and M. H. Miller, "The Cost of Capital, Corporation Finance and the Theory of Investment," *American Economic Review, 48:* 261-297, June 1958.

Mollenhoff, Clark, "Presidential Guile," *Harpers,* 38-42, June 1973.

Mueller, Willard F., "The Origins of the Basic Inventions Underlying DuPont's Major Product and Process Innovations, 1920 to 1950." *The Rate and Direction of Inventive Activity.* Princeton: Princeton University Press, 1962, pp. 323-346.

Neal, P. C. et al., "White House Task Force on Antitrust Policy," *Antitrust and Trade Regulation Report,* no. 411, Special Supplement, part II, May 27, 1969.

Nelson, Richard R., "Intellectualizing About the Moon-Ghetto Metaphor: A Study of the Current Malaise of Rational Analysis of Social Problems," Working Paper W3-28 (Revised), Center for the Study of the City and Its Environment, New Haven: Yale University, February, 1974.

———, M. J. Peck and E. D. Kalachek, *Technology, Economic Growth and Public Policy.* Washington: Brookings Institution, 1967.

_____ and S. Winter, "Toward an Evolutionary Theory of Economic Capabilities," *American Economic Review. 63:* 440-449, May 1973.

Nordhaus, William D., *Invention, Growth and Welfare.* Cambridge: Massachusetts Institute of Technology Press, 1969.

Olson, Mancur, Jr., *The Logic of Collective Action.* New York: Schocken Books. Inc., 1968.

Patinkin, D., "Multiple-Plant Firms, Cartels, and Imperfect Competition," *Quarterly Journal of Economics. 61:* 173-205, February 1947.

Pauly, M., "The Economics of Moral Hazard," *American Economic Review. 58:* 531-537, June 1968.

Peck, M. J., "Inventions in the Postwar American Aluminum Industry," *The Rate and Direction of Inventive Activity.* Princeton: Princeton University Press, 1962. pp. 279-298.

Peterson, S., "Corporate Control and Capitalism," *Quarterly Journal of Economics, 79:* 1019, February 1965.

Phillips, Almarin, *Market Structure, Organization, and Performance.* Cambridge: Harvard University Press, 1962.

_____, "Patents, Potential Competition and Technical Progress," *American Economic Review. 56:* 301-310, May 1966.

_____, *Technological Change and Market Structure: A Case Study of the Market for Commercial Aircraft.* Boston: D. C. Heath and Company, 1970.

Pigou, A. C., ed., *Memorials of Alfred Marshall.* New York: Kelley and Millman, 1956.

Piore, M., "Fragments of a 'Sociological' Theory of Wages," *Papers and Proceedings of the American Economic Association. 63:* 377-384, May 1973.

Posner. R. A., "Natural Monopoly and its Regulation," *Stanford Law Review, 21:* 548-643, February 1969.

_____, "Oligopoly and the Antitrust Laws: A Suggested Approach," *Stanford Law Review. 21:* 1562-1606, June 1969.

_____, "A Statistical Study of Antitrust Enforcement," *Journal of Law and Economics. 13:* 365-420, October 1970.

_____, *Economic Analysis of Law.* Boston: Little, Brown & Co., 1972.

Radner, R., "Competitive Equilibrium Under Uncertainty," *Econometrica, 36:* 31-58. January 1968.

_____, "Problems in the Theory of Markets Under Uncertainty," *American Economic Review. 60:* 454-460, May 1970.

_____, "Existence of Equilibrium of Plans. Prices, and Price Expectations in a Sequence of Markets," *Econometrica. 40:* 289-304, March 1972.

Raimon, R., "The Indeterminateness of Wages of Semiskilled Workers," *Industrial and Labor Relations Review. 6:* 180-194, January 1953.

Regan, D. H., "The Problem of Social Cost Revisited," *Journal of Law and Economics. 15:* 427-438, October 1972.

Reid, S. R., *Mergers, Managers and the Economy.* New York: McGraw-Hill Book Company, 1968.

Richardson, G. B., *Information and Investment.* London: Oxford University Press, 1960.

_____, "The Organization of Industry," *Economic Journal. 82:* 883-896, September 1972.

Ross. A.. "Do We Have a New Industrial Feudalism?" *American Economic Review,* 48: 903-920, December 1958.

Sabin, Sharon. "At Nuclepore, They Don't Work for G. E. Anymore," *Fortune, 88:* 144-153, December 1973.

Sampson, Anthony, *The Sovereign State of I.T.T.* New York: Stein and Day Incorporated, 1973.

Samuelson, P. A., "The Pure Theory of Public Expenditure," *The Review of Economics and Statistics, 36:* 387-389, November 1954.

_____, Foreword to A. Lindbeck, *Political Economy of the New Left: An Outsider's View.* New York: Harper & Row, Publishers, Incorporated, 1971.

Schelling, T. C., *The Strategy of Conflict.* Cambridge: Harvard University Press, 1960.

_____, "On the Ecology of Micromotives," *Public Interest, 25:* 61-98 Fall 1971.

Scherer, F. M., "Size of Firm, Oligopoly and Research: A Comment," *Canadian Journal of Economics and Political Science. 31:* 256-266, May 1965.

_____, "Firm Size, Market Structure, Opportunity and the Output of Patented Inventions," *American Economic Review, 55:* 1098-1125, December 1965.

_____, "Research and Development Resource Allocation Under Rivalry," *Quarterly Journal of Economics. 81:* 359-394, August 1967.

_____, *Industrial Market Structure and Economic Performance.* Chicago: Rand McNally & Company, 1970.

Schlesinger, James R., "Organizational Structures and Planning," in Roland N. McKean, ed., *Issues in Defense Economics.* New York: National Bureau of Economic Research, Inc. 1967, pp. 185-216.

Schmalensee, R.. "A Note on the Theory of Vertical Integration," *Journal of Political Economy. 81:* 442-449, March/April 1973.

Schmookler, J., "Inventors Past and Present," *Review of Economics and Statistics, 39:* 321-333, August 1957.

Schumpeter, J. A., *Capitalism, Socialism, and Democracy.* New York: Harper & Row, Publishers, Incorporated, 1942.

_____, *The Theory of Economic Development.* New York: Oxford University Press, 1961.

Scott, B. R., "The Industrial State: Old Myths and New Realities," *Harvard Business Review. 51:* 133-149, March/April 1973.

Sheehan, Neil, et al., *The Pentagon Papers.* New York: Bantam Books, Inc., 1971.

Shepherd, W. G., *Market Power and Economic Welfare.* New York: Random House, Inc., 1970.

Shubik, M., "Information, Duopoly, and Competitive Markets: A Sensitivity Analysis," *Kyklos, Fasc, 4, 26:* 736-761, 1973.

Simon, H. A., *Models of Man.* New York: John Wiley & Sons. Inc., 1957.

_____, *Administrative Behavior.* 2d ed., New York: The Macmillan Company, 1961.

_____, "The Architecture of Complexity," *Proceedings of the American Philosophical Society, 106:* 467-482, December 1962.

_____, *The Sciences of the Artificial.* Cambridge: Massachusetts Institute of Technology Press, 1969.

_____, "Theories of Bounded Rationality," in C. McGuire and R. Radner, eds., *Decision and Organization.* Amsterdam: North-Holland Publishing Company, 1972, pp. 161-176.

_____ and C. P. Bonini, "The Size Distribution of Business Firms," *American Economic Review, 48:* 607-617, September 1958.

Smiley, Robert, *The Economics of Tender Offers.* Unpublished Ph.D. dessertation, Stanford University, 1973.

Smith, K. V., and J. C. Schreiner, "A Portfolio Analysis of Conglomerate Diversification," *Journal of Finance. 24:* 413-429, June 1969.

Smith, R.A., *Corporations in Crisis.* New York: Doubleday & Company, Inc., Anchor Books Edition, 1966.

Solo, Robert A., "New Maths and Old Sterilities," *Saturday Review,* January 22, 1972, pp. 47-48.

Stigler, George J., "The Division of Labor is Limited by the Extent of the Market," *Journal of Political Economy, 59:* 185-193, June 1951.

_____, "Industrial Organization and Economic Progress," in L. D. White, ed., *The State of the Social Sciences.* Chicago: University of Chicago Press. 1956. pp. 269-282.

_____, "A Theory of Oligopoly," *Journal of Political Economy. 22:* 44-61, February 1964.

_____, *The Organization of Industry.* Homewood, Ill.: Richard D. Irwin, Inc., 1968.

Summers, C., "Collective Agreements and the Law of Contracts," *Yale Law Journal, 78:* 527-575, March 1969.

Sylos-Labini, Paolo, *Oligopoly and Technical Progress.* (Translated by Elizabeth Henderson), Cambridge: Harvard University Press, 1962.

"Symposium: Economics of the New Left," *Quarterly Journal of Economics. 85:* 632-683, November 1972.

Telser, Lester, *Competition, Collusion, and Game Theory.* Chicago: Aldine-Atherton, Inc., 1972.

Thurow, L., "Measuring the Economic Benefits of Education," Carnegie Commission on Higher Education, December, 1971.

Titmuss, R. M., *The Gift Relationship: from Human Blood to Social Policy.* New York: Pantheon Books, Inc., 1971.

Troxel, C. Emery, "Telephone Regulation in Michigan," in W. G. Shepherd and T. G. Gies, eds., *Utility Regulation.* New York: Random House, Inc., 1966, pp. 141-186.

Turner, D. F., "The Definition of Agreement Under the Sherman Act: Conscious Parallelism and Refusals to Deal," *Harvard Law Review, 75:* 655-706, February 1962.

_____, "Conglomerate Mergers and Section 7 of the Clayton Act," *Harvard Law Review 78:* 1313-1395, May 1965.

_____, "The Scope of Antitrust and Other Economic Regulatory Policies," *Harvard Law Review, 82:* 1207-1244, April 1969.

_____ and O. E. Williamson, "Market Structure in Relation to Technical and Organizational Innovation," in J. B. Heath, ed., *International Conference on Monopolies, Mergers and Restrictive Practices.* London: HMSO, 1971, pp. 127-144.

U.S. Bureau of the Census, "Concentration Ratios in Manufacturing Industry 1963," *Report prepared by the Bureau of the Census for the Subcommittee on Antitrust and Monopoly of the Committee on the Judiciary,* U.S. Senate, Washington, D.C., 1966.

U.S. Department of Justice, *United States vs. United Shore Machinery Corporation*, "Brief for the United States on Relief," 1952.

U.S. Federal Trade Commission, "Economic Report on Corporate Mergers," *Staff Report of the Federal Trade Commission* (*Economic Concentration, part 8a, Hearings Before the Subcommittee of Antitrust and Monopoly*, Committee on the Judiciary, U.S. Senate, 91st Cong., 1st Sess.), Washington, D.C., 1969.

_____, "Conglomerate Merger Performance: An Empirical Analysis of Nine Corporations," *Staff Report of the Federal Trade Commission*, Washington, D.C., November 1972.

_____, Official Transcript of the Proceedings Before the Federal Trade Commission, Docket #8767, on the matter of Allied Chemical Corporation et al., Washington, D.C., August 1969.

Usher, D., "The Welfare Economics of Invention," *Economica, 31:* 279-287, August 1964.

Varaiya, Pravin, "Trends in the Theory of Decision Making in Large Systems," *Annals of Economic and Social Measurement, 1:* 493-500, October 1972.

Vernon, J. M. and P. A. Gordon, "Profitability of Monopolization by Vertical Integration," *The Journal of Political Economy,* No. 4, *79:* 924-925. July/August 1971.

Vladeck, S., "Labor Arbitration and Concensus," *Stanford Law Review, 19:* 719-722, February 1967.

Von Neumann, J. and O. Morgenstern, *Theory of Games and Economic Behavior.* Princeton: Princeton University Press, 1953.

Wachtel, H. and C. Betsy, "Employment at Low Wages," *Review of Economics and Statistics, 54:* 121-129, May 1972.

Ward, B. N., *The Socialist Economy: A Study of Organizational Alternatives.* New York: Random House, Inc., 1967.

_____ "Organization and Comparative Economics: Some Approaches," in A. Eckstein, ed., *Comparison of Economic Systems.* Berkeley: University of California Press, 1971, pp. 103-121.

Warren-Boulton, F. R., "Vertical Control with Variable Proportions," *Journal of Political Economy, 82:* 783-802, July/August 1974.

Weisbrod, Burton A., "Collective-Consumption Services of Individual-Consumption Goods," *Quarterly Journal of Economics, 78:* 471-477, August 1964.

Weiss, Leonard, "Quantitative Studies of Industrial Organization," in M. D. Intrilligator, ed., *Frontiers of Quantitative Economics.* Amsterdam: North-Holland Publishing Company, 1971, pp. 362-403.

Westerfield, Randolph, "A Note on the Measure of Conglomerate Diversification," *Journal of Finance, 25:* 904-914.

Westfield, Fred M., "Regulation and Conspiracy," *American Economic Review, 60:* 424-443, June 1965.

Weston, J. Fred, "Diversification and Merger Trends," *Business Economics, 5:* 50-57, January 1970.

_____ and S. K. Mansinghka, "Tests of the Efficiency Performance of Conglomerate Firms," *Journal of Finance, 26:* 919-936, September 1971.

_____, K. V. Smith and R. E. Shrieves, "Conglomerate Performance Using the Capital Asset Pricing Model," *The Review of Economics and Statistics,* No. 4, *54:* 357-363.

Whinston, A., "Price Guides in Decentralized Organizations," in W. W. Cooper, H. J. Leavitt and M. W. Shelly, eds., *New Perspectives in Organization Research*. New York: John Wiley & Sons, Inc., 1964, pp. 405-448.

Williamson, O. E., *The Economics of Discretionary Behavior: Managerial Objectives in a Theory of the Firm*. Englewood Cliffs, N. J.: Prentice-Hall, 1964.

_____, "Innovation and Market Structure," *Journal of Political Economy*, 73: 67-73, February 1965.

_____, "The Economics of Defense Contracting: Incentives and Performance," in Roland N. NcKean, ed., *Issues in Defense Economics*. New York: National Bureau of Economic Research, Inc., 1967, 218-256.

_____, "Hierarchical Control and Optimum Firm Size," *Journal of Political Economy*, 75: 123-138, April 1967.

_____, "Wage Rates as a Barrier to Entry: The Pennington Case in Perspective," *Quarterly Journal of Economics*, 82: 85-116, February 1968.

_____, *Corporate Control and Business Behavior*. Englewood Cliffs, N.J.: Prentice-Hall, Inc., 1970.

_____, "Administrative Decision Making and Pricing: Externality and Compensation Analysis Applied," in Julius Margolis, ed., *The Analysis of Public Output*. New York: National Bureau of Economic Research, Inc., 1970, pp. 115-135.

_____, "The Vertical Integration of Production: Market Failure Considerations," *American Economic Review*, 61: 112-123, May 1971.

_____, "Antitrust Enforcement and the Modern Corporation," in V. R. Fuchs, ed., *Policy Issues and Research Opportunities in Industrial Organization*. New York: National Bureau of Economic Research, Inc., 1972, pp. 16-33.

_____, "Some Notes on the Economics of Atmosphere," Discussion Paper #29, Fels Center of Government, University of Pennsylvania, Philadelphia, March 1973.

_____, "Markets and Hierarchies: Some Elementary Considerations," *American Economic Review*, 63: 316-325, May 1973.

_____, "The Economics of Antitrust: Transaction Cost Considerations," *University of Pennsylvania Law Review*, 122: 1439-1496, June 1974.

_____ and N. Bhargava, "Assessing and Classifying the Internal Structure and Control Apparatus of the Modern Corporation," in Keith Cowling, ed., *Market Structure and Corporate Behavior Theory and Empirical Analysis of the Firm*. London: Gray-Mills Publishing Ltd., 1972, pp. 125-148.

_____, M. L. Wachter and J. E. Harris, "Understanding the Employment Relation: The Analysis of Idiosyncratic Exchange," *Bell Journal of Economics*, 6: 250-280, Spring 1975.

Winter, Sidney, "Satisficing Selection and the Innovating Remnant," *Quarterly Journal of Economics*, 85: 237-261, May 1971.

Wolf, Charles, "Symposium: Time in Economic Life: Comment," *Quarterly Journal of Economics*, 87: 661-667, November 1973.

Woods, Donald H., "Improving Estimates that Involve Uncertainty," *Harvard Business Review*, 44: 91-98, July 1966.

Index